HOAX HUNTERS™

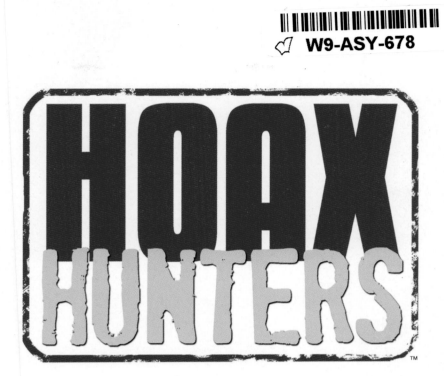

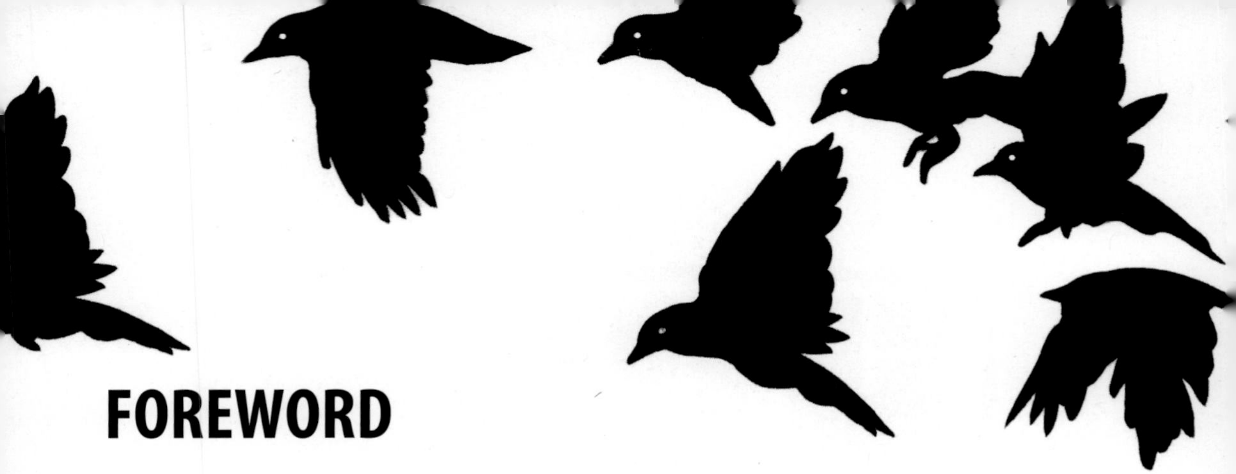

FOREWORD

What is *real* and how much do we *really* understand about our world? Is mainstream science dedicated to the study of *all* the wonders of the universe or does it pick and choose which mysteries fit within contemporary theory; then dismiss or ridicule the shocking, the unbelievable, the sort of things we were taught not to believe in as children?

Most people know me as the lead host and investigator of SyFy Channel's hit TV reality show *Fact or Faked: Paranormal Files.* Much in the same way Jack and the *Hoax Hunters* team scour the globe investigating claims of the paranormal, my team also deploys in response to bizarre stories found on the Internet. When I was a young, I watched cartoons like *Casper the Friendly Ghost,* movies like *Ghostbusters,* and TV shows like *The X-Files.* I had a strong belief in the afterlife and in life on other worlds, but the subjects of ghosts, UFOs, and strange cryptids weren't topics I freely discussed with friends. After all, hauntings and swamp creatures only exist in the movies, right? I collected newspaper clippings about UFOs. I read books which I hid from my friends when they came to visit. As I grew older, I naturally assumed that I would trade these curiosities for the hard realities of adulthood. Never in my wildest dreams did I think I would one day be working full-time as an investigator of the unknown and witnessing the incredible things I've seen! Ironically, I'm now compelled to reserve more open-mindedness to unexplained phenomena than when I was a child. Yes, the taunters are still busy ridiculing, ignoring, and providing improbable explanations for many unusual events; but like me, there are also those who cannot deny what they've witnessed. We may not have all of the answers. However, *facts do not cease to exist because they are ignored.* If there's one thing that we've learned about history; it's that it's *history.* Science has often been right. Some theories that have been unquestioned for millennia have also been proven wrong. Given our short existence on this planet, let us not be so arrogant to presume there are no mysteries of the universe still beyond our grasp.

I hope that you enjoy *Hoax Hunters* as much as I have. It's smart, outrageously creative, and creepily entertaining. Jack and I share a common background, but what you didn't know is that I taught him everything he knows *(laughing).* Consider for a moment the idea that just perhaps there are mysteries too big, too unusual for us to comprehend... or at least too big that others think we can't comprehend. How would the secret keepers go about keeping those secrets? If seeing is believing, then seeing a mysterious event should provide us undeniable proof... right? If we're not present to witness it, then a video offers near-perfect proof that something does or doesn't exist, correct? How easy is it to hoax a paranormal video and what would motivate someone to do it? These are riveting themes explored by both *Hoax Hunters* and my show *Fact or Faked.* I've traveled the world looking for answers to such questions. I've found reasonable explanations to most of the phenomena I've investigated; but I've also pinched myself and blinked hard at times to verify I wasn't dreaming. Many of those experiences simply *blew me away.* Yet looking back, I confess I wasn't terribly surprised. Somehow I always knew I would witness evidence supporting my premonitions. It's possible that you too have are searching for what to believe. The relationship between seeing and believing fascinates me. I'm now convinced that our deep understanding of the universe rarely begins with seeing, but rather with believing. Years ago I had a phrase translated for me into Latin, *"Aliquando videre non est satis."* It means "Sometimes seeing is not enough." May we always continue to ask questions. May we always continue to be curious. In so doing, we will never be bored.

— Ben Hansen
Host of SyFy's Fact or Faked

HOAX HUNTERS

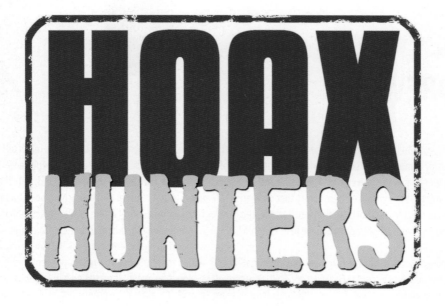

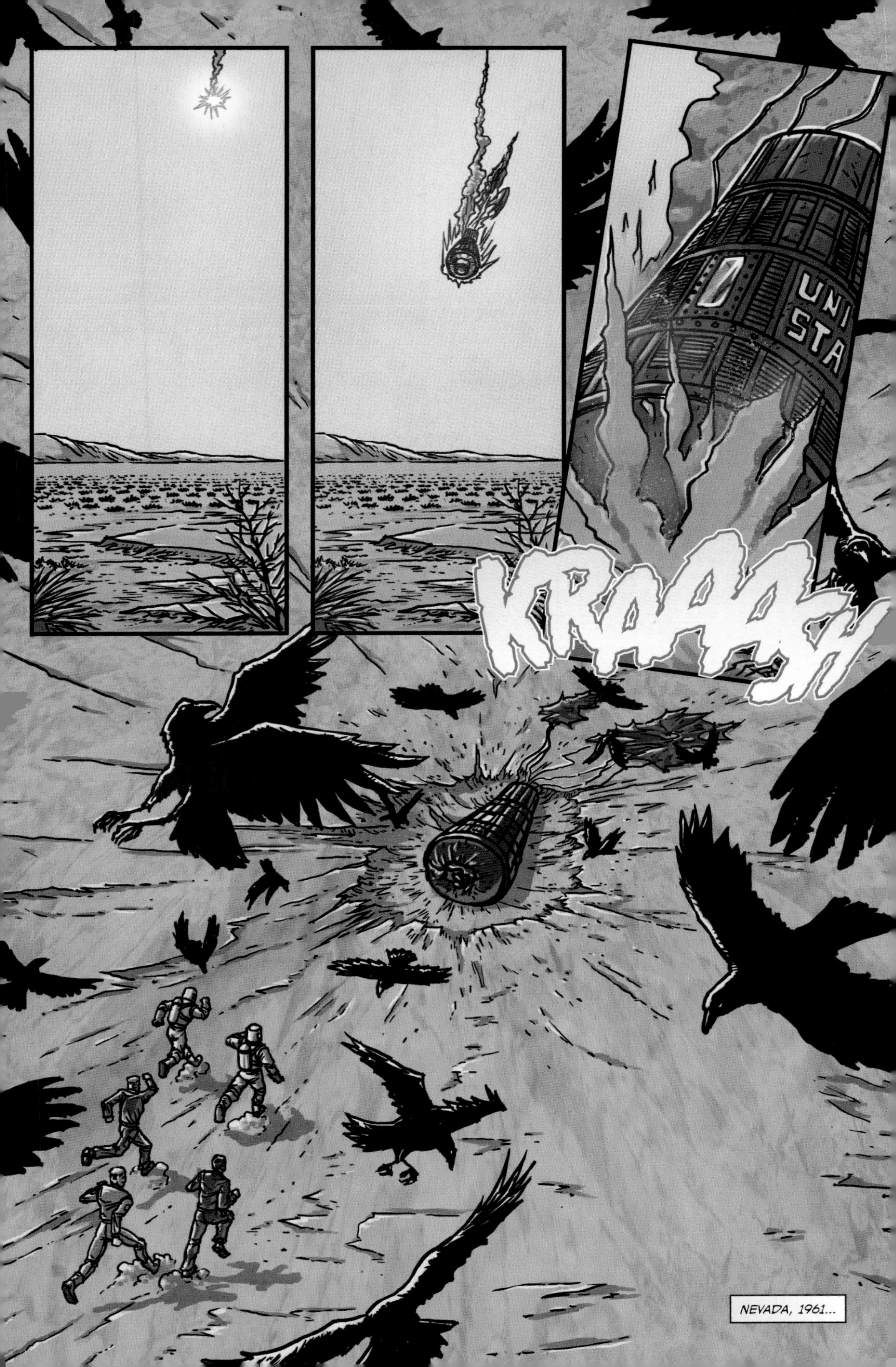
UNI
STA
KRAAASH
NEVADA, 1961...

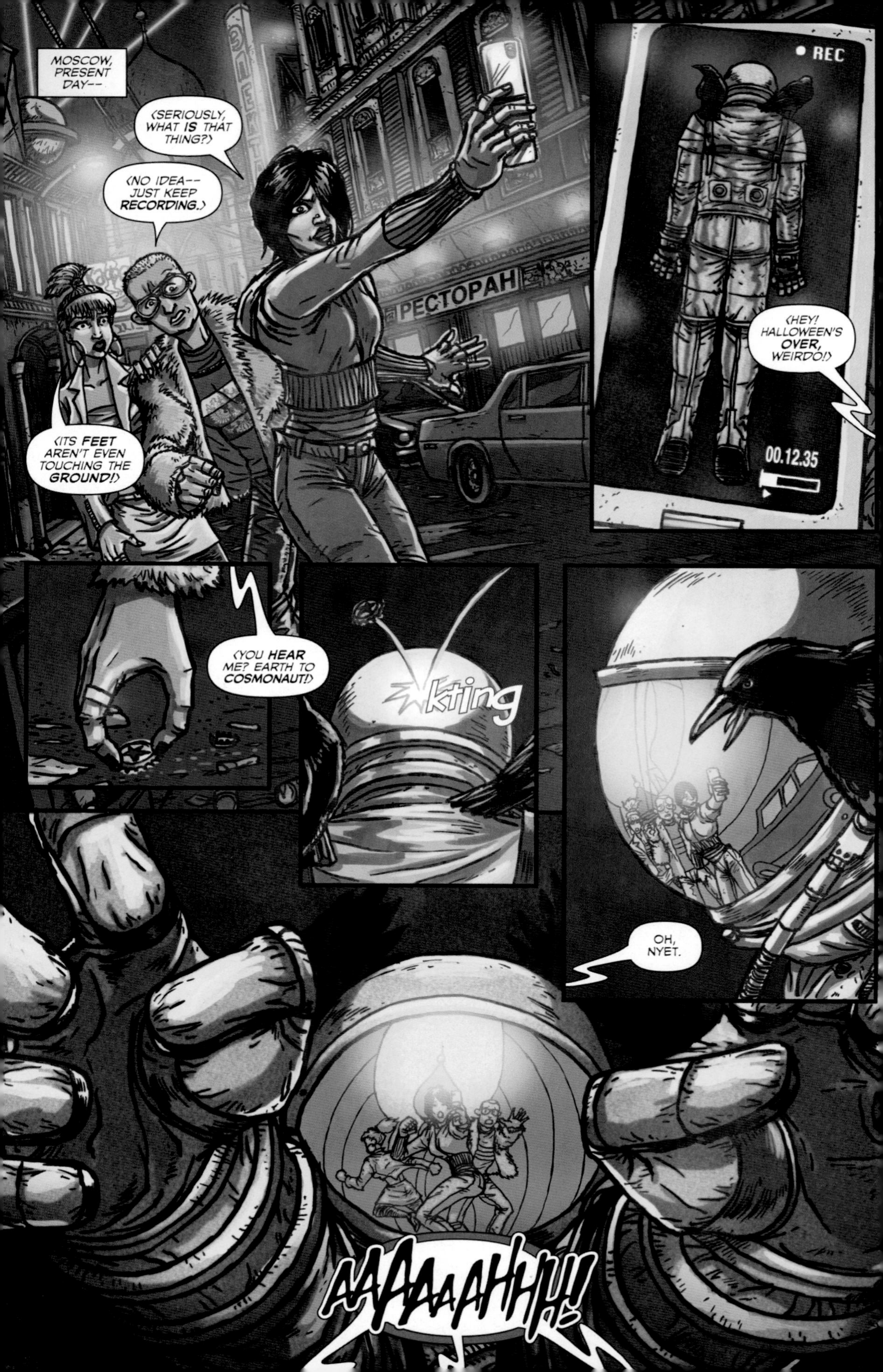
MOSCOW, PRESENT DAY--
‹SERIOUSLY, WHAT IS THAT THING?›
‹NO IDEA-- JUST KEEP RECORDING.›
‹ITS FEET AREN'T EVEN TOUCHING THE GROUND!›
РЕСТОРАН
REC
00.12.35
‹HEY! HALLOWEEN'S OVER, WEIRDO!›
‹YOU HEAR ME? EARTH TO COSMONAUT!›
kting
OH, NYET.
AAAAAAHHH!!

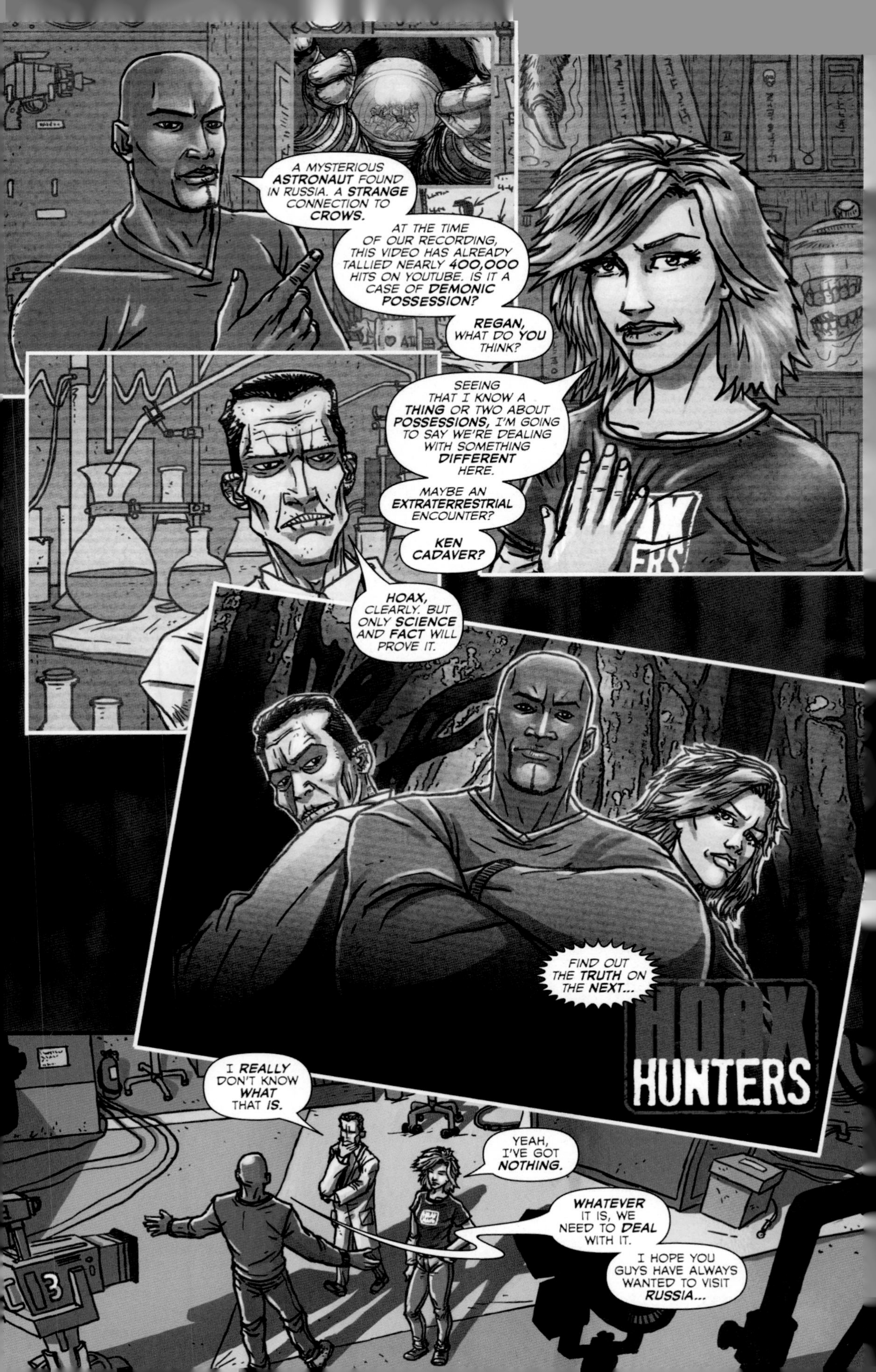
A MYSTERIOUS ASTRONAUT FOUND IN RUSSIA. A STRANGE CONNECTION TO CROWS.
AT THE TIME OF OUR RECORDING, THIS VIDEO HAS ALREADY TALLIED NEARLY 400,000 HITS ON YOUTUBE. IS IT A CASE OF DEMONIC POSSESSION?
REGAN, WHAT DO YOU THINK?
SEEING THAT I KNOW A THING OR TWO ABOUT POSSESSIONS, I'M GOING TO SAY WE'RE DEALING WITH SOMETHING DIFFERENT HERE.
MAYBE AN EXTRATERRESTRIAL ENCOUNTER?
KEN CADAVER?
HOAX, CLEARLY. BUT ONLY SCIENCE AND FACT WILL PROVE IT.
FIND OUT THE TRUTH ON THE NEXT...
HOAX HUNTERS
I REALLY DON'T KNOW WHAT THAT IS.
YEAH, I'VE GOT NOTHING.
WHATEVER IT IS, WE NEED TO DEAL WITH IT.
I HOPE YOU GUYS HAVE ALWAYS WANTED TO VISIT RUSSIA...

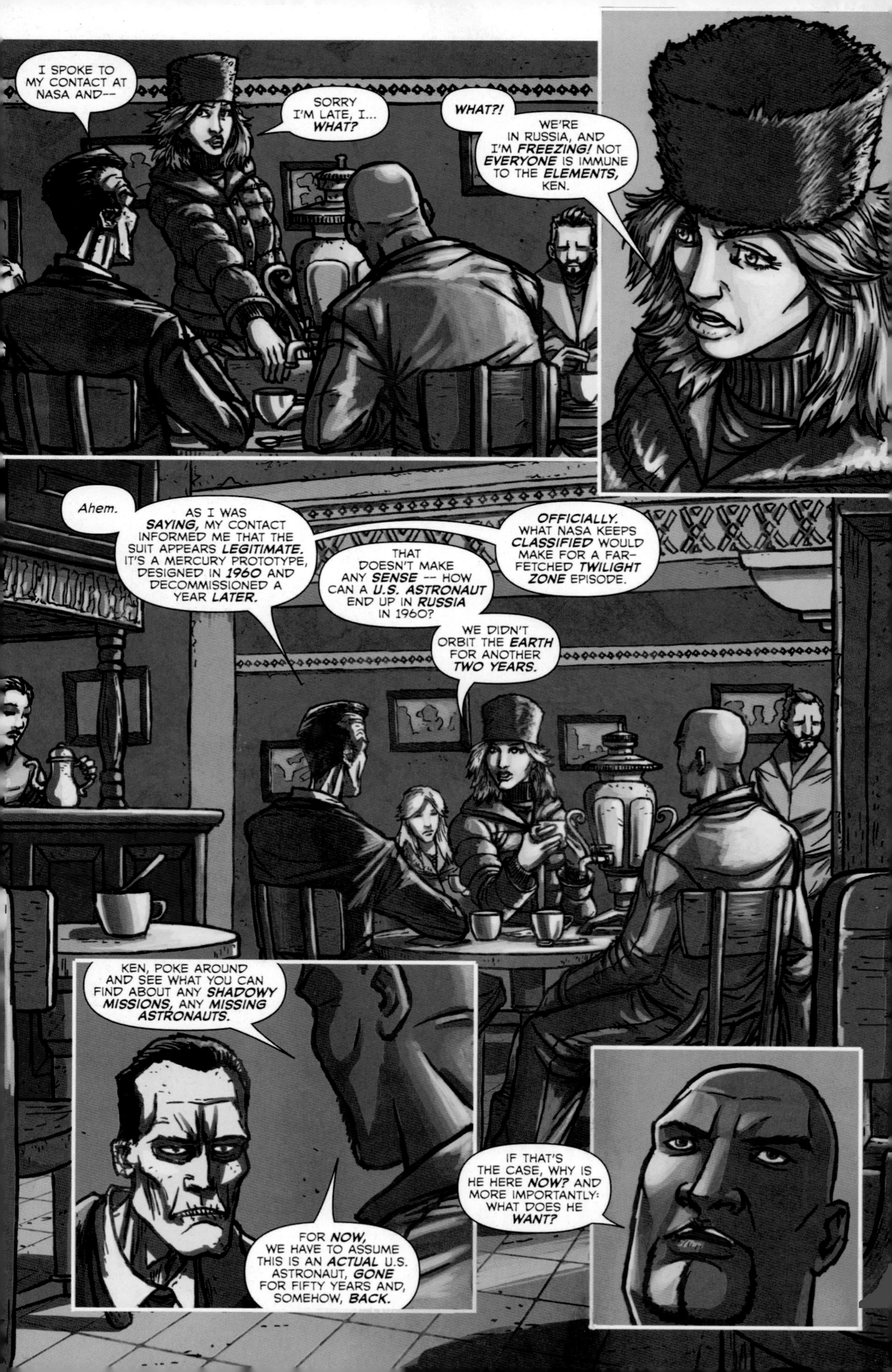
I SPOKE TO MY CONTACT AT NASA AND--
SORRY I'M LATE, I... WHAT?
WHAT?!
WE'RE IN RUSSIA, AND I'M FREEZING! NOT EVERYONE IS IMMUNE TO THE ELEMENTS, KEN.
Ahem.
AS I WAS SAYING, MY CONTACT INFORMED ME THAT THE SUIT APPEARS LEGITIMATE. IT'S A MERCURY PROTOTYPE, DESIGNED IN 1960 AND DECOMMISSIONED A YEAR LATER.
OFFICIALLY. WHAT NASA KEEPS CLASSIFIED WOULD MAKE FOR A FAR-FETCHED TWILIGHT ZONE EPISODE.
THAT DOESN'T MAKE ANY SENSE -- HOW CAN A U.S. ASTRONAUT END UP IN RUSSIA IN 1960?
WE DIDN'T ORBIT THE EARTH FOR ANOTHER TWO YEARS.
KEN, POKE AROUND AND SEE WHAT YOU CAN FIND ABOUT ANY SHADOWY MISSIONS, ANY MISSING ASTRONAUTS.
FOR NOW, WE HAVE TO ASSUME THIS IS AN ACTUAL U.S. ASTRONAUT, GONE FOR FIFTY YEARS AND, SOMEHOW, BACK.
IF THAT'S THE CASE, WHY IS HE HERE NOW? AND MORE IMPORTANTLY: WHAT DOES HE WANT?

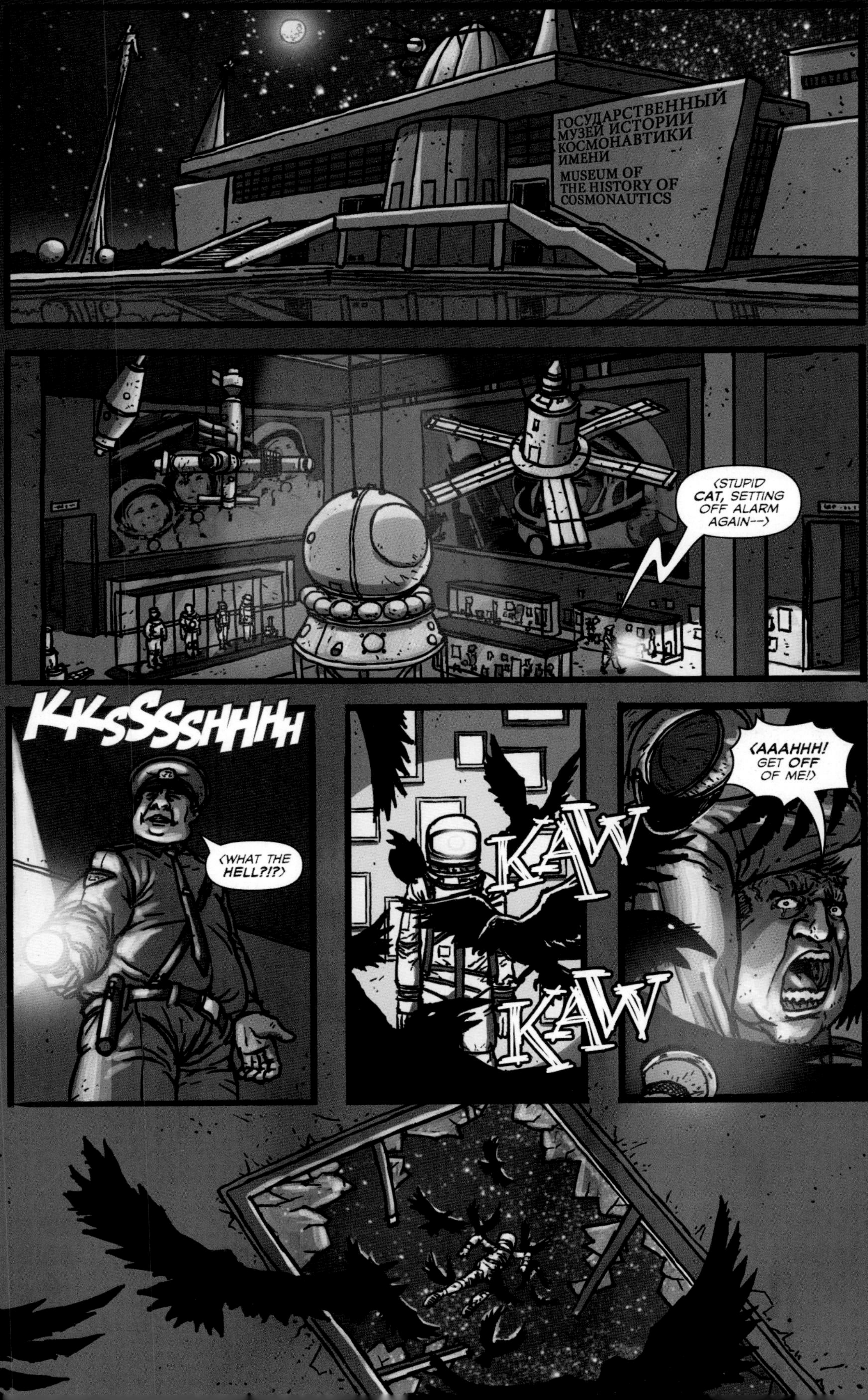
ГОСУДАРСТВЕННЫЙ МУЗЕЙ ИСТОРИИ КОСМОНАВТИКИ ИМЕНИ
MUSEUM OF THE HISTORY OF COSMONAUTICS
‹STUPID CAT, SETTING OFF ALARM AGAIN--›
KKSSSSHHHH
‹WHAT THE HELL?!?›
KAW
KAW
‹AAAHHH! GET OFF OF ME!›

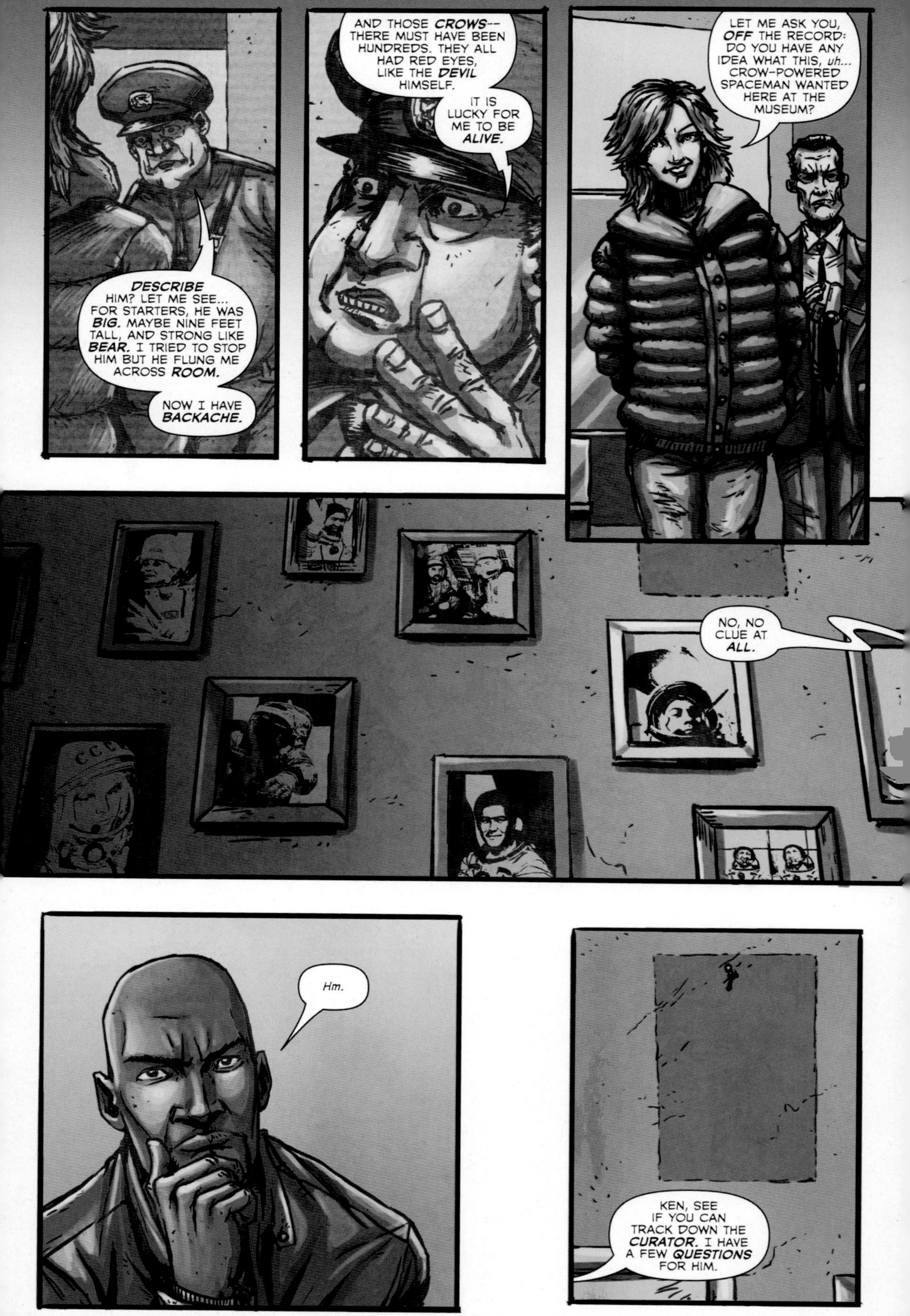
DESCRIBE HIM? LET ME SEE... FOR STARTERS, HE WAS BIG. MAYBE NINE FEET TALL, AND STRONG LIKE BEAR. I TRIED TO STOP HIM BUT HE FLUNG ME ACROSS ROOM.
NOW I HAVE BACKACHE.
AND THOSE CROWS-- THERE MUST HAVE BEEN HUNDREDS. THEY ALL HAD RED EYES, LIKE THE DEVIL HIMSELF.
IT IS LUCKY FOR ME TO BE ALIVE.
LET ME ASK YOU, OFF THE RECORD: DO YOU HAVE ANY IDEA WHAT THIS, uh... CROW-POWERED SPACEMAN WANTED HERE AT THE MUSEUM?
NO, NO CLUE AT ALL.
Hm.
KEN, SEE IF YOU CAN TRACK DOWN THE CURATOR. I HAVE A FEW QUESTIONS FOR HIM.

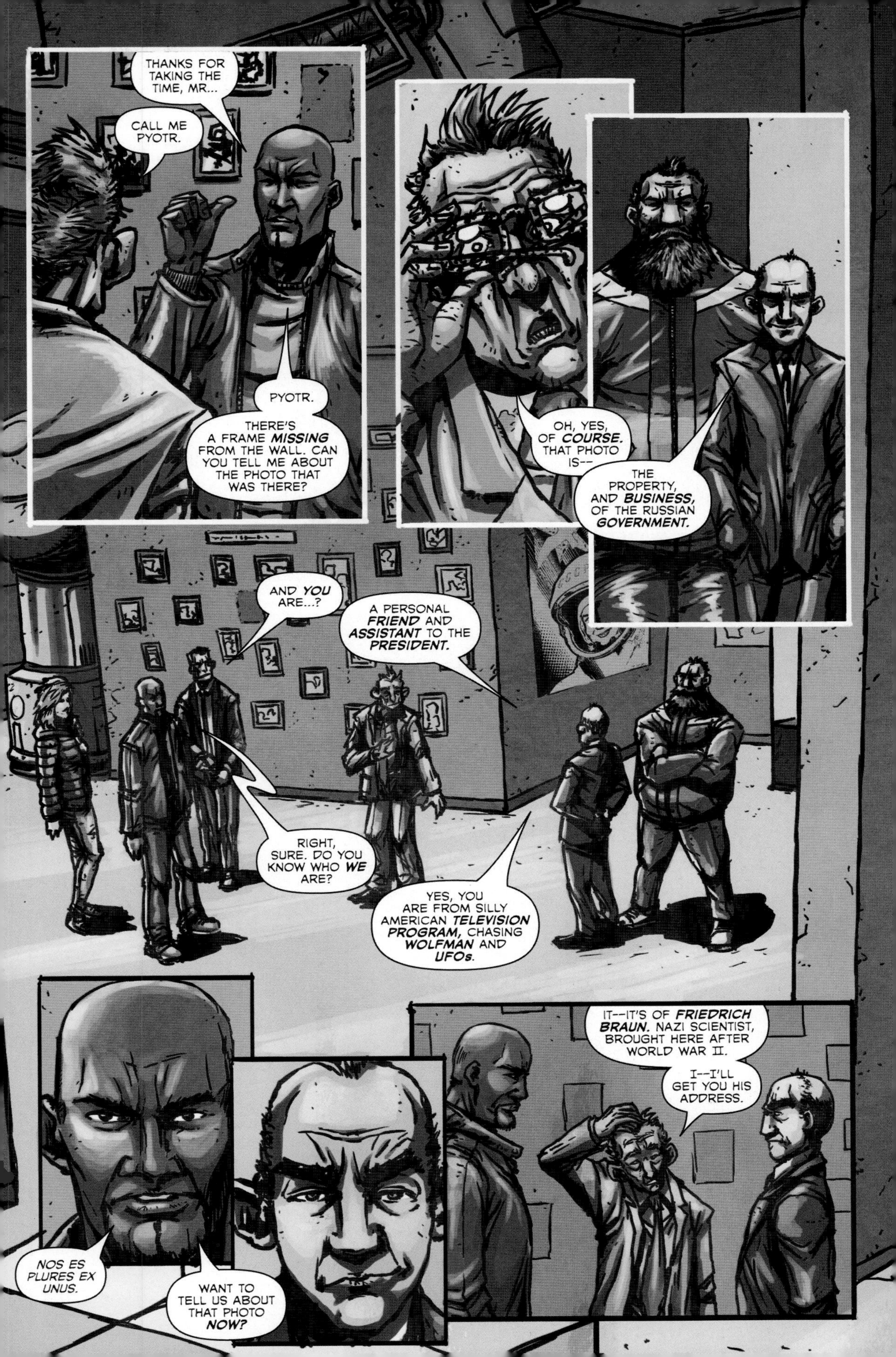
THANKS FOR TAKING THE TIME, MR...
CALL ME PYOTR.
PYOTR.
THERE'S A FRAME MISSING FROM THE WALL. CAN YOU TELL ME ABOUT THE PHOTO THAT WAS THERE?
OH, YES, OF COURSE. THAT PHOTO IS--
THE PROPERTY, AND BUSINESS, OF THE RUSSIAN GOVERNMENT.
AND YOU ARE...?
A PERSONAL FRIEND AND ASSISTANT TO THE PRESIDENT.
RIGHT, SURE. DO YOU KNOW WHO WE ARE?
YES, YOU ARE FROM SILLY AMERICAN TELEVISION PROGRAM, CHASING WOLFMAN AND UFOs.
NOS ES PLURES EX UNUS.
WANT TO TELL US ABOUT THAT PHOTO NOW?
IT--IT'S OF FRIEDRICH BRAUN. NAZI SCIENTIST, BROUGHT HERE AFTER WORLD WAR II.
I--I'LL GET YOU HIS ADDRESS.

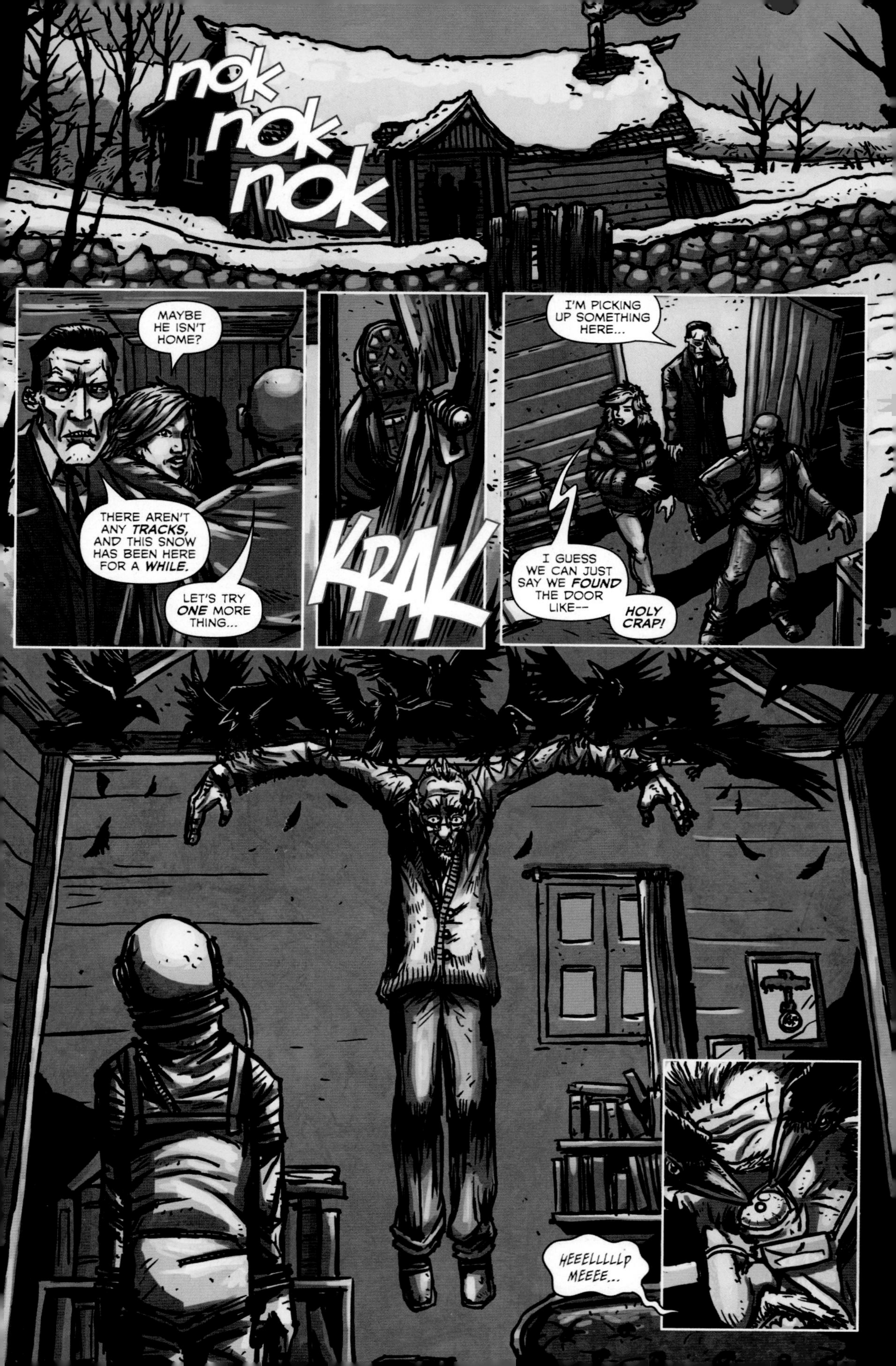
nok
nok
nok
MAYBE HE ISN'T HOME?
THERE AREN'T ANY *TRACKS,* AND THIS SNOW HAS BEEN HERE FOR A *WHILE.*
LET'S TRY *ONE* MORE THING...
KRAK
I'M PICKING UP SOMETHING HERE...
I GUESS WE CAN JUST SAY WE *FOUND* THE DOOR LIKE--
HOLY CRAP!
HEEELLLLLP MEEEE...

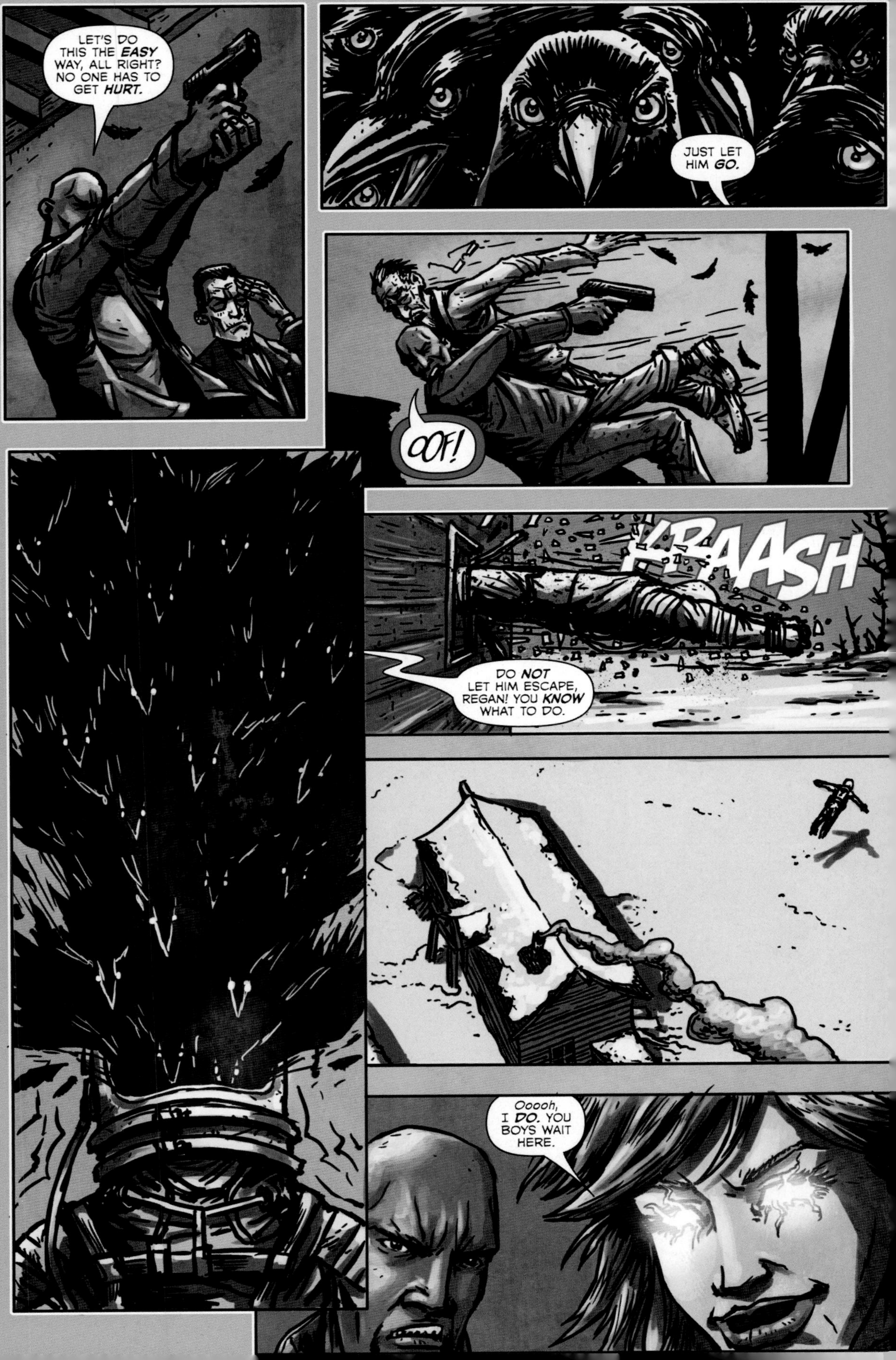
LET'S DO THIS THE EASY WAY, ALL RIGHT? NO ONE HAS TO GET HURT.
JUST LET HIM GO.
OOF!
KRAASH
DO NOT LET HIM ESCAPE, REGAN! YOU KNOW WHAT TO DO.
Ooooh, I DO. YOU BOYS WAIT HERE.

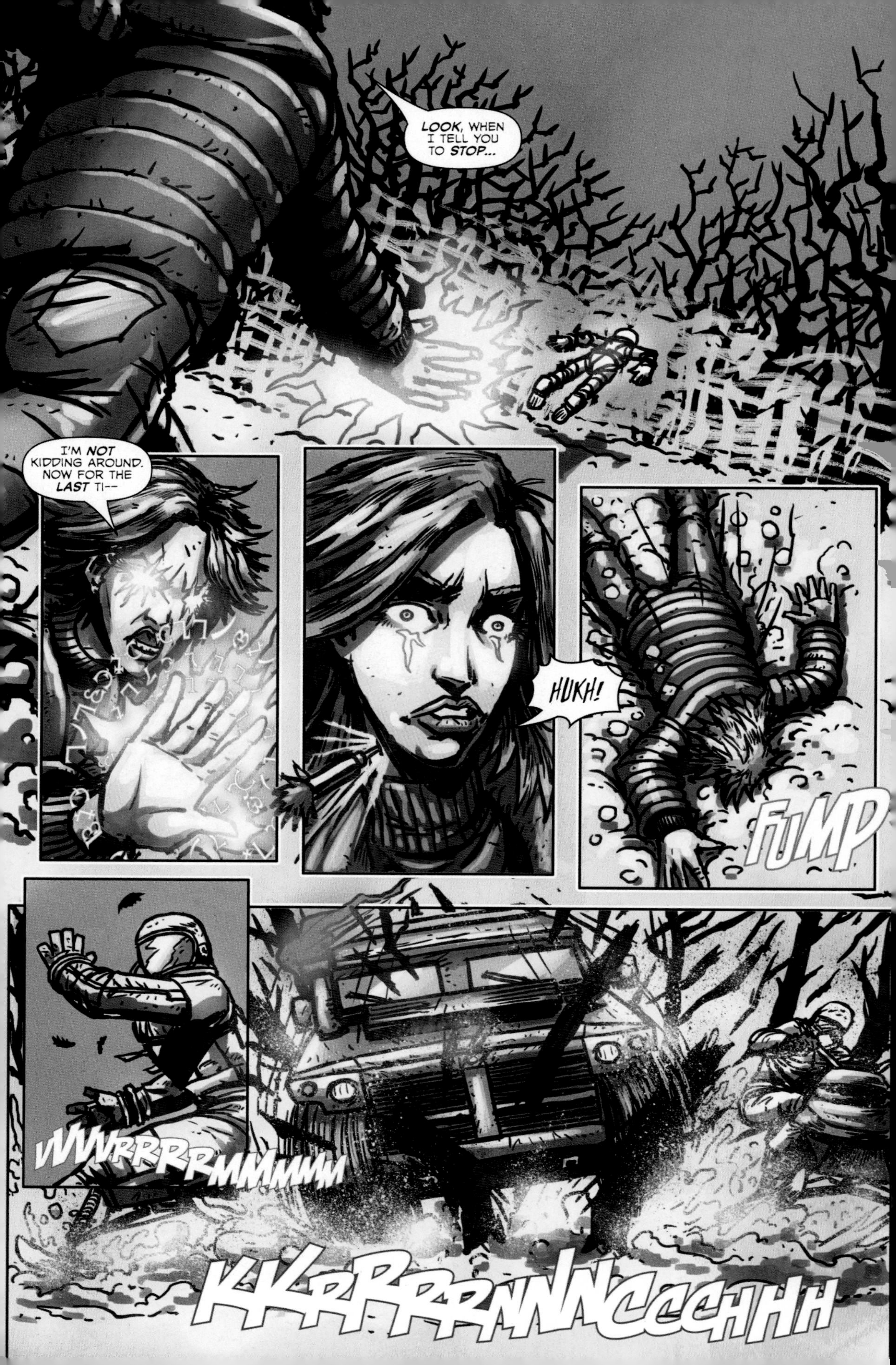
LOOK, WHEN I TELL YOU TO STOP...
I'M NOT KIDDING AROUND. NOW FOR THE LAST TI--
HUKH!
FUMP
VVVVRRRRMMMMMM
KKRRRRRNNNCCCHHH

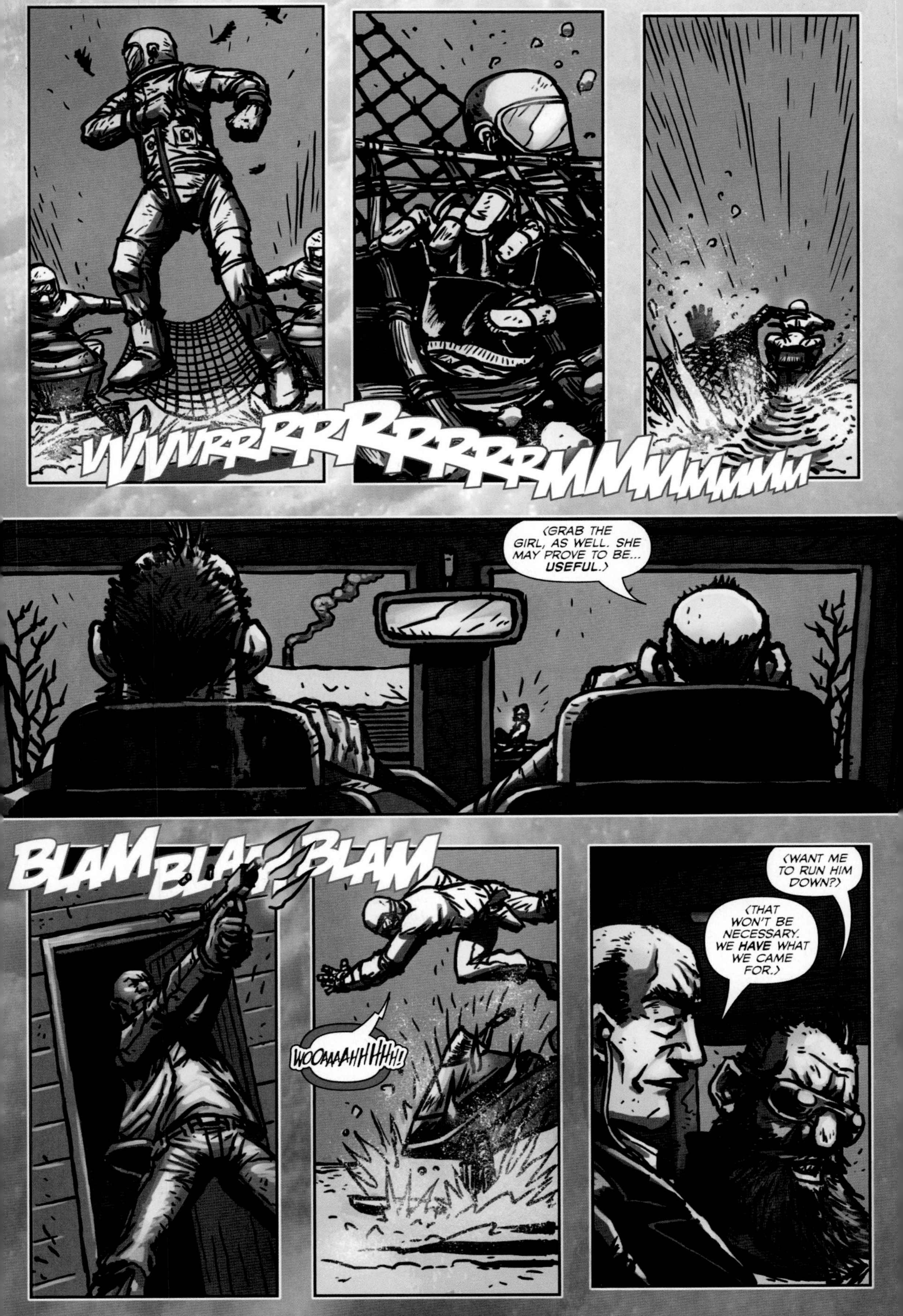
VVVVVRRRRRRRRRRRRRMMMMMMMM
⟨GRAB THE GIRL, AS WELL. SHE MAY PROVE TO BE... USEFUL.⟩
BLAM BLAM BLAM
WOOAAAAHHHHH!
⟨WANT ME TO RUN HIM DOWN?⟩
⟨THAT WON'T BE NECESSARY. WE HAVE WHAT WE CAME FOR.⟩

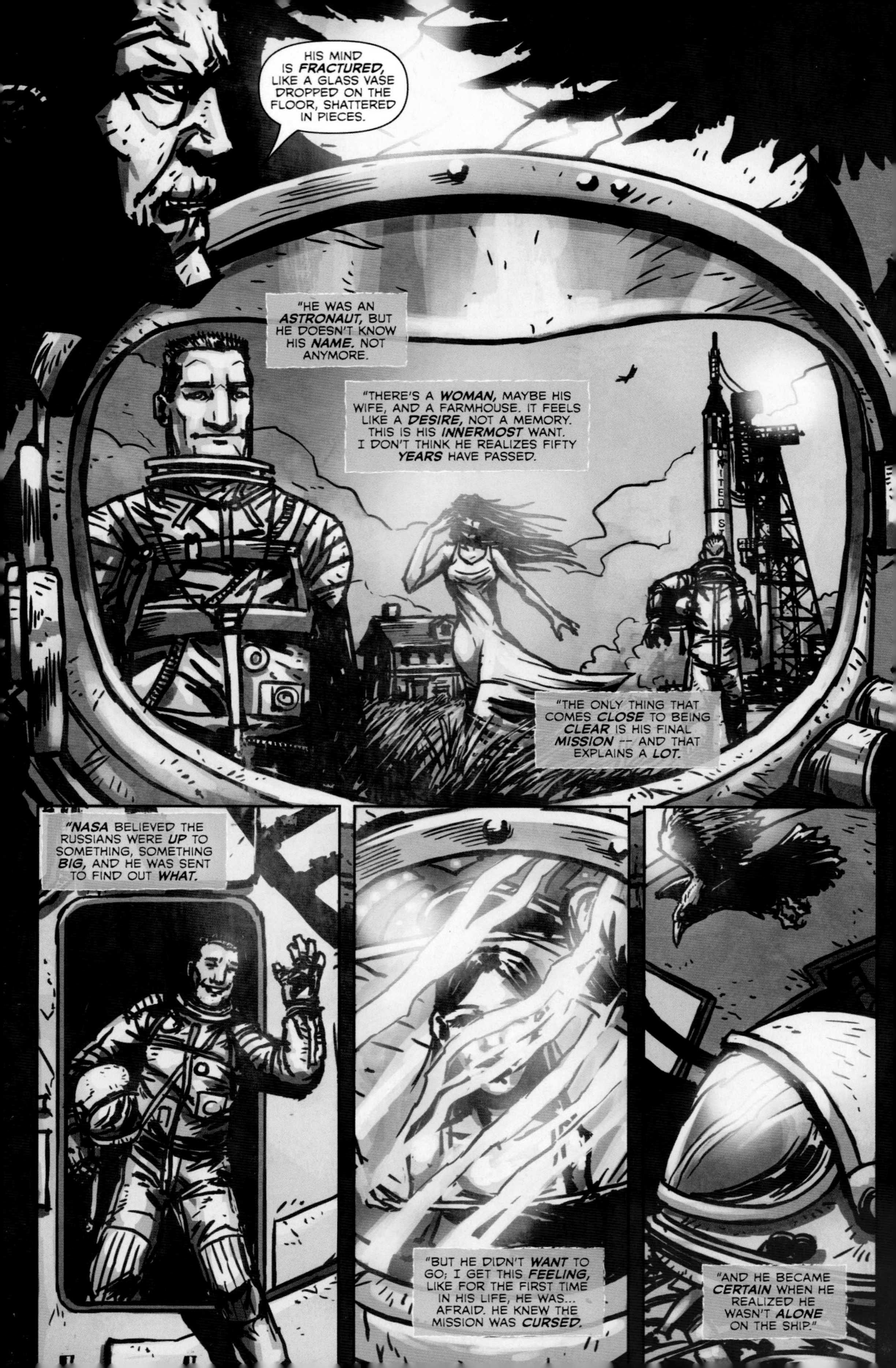
HIS MIND IS FRACTURED, LIKE A GLASS VASE DROPPED ON THE FLOOR, SHATTERED IN PIECES.
"HE WAS AN ASTRONAUT, BUT HE DOESN'T KNOW HIS NAME. NOT ANYMORE.
"THERE'S A WOMAN, MAYBE HIS WIFE, AND A FARMHOUSE. IT FEELS LIKE A DESIRE, NOT A MEMORY. THIS IS HIS INNERMOST WANT. I DON'T THINK HE REALIZES FIFTY YEARS HAVE PASSED.
"THE ONLY THING THAT COMES CLOSE TO BEING CLEAR IS HIS FINAL MISSION -- AND THAT EXPLAINS A LOT.
"NASA BELIEVED THE RUSSIANS WERE UP TO SOMETHING, SOMETHING BIG, AND HE WAS SENT TO FIND OUT WHAT.
"BUT HE DIDN'T WANT TO GO; I GET THIS FEELING, LIKE FOR THE FIRST TIME IN HIS LIFE, HE WAS... AFRAID. HE KNEW THE MISSION WAS CURSED.
"AND HE BECAME CERTAIN WHEN HE REALIZED HE WASN'T ALONE ON THE SHIP."

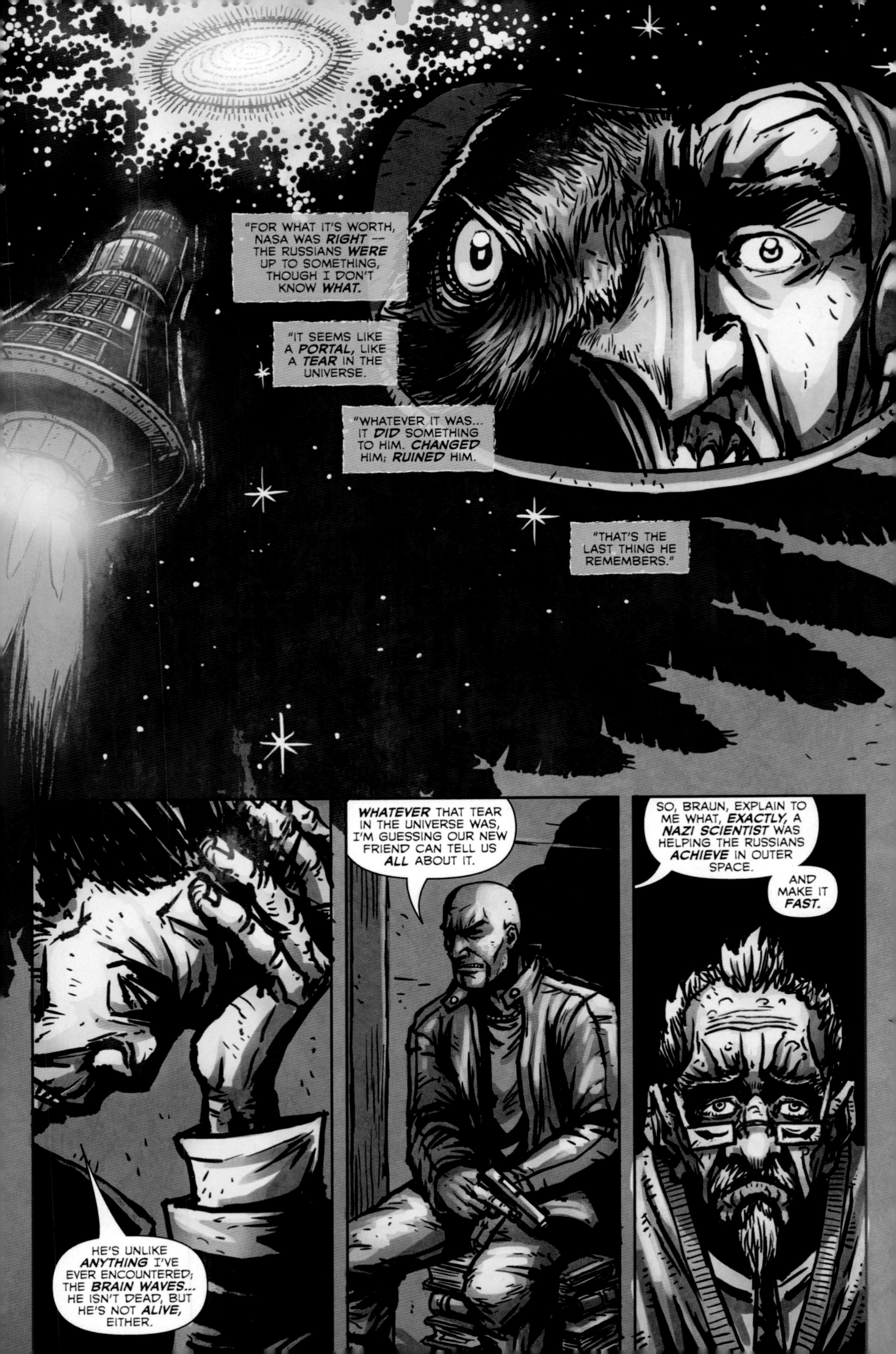
"FOR WHAT IT'S WORTH, NASA WAS RIGHT -- THE RUSSIANS WERE UP TO SOMETHING, THOUGH I DON'T KNOW WHAT.
"IT SEEMS LIKE A PORTAL, LIKE A TEAR IN THE UNIVERSE.
"WHATEVER IT WAS... IT DID SOMETHING TO HIM. CHANGED HIM; RUINED HIM.
"THAT'S THE LAST THING HE REMEMBERS."
HE'S UNLIKE ANYTHING I'VE EVER ENCOUNTERED; THE BRAIN WAVES... HE ISN'T DEAD, BUT HE'S NOT ALIVE, EITHER.
WHATEVER THAT TEAR IN THE UNIVERSE WAS, I'M GUESSING OUR NEW FRIEND CAN TELL US ALL ABOUT IT.
SO, BRAUN, EXPLAIN TO ME WHAT, EXACTLY, A NAZI SCIENTIST WAS HELPING THE RUSSIANS ACHIEVE IN OUTER SPACE.
AND MAKE IT FAST.

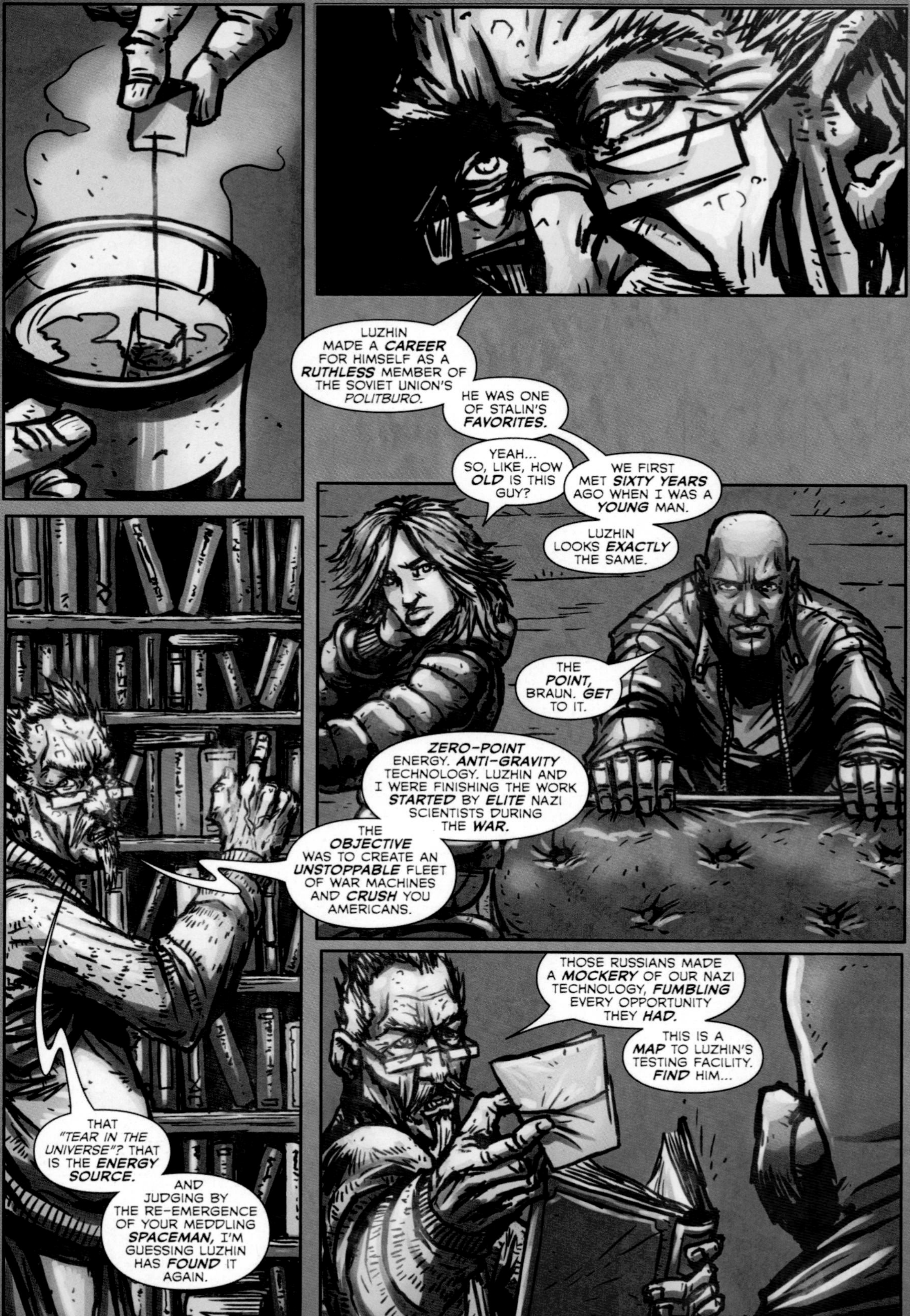
LUZHIN MADE A CAREER FOR HIMSELF AS A RUTHLESS MEMBER OF THE SOVIET UNION'S POLITBURO.
HE WAS ONE OF STALIN'S FAVORITES.
YEAH... SO, LIKE, HOW OLD IS THIS GUY?
WE FIRST MET SIXTY YEARS AGO WHEN I WAS A YOUNG MAN.
LUZHIN LOOKS EXACTLY THE SAME.
THE POINT, BRAUN. GET TO IT.
ZERO-POINT ENERGY. ANTI-GRAVITY TECHNOLOGY. LUZHIN AND I WERE FINISHING THE WORK STARTED BY ELITE NAZI SCIENTISTS DURING THE WAR.
THE OBJECTIVE WAS TO CREATE AN UNSTOPPABLE FLEET OF WAR MACHINES AND CRUSH YOU AMERICANS.
THAT "TEAR IN THE UNIVERSE"? THAT IS THE ENERGY SOURCE.
AND JUDGING BY THE RE-EMERGENCE OF YOUR MEDDLING SPACEMAN, I'M GUESSING LUZHIN HAS FOUND IT AGAIN.
THOSE RUSSIANS MADE A MOCKERY OF OUR NAZI TECHNOLOGY, FUMBLING EVERY OPPORTUNITY THEY HAD.
THIS IS A MAP TO LUZHIN'S TESTING FACILITY. FIND HIM...

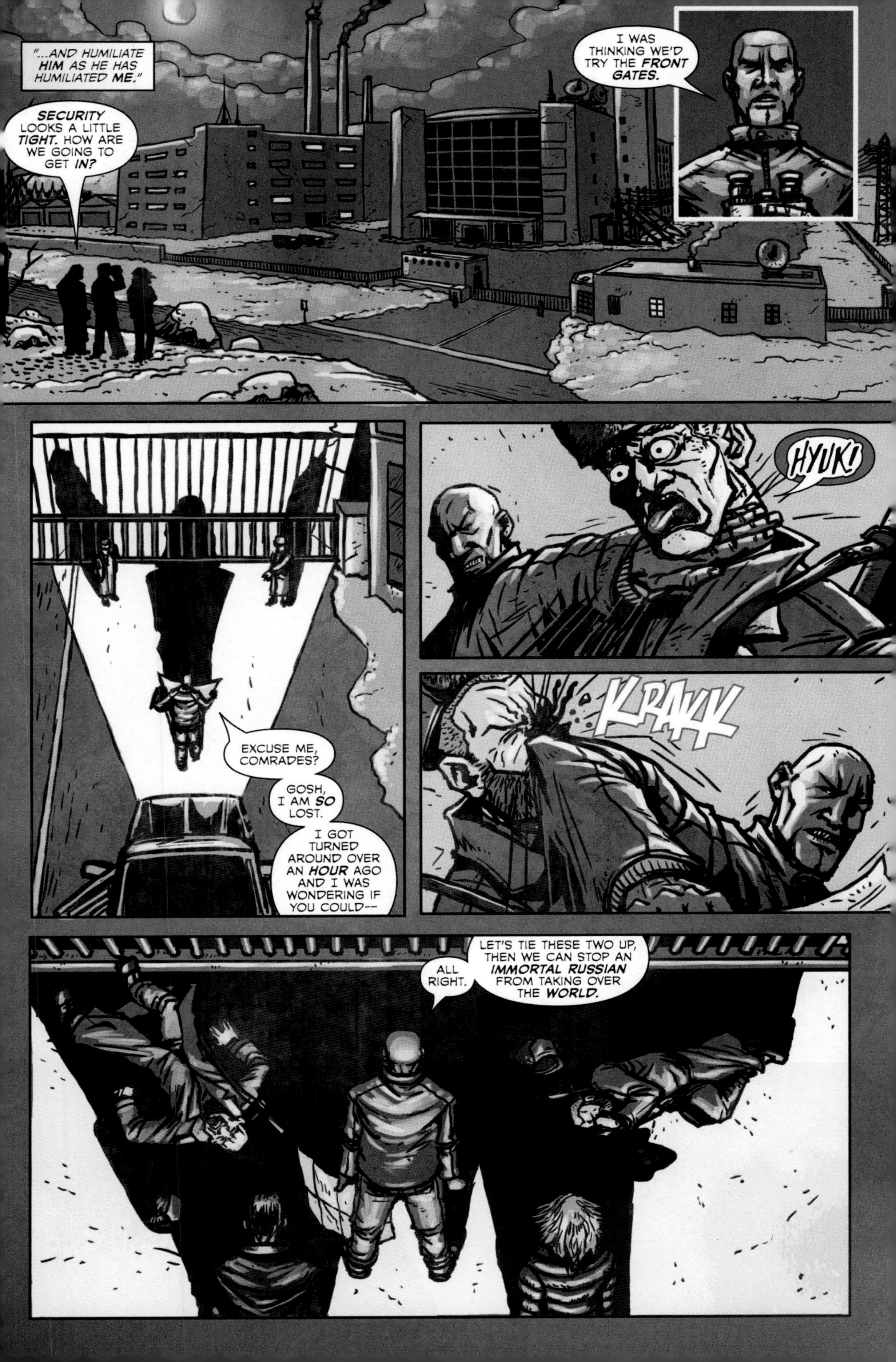
"...AND HUMILIATE HIM AS HE HAS HUMILIATED ME."
SECURITY LOOKS A LITTLE TIGHT. HOW ARE WE GOING TO GET IN?
I WAS THINKING WE'D TRY THE FRONT GATES.
EXCUSE ME, COMRADES?
GOSH, I AM SO LOST.
I GOT TURNED AROUND OVER AN HOUR AGO AND I WAS WONDERING IF YOU COULD--
HYUK!
KRAKK
LET'S TIE THESE TWO UP, THEN WE CAN STOP AN IMMORTAL RUSSIAN FROM TAKING OVER THE WORLD.
ALL RIGHT.

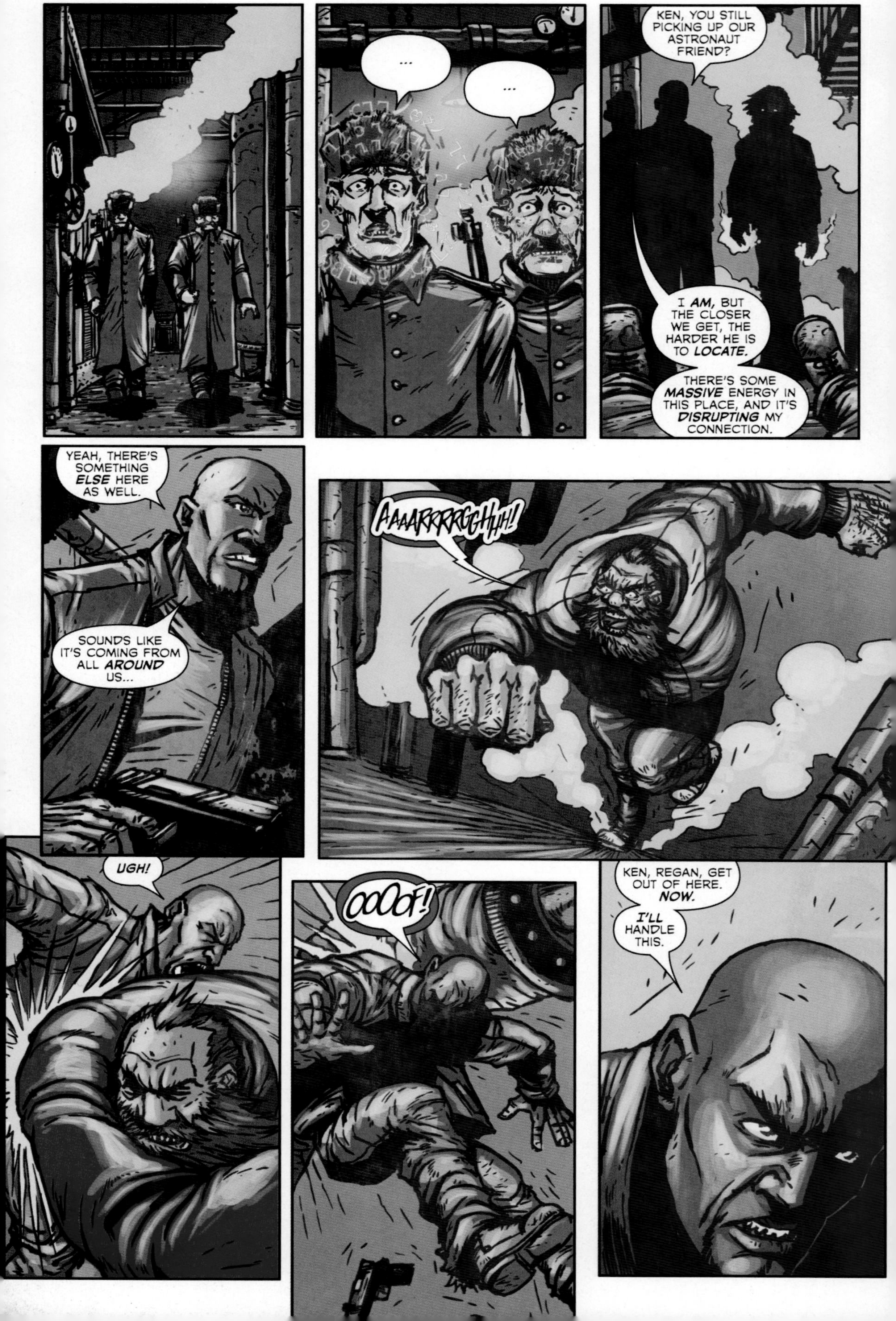
...
...
KEN, YOU STILL PICKING UP OUR ASTRONAUT FRIEND?
I **AM,** BUT THE CLOSER WE GET, THE HARDER HE IS TO **LOCATE.**
THERE'S SOME **MASSIVE** ENERGY IN THIS PLACE, AND IT'S **DISRUPTING** MY CONNECTION.
YEAH, THERE'S SOMETHING **ELSE** HERE AS WELL.
SOUNDS LIKE IT'S COMING FROM ALL **AROUND** US...
AAAARRRRGGHHH!
UGH!
OOOOF!
KEN, REGAN, GET OUT OF HERE. **NOW.**
I'LL HANDLE THIS.

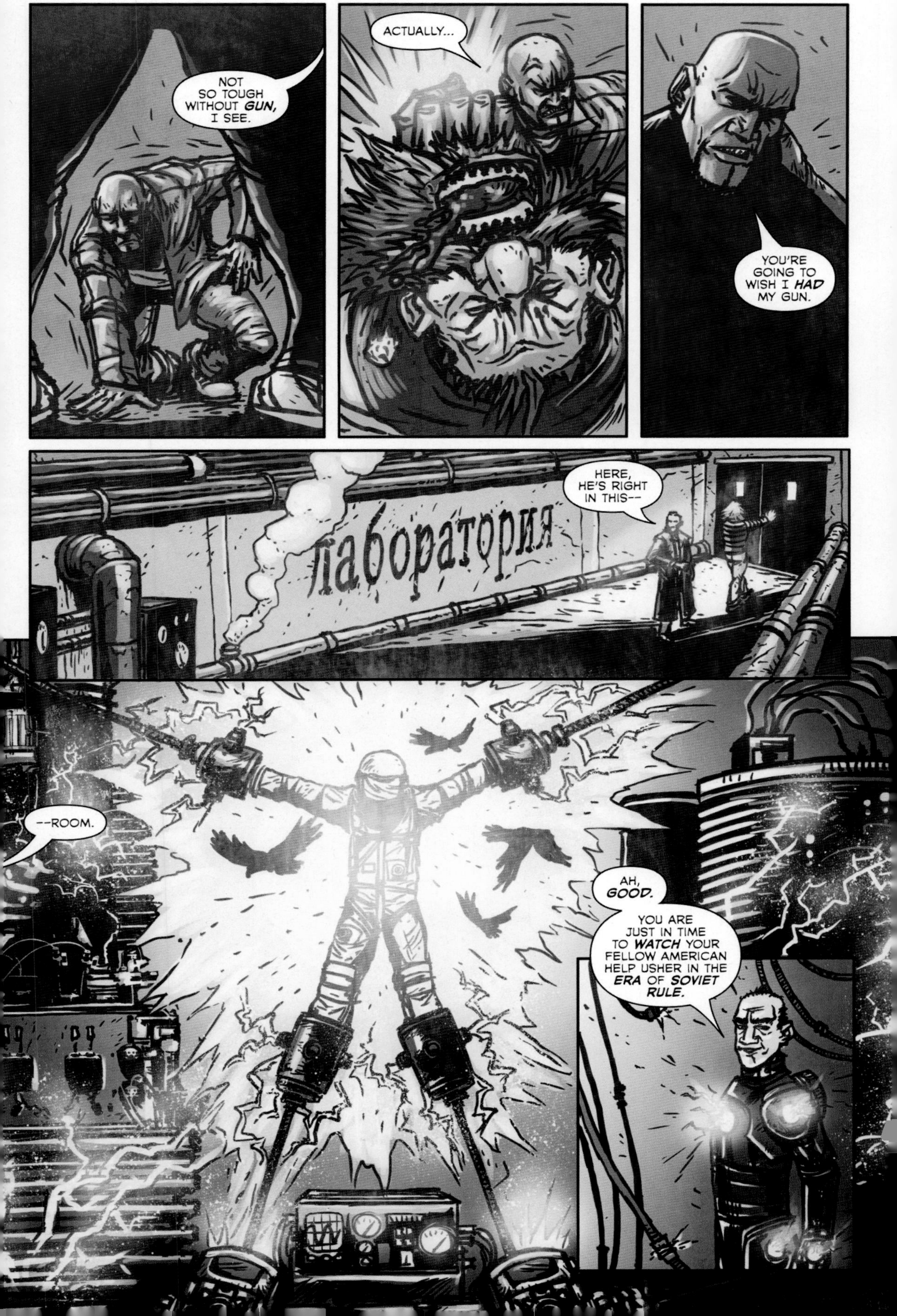
NOT SO TOUGH WITHOUT *GUN,* I SEE.
ACTUALLY...
YOU'RE GOING TO WISH I *HAD* MY GUN.
Лаборатория
HERE, HE'S RIGHT IN THIS--
--ROOM.
AH, *GOOD.*
YOU ARE JUST IN TIME TO *WATCH* YOUR FELLOW AMERICAN HELP USHER IN THE *ERA* OF *SOVIET RULE.*

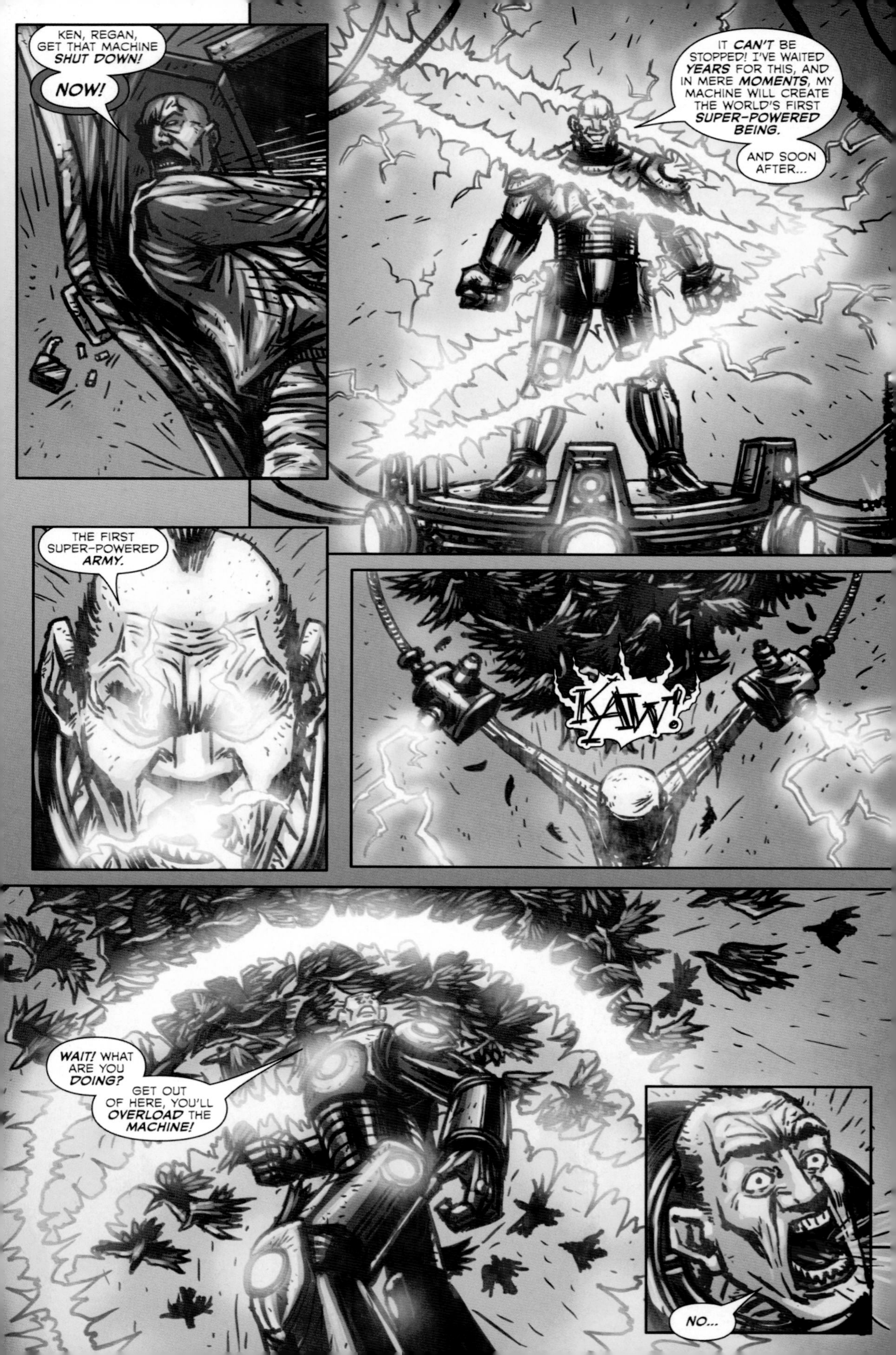
KEN, REGAN, GET THAT MACHINE SHUT DOWN!
NOW!
IT CAN'T BE STOPPED! I'VE WAITED YEARS FOR THIS, AND IN MERE MOMENTS, MY MACHINE WILL CREATE THE WORLD'S FIRST SUPER-POWERED BEING.
AND SOON AFTER...
THE FIRST SUPER-POWERED ARMY.
KAW!
WAIT! WHAT ARE YOU DOING?
GET OUT OF HERE, YOU'LL OVERLOAD THE MACHINE!
NO...

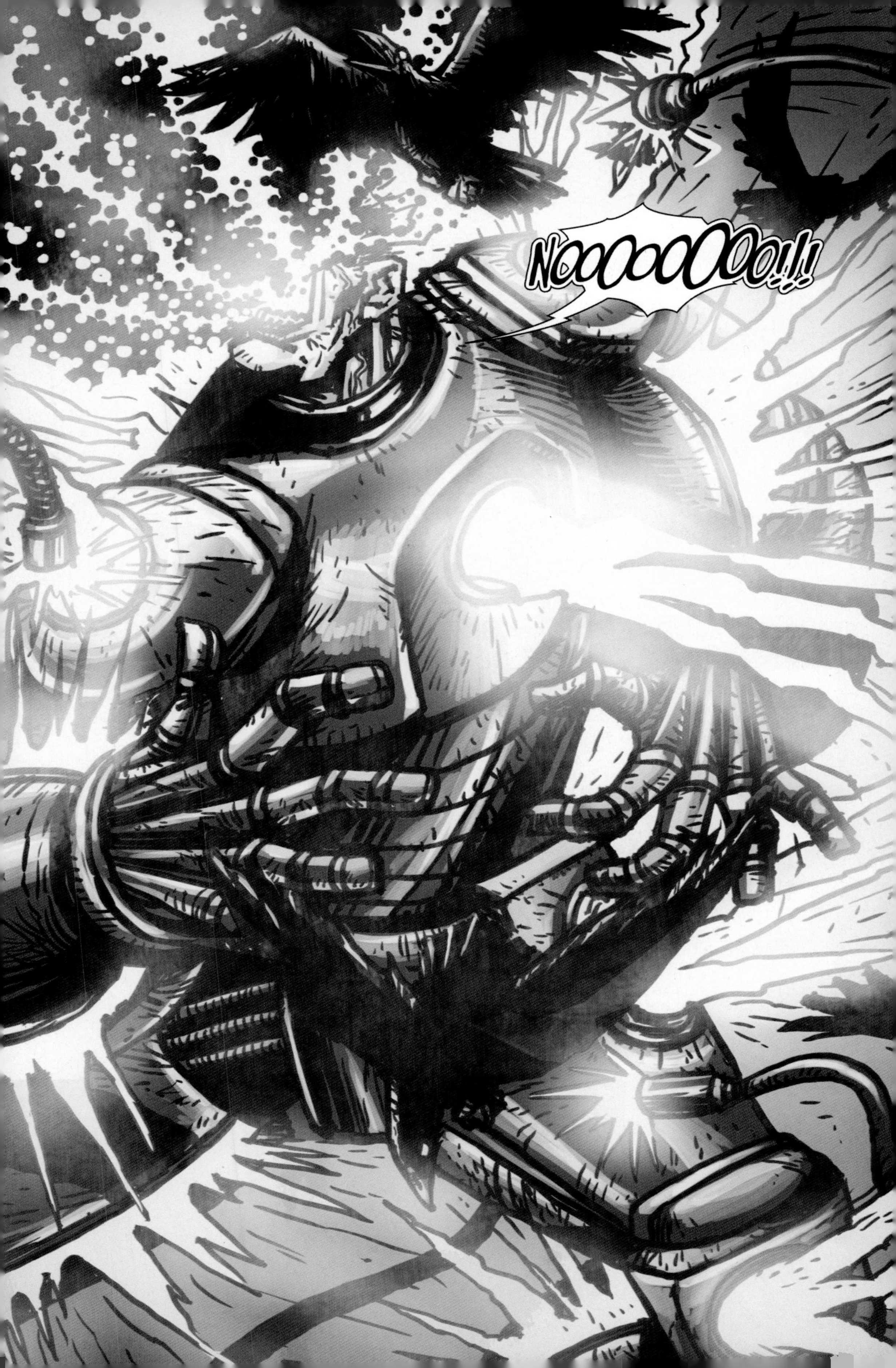
NOOOOOOOO!!!

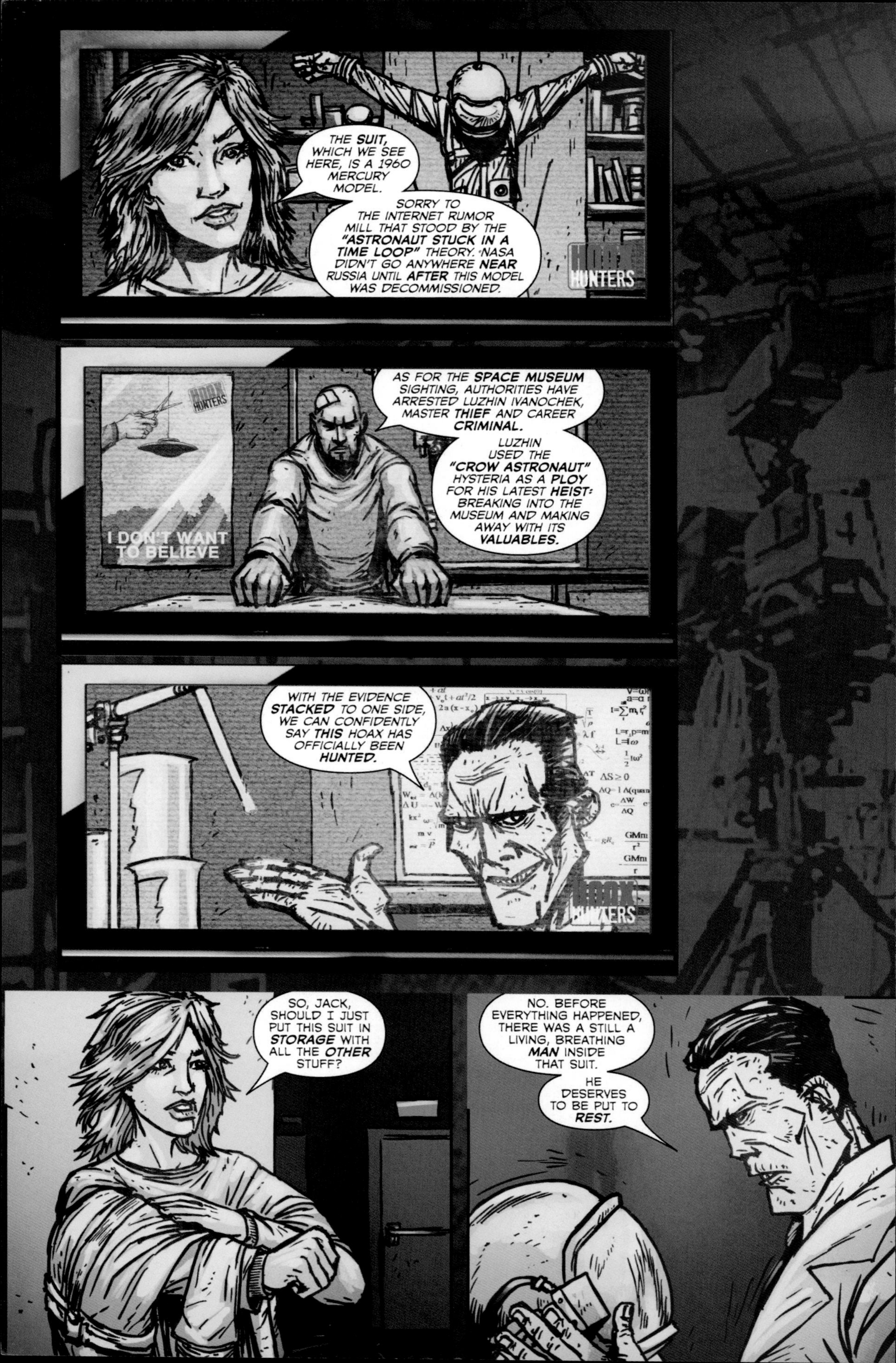
THE SUIT, WHICH WE SEE HERE, IS A 1960 MERCURY MODEL.
SORRY TO THE INTERNET RUMOR MILL THAT STOOD BY THE "ASTRONAUT STUCK IN A TIME LOOP" THEORY. NASA DIDN'T GO ANYWHERE NEAR RUSSIA UNTIL AFTER THIS MODEL WAS DECOMMISSIONED.
HOAX HUNTERS
HOAX HUNTERS
I DON'T WANT TO BELIEVE
AS FOR THE SPACE MUSEUM SIGHTING, AUTHORITIES HAVE ARRESTED LUZHIN IVANOCHEK, MASTER THIEF AND CAREER CRIMINAL.
LUZHIN USED THE "CROW ASTRONAUT" HYSTERIA AS A PLOY FOR HIS LATEST HEIST: BREAKING INTO THE MUSEUM AND MAKING AWAY WITH ITS VALUABLES.
WITH THE EVIDENCE STACKED TO ONE SIDE, WE CAN CONFIDENTLY SAY THIS HOAX HAS OFFICIALLY BEEN HUNTED.
SO, JACK, SHOULD I JUST PUT THIS SUIT IN STORAGE WITH ALL THE OTHER STUFF?
NO. BEFORE EVERYTHING HAPPENED, THERE WAS A STILL A LIVING, BREATHING MAN INSIDE THAT SUIT.
HE DESERVES TO BE PUT TO REST.

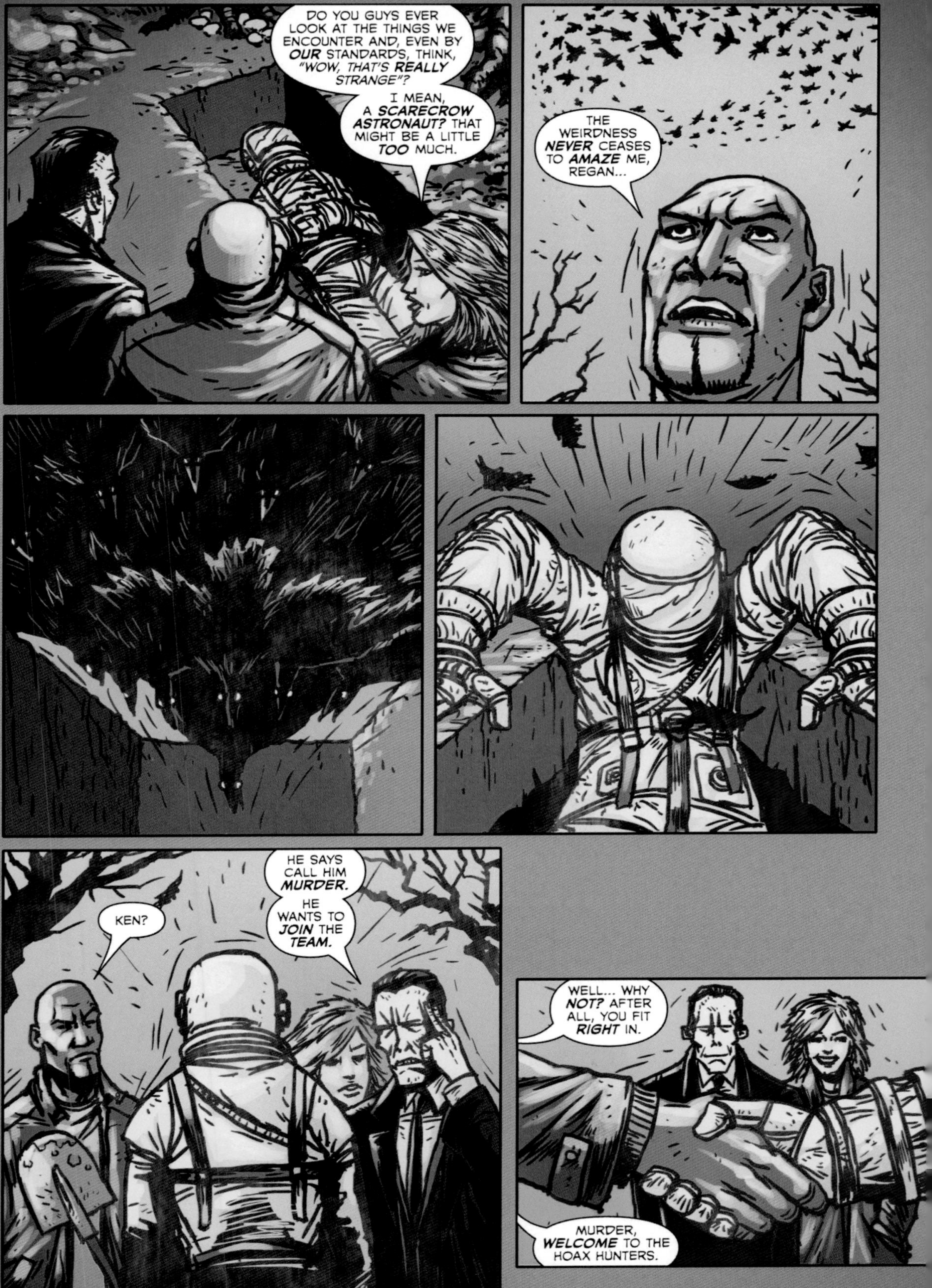
DO YOU GUYS EVER LOOK AT THE THINGS WE ENCOUNTER AND, EVEN BY *OUR* STANDARDS, THINK, *"WOW, THAT'S REALLY STRANGE"?*
I MEAN, A **SCARECROW ASTRONAUT?** THAT MIGHT BE A LITTLE **TOO** MUCH.
THE WEIRDNESS **NEVER** CEASES TO **AMAZE** ME, REGAN...
KEN?
HE SAYS CALL HIM **MURDER.**
HE WANTS TO **JOIN** THE **TEAM.**
WELL... WHY **NOT?** AFTER ALL, YOU FIT **RIGHT** IN.
MURDER, **WELCOME** TO THE HOAX HUNTERS.
THE STORY **CONTINUES** *IN* **HOAX HUNTERS #1...**

HOAX HUNTERS

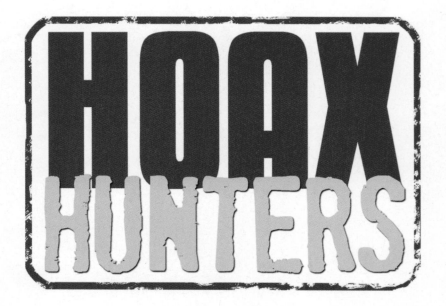

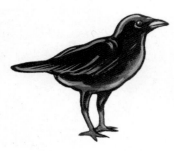

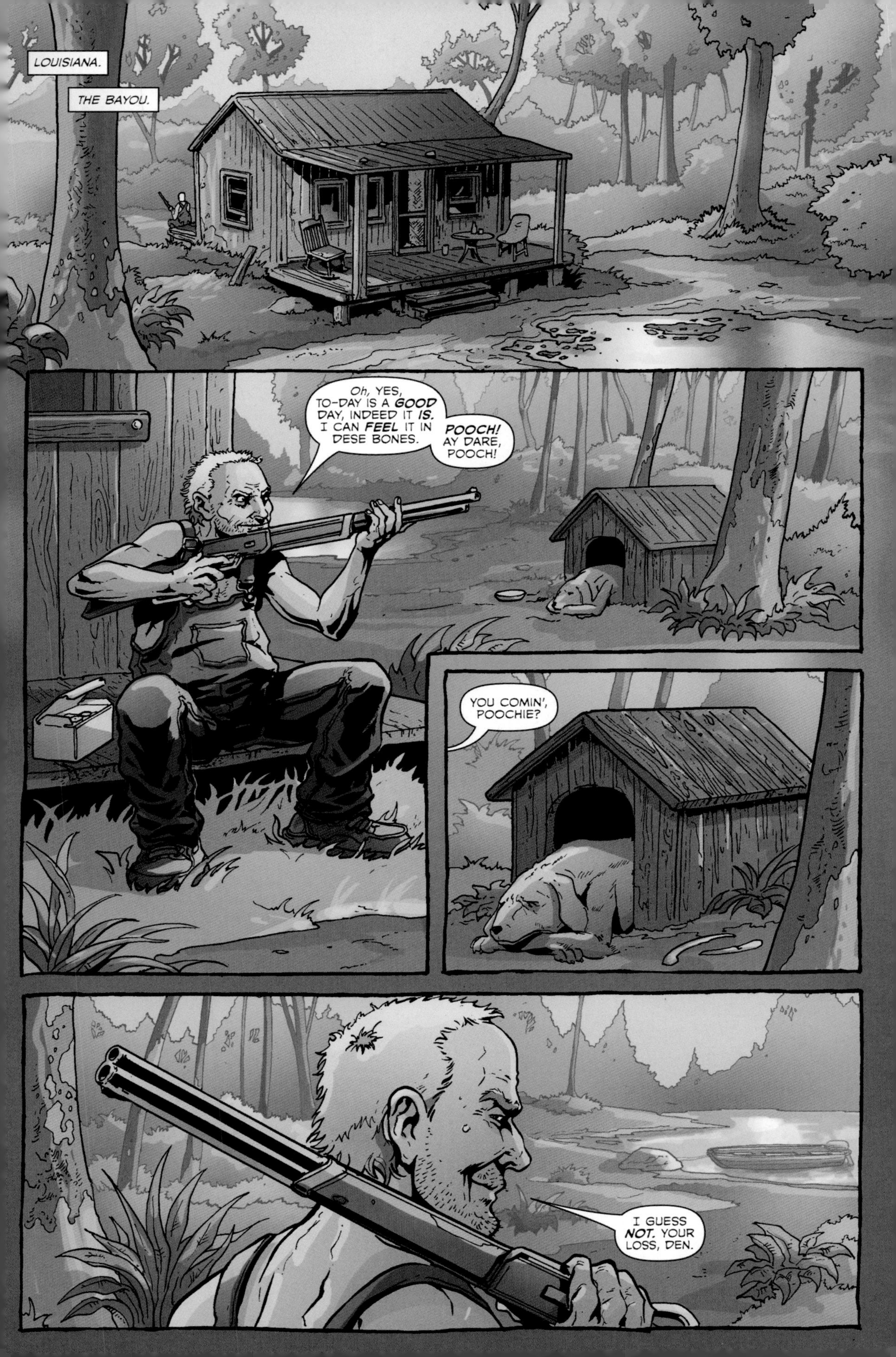
LOUISIANA.
THE BAYOU.
Oh, YES, TO-DAY IS A GOOD DAY, INDEED IT IS. I CAN FEEL IT IN DESE BONES.
POOCH! AY DARE, POOCH!
YOU COMIN', POOCHIE?
I GUESS NOT. YOUR LOSS, DEN.

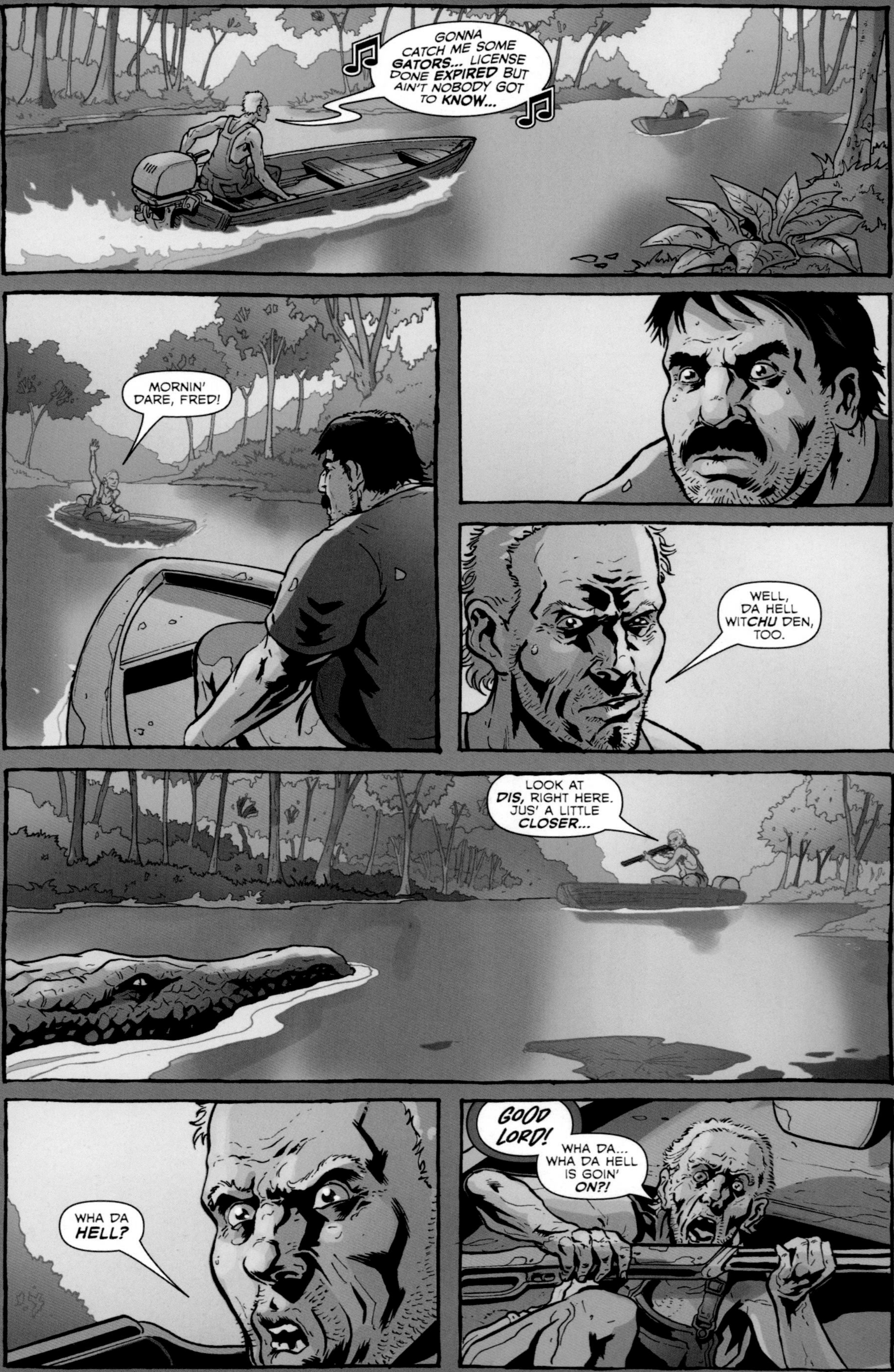
GONNA CATCH ME SOME GATORS... LICENSE DONE EXPIRED BUT AIN'T NOBODY GOT TO KNOW...
MORNIN' DARE, FRED!
WELL, DA HELL WITCHU DEN, TOO.
LOOK AT DIS, RIGHT HERE. JUS' A LITTLE CLOSER...
WHA DA HELL?
GOOD LORD!
WHA DA... WHA DA HELL IS GOIN' ON?!

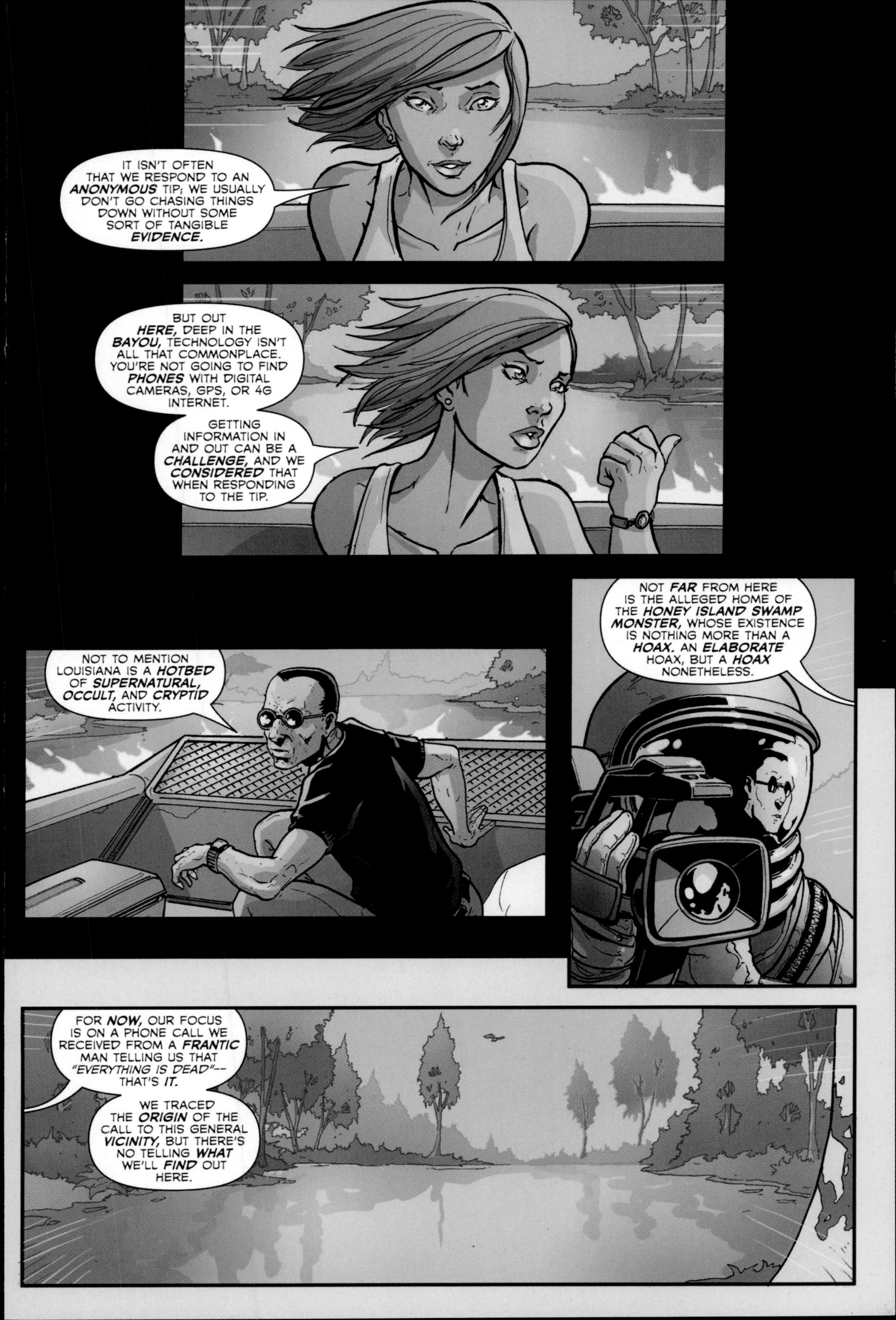

IT ISN'T OFTEN THAT WE RESPOND TO AN ANONYMOUS TIP; WE USUALLY DON'T GO CHASING THINGS DOWN WITHOUT SOME SORT OF TANGIBLE EVIDENCE.
BUT OUT HERE, DEEP IN THE BAYOU, TECHNOLOGY ISN'T ALL THAT COMMONPLACE. YOU'RE NOT GOING TO FIND PHONES WITH DIGITAL CAMERAS, GPS, OR 4G INTERNET.
GETTING INFORMATION IN AND OUT CAN BE A CHALLENGE, AND WE CONSIDERED THAT WHEN RESPONDING TO THE TIP.
NOT TO MENTION LOUISIANA IS A HOTBED OF SUPERNATURAL, OCCULT, AND CRYPTID ACTIVITY.
NOT FAR FROM HERE IS THE ALLEGED HOME OF THE HONEY ISLAND SWAMP MONSTER, WHOSE EXISTENCE IS NOTHING MORE THAN A HOAX. AN ELABORATE HOAX, BUT A HOAX NONETHELESS.
FOR NOW, OUR FOCUS IS ON A PHONE CALL WE RECEIVED FROM A FRANTIC MAN TELLING US THAT "EVERYTHING IS DEAD"-- THAT'S IT.
WE TRACED THE ORIGIN OF THE CALL TO THIS GENERAL VICINITY, BUT THERE'S NO TELLING WHAT WE'LL FIND OUT HERE.

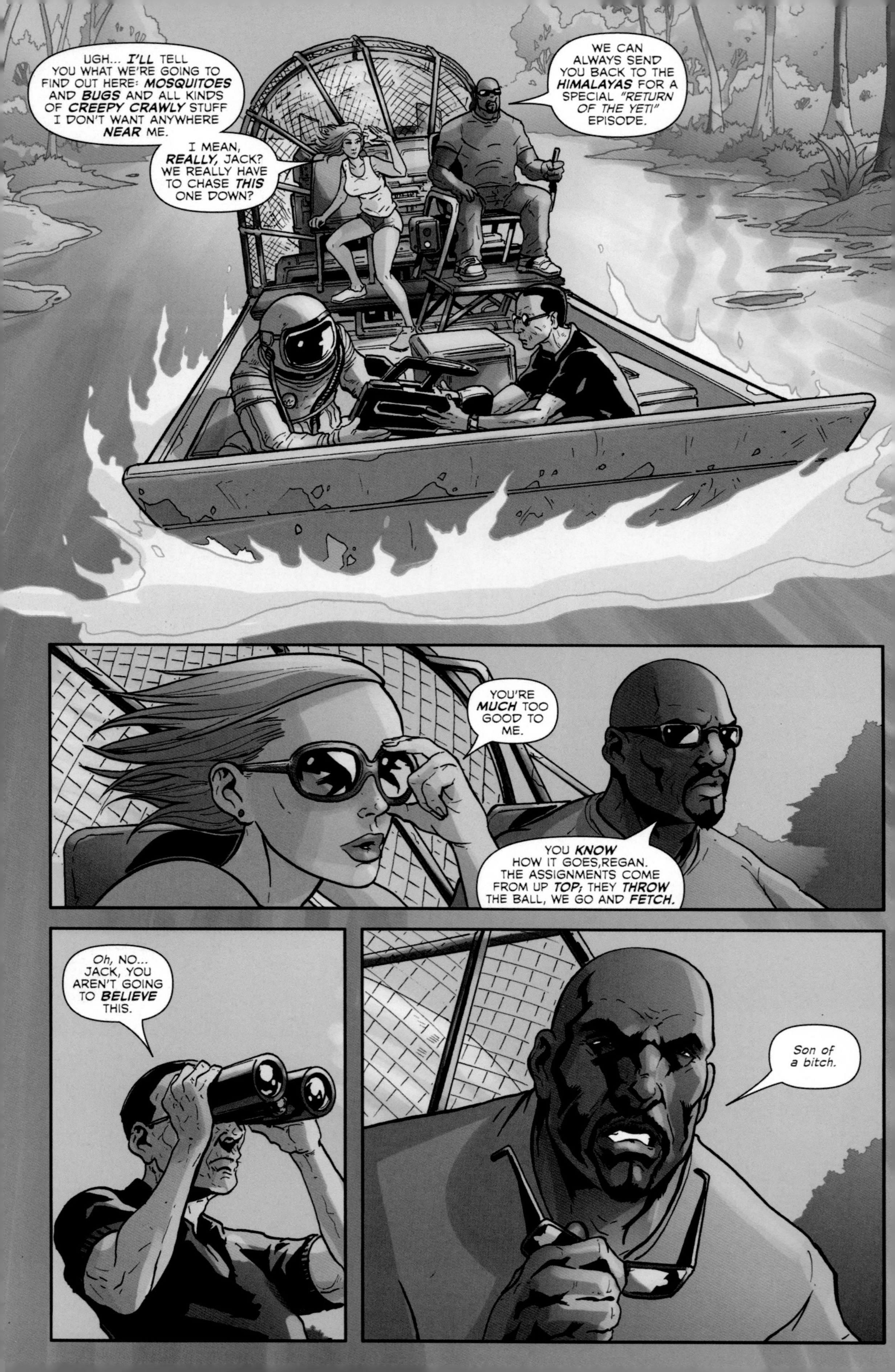

UGH... *I'LL* TELL YOU WHAT WE'RE GOING TO FIND OUT HERE: *MOSQUITOES* AND *BUGS* AND ALL KINDS OF *CREEPY CRAWLY* STUFF I DON'T WANT ANYWHERE *NEAR* ME.
I MEAN, *REALLY,* JACK? WE REALLY HAVE TO CHASE *THIS* ONE DOWN?
WE CAN ALWAYS SEND YOU BACK TO THE *HIMALAYAS* FOR A SPECIAL *"RETURN OF THE YETI!"* EPISODE.
YOU'RE *MUCH* TOO GOOD TO ME.
YOU *KNOW* HOW IT GOES,REGAN. THE ASSIGNMENTS COME FROM UP *TOP;* THEY *THROW* THE BALL, WE GO AND *FETCH.*
Oh, NO... JACK, YOU AREN'T GOING TO *BELIEVE* THIS.
Son of a bitch.

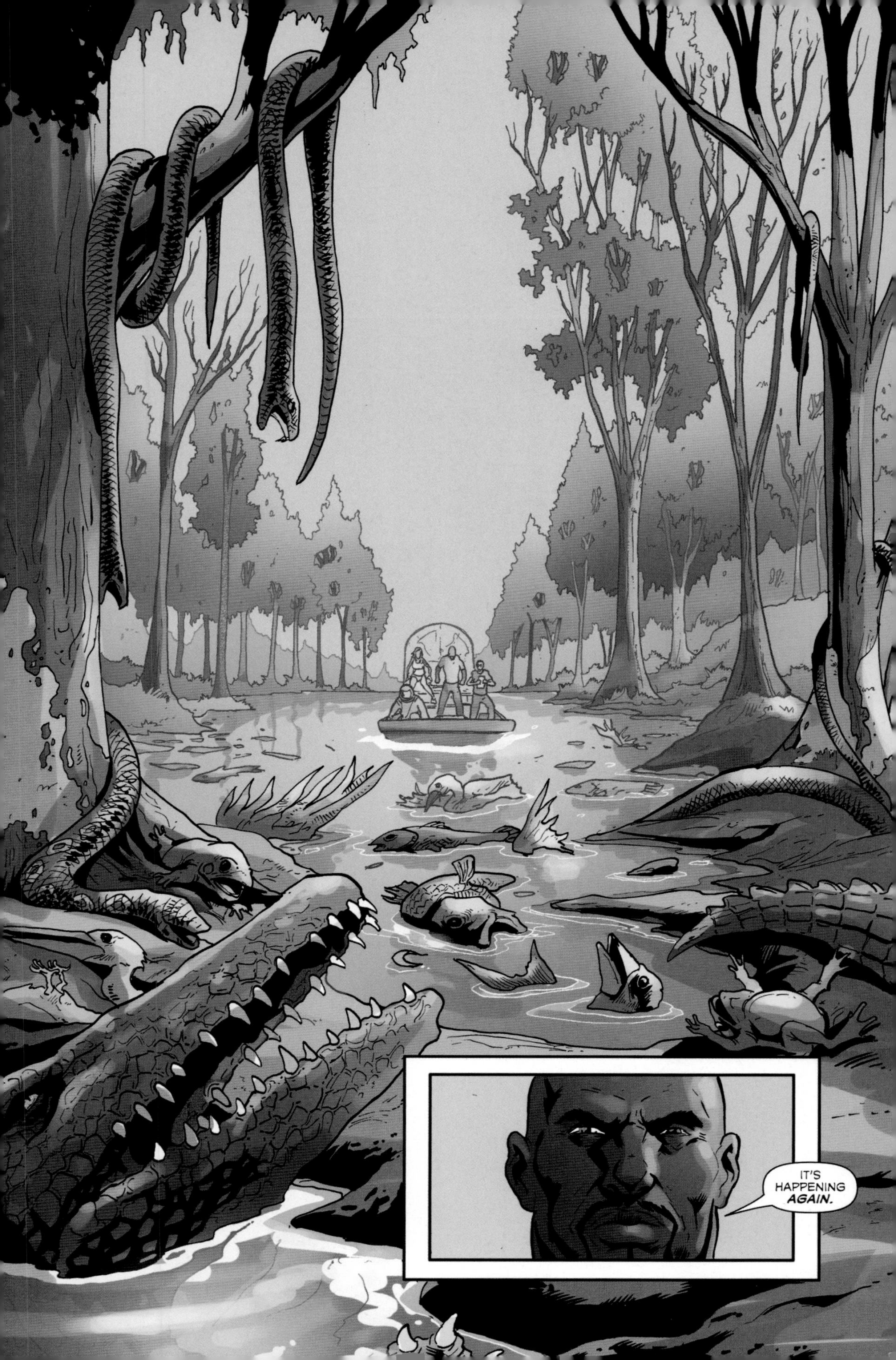
IT'S HAPPENING *AGAIN.*

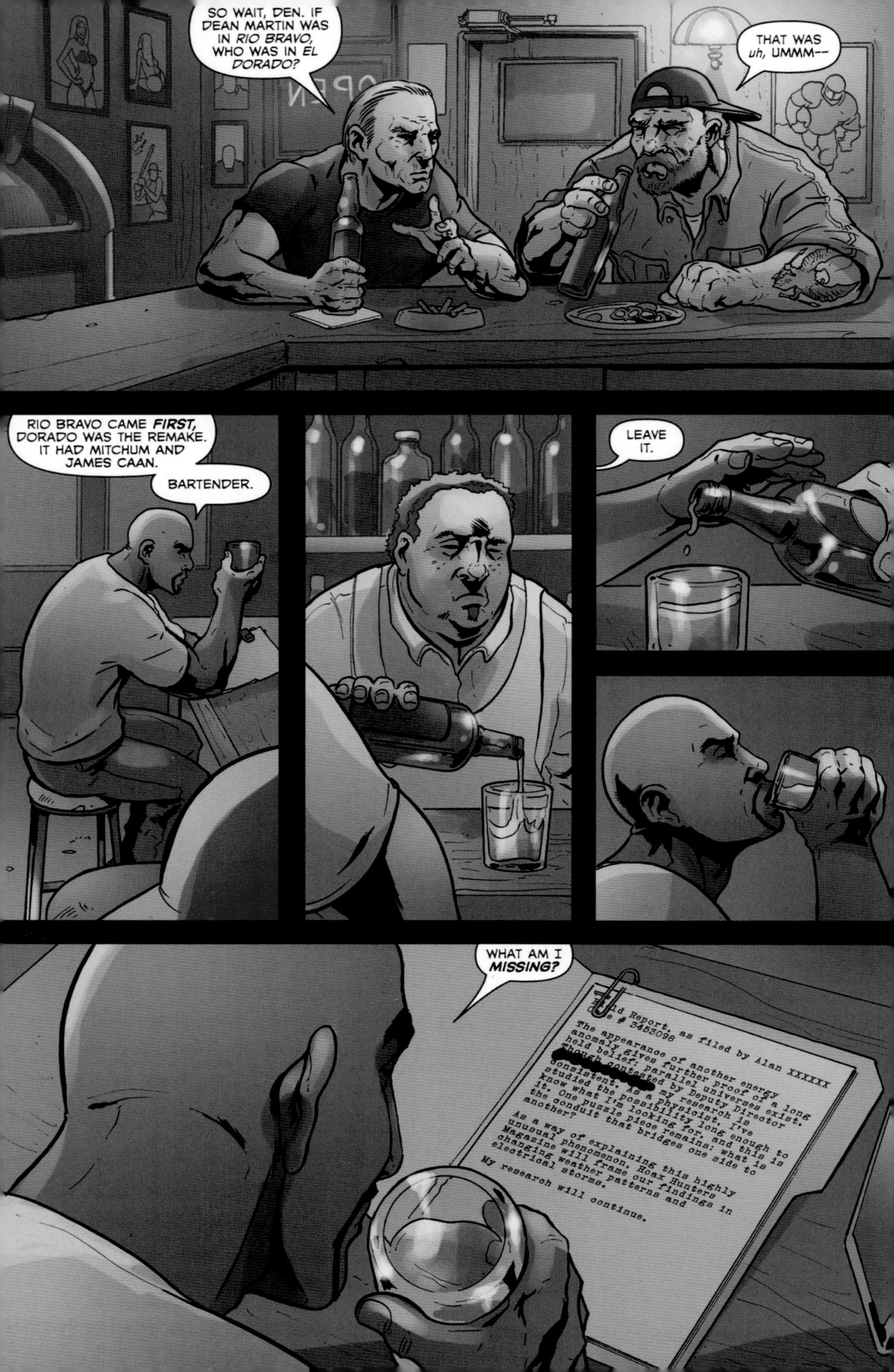

SO WAIT, DEN. IF DEAN MARTIN WAS IN *RIO BRAVO*, WHO WAS IN *EL DORADO*?
THAT WAS *uh*, UMMM--
RIO BRAVO CAME ***FIRST***, DORADO WAS THE REMAKE. IT HAD MITCHUM AND JAMES CAAN.
BARTENDER.
LEAVE IT.
WHAT AM I ***MISSING?***
ld Report, as filed by Alan XXXXXX
e # 3453098
The appearance of another energy anomaly gives further proof of a long held belief: parallel universes exist. [redacted] by Deputy Director consistent. As a physicist, I've studied the possibility long enough to know what I'm looking for, and this is it. One puzzle piece remains: what is the conduit that bridges one side to another?
As a way of explaining this highly unusual phenomenon, Hoax Hunters Magazine will frame our findings in changing weather patterns and electrical storms.
My research will continue.

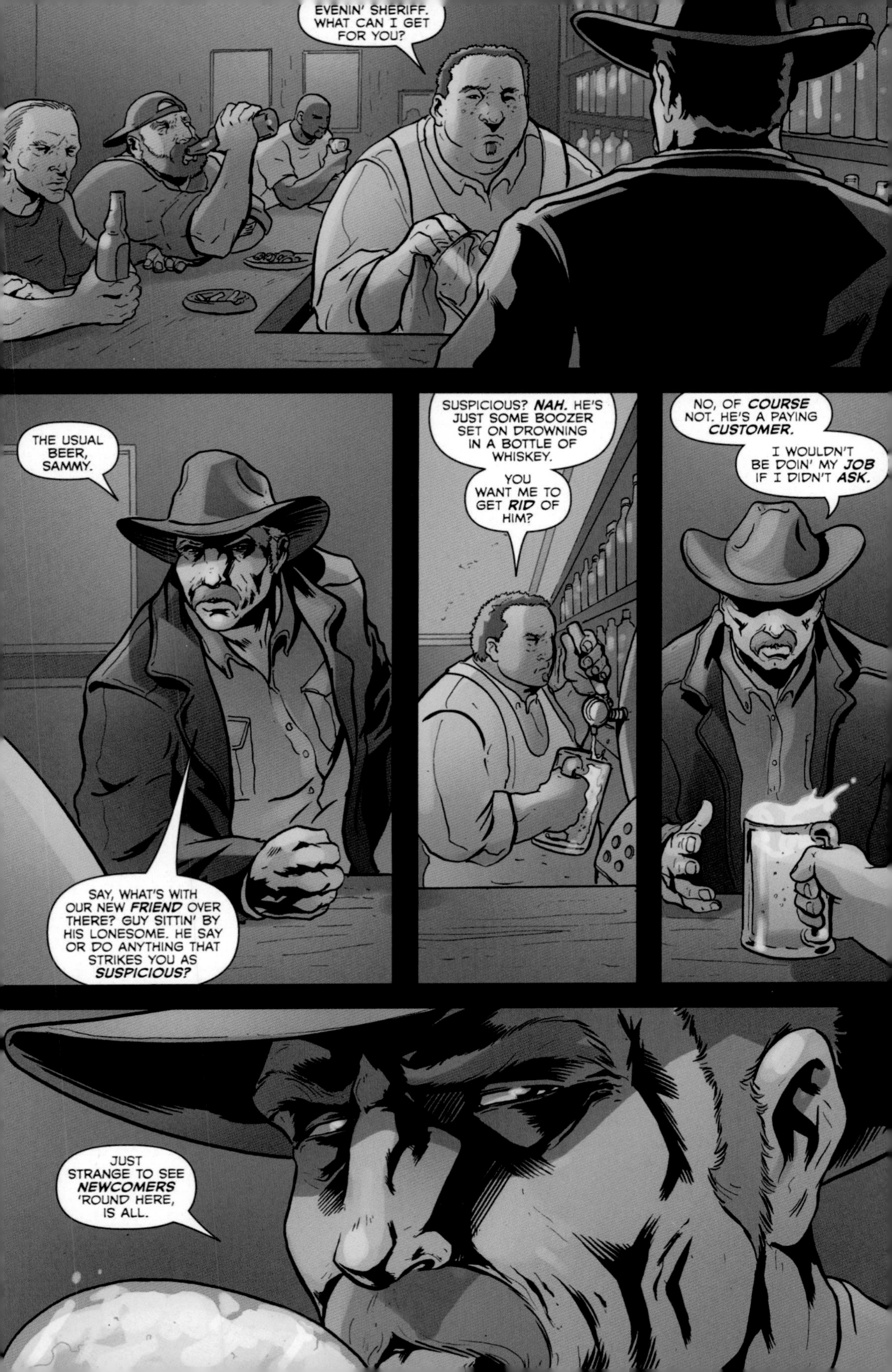
EVENIN' SHERIFF. WHAT CAN I GET FOR YOU?
THE USUAL BEER, SAMMY.
SAY, WHAT'S WITH OUR NEW FRIEND OVER THERE? GUY SITTIN' BY HIS LONESOME. HE SAY OR DO ANYTHING THAT STRIKES YOU AS SUSPICIOUS?
SUSPICIOUS? NAH. HE'S JUST SOME BOOZER SET ON DROWNING IN A BOTTLE OF WHISKEY.
YOU WANT ME TO GET RID OF HIM?
NO, OF COURSE NOT. HE'S A PAYING CUSTOMER.
I WOULDN'T BE DOIN' MY JOB IF I DIDN'T ASK.
JUST STRANGE TO SEE NEWCOMERS 'ROUND HERE, IS ALL.

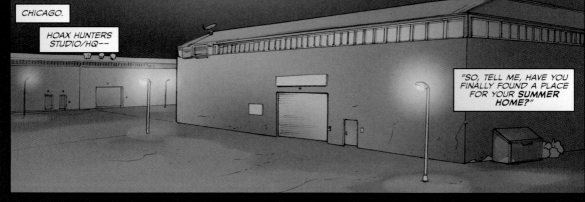

CHICAGO.

HOAX HUNTERS STUDIO/HQ--

"SO, TELL ME, HAVE YOU FINALLY FOUND A PLACE FOR YOUR *SUMMER HOME?*"

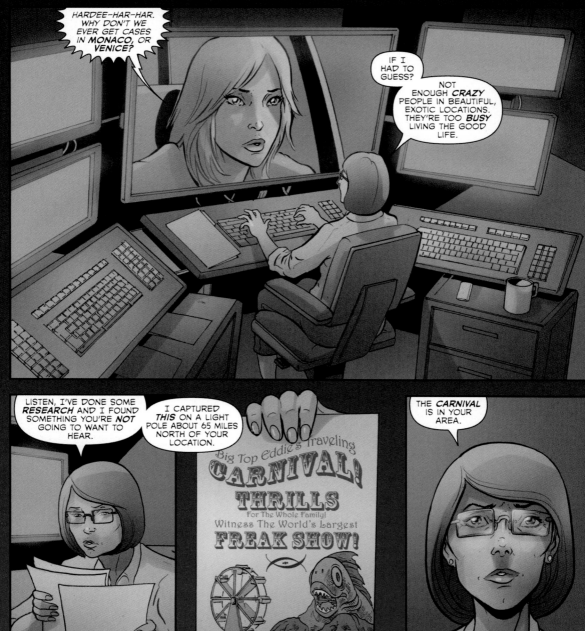

HARDEE-HAR-HAR. WHY DON'T WE EVER GET CASES IN *MONACO,* OR *VENICE?*

IF I HAD TO GUESS?

NOT ENOUGH *CRAZY* PEOPLE IN BEAUTIFUL, EXOTIC LOCATIONS. THEY'RE TOO *BUSY* LIVING THE GOOD LIFE.

LISTEN, I'VE DONE SOME *RESEARCH* AND I FOUND SOMETHING YOU'RE *NOT* GOING TO WANT TO HEAR.

I CAPTURED *THIS* ON A LIGHT POLE ABOUT 65 MILES NORTH OF YOUR LOCATION.

Big Top Eddie's Traveling
CARNIVAL!
THRILLS
For The Whole Family!
Witness The World's Largest
FREAK SHOW!

THE *CARNIVAL* IS IN YOUR AREA.

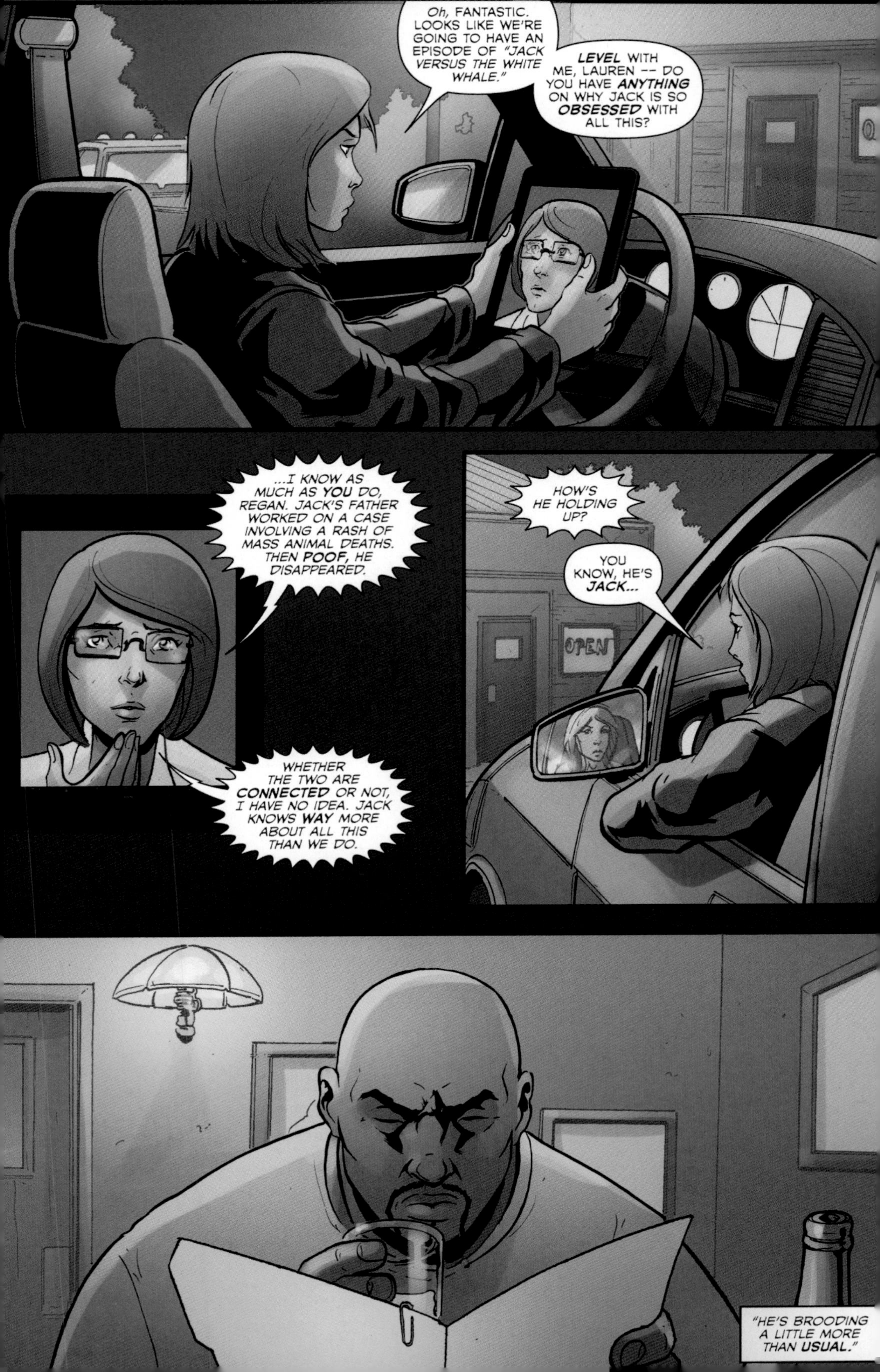
Oh, FANTASTIC. LOOKS LIKE WE'RE GOING TO HAVE AN EPISODE OF *"JACK VERSUS THE WHITE WHALE."*
LEVEL WITH ME, LAUREN -- DO YOU HAVE **ANYTHING** ON WHY JACK IS SO **OBSESSED** WITH ALL THIS?
...I KNOW AS MUCH AS **YOU** *DO, REGAN. JACK'S FATHER WORKED ON A CASE INVOLVING A RASH OF MASS ANIMAL DEATHS. THEN* **POOF,** *HE DISAPPEARED.*
WHETHER THE TWO ARE **CONNECTED** OR NOT, I HAVE NO IDEA. JACK KNOWS **WAY** MORE ABOUT ALL THIS THAN WE DO.
HOW'S HE HOLDING UP?
YOU KNOW, HE'S **JACK...**
OPEN
"HE'S BROODING A LITTLE MORE THAN **USUAL.**"

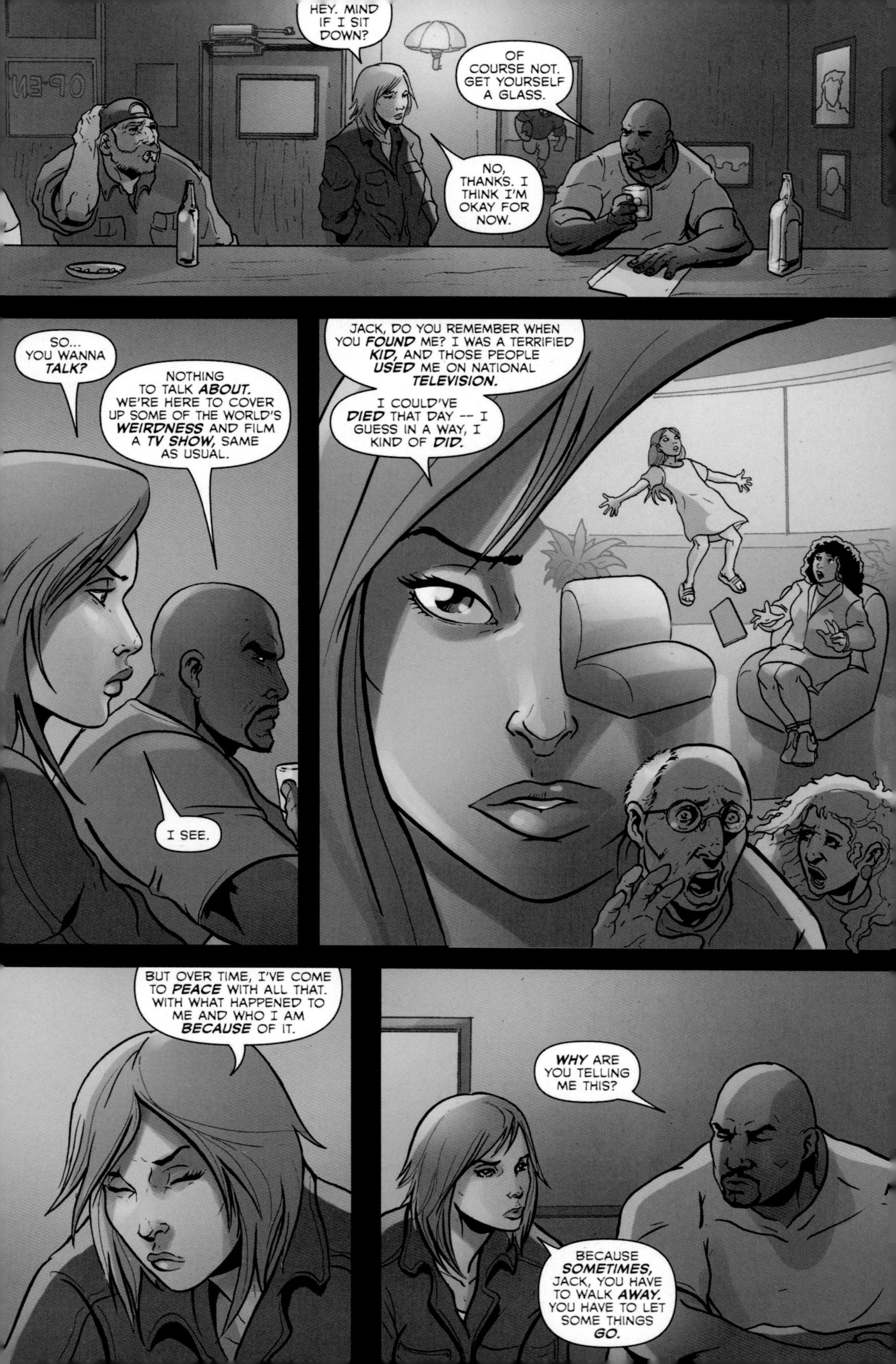

HEY. MIND IF I SIT DOWN?
OF COURSE NOT. GET YOURSELF A GLASS.
NO, THANKS. I THINK I'M OKAY FOR NOW.
SO... YOU WANNA TALK?
NOTHING TO TALK ABOUT. WE'RE HERE TO COVER UP SOME OF THE WORLD'S WEIRDNESS AND FILM A TV SHOW, SAME AS USUAL.
I SEE.
JACK, DO YOU REMEMBER WHEN YOU FOUND ME? I WAS A TERRIFIED KID, AND THOSE PEOPLE USED ME ON NATIONAL TELEVISION.
I COULD'VE DIED THAT DAY -- I GUESS IN A WAY, I KIND OF DID.
BUT OVER TIME, I'VE COME TO PEACE WITH ALL THAT. WITH WHAT HAPPENED TO ME AND WHO I AM BECAUSE OF IT.
WHY ARE YOU TELLING ME THIS?
BECAUSE SOMETIMES, JACK, YOU HAVE TO WALK AWAY. YOU HAVE TO LET SOME THINGS GO.

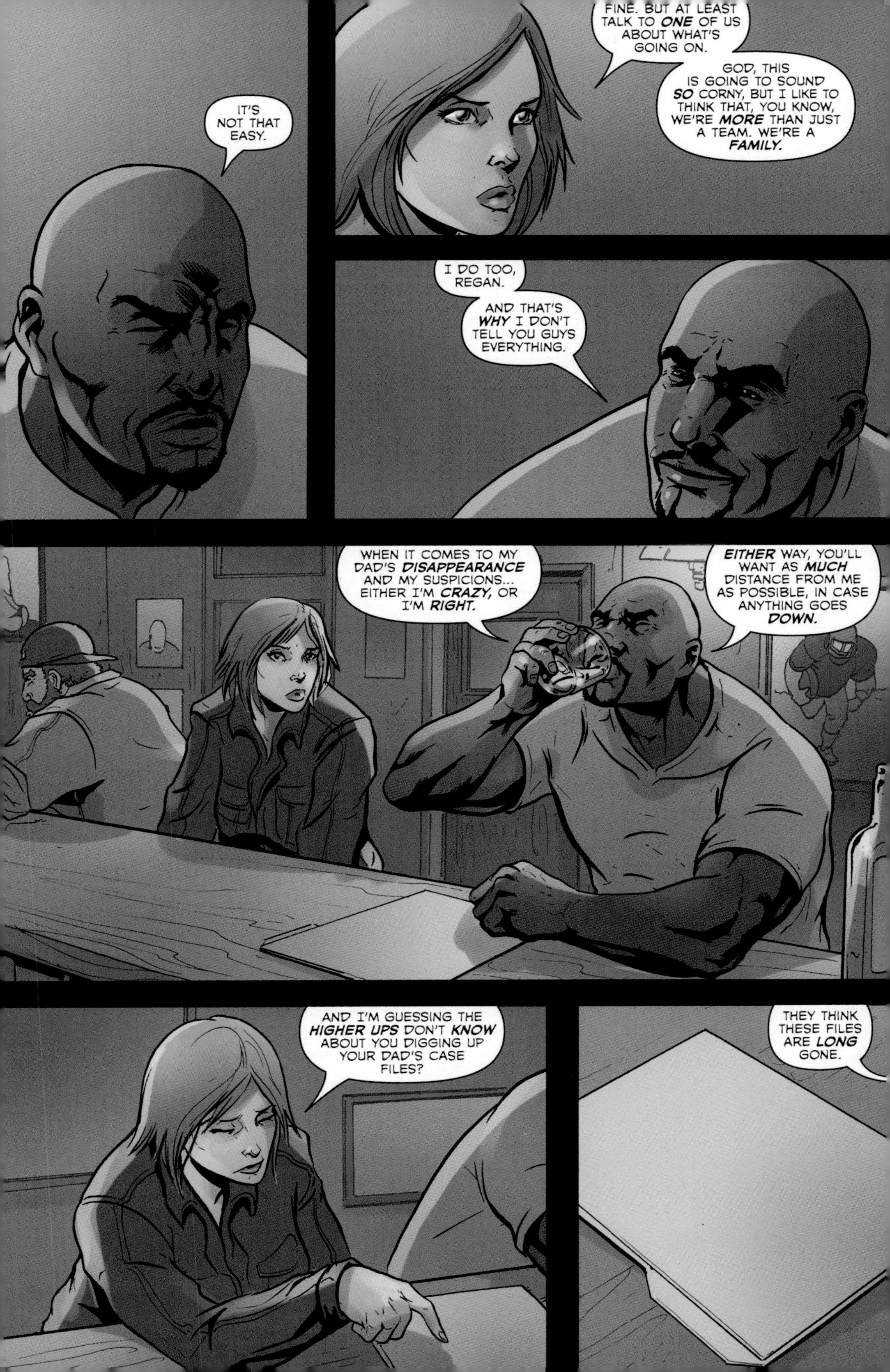
IT'S NOT THAT EASY.
FINE. BUT AT LEAST TALK TO ONE OF US ABOUT WHAT'S GOING ON.
GOD, THIS IS GOING TO SOUND SO CORNY, BUT I LIKE TO THINK THAT, YOU KNOW, WE'RE MORE THAN JUST A TEAM. WE'RE A FAMILY.
I DO TOO, REGAN.
AND THAT'S WHY I DON'T TELL YOU GUYS EVERYTHING.
WHEN IT COMES TO MY DAD'S DISAPPEARANCE AND MY SUSPICIONS... EITHER I'M CRAZY, OR I'M RIGHT.
EITHER WAY, YOU'LL WANT AS MUCH DISTANCE FROM ME AS POSSIBLE, IN CASE ANYTHING GOES DOWN.
AND I'M GUESSING THE HIGHER UPS DON'T KNOW ABOUT YOU DIGGING UP YOUR DAD'S CASE FILES?
THEY THINK THESE FILES ARE LONG GONE.

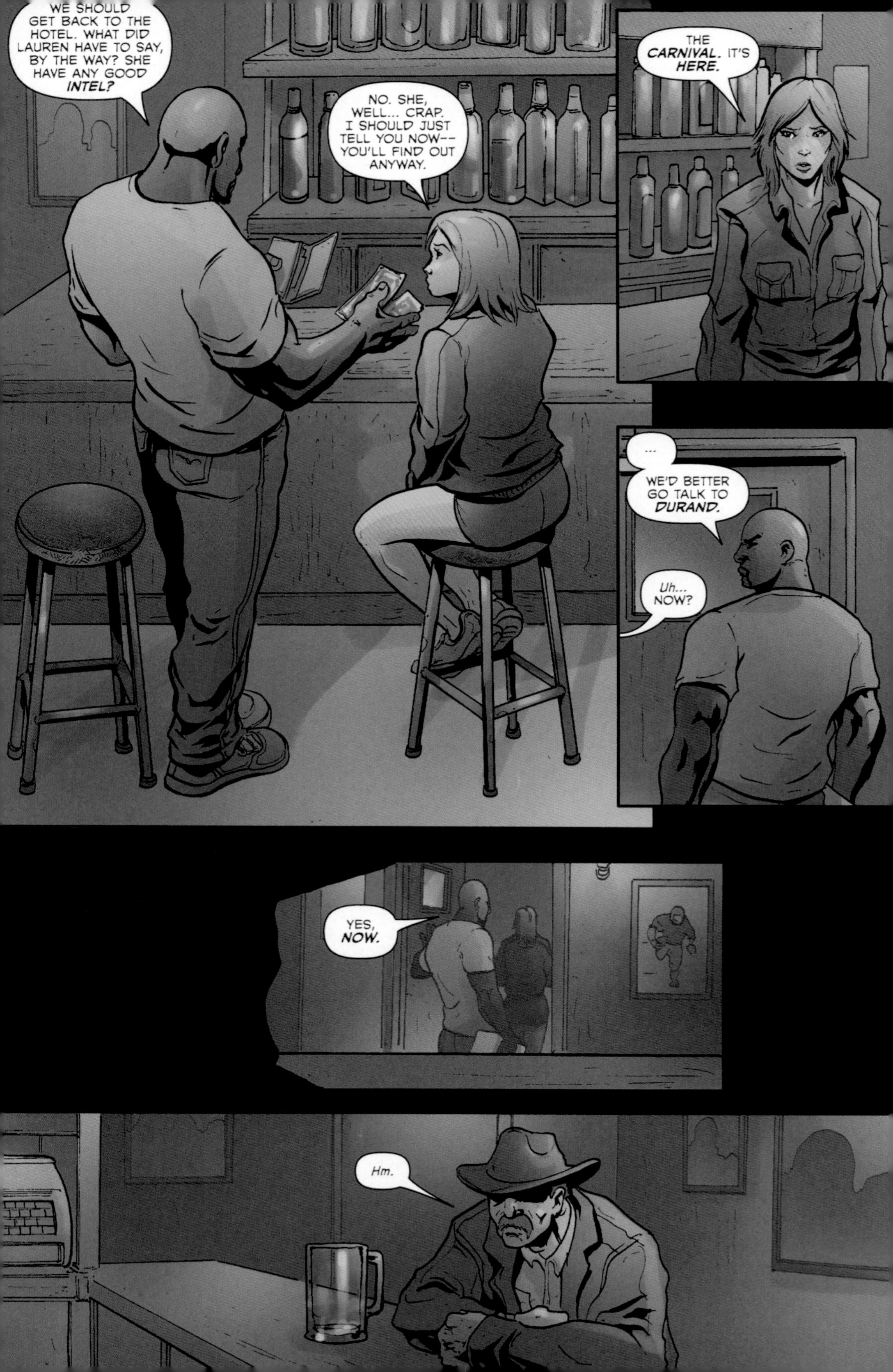
WE SHOULD GET BACK TO THE HOTEL. WHAT DID LAUREN HAVE TO SAY, BY THE WAY? SHE HAVE ANY GOOD INTEL?
NO. SHE, WELL... CRAP. I SHOULD JUST TELL YOU NOW-- YOU'LL FIND OUT ANYWAY.
THE CARNIVAL. IT'S HERE.
...
WE'D BETTER GO TALK TO DURAND.
Uh... NOW?
YES, NOW.
Hm.

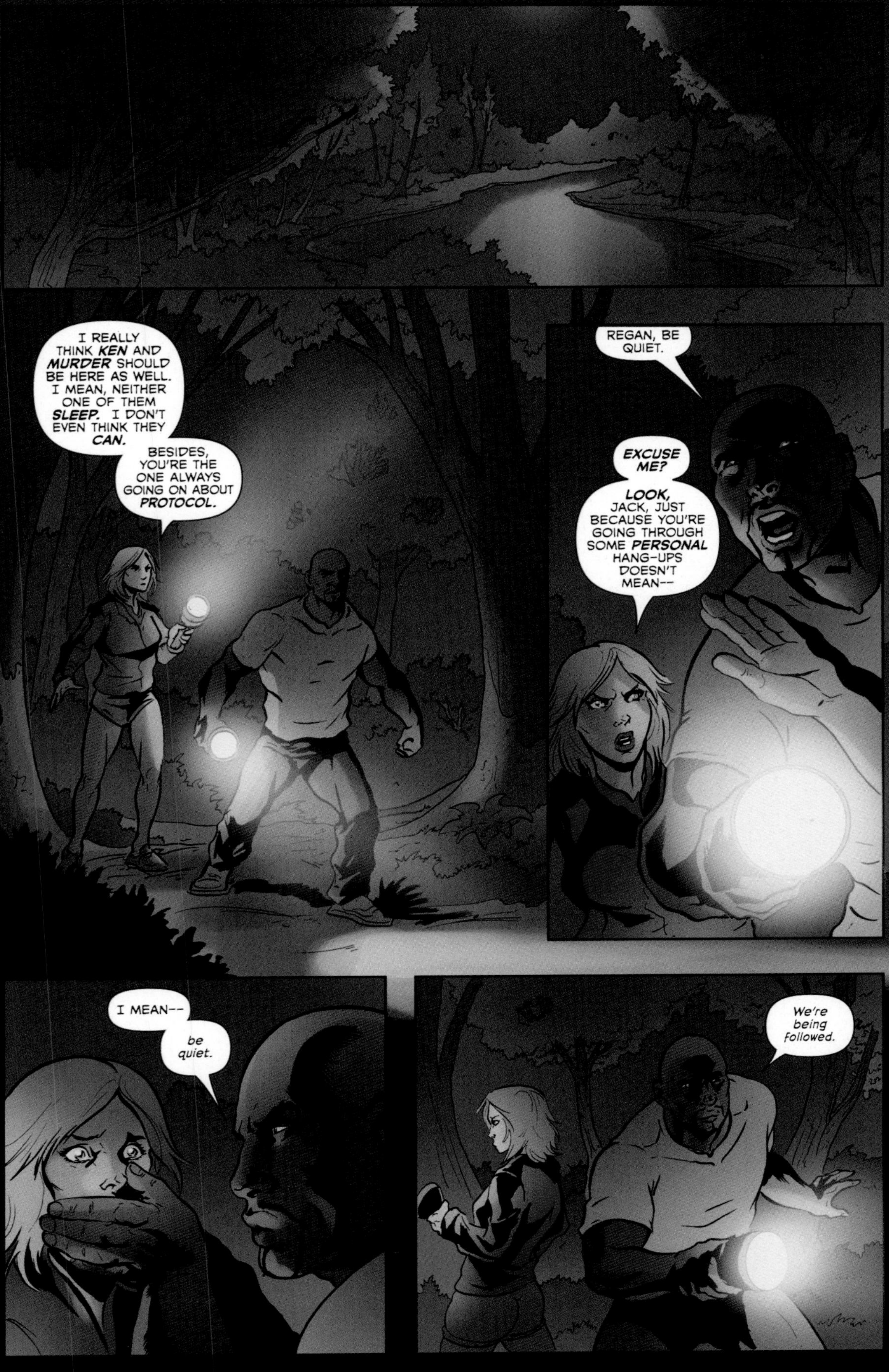

I REALLY THINK **KEN** AND **MURDER** SHOULD BE HERE AS WELL. I MEAN, NEITHER ONE OF THEM **SLEEP.** I DON'T EVEN THINK THEY **CAN.**
BESIDES, YOU'RE THE ONE ALWAYS GOING ON ABOUT **PROTOCOL.**
REGAN, BE QUIET.
EXCUSE ME?
LOOK, JACK, JUST BECAUSE YOU'RE GOING THROUGH SOME **PERSONAL** HANG-UPS DOESN'T MEAN--
I MEAN--
be quiet.
We're being followed.

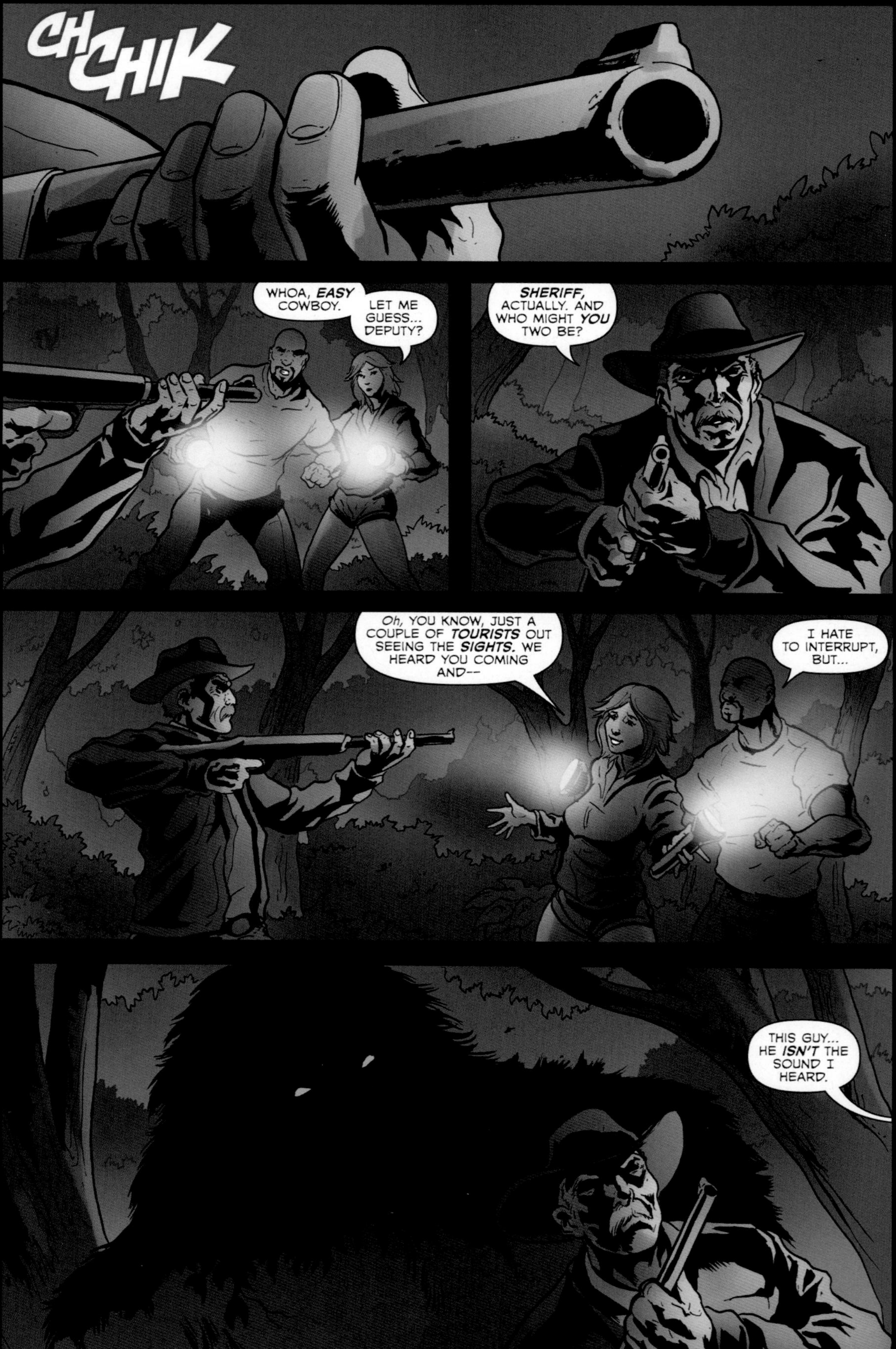
CH CHIK
WHOA, EASY COWBOY.
LET ME GUESS... DEPUTY?
SHERIFF, ACTUALLY. AND WHO MIGHT YOU TWO BE?
Oh, YOU KNOW, JUST A COUPLE OF TOURISTS OUT SEEING THE SIGHTS. WE HEARD YOU COMING AND--
I HATE TO INTERRUPT, BUT...
THIS GUY... HE ISN'T THE SOUND I HEARD.

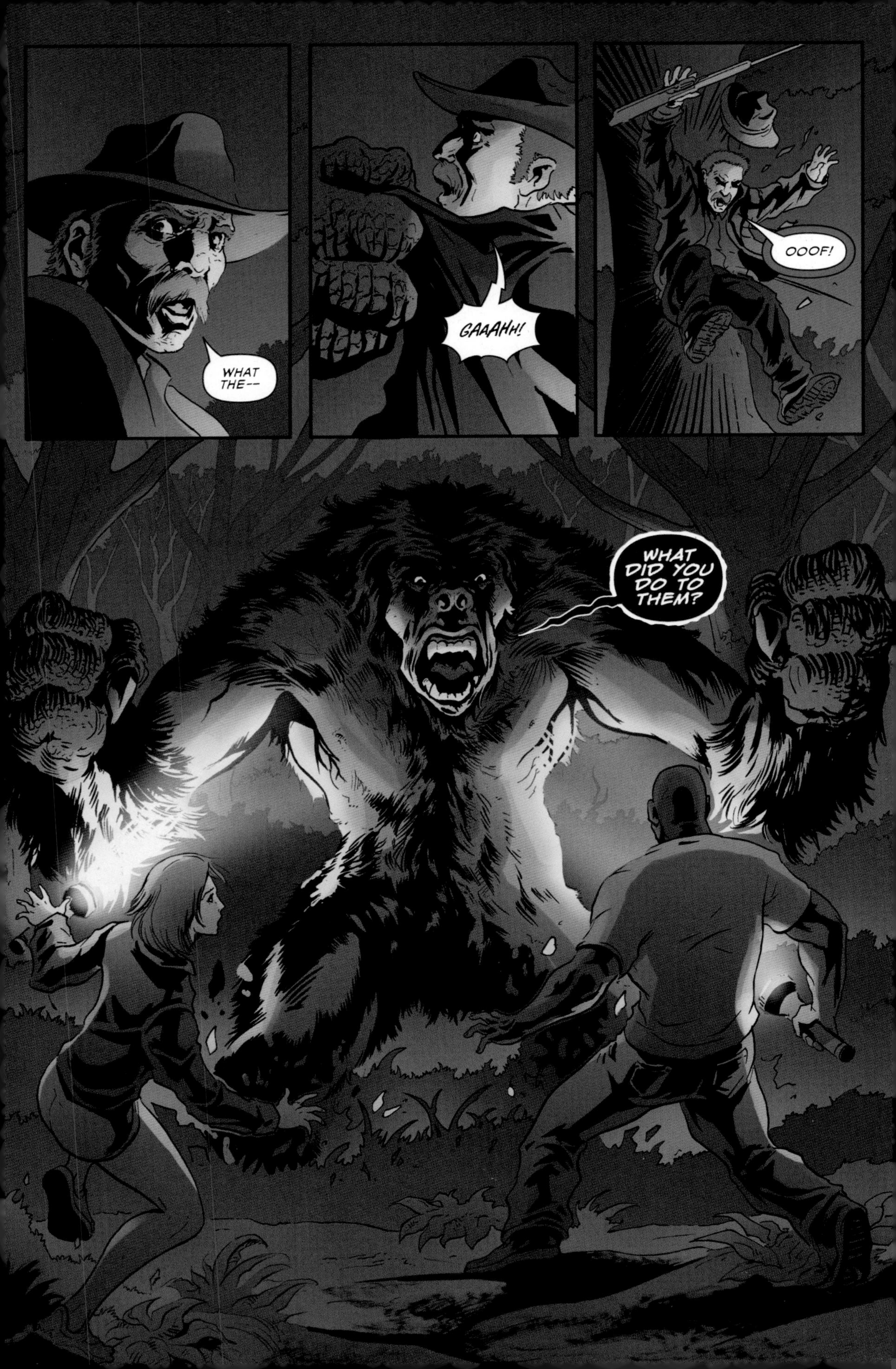
WHAT THE--
GAAAHH!
OOOF!
WHAT DID YOU DO TO THEM?

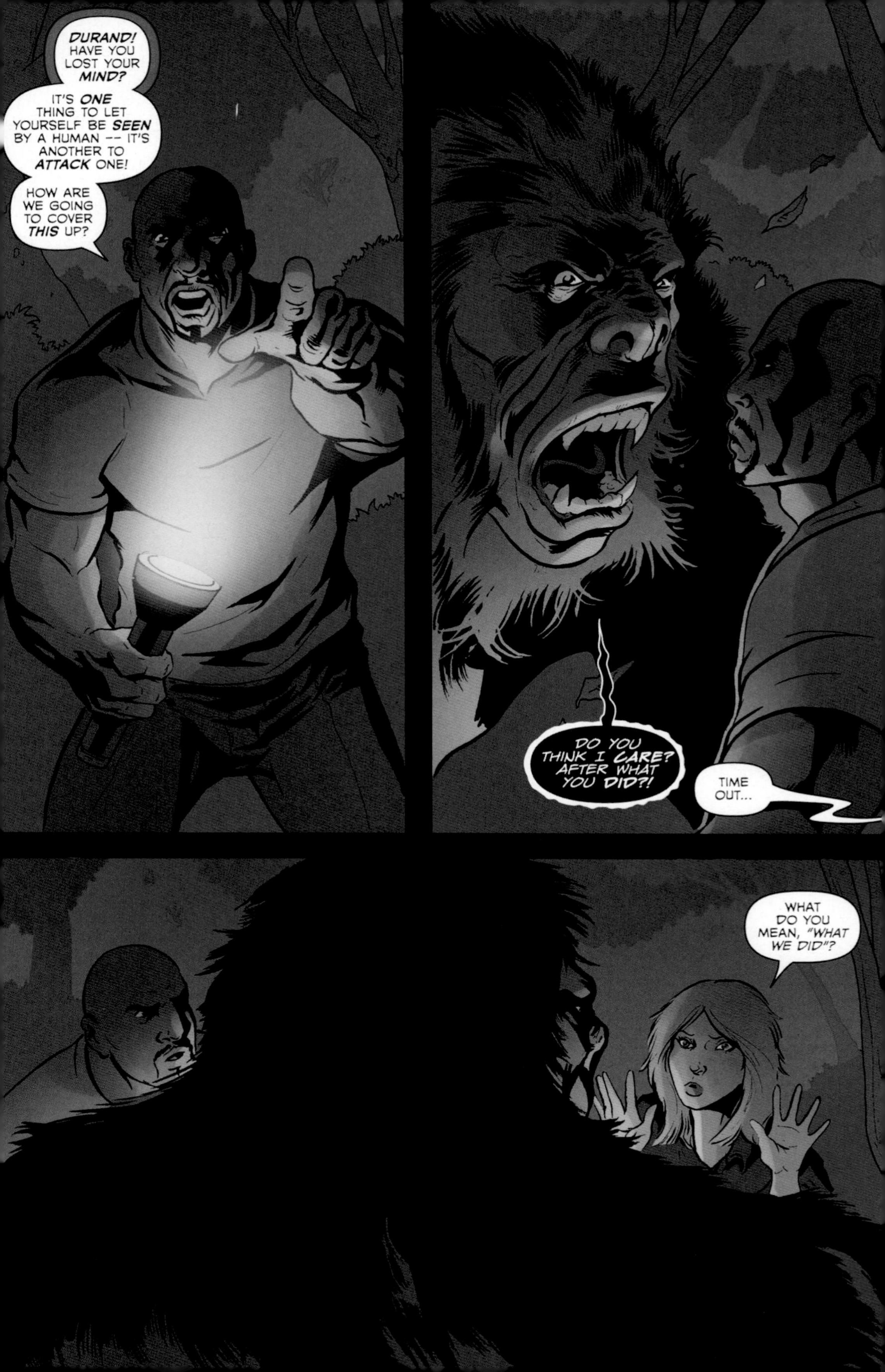
DURAND! HAVE YOU LOST YOUR MIND?
IT'S ONE THING TO LET YOURSELF BE SEEN BY A HUMAN -- IT'S ANOTHER TO ATTACK ONE!
HOW ARE WE GOING TO COVER THIS UP?
DO YOU THINK I CARE? AFTER WHAT YOU DID?!
TIME OUT...
WHAT DO YOU MEAN, "WHAT WE DID"?

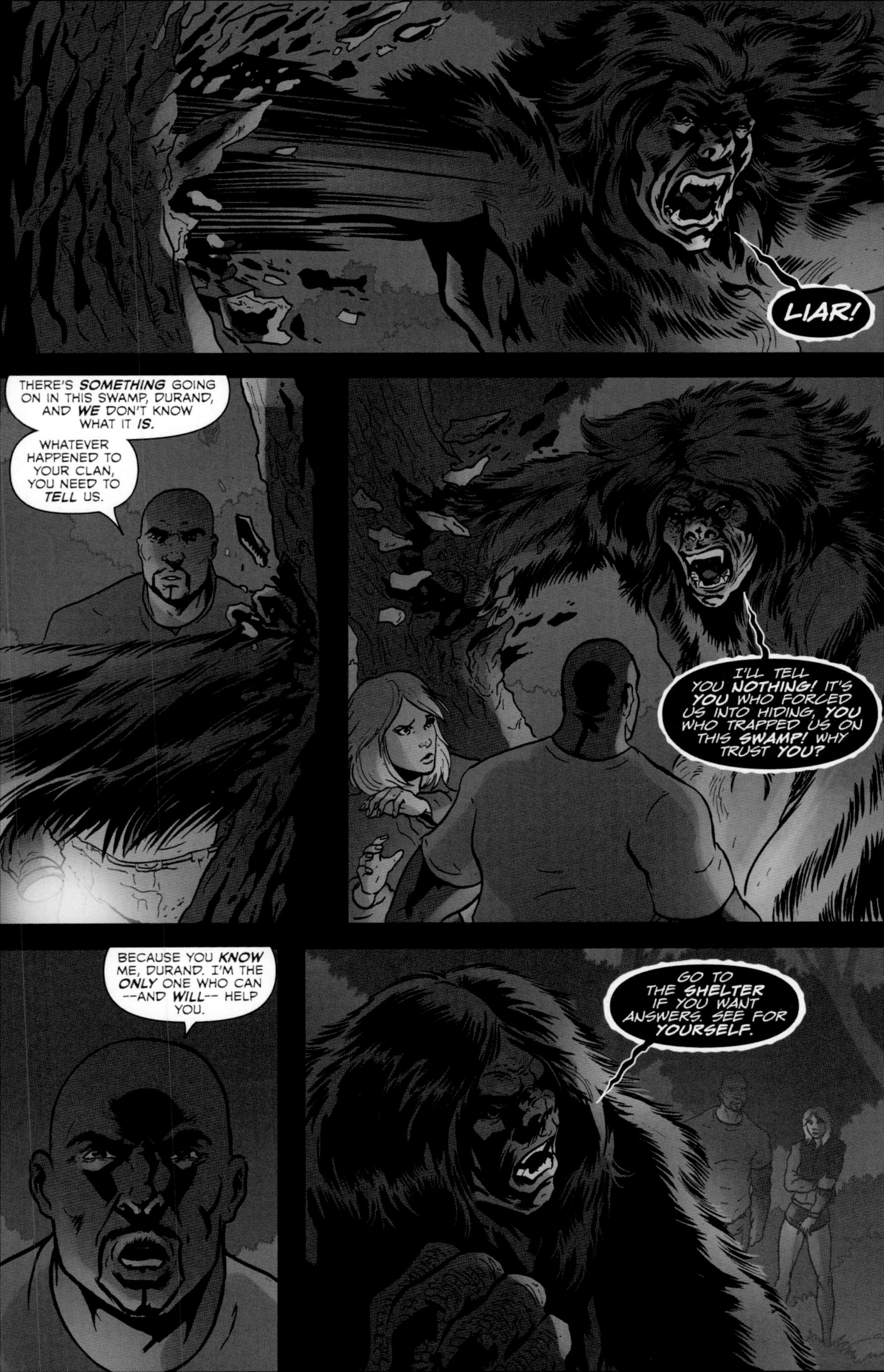
LIAR!
THERE'S SOMETHING GOING ON IN THIS SWAMP, DURAND, AND WE DON'T KNOW WHAT IT IS.
WHATEVER HAPPENED TO YOUR CLAN, YOU NEED TO TELL US.
I'LL TELL YOU NOTHING! IT'S YOU WHO FORCED US INTO HIDING, YOU WHO TRAPPED US ON THIS SWAMP! WHY TRUST YOU?
BECAUSE YOU KNOW ME, DURAND. I'M THE ONLY ONE WHO CAN --AND WILL-- HELP YOU.
GO TO THE SHELTER IF YOU WANT ANSWERS. SEE FOR YOURSELF.

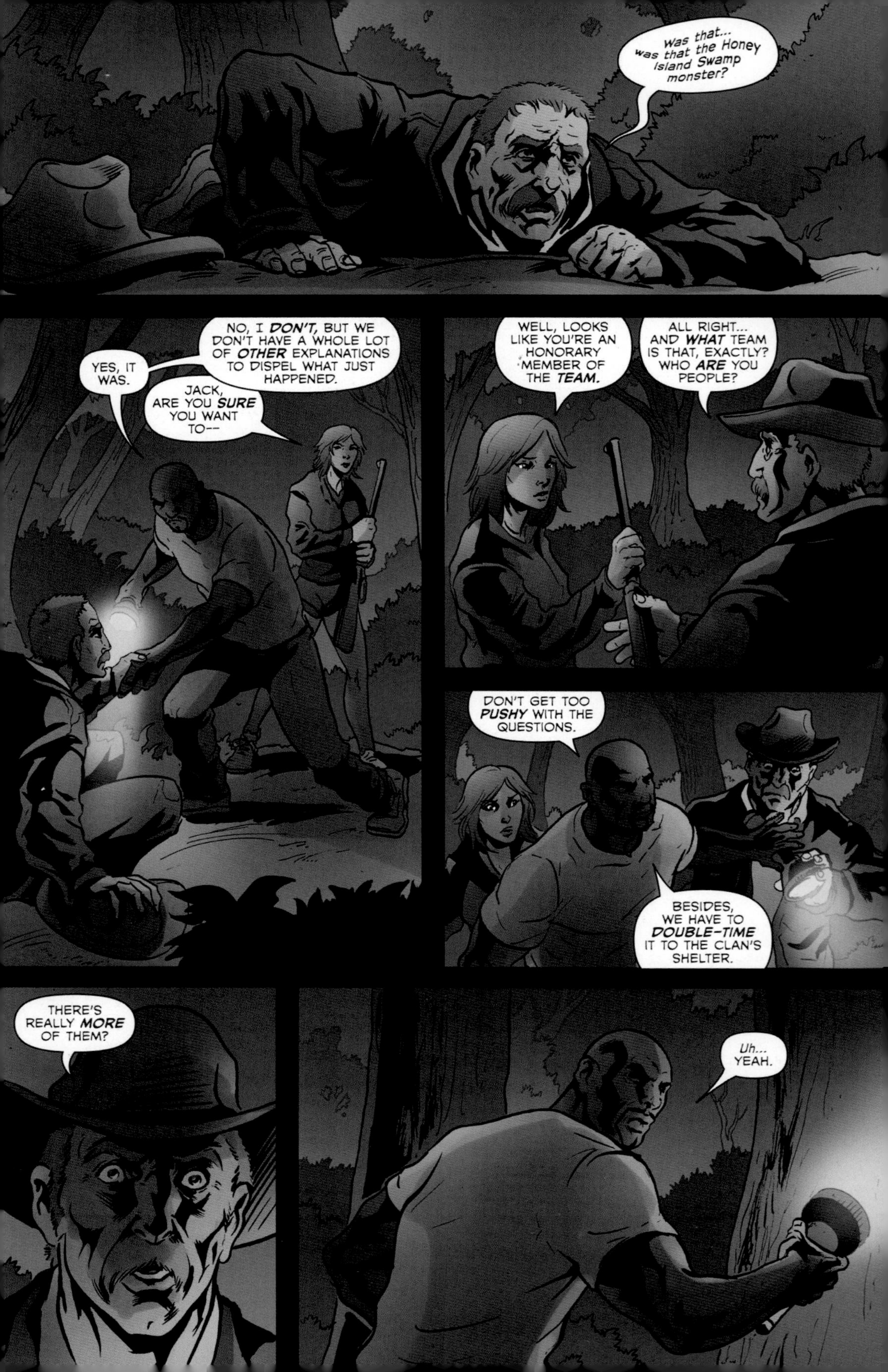

Was that... was that the Honey Island Swamp monster?
YES, IT WAS.
NO, I DON'T, BUT WE DON'T HAVE A WHOLE LOT OF OTHER EXPLANATIONS TO DISPEL WHAT JUST HAPPENED.
JACK, ARE YOU SURE YOU WANT TO--
WELL, LOOKS LIKE YOU'RE AN HONORARY MEMBER OF THE TEAM.
ALL RIGHT... AND WHAT TEAM IS THAT, EXACTLY? WHO ARE YOU PEOPLE?
DON'T GET TOO PUSHY WITH THE QUESTIONS.
BESIDES, WE HAVE TO DOUBLE-TIME IT TO THE CLAN'S SHELTER.
THERE'S REALLY MORE OF THEM?
Uh... YEAH.

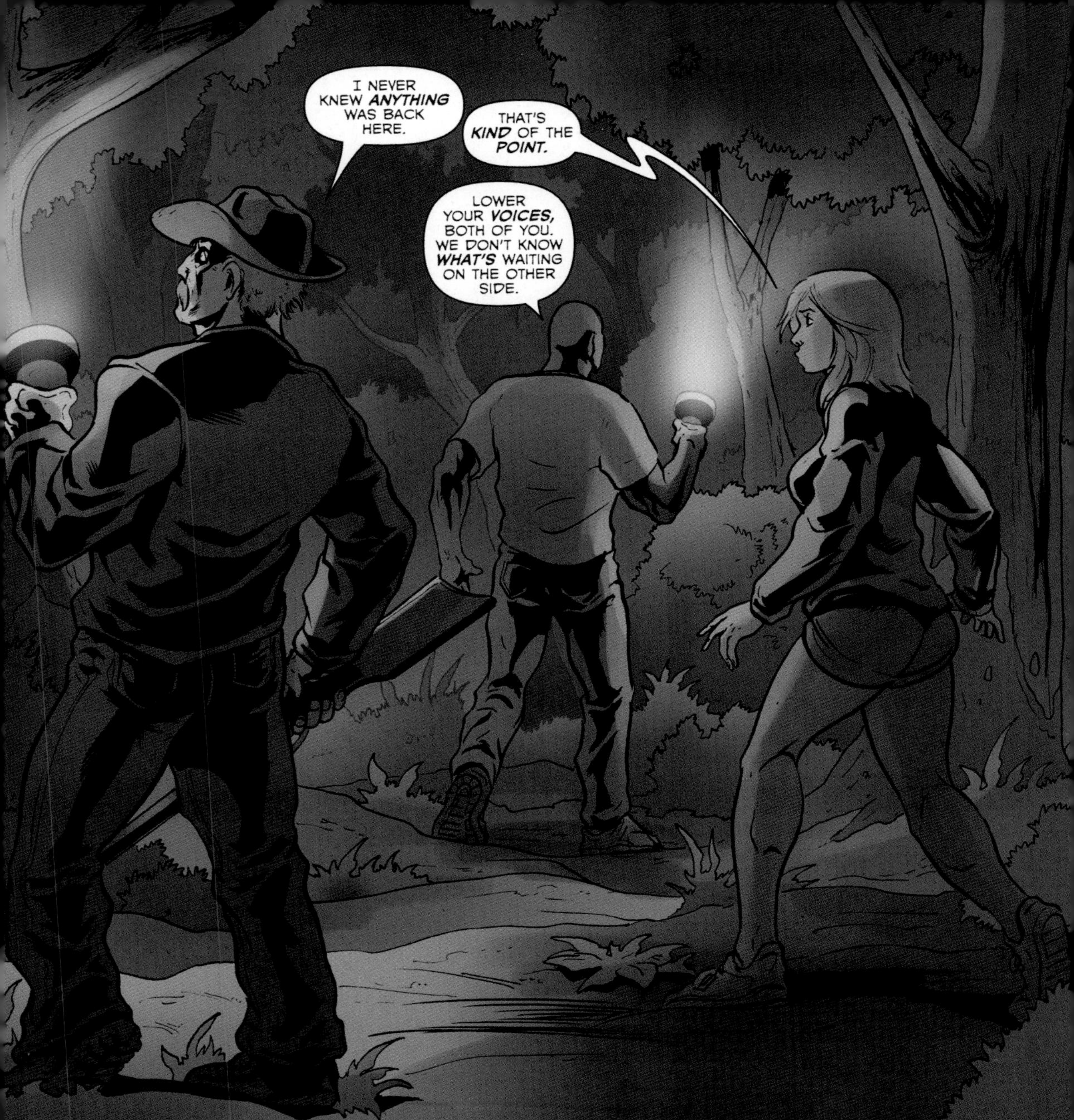
I NEVER KNEW ANYTHING WAS BACK HERE.
THAT'S KIND OF THE POINT.
LOWER YOUR VOICES, BOTH OF YOU. WE DON'T KNOW WHAT'S WAITING ON THE OTHER SIDE.

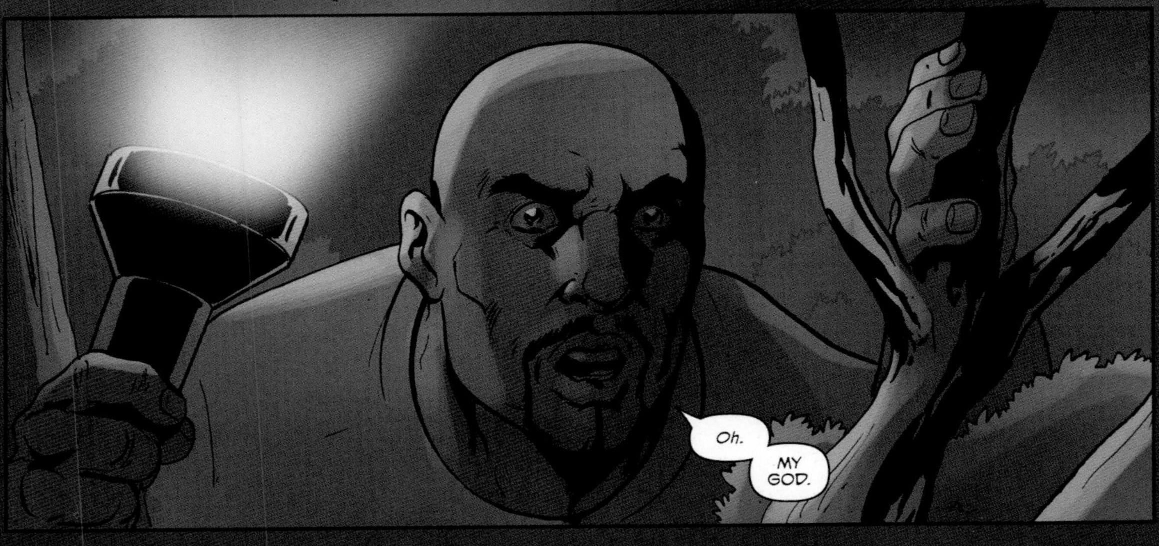
Oh.
MY GOD.

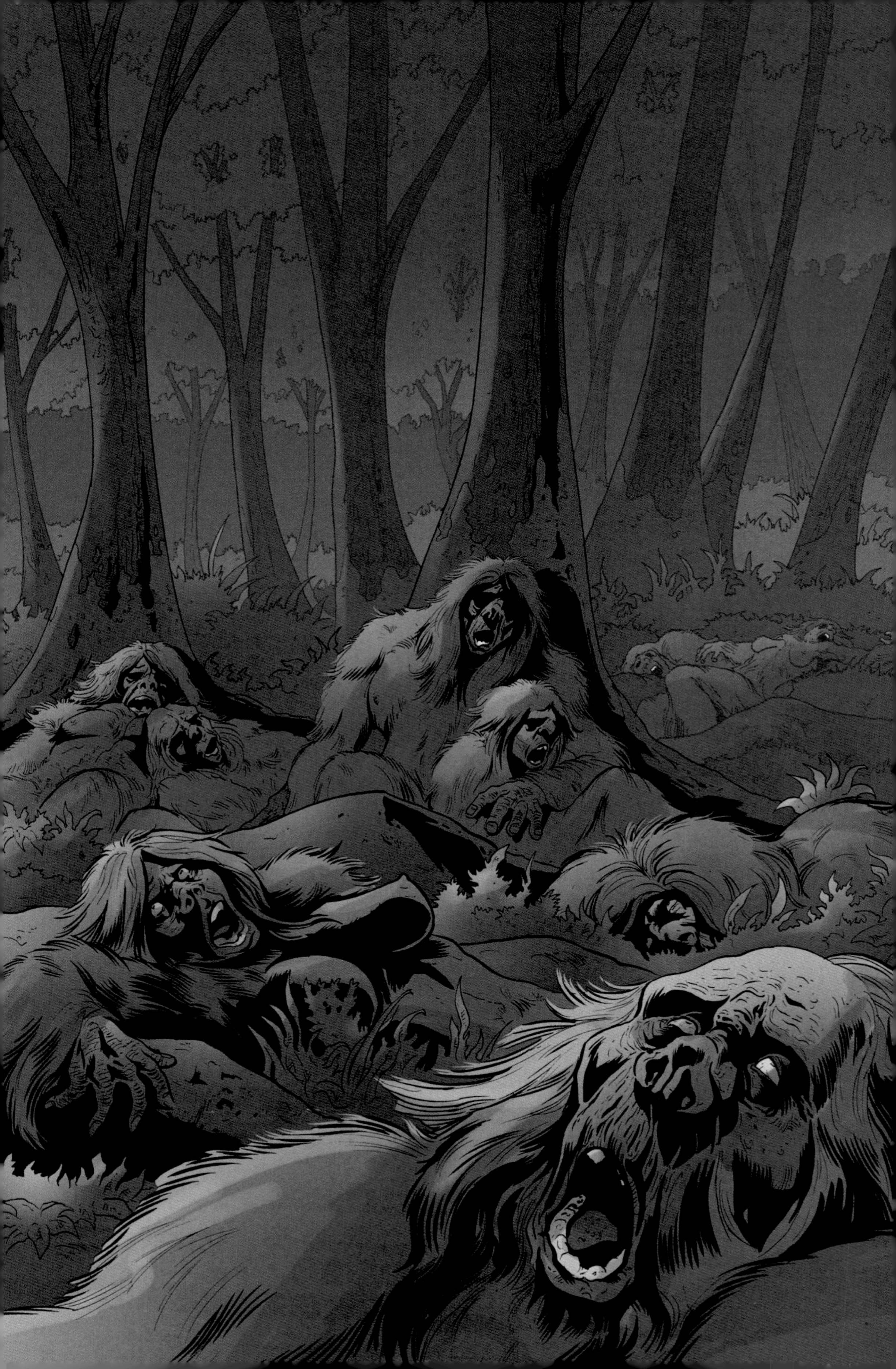

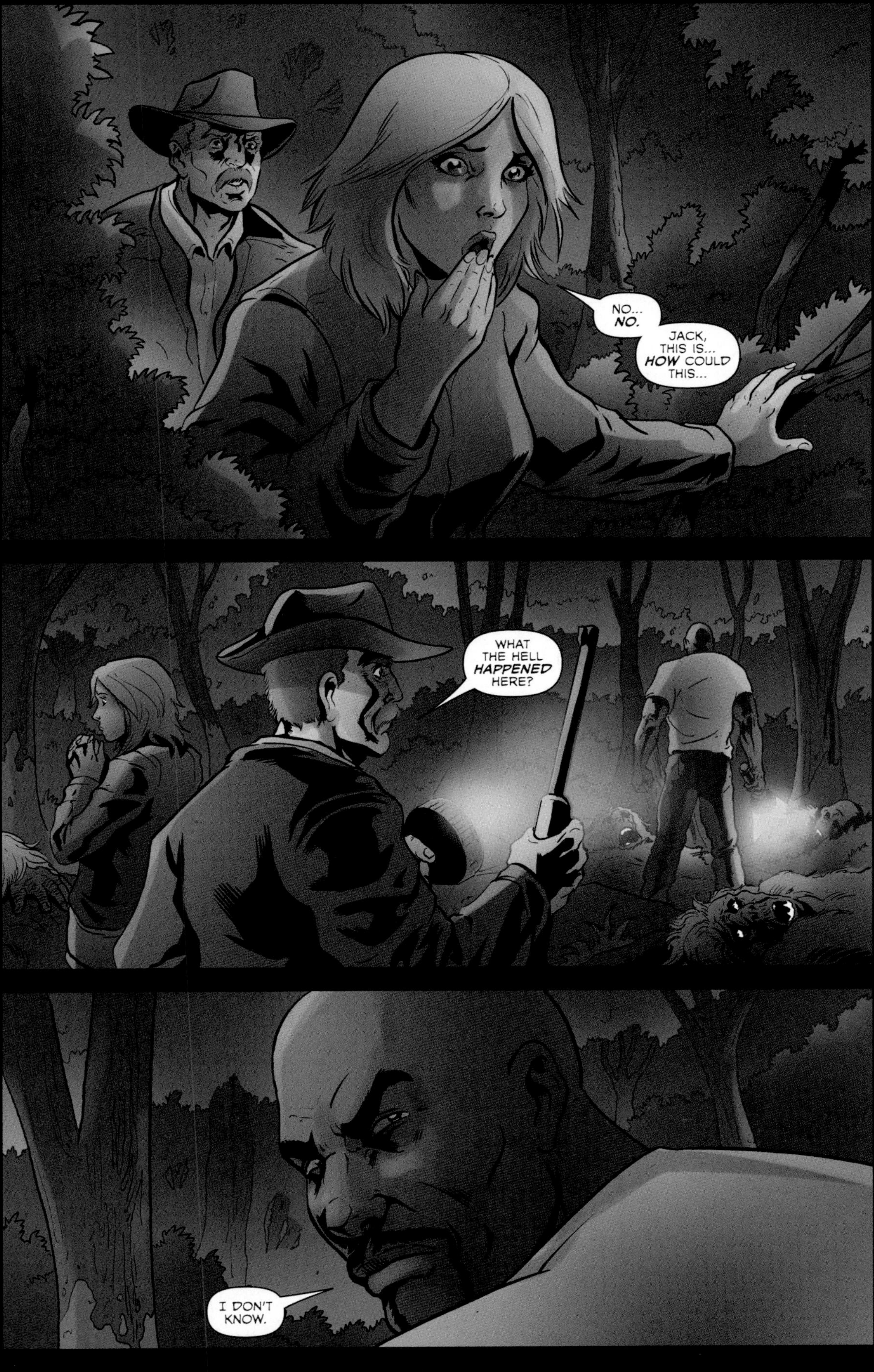
NO... NO.
JACK, THIS IS... HOW COULD THIS...
WHAT THE HELL HAPPENED HERE?
I DON'T KNOW.

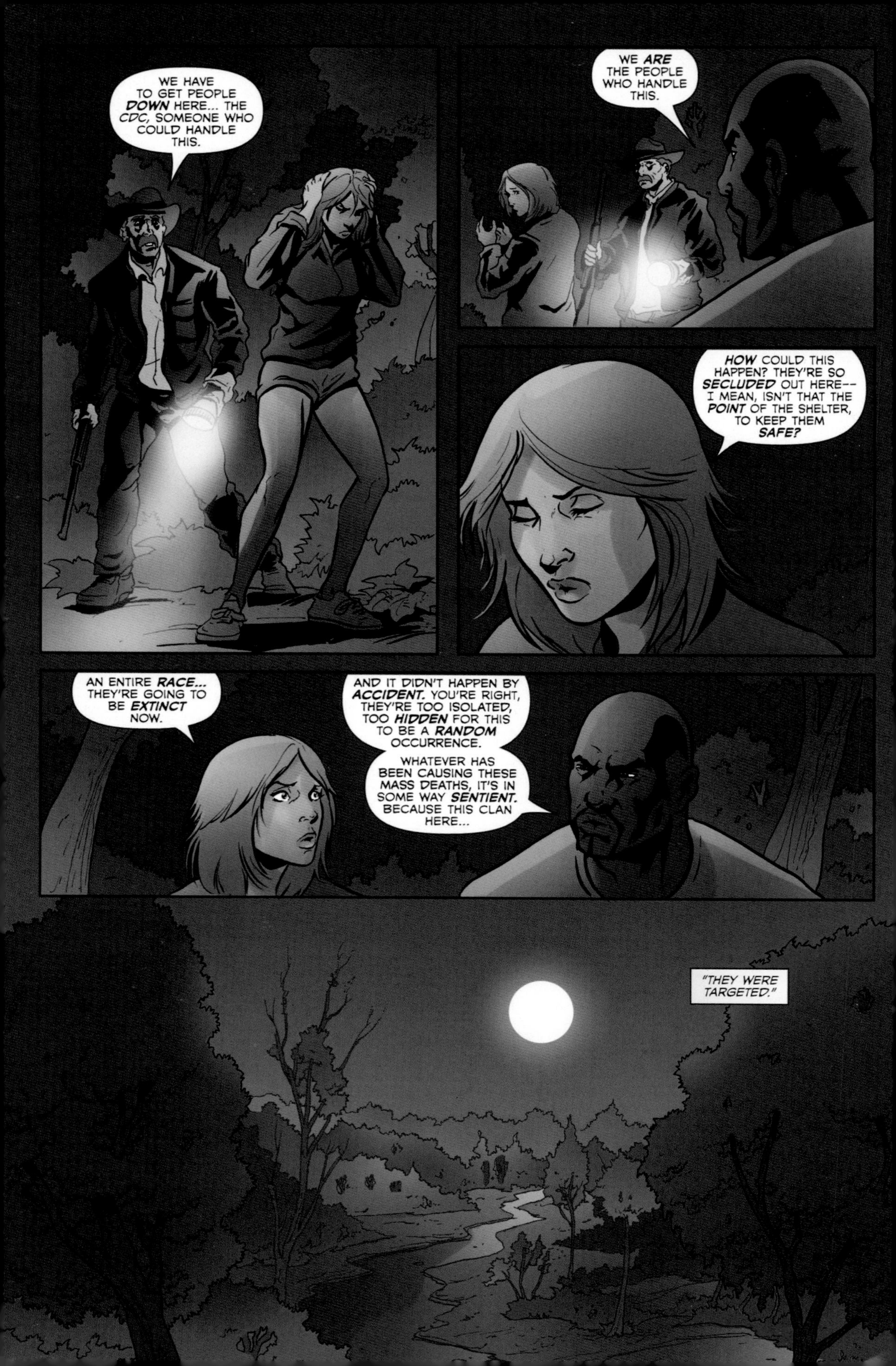

WE HAVE TO GET PEOPLE DOWN HERE... THE CDC, SOMEONE WHO COULD HANDLE THIS.
WE ARE THE PEOPLE WHO HANDLE THIS.
HOW COULD THIS HAPPEN? THEY'RE SO SECLUDED OUT HERE-- I MEAN, ISN'T THAT THE POINT OF THE SHELTER, TO KEEP THEM SAFE?
AN ENTIRE RACE... THEY'RE GOING TO BE EXTINCT NOW.
AND IT DIDN'T HAPPEN BY ACCIDENT. YOU'RE RIGHT, THEY'RE TOO ISOLATED, TOO HIDDEN FOR THIS TO BE A RANDOM OCCURRENCE.
WHATEVER HAS BEEN CAUSING THESE MASS DEATHS, IT'S IN SOME WAY SENTIENT. BECAUSE THIS CLAN HERE...
"THEY WERE TARGETED."

HOAX HUNTERS

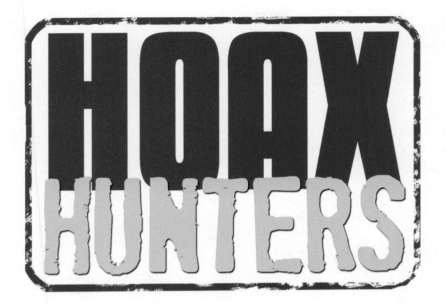

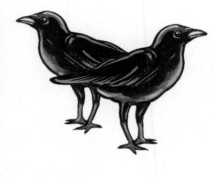

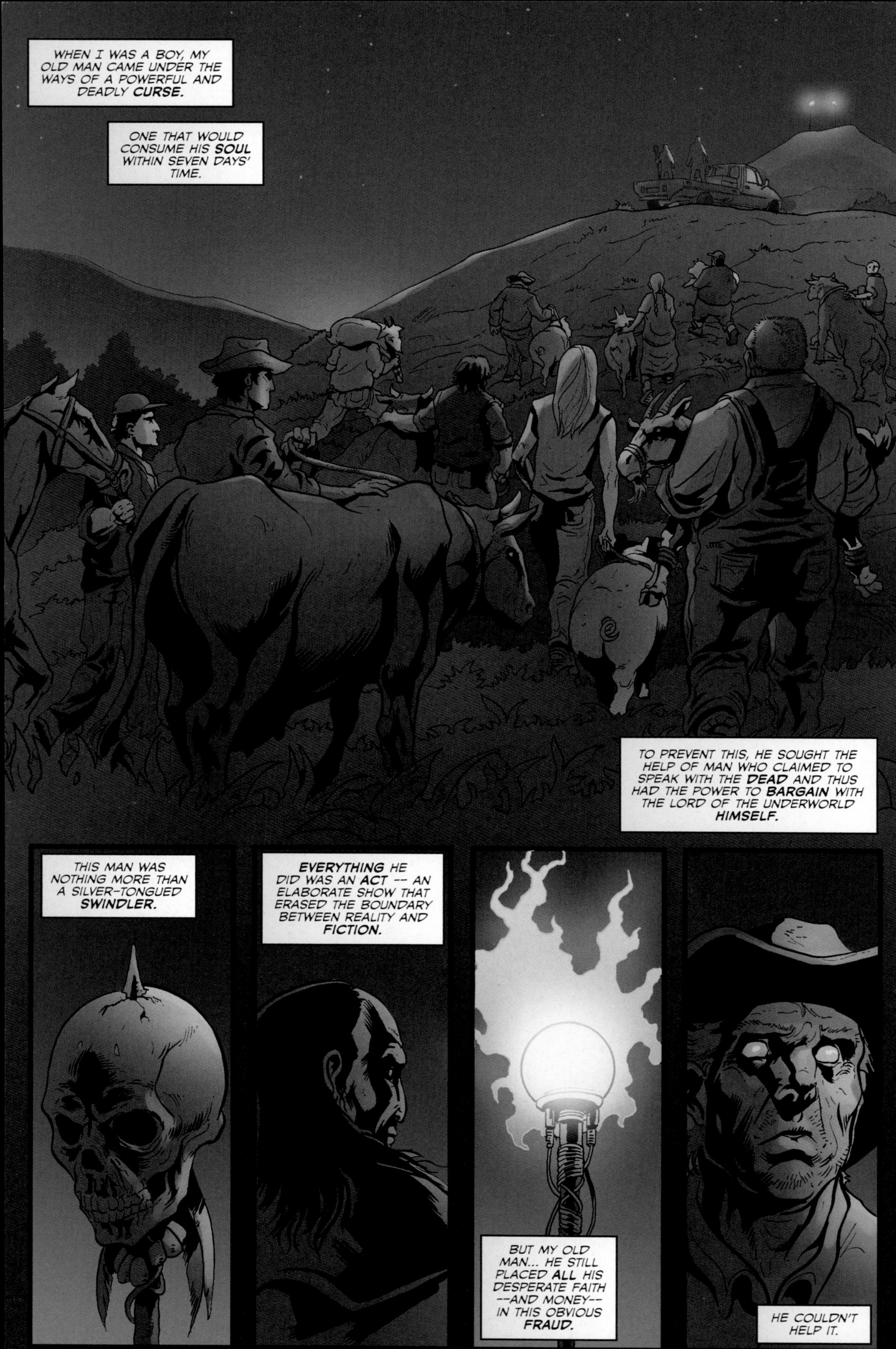
WHEN I WAS A BOY, MY OLD MAN CAME UNDER THE WAYS OF A POWERFUL AND DEADLY CURSE.
ONE THAT WOULD CONSUME HIS SOUL WITHIN SEVEN DAYS' TIME.
TO PREVENT THIS, HE SOUGHT THE HELP OF MAN WHO CLAIMED TO SPEAK WITH THE DEAD AND THUS HAD THE POWER TO BARGAIN WITH THE LORD OF THE UNDERWORLD HIMSELF.
THIS MAN WAS NOTHING MORE THAN A SILVER-TONGUED SWINDLER.
EVERYTHING HE DID WAS AN ACT -- AN ELABORATE SHOW THAT ERASED THE BOUNDARY BETWEEN REALITY AND FICTION.
BUT MY OLD MAN... HE STILL PLACED ALL HIS DESPERATE FAITH --AND MONEY-- IN THIS OBVIOUS FRAUD.
HE COULDN'T HELP IT.

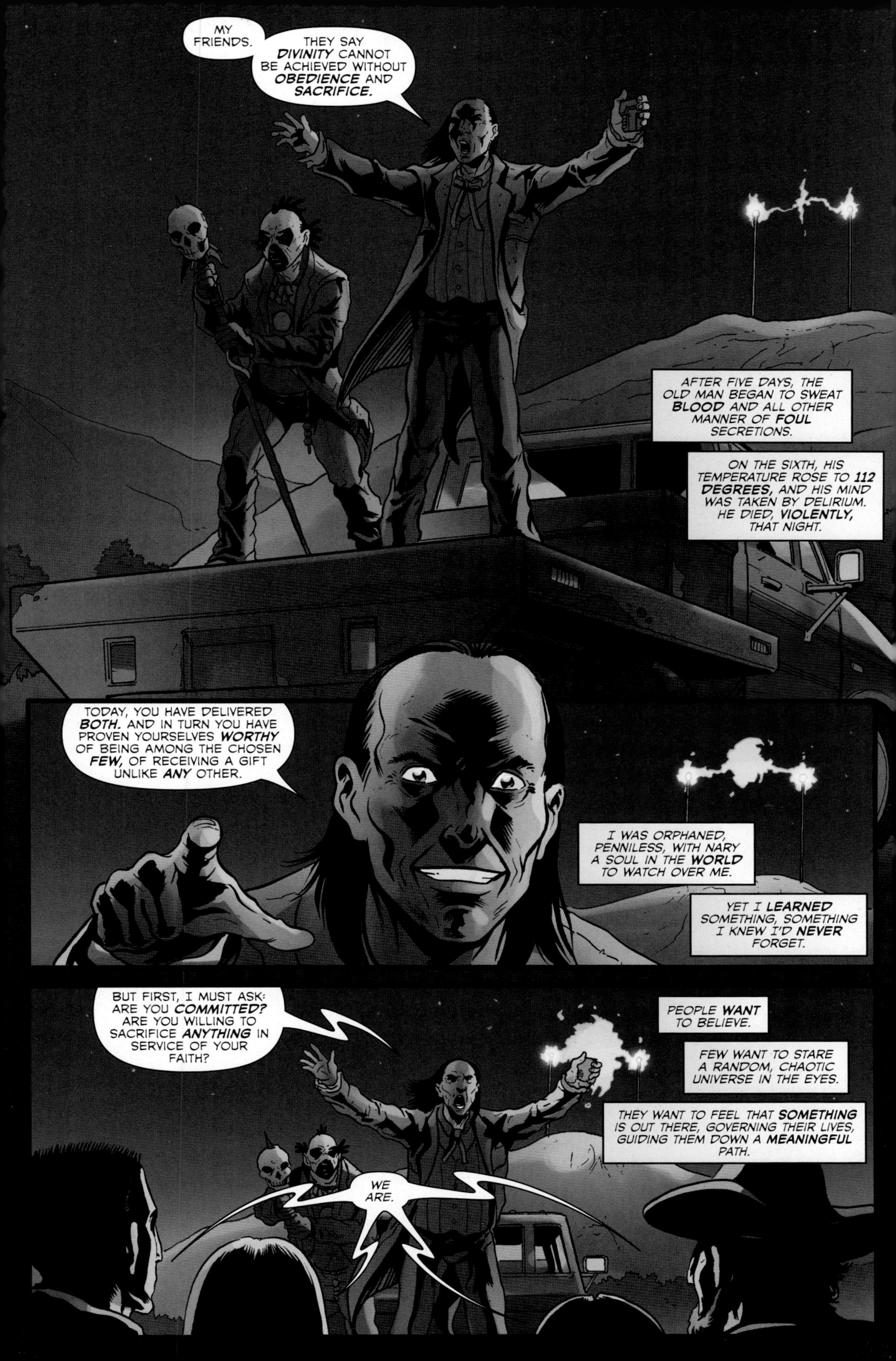

MY FRIENDS.
THEY SAY DIVINITY CANNOT BE ACHIEVED WITHOUT OBEDIENCE AND SACRIFICE.
AFTER FIVE DAYS, THE OLD MAN BEGAN TO SWEAT BLOOD AND ALL OTHER MANNER OF FOUL SECRETIONS.
ON THE SIXTH, HIS TEMPERATURE ROSE TO 112 DEGREES, AND HIS MIND WAS TAKEN BY DELIRIUM. HE DIED, VIOLENTLY, THAT NIGHT.
TODAY, YOU HAVE DELIVERED BOTH. AND IN TURN YOU HAVE PROVEN YOURSELVES WORTHY OF BEING AMONG THE CHOSEN FEW, OF RECEIVING A GIFT UNLIKE ANY OTHER.
I WAS ORPHANED, PENNILESS, WITH NARY A SOUL IN THE WORLD TO WATCH OVER ME.
YET I LEARNED SOMETHING, SOMETHING I KNEW I'D NEVER FORGET.
BUT FIRST, I MUST ASK: ARE YOU COMMITTED? ARE YOU WILLING TO SACRIFICE ANYTHING IN SERVICE OF YOUR FAITH?
PEOPLE WANT TO BELIEVE.
FEW WANT TO STARE A RANDOM, CHAOTIC UNIVERSE IN THE EYES.
THEY WANT TO FEEL THAT SOMETHING IS OUT THERE, GOVERNING THEIR LIVES, GUIDING THEM DOWN A MEANINGFUL PATH.
WE ARE.

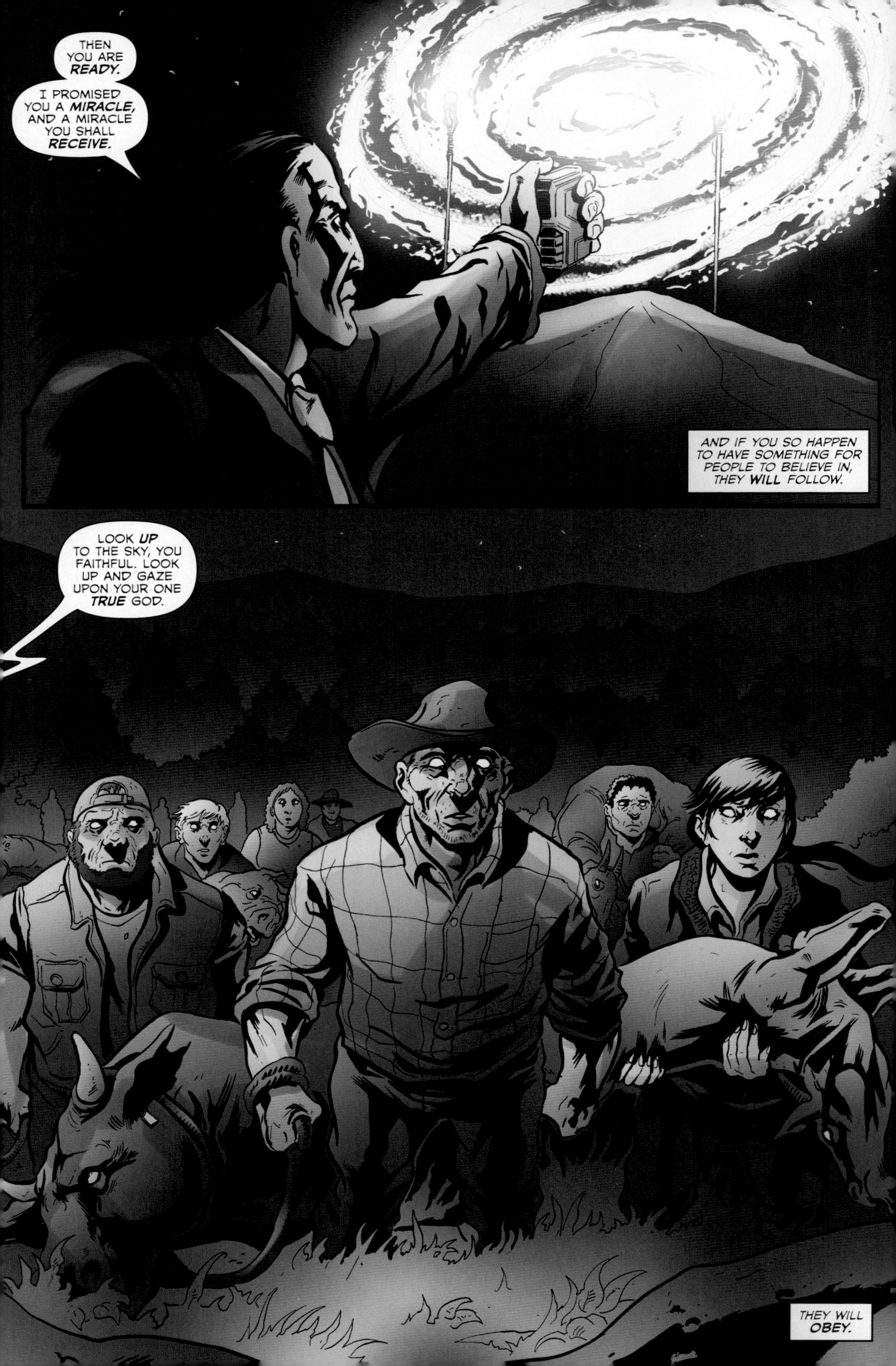
THEN YOU ARE READY.
I PROMISED YOU A MIRACLE, AND A MIRACLE YOU SHALL RECEIVE.
AND IF YOU SO HAPPEN TO HAVE SOMETHING FOR PEOPLE TO BELIEVE IN, THEY WILL FOLLOW.
LOOK UP TO THE SKY, YOU FAITHFUL. LOOK UP AND GAZE UPON YOUR ONE TRUE GOD.
THEY WILL OBEY.

Grand CROSSING

"SO, LET ME GET THIS STRAIGHT, JUST SO I'M CLEAR..."

LAST NIGHT, YOU TWO WENT OUT TO THE SWAMP -- WITHOUT TELLING **ANYONE** ELSE -- AND LAUNCHED YOUR **OWN** INVESTIGATION.

IS **THIS** HOW WE OPERATE NOW? LOOSE AND FREE WITH **RULES** AND **PROCEDURES?**

I **SAID** WE SHOULD CALL...

I USED MY **JUDGMENT**, KEN. THAT'S ALL THERE IS TO IT.

GIVEN YOUR **HISTORY** ON THIS, JACK, YOUR JUDGMENT DOESN'T INSTILL MUCH **CONFIDENCE.**

THAT **ASIDE,** LET ME ASK YOU THIS: WHAT INFORMATION **DID** YOU HOPE TO OBTAIN, IN THE SWAMP, IN THE PITCH BLACK DEAD OF **NIGHT?**

I WASN'T LOOKING FOR **INFORMATION,** WE WERE CHECKING ON **DURAND** AND HIS CLAN.

ALL OF WHOM ARE **DEAD,** A FACT I **HOPE** UPSETS YOU **MORE** THAN YOU'RE LETTING ON.

MY FEELINGS AREN'T THE **POINT.** WHAT I'M SAYING--

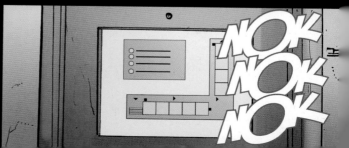

NOK NOK NOK

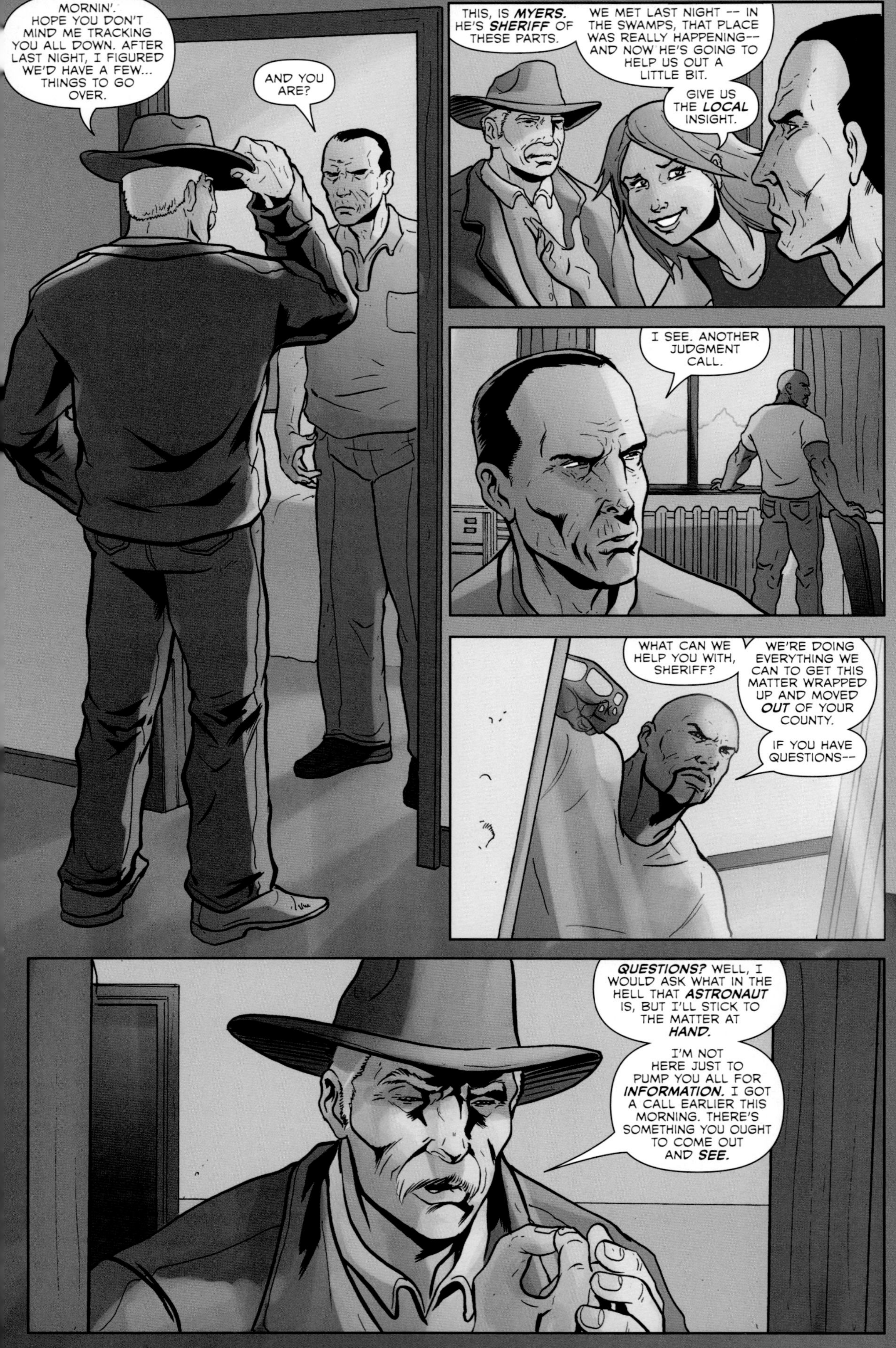
MORNIN'. HOPE YOU DON'T MIND ME TRACKING YOU ALL DOWN. AFTER LAST NIGHT, I FIGURED WE'D HAVE A FEW... THINGS TO GO OVER.
AND YOU ARE?
THIS, IS MYERS. HE'S SHERIFF OF THESE PARTS.
WE MET LAST NIGHT -- IN THE SWAMPS, THAT PLACE WAS REALLY HAPPENING-- AND NOW HE'S GOING TO HELP US OUT A LITTLE BIT.
GIVE US THE LOCAL INSIGHT.
I SEE. ANOTHER JUDGMENT CALL.
WHAT CAN WE HELP YOU WITH, SHERIFF?
WE'RE DOING EVERYTHING WE CAN TO GET THIS MATTER WRAPPED UP AND MOVED OUT OF YOUR COUNTY.
IF YOU HAVE QUESTIONS--
QUESTIONS? WELL, I WOULD ASK WHAT IN THE HELL THAT ASTRONAUT IS, BUT I'LL STICK TO THE MATTER AT HAND.
I'M NOT HERE JUST TO PUMP YOU ALL FOR INFORMATION. I GOT A CALL EARLIER THIS MORNING. THERE'S SOMETHING YOU OUGHT TO COME OUT AND SEE.

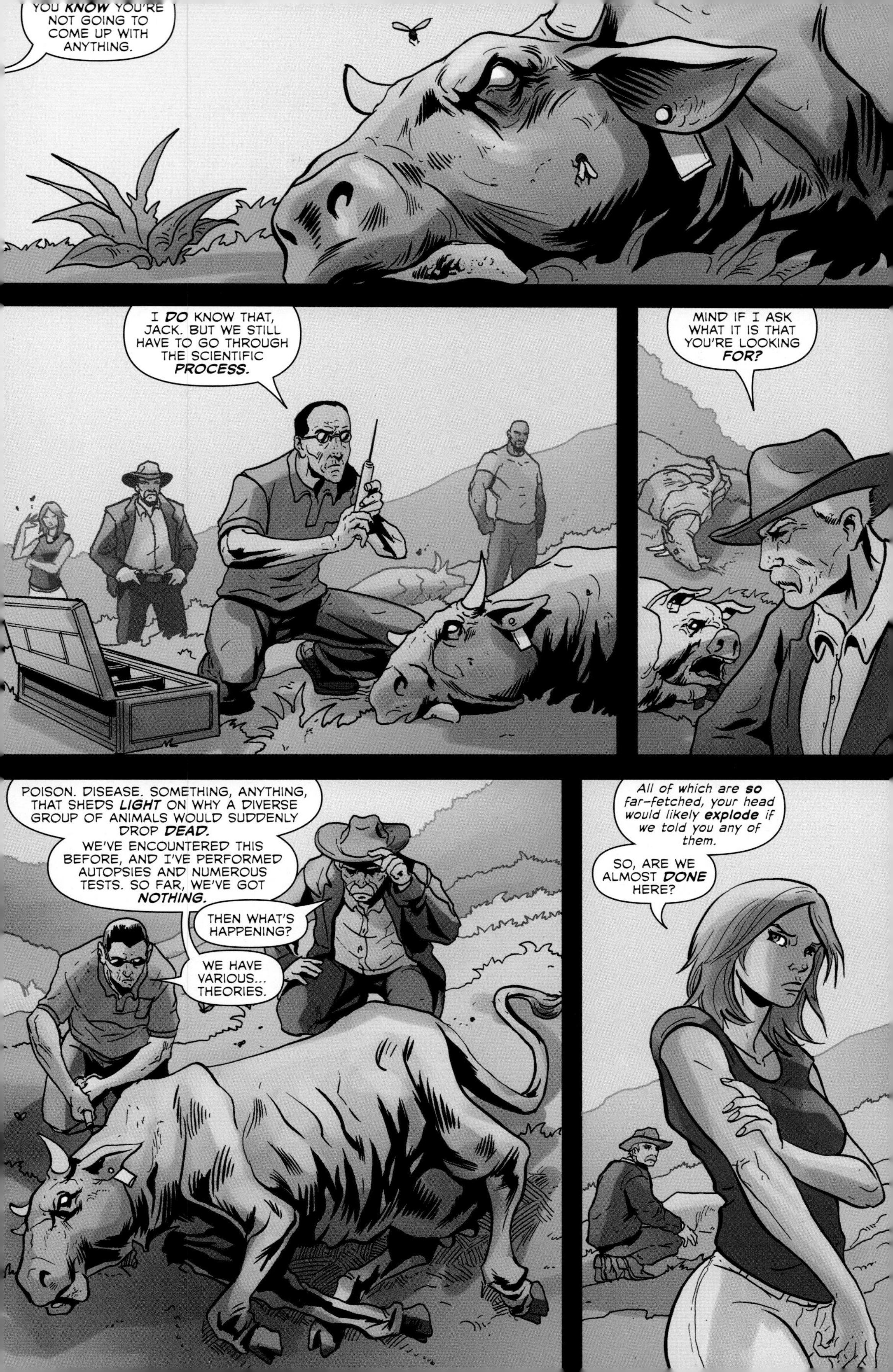

YOU **KNOW** YOU'RE NOT GOING TO COME UP WITH ANYTHING.
I **DO** KNOW THAT, JACK. BUT WE STILL HAVE TO GO THROUGH THE SCIENTIFIC **PROCESS.**
MIND IF I ASK WHAT IT IS THAT YOU'RE LOOKING **FOR?**
POISON. DISEASE. SOMETHING, ANYTHING, THAT SHEDS **LIGHT** ON WHY A DIVERSE GROUP OF ANIMALS WOULD SUDDENLY DROP **DEAD.**
WE'VE ENCOUNTERED THIS BEFORE, AND I'VE PERFORMED AUTOPSIES AND NUMEROUS TESTS. SO FAR, WE'VE GOT **NOTHING.**
THEN WHAT'S HAPPENING?
WE HAVE VARIOUS... THEORIES.
*All of which are **so** far-fetched, your head would likely **explode** if we told you any of them.*
SO, ARE WE ALMOST **DONE** HERE?

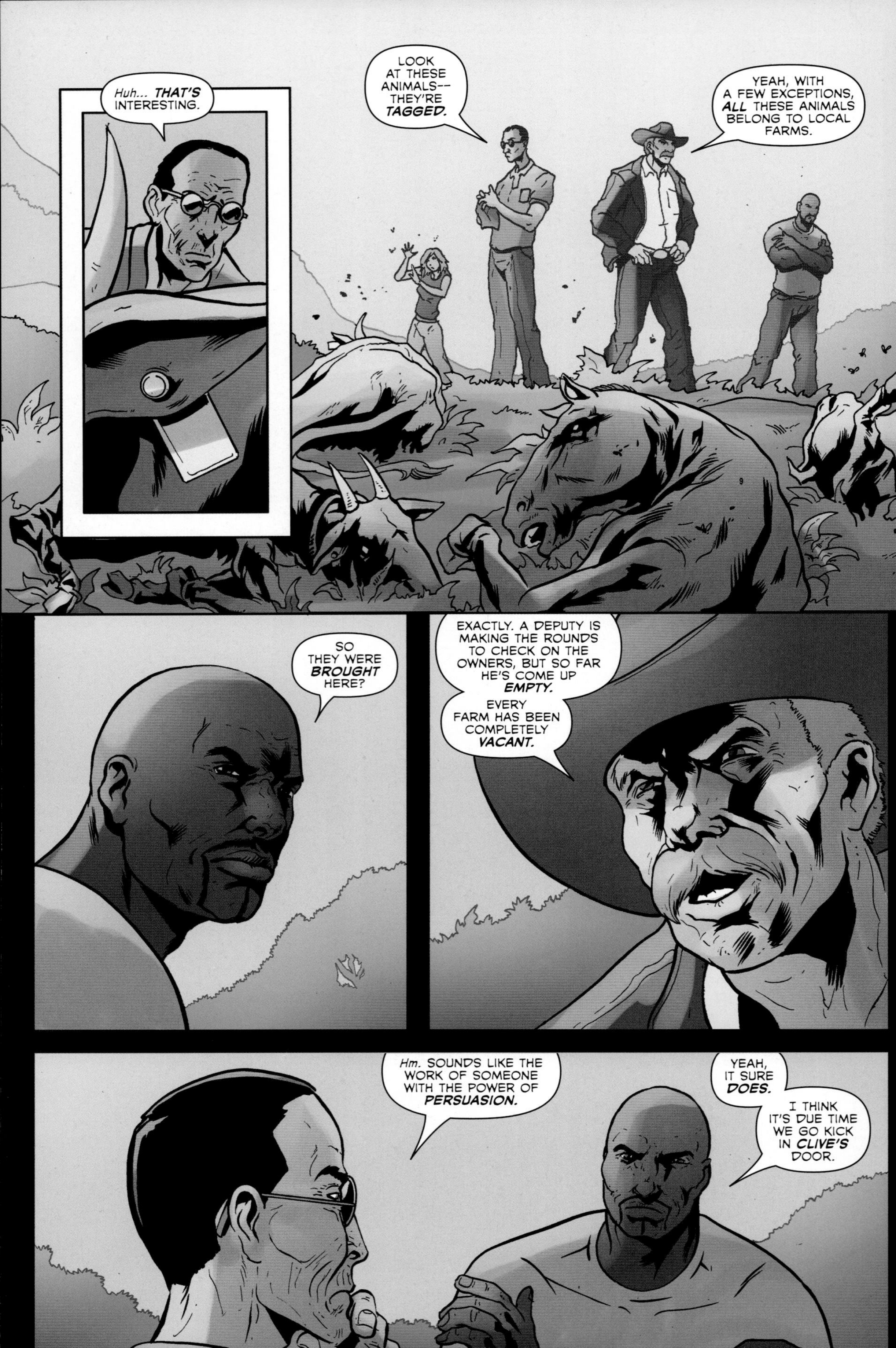

Huh... THAT'S INTERESTING.
LOOK AT THESE ANIMALS-- THEY'RE TAGGED.
YEAH, WITH A FEW EXCEPTIONS, ALL THESE ANIMALS BELONG TO LOCAL FARMS.
SO THEY WERE BROUGHT HERE?
EXACTLY. A DEPUTY IS MAKING THE ROUNDS TO CHECK ON THE OWNERS, BUT SO FAR HE'S COME UP EMPTY.
EVERY FARM HAS BEEN COMPLETELY VACANT.
Hm. SOUNDS LIKE THE WORK OF SOMEONE WITH THE POWER OF PERSUASION.
YEAH, IT SURE DOES.
I THINK IT'S DUE TIME WE GO KICK IN CLIVE'S DOOR.

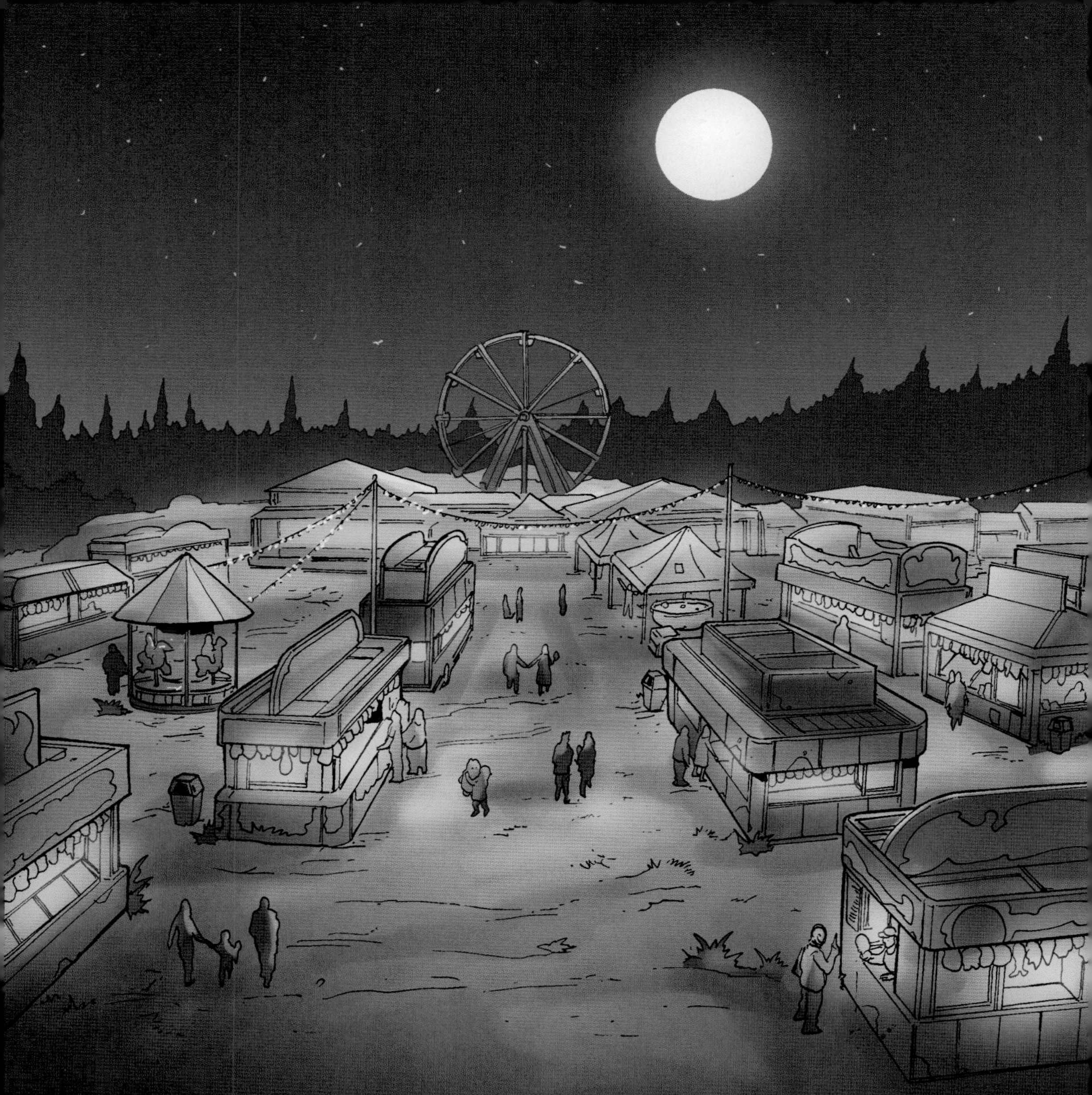

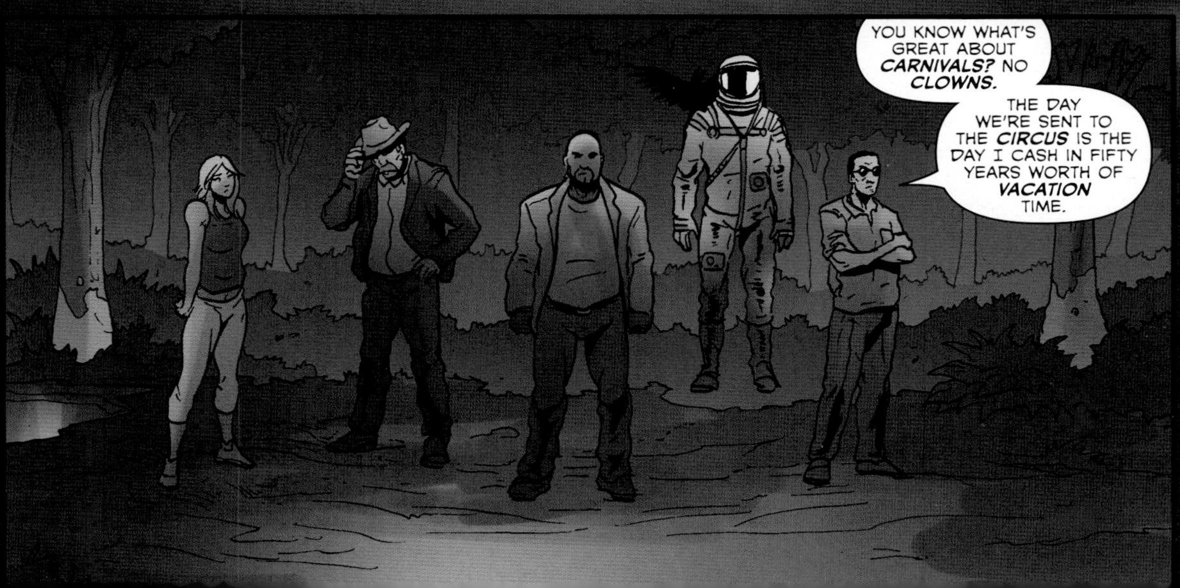
YOU KNOW WHAT'S GREAT ABOUT CARNIVALS? NO CLOWNS.
THE DAY WE'RE SENT TO THE CIRCUS IS THE DAY I CASH IN FIFTY YEARS WORTH OF VACATION TIME.

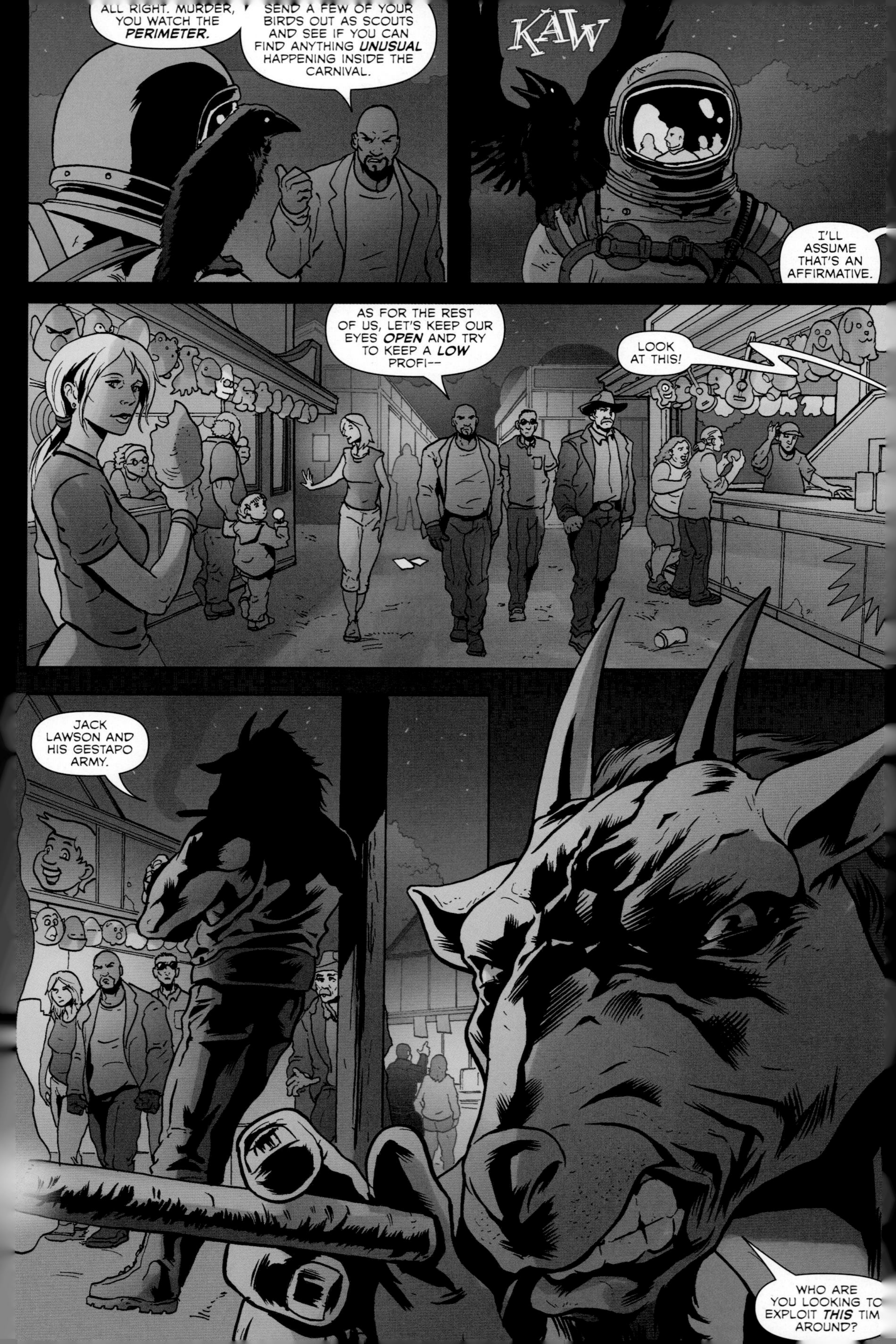
ALL RIGHT. MURDER, YOU WATCH THE PERIMETER.
SEND A FEW OF YOUR BIRDS OUT AS SCOUTS AND SEE IF YOU CAN FIND ANYTHING UNUSUAL HAPPENING INSIDE THE CARNIVAL.
KAW
I'LL ASSUME THAT'S AN AFFIRMATIVE.
AS FOR THE REST OF US, LET'S KEEP OUR EYES OPEN AND TRY TO KEEP A LOW PROFI--
LOOK AT THIS!
JACK LAWSON AND HIS GESTAPO ARMY.
WHO ARE YOU LOOKING TO EXPLOIT THIS TIM AROUND?

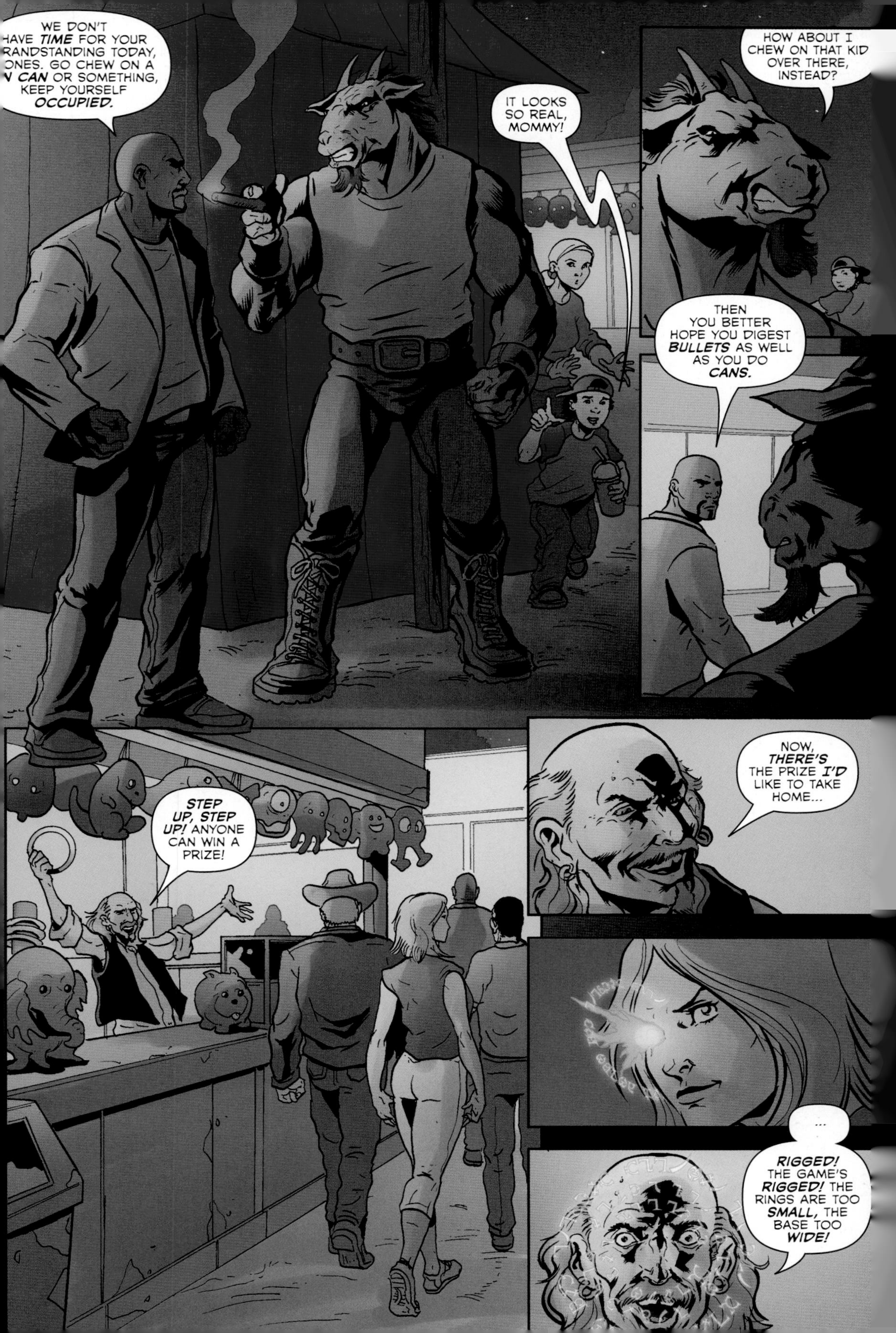
WE DON'T HAVE TIME FOR YOUR RANDSTANDING TODAY, ONES. GO CHEW ON A N CAN OR SOMETHING, KEEP YOURSELF OCCUPIED.
IT LOOKS SO REAL, MOMMY!
HOW ABOUT I CHEW ON THAT KID OVER THERE, INSTEAD?
THEN YOU BETTER HOPE YOU DIGEST BULLETS AS WELL AS YOU DO CANS.
STEP UP, STEP UP! ANYONE CAN WIN A PRIZE!
NOW, THERE'S THE PRIZE I'D LIKE TO TAKE HOME...
...
RIGGED! THE GAME'S RIGGED! THE RINGS ARE TOO SMALL, THE BASE TOO WIDE!

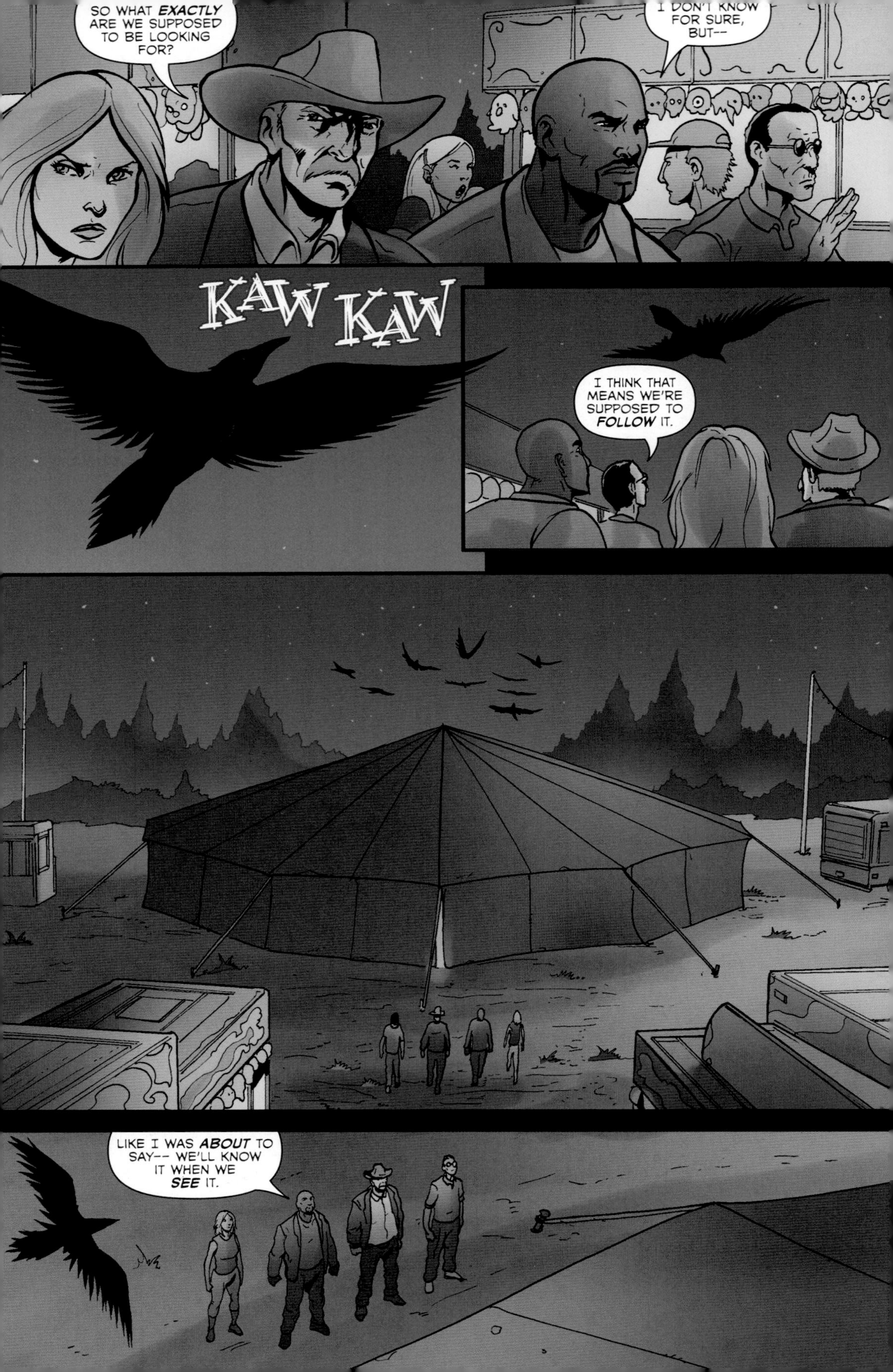
SO WHAT *EXACTLY* ARE WE SUPPOSED TO BE LOOKING FOR?
I DON'T KNOW FOR SURE, BUT--
KAW KAW
I THINK THAT MEANS WE'RE SUPPOSED TO *FOLLOW* IT.
LIKE I WAS *ABOUT* TO SAY-- WE'LL KNOW IT WHEN WE *SEE* IT.

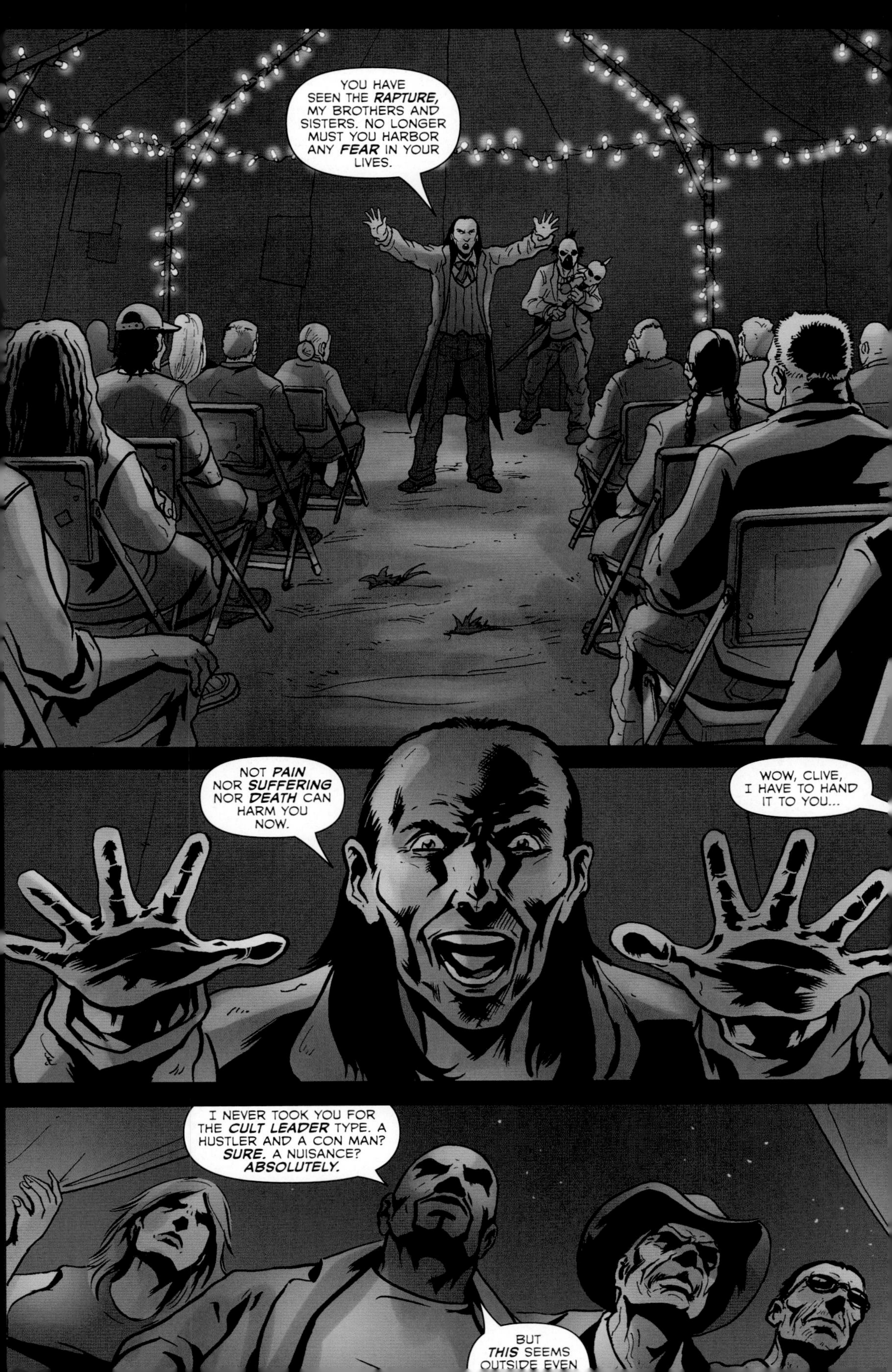
YOU HAVE SEEN THE *RAPTURE,* MY BROTHERS AND SISTERS. NO LONGER MUST YOU HARBOR ANY *FEAR* IN YOUR LIVES.
NOT *PAIN* NOR *SUFFERING* NOR *DEATH* CAN HARM YOU NOW.
WOW, CLIVE, I HAVE TO HAND IT TO YOU...
I NEVER TOOK YOU FOR THE *CULT LEADER* TYPE. A HUSTLER AND A CON MAN? *SURE.* A NUISANCE? *ABSOLUTELY.*
BUT *THIS* SEEMS OUTSIDE EVEN

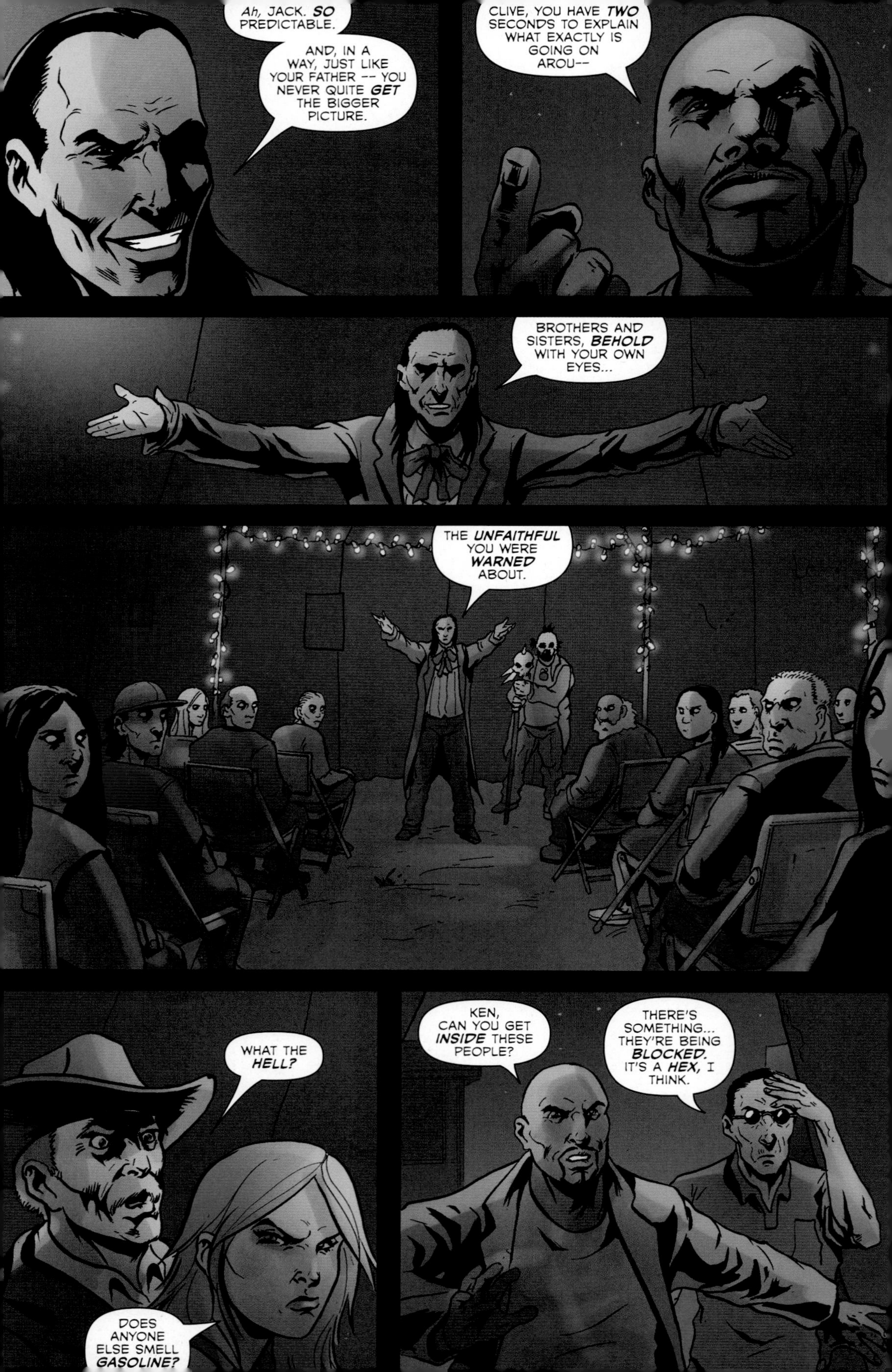

Ah, JACK. SO PREDICTABLE.
AND, IN A WAY, JUST LIKE YOUR FATHER -- YOU NEVER QUITE GET THE BIGGER PICTURE.
CLIVE, YOU HAVE TWO SECONDS TO EXPLAIN WHAT EXACTLY IS GOING ON AROU--
BROTHERS AND SISTERS, BEHOLD WITH YOUR OWN EYES...
THE UNFAITHFUL YOU WERE WARNED ABOUT.
WHAT THE HELL?
DOES ANYONE ELSE SMELL GASOLINE?
KEN, CAN YOU GET INSIDE THESE PEOPLE?
THERE'S SOMETHING... THEY'RE BEING BLOCKED. IT'S A HEX, I THINK.

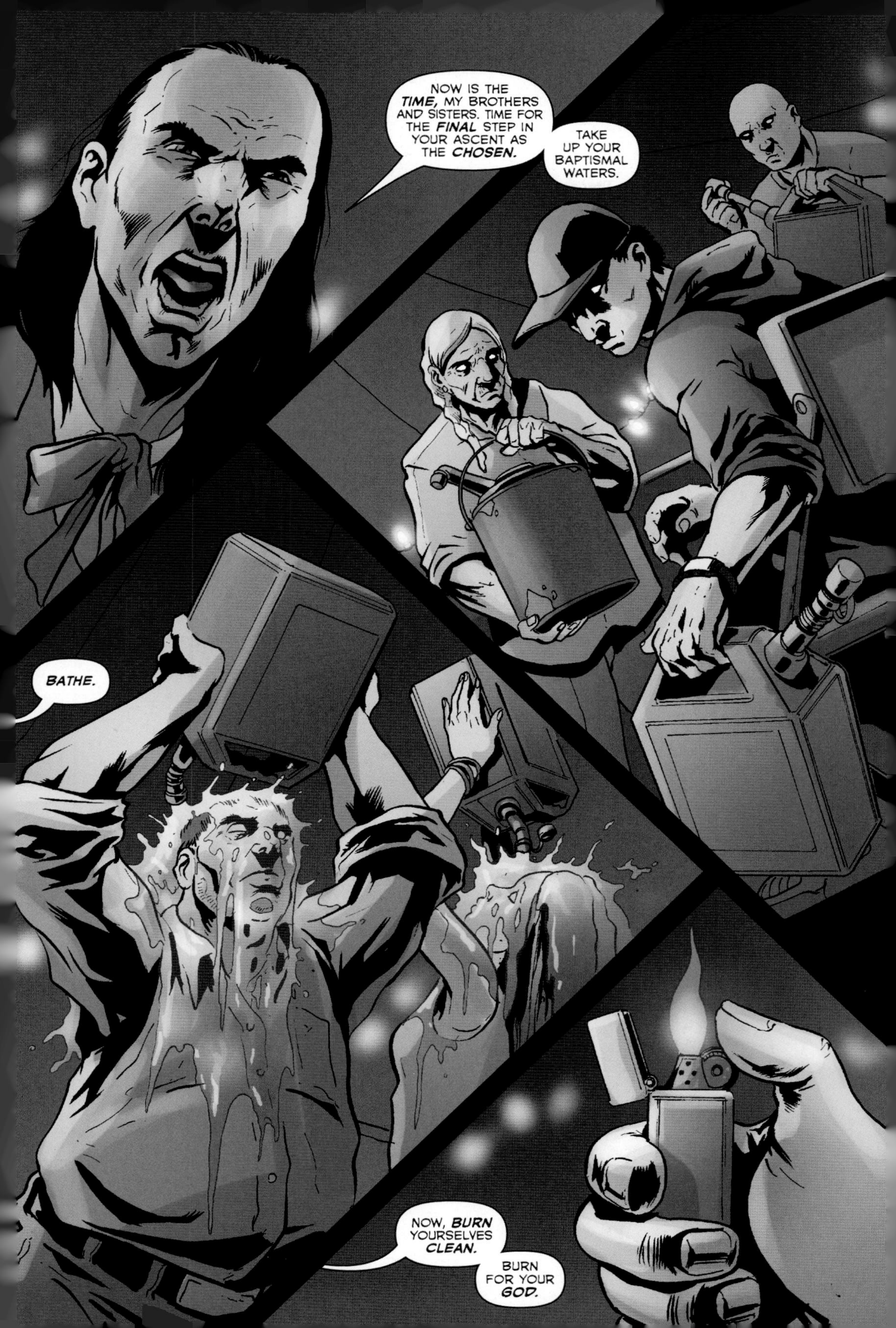
NOW IS THE TIME, MY BROTHERS AND SISTERS. TIME FOR THE FINAL STEP IN YOUR ASCENT AS THE CHOSEN.
TAKE UP YOUR BAPTISMAL WATERS.
BATHE.
NOW, BURN YOURSELVES CLEAN.
BURN FOR YOUR GOD.

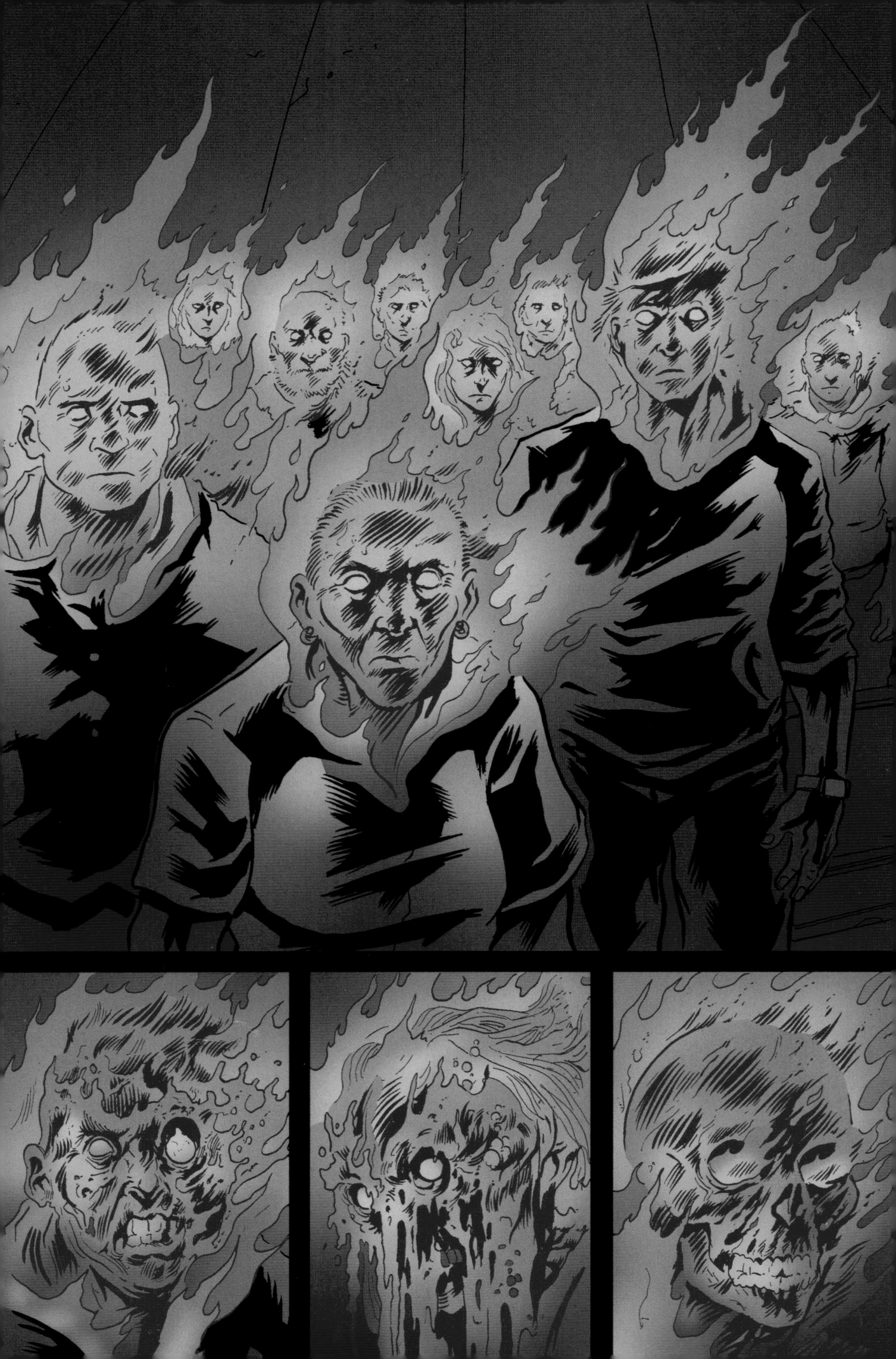

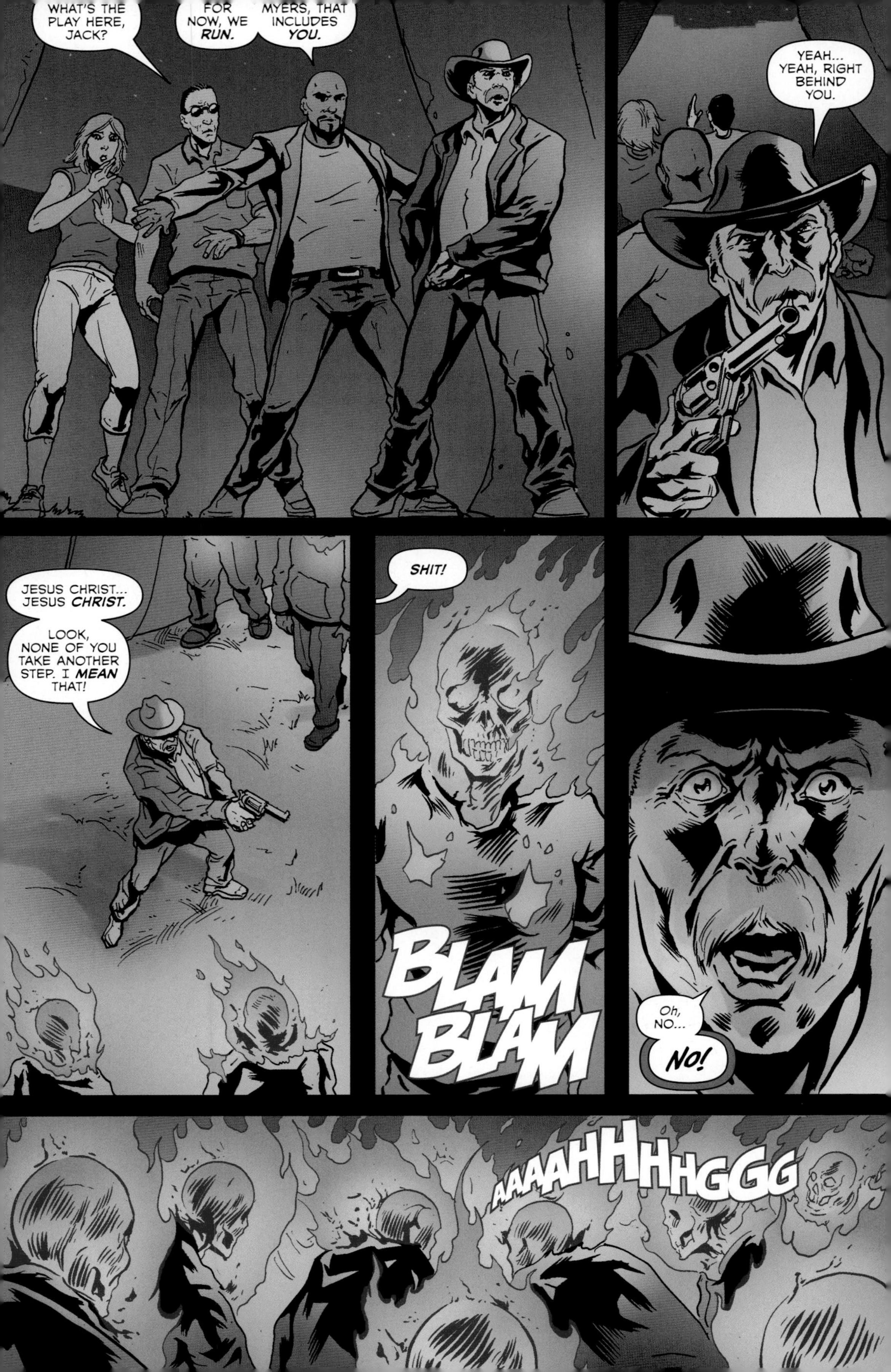
WHAT'S THE PLAY HERE, JACK?
FOR NOW, WE RUN.
MYERS, THAT INCLUDES YOU.
YEAH... YEAH, RIGHT BEHIND YOU.
JESUS CHRIST... JESUS CHRIST.
LOOK, NONE OF YOU TAKE ANOTHER STEP. I MEAN THAT!
SHIT!
BLAM BLAM
Oh, NO...
NO!
AAAAHHHHGGG

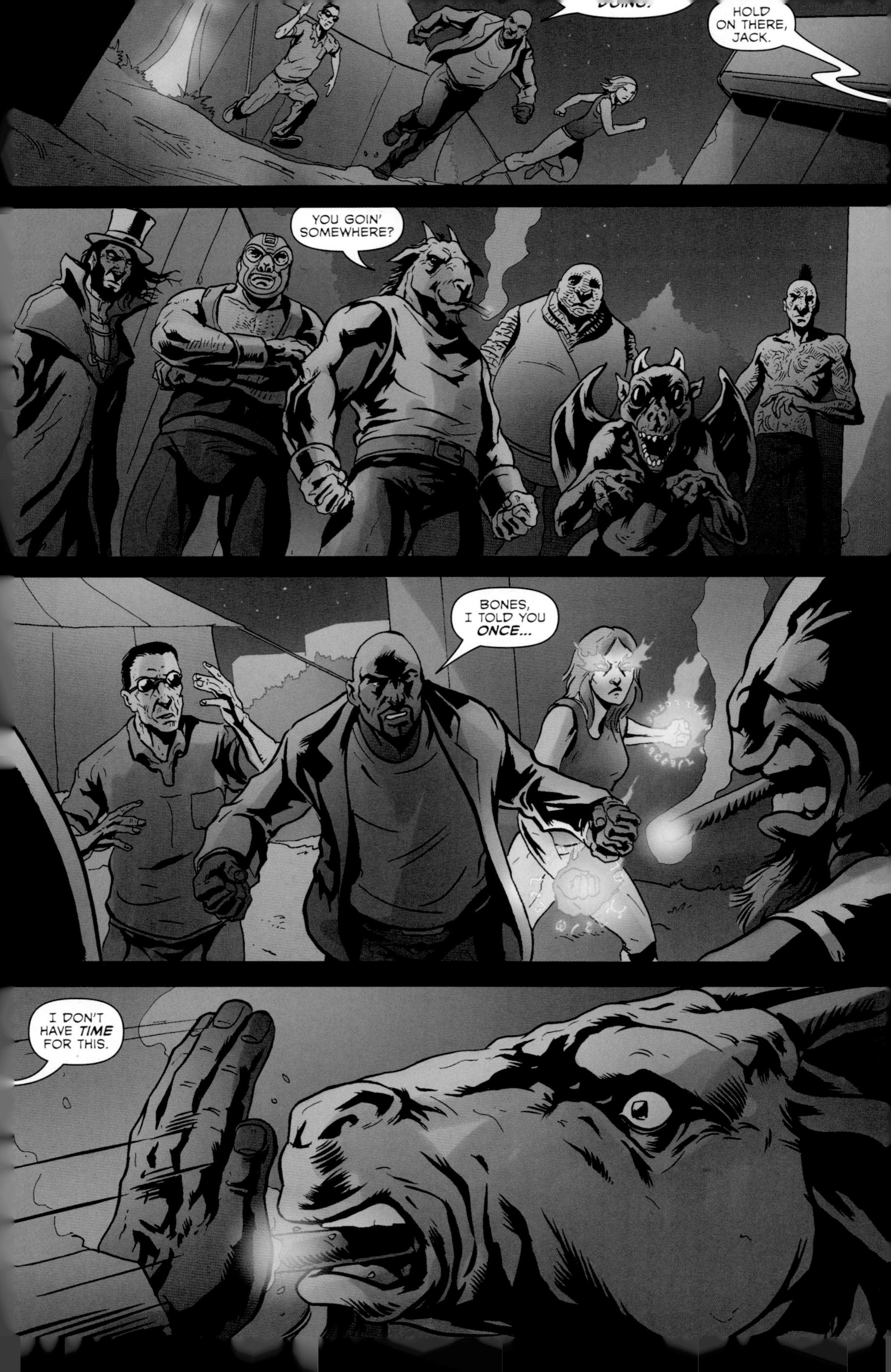
HOLD ON THERE, JACK.
YOU GOIN' SOMEWHERE?
BONES, I TOLD YOU *ONCE*...
I DON'T HAVE *TIME* FOR THIS.

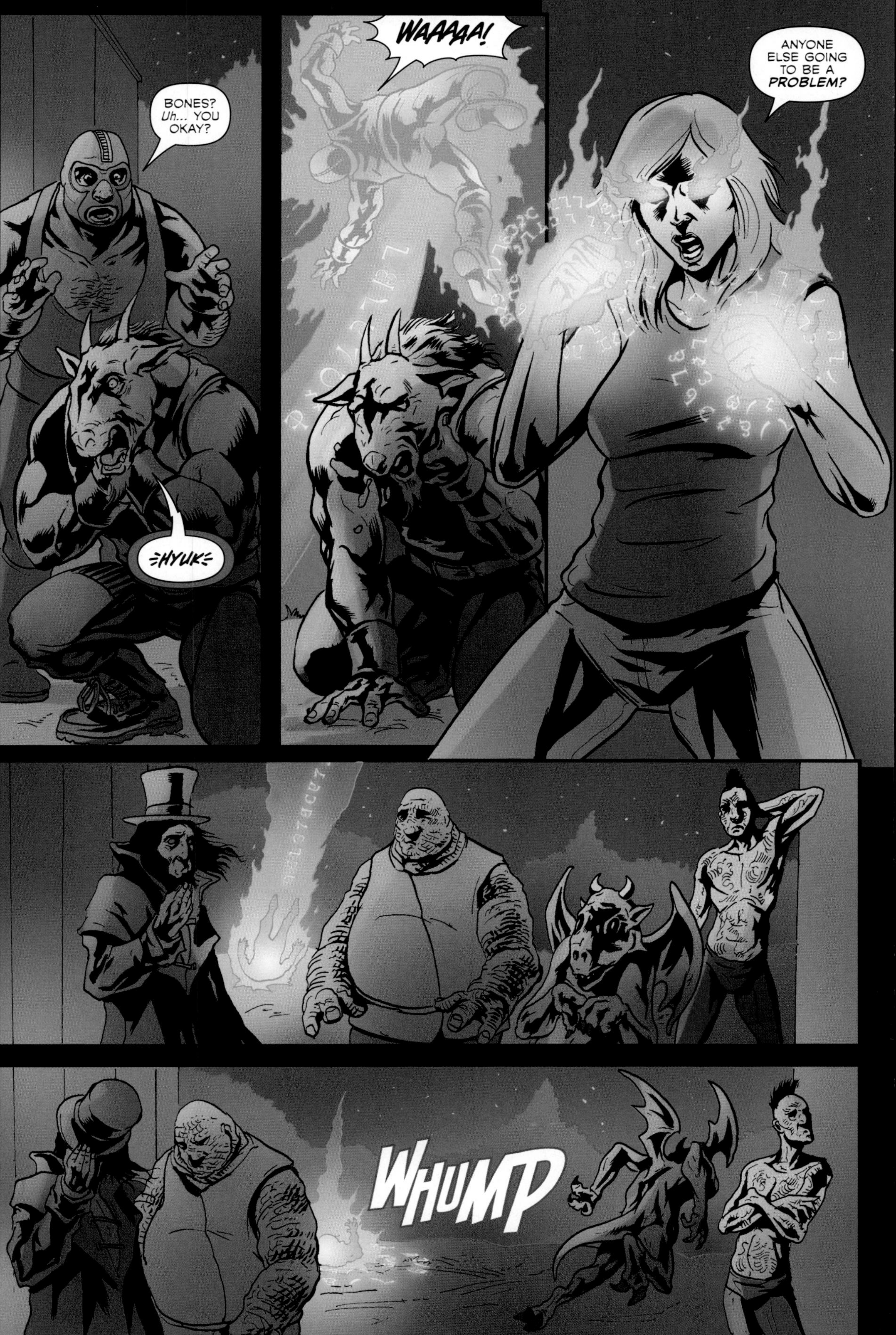
BONES? Uh... YOU OKAY?
HYUK
WAAAAA!
ANYONE ELSE GOING TO BE A PROBLEM?
WHUMP

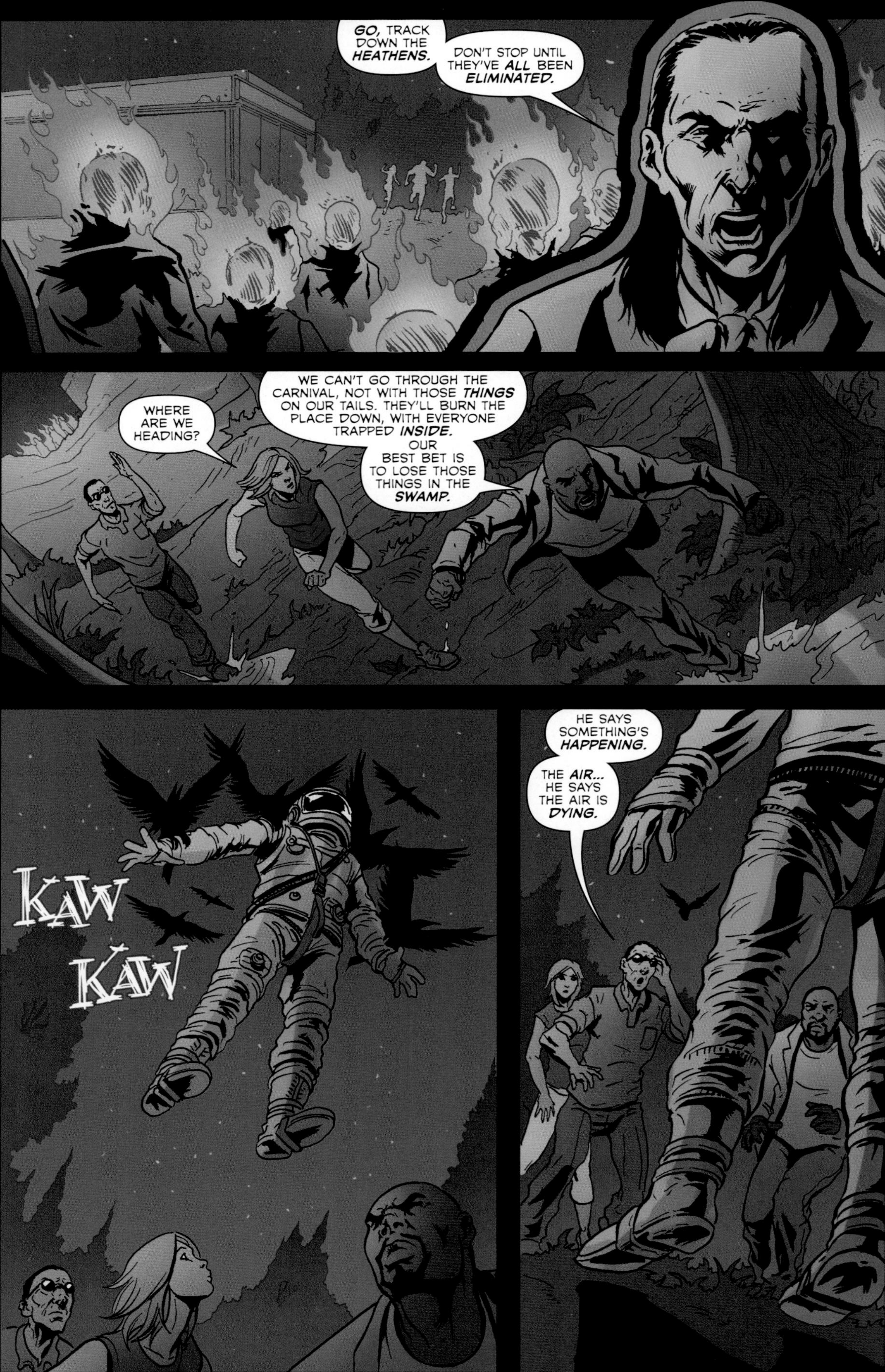
GO, TRACK DOWN THE HEATHENS.
DON'T STOP UNTIL THEY'VE ALL BEEN ELIMINATED.
WHERE ARE WE HEADING?
WE CAN'T GO THROUGH THE CARNIVAL, NOT WITH THOSE THINGS ON OUR TAILS. THEY'LL BURN THE PLACE DOWN, WITH EVERYONE TRAPPED INSIDE.
OUR BEST BET IS TO LOSE THOSE THINGS IN THE SWAMP.
KAW
KAW
HE SAYS SOMETHING'S HAPPENING.
THE AIR... HE SAYS THE AIR IS DYING.

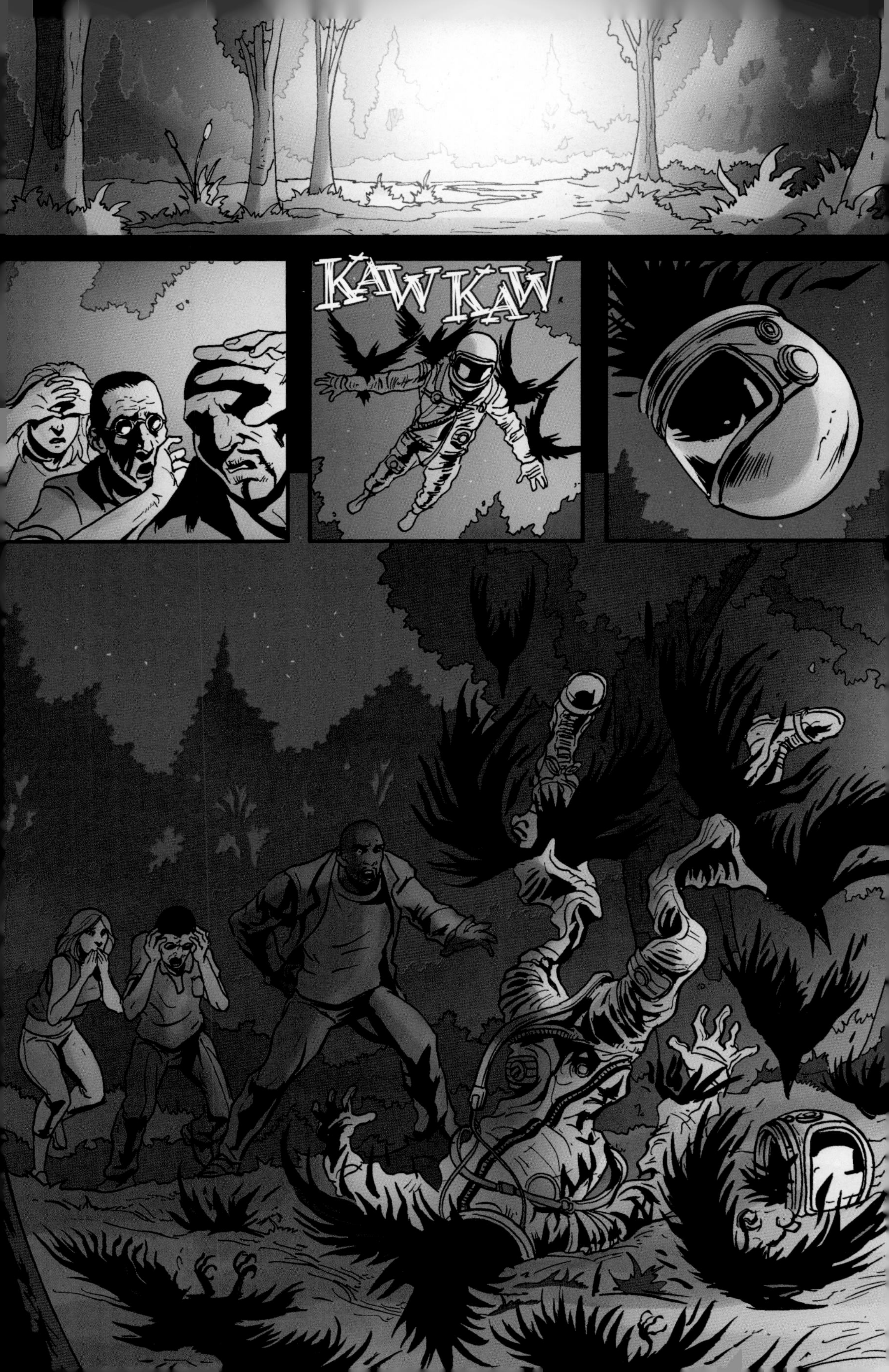
KAW KAW

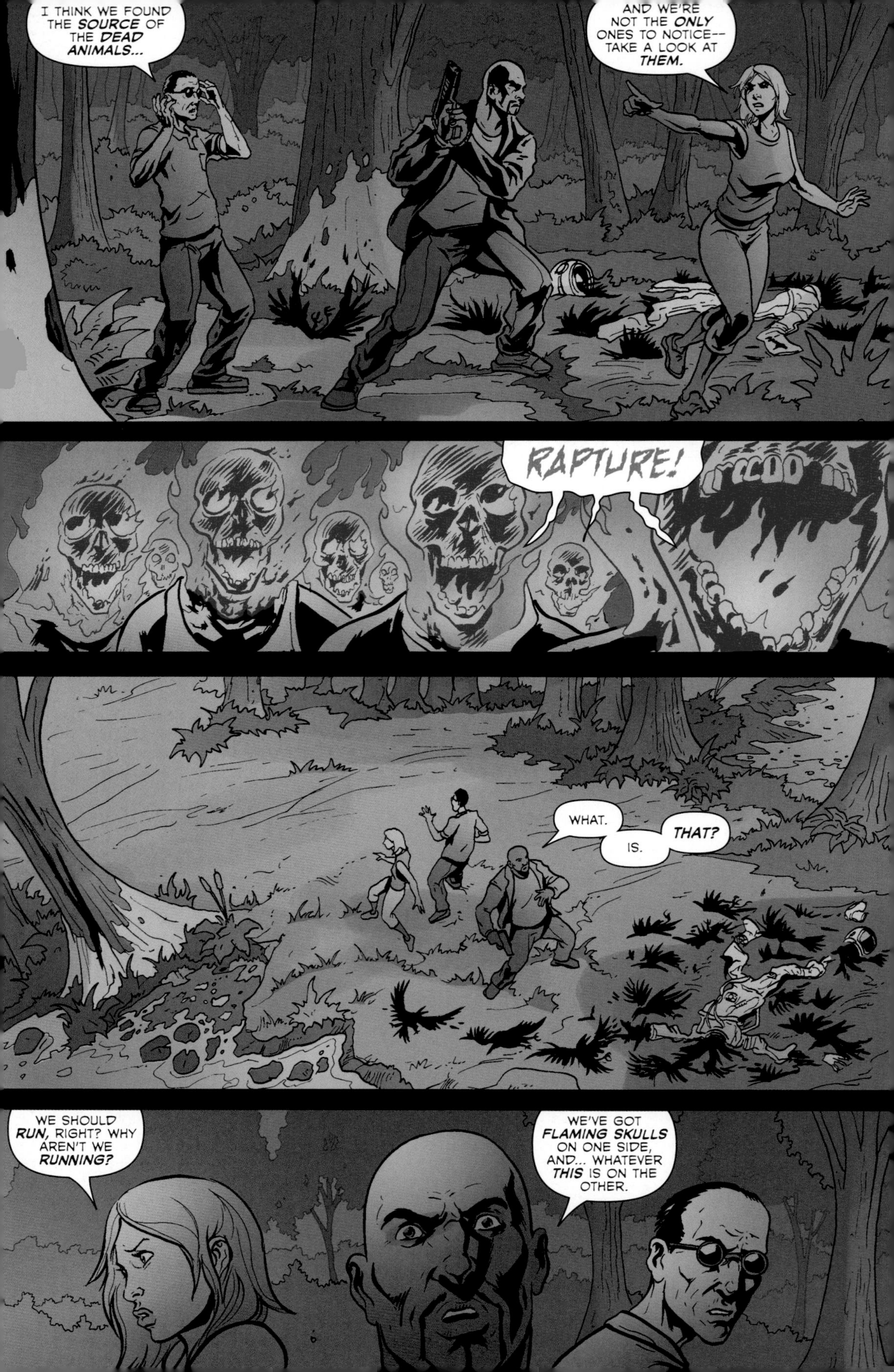
I THINK WE FOUND THE SOURCE OF THE DEAD ANIMALS...
AND WE'RE NOT THE ONLY ONES TO NOTICE-- TAKE A LOOK AT THEM.
RAPTURE!
WHAT.
IS.
THAT?
WE SHOULD RUN, RIGHT? WHY AREN'T WE RUNNING?
WE'VE GOT FLAMING SKULLS ON ONE SIDE, AND... WHATEVER THIS IS ON THE OTHER.

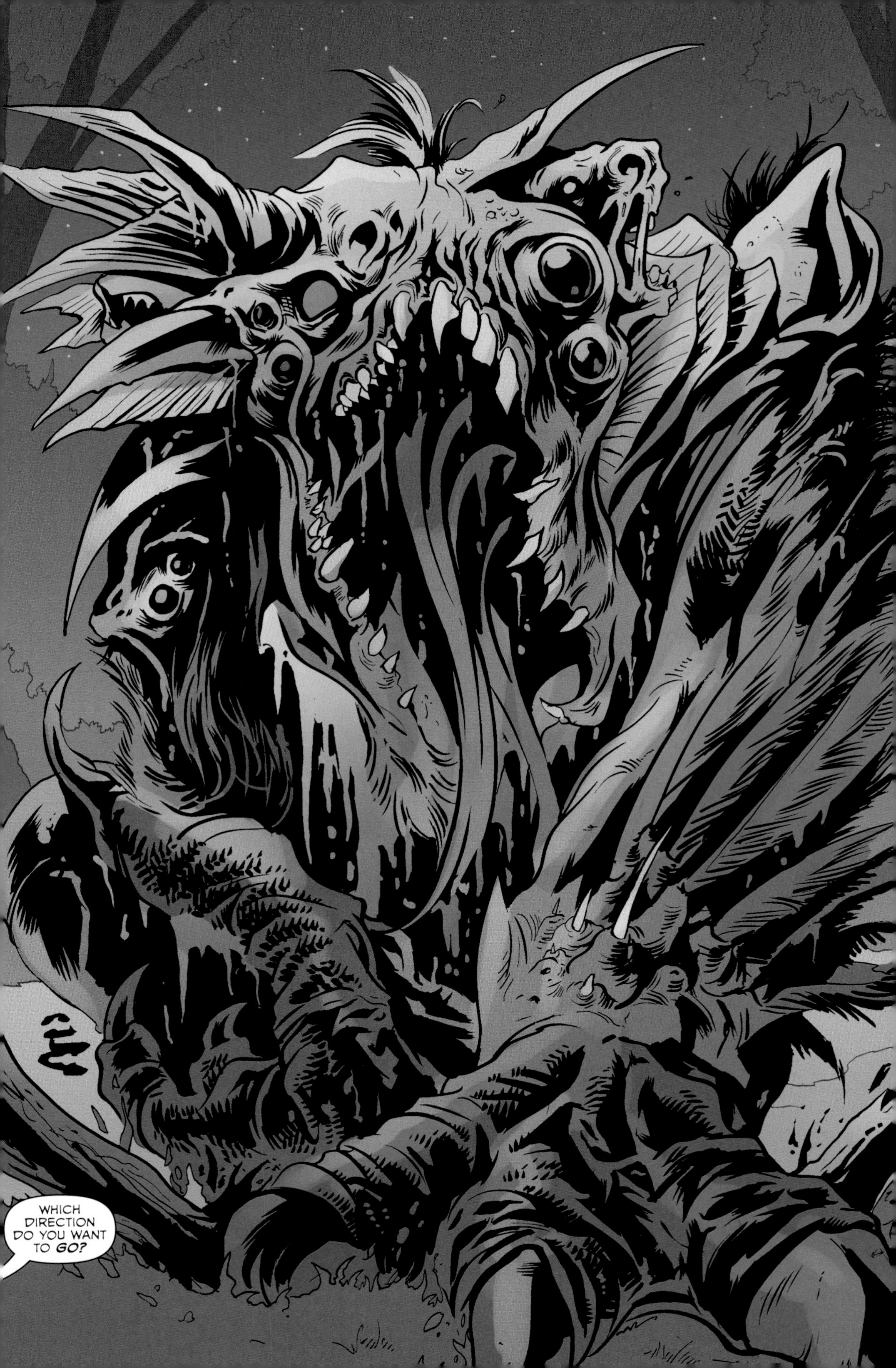
WHICH DIRECTION DO YOU WANT TO GO?

HOAX HUNTERS

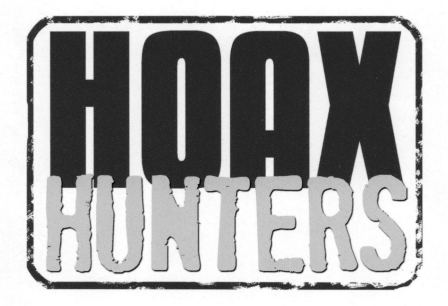

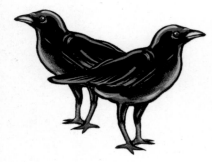

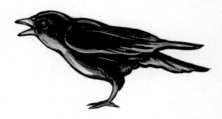

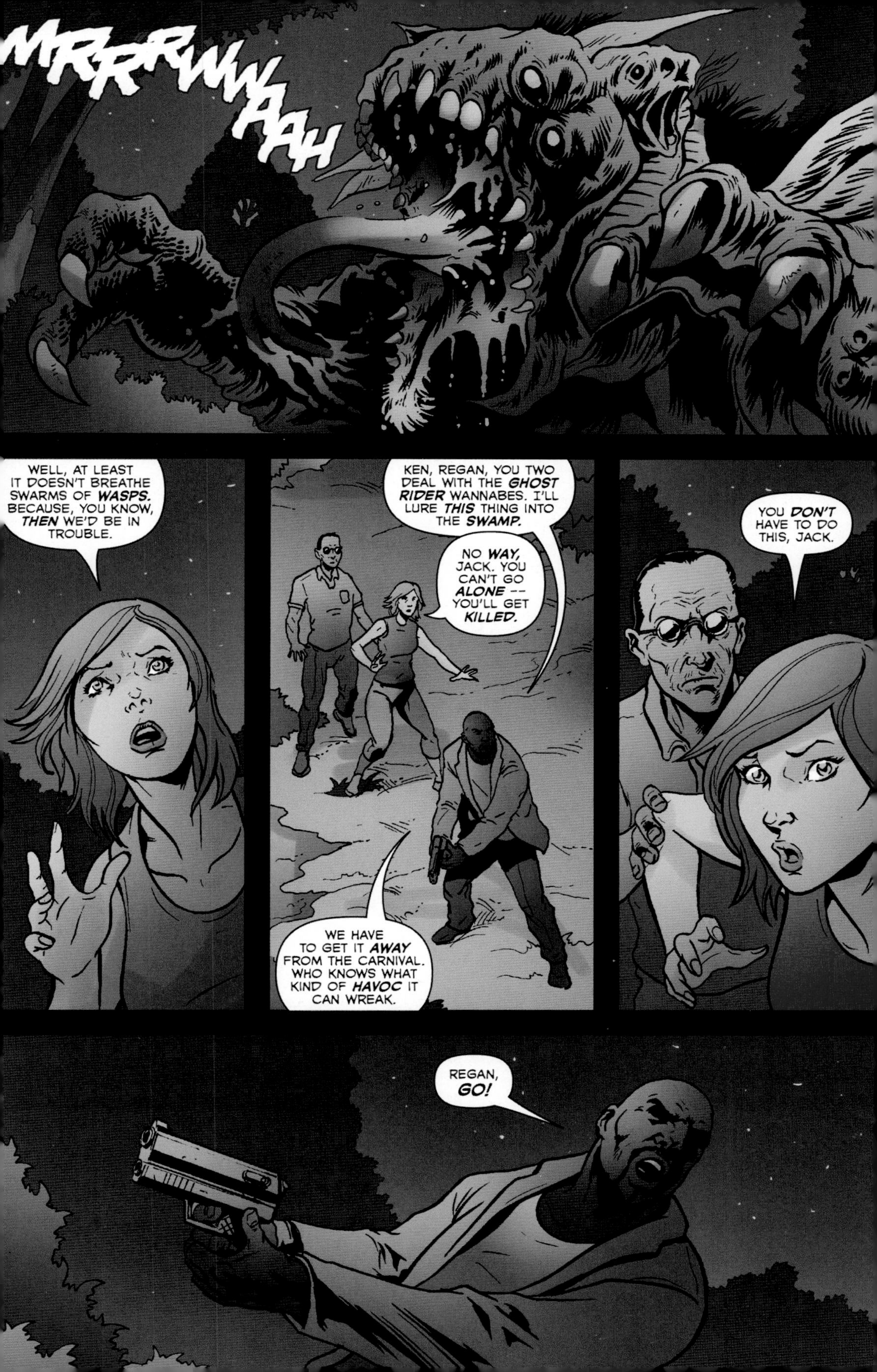
MRRRWWAAH
WELL, AT LEAST IT DOESN'T BREATHE SWARMS OF WASPS. BECAUSE, YOU KNOW, THEN WE'D BE IN TROUBLE.
KEN, REGAN, YOU TWO DEAL WITH THE GHOST RIDER WANNABES. I'LL LURE THIS THING INTO THE SWAMP.
NO WAY, JACK. YOU CAN'T GO ALONE -- YOU'LL GET KILLED.
WE HAVE TO GET IT AWAY FROM THE CARNIVAL. WHO KNOWS WHAT KIND OF HAVOC IT CAN WREAK.
YOU DON'T HAVE TO DO THIS, JACK.
REGAN, GO!

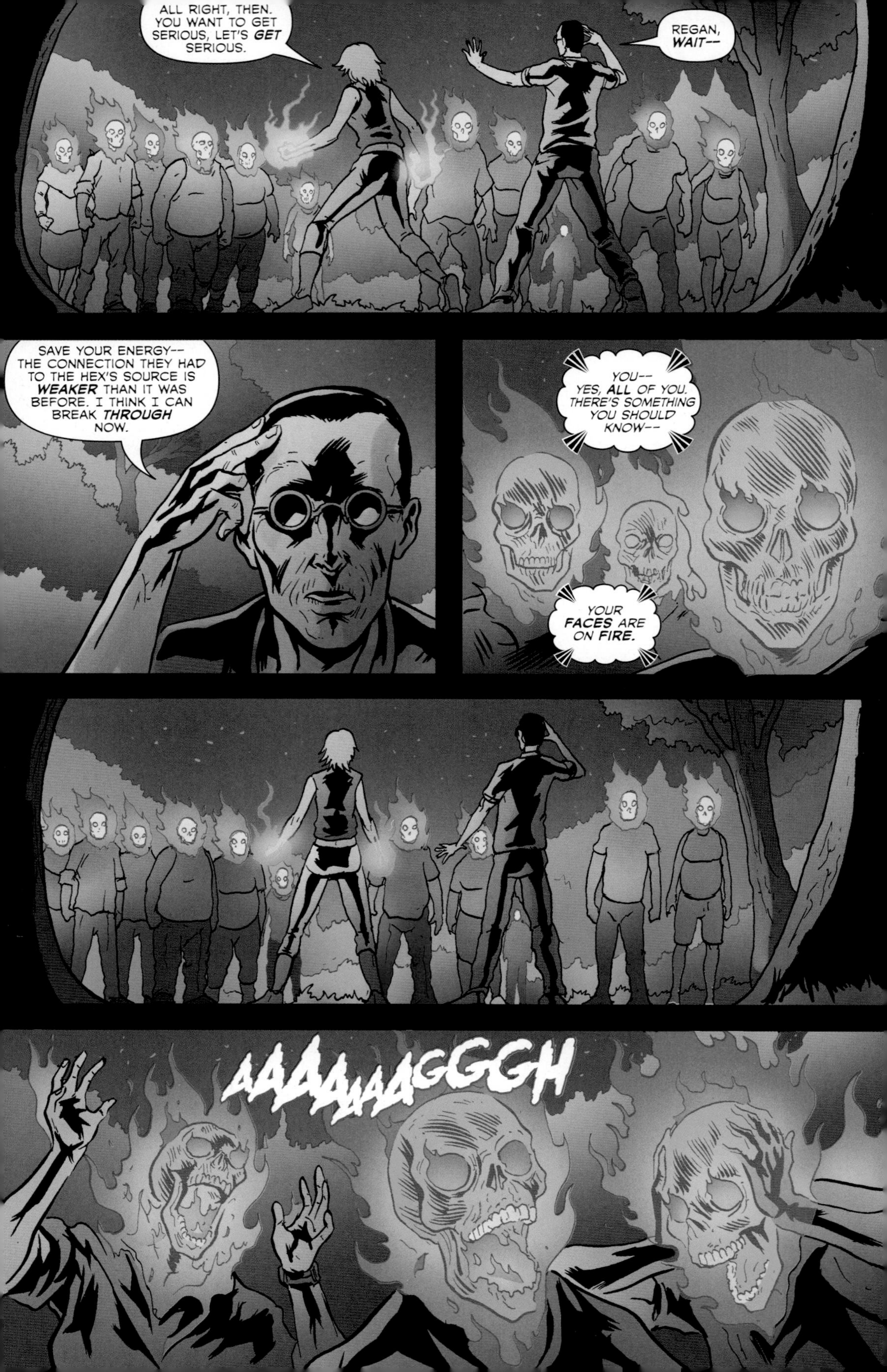
ALL RIGHT, THEN. YOU WANT TO GET SERIOUS, LET'S GET SERIOUS.
REGAN, WAIT--
SAVE YOUR ENERGY-- THE CONNECTION THEY HAD TO THE HEX'S SOURCE IS WEAKER THAN IT WAS BEFORE. I THINK I CAN BREAK THROUGH NOW.
YOU-- YES, ALL OF YOU. THERE'S SOMETHING YOU SHOULD KNOW--
YOUR FACES ARE ON FIRE.
AAAAAAAGGGH

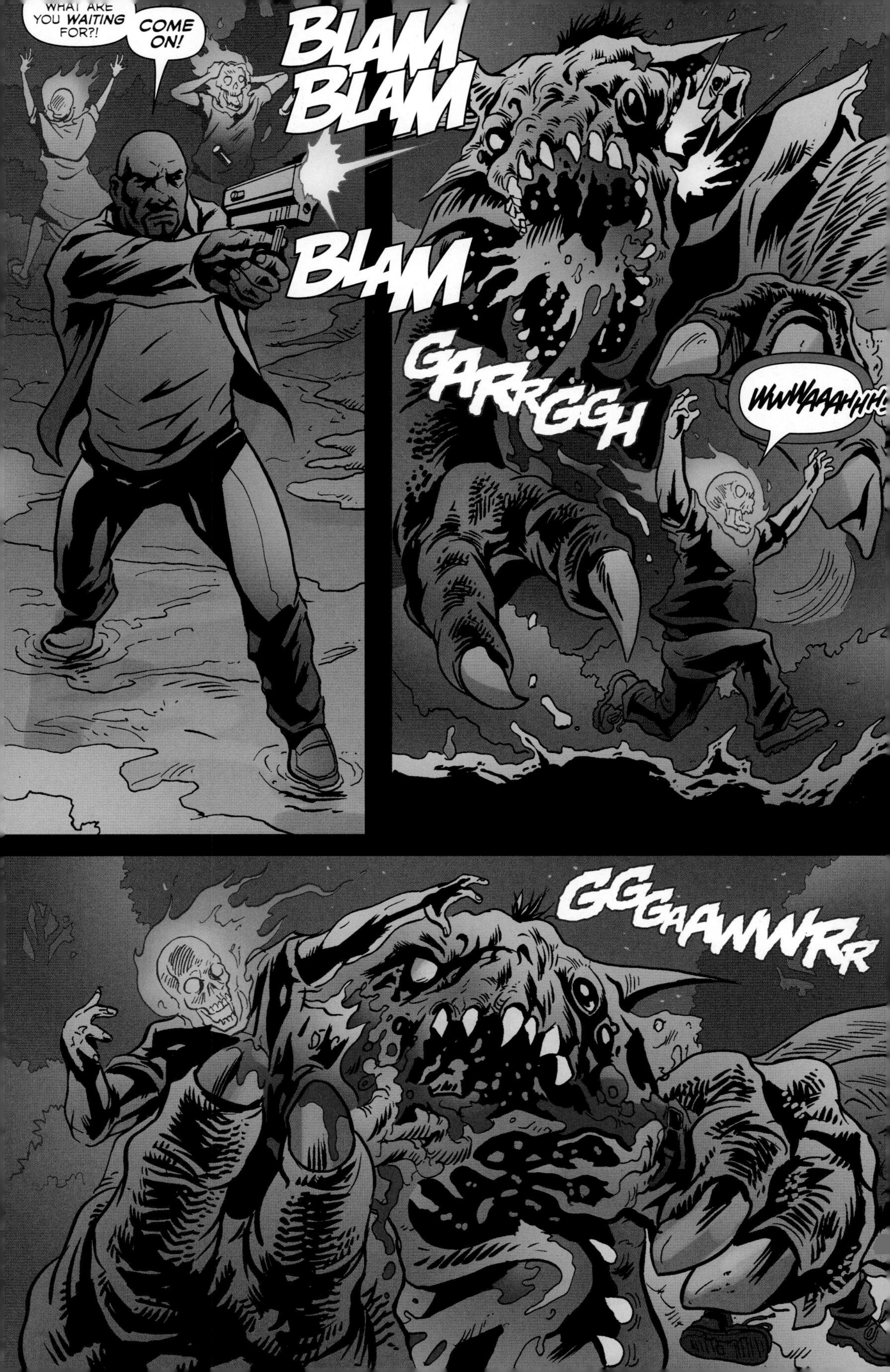
WHAT ARE YOU WAITING FOR?!
COME ON!
BLAM BLAM
BLAM
GARRGGH
WWWAAAHHH!
GGGAAWWRR

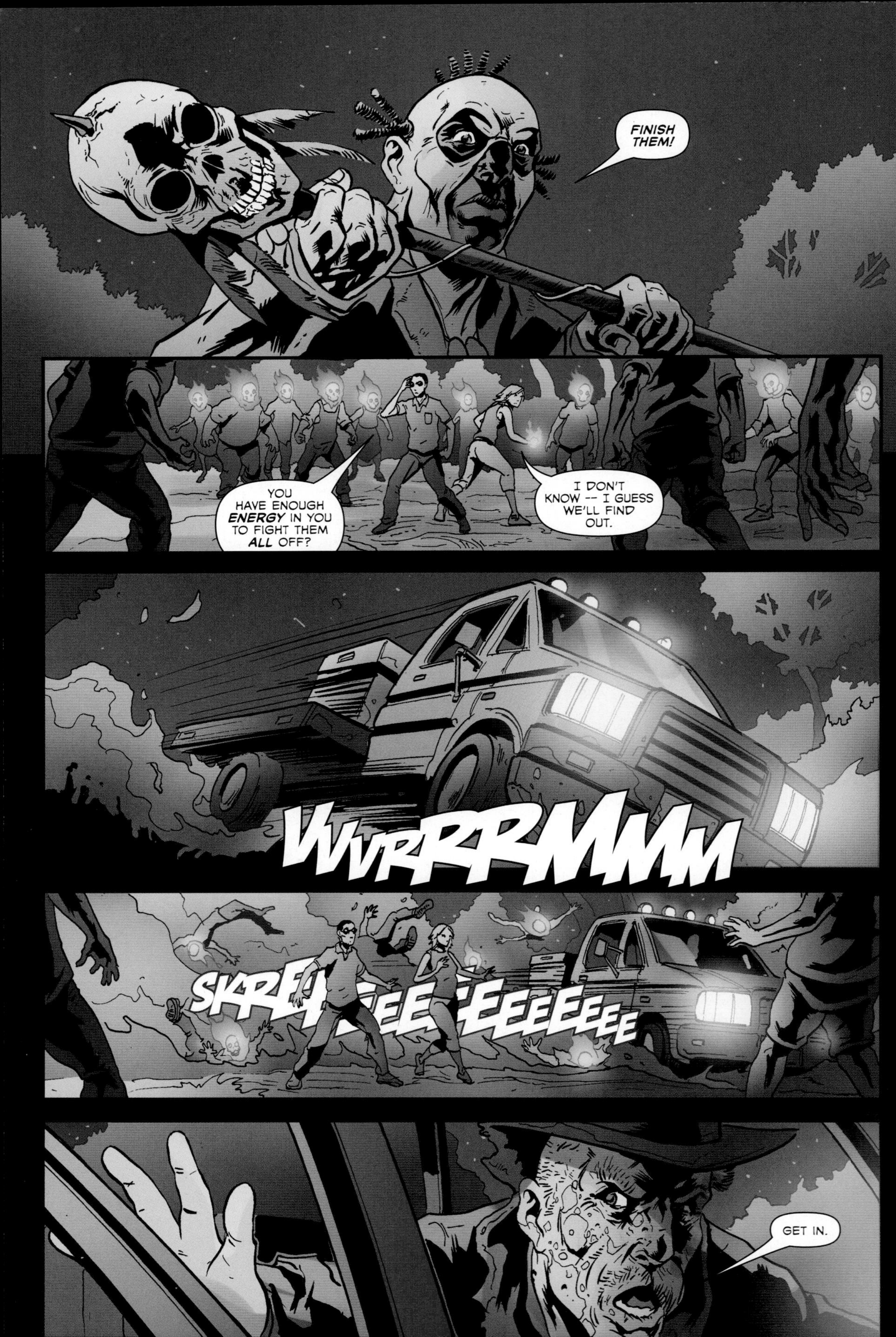
FINISH THEM!
YOU HAVE ENOUGH ENERGY IN YOU TO FIGHT THEM ALL OFF?
I DON'T KNOW -- I GUESS WE'LL FIND OUT.
VVVRRRMMMM
SKREEEEEEEEEEEEeee
GET IN.

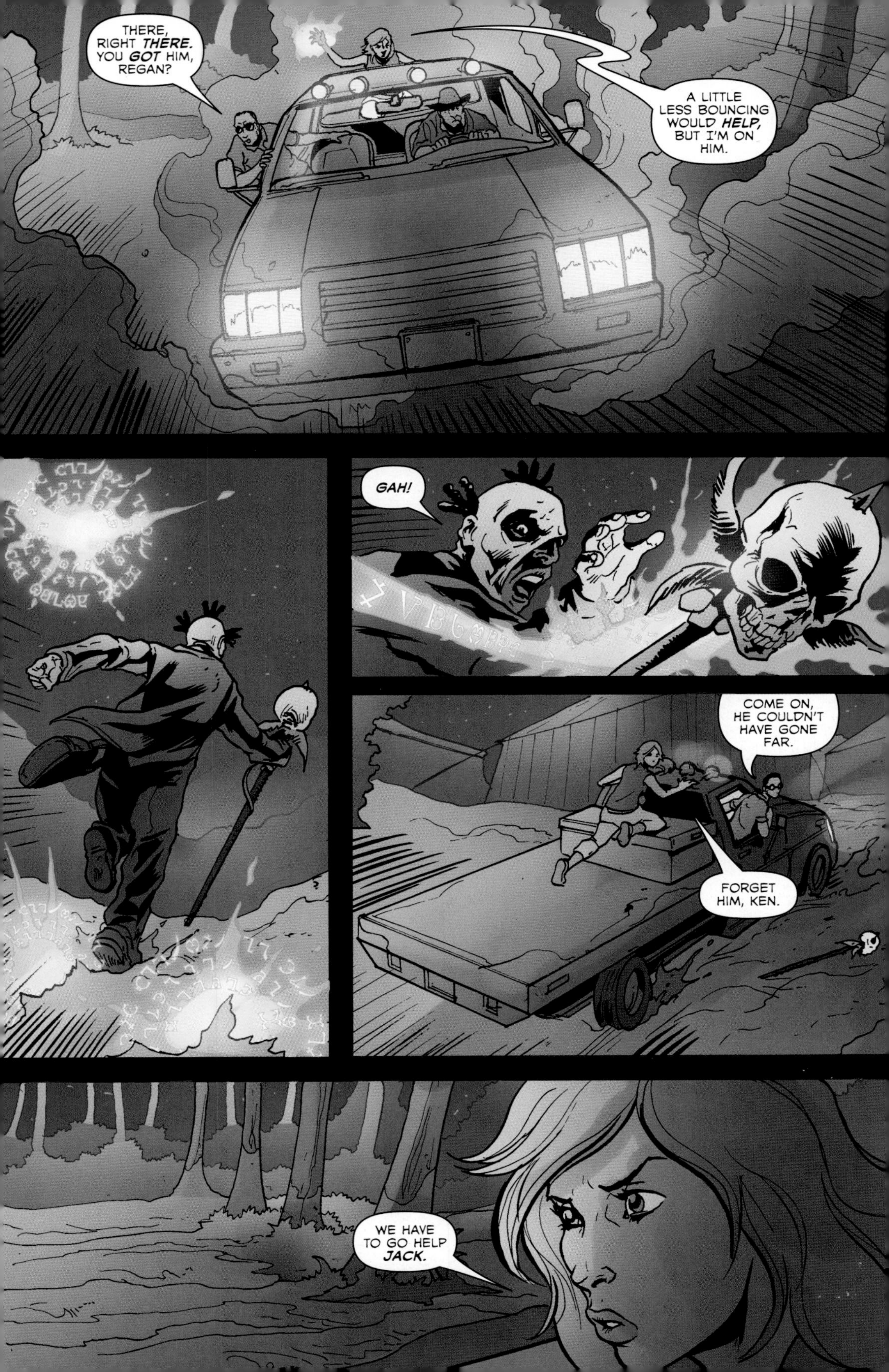
THERE, RIGHT THERE. YOU GOT HIM, REGAN?
A LITTLE LESS BOUNCING WOULD HELP, BUT I'M ON HIM.
GAH!
COME ON, HE COULDN'T HAVE GONE FAR.
FORGET HIM, KEN.
WE HAVE TO GO HELP JACK.

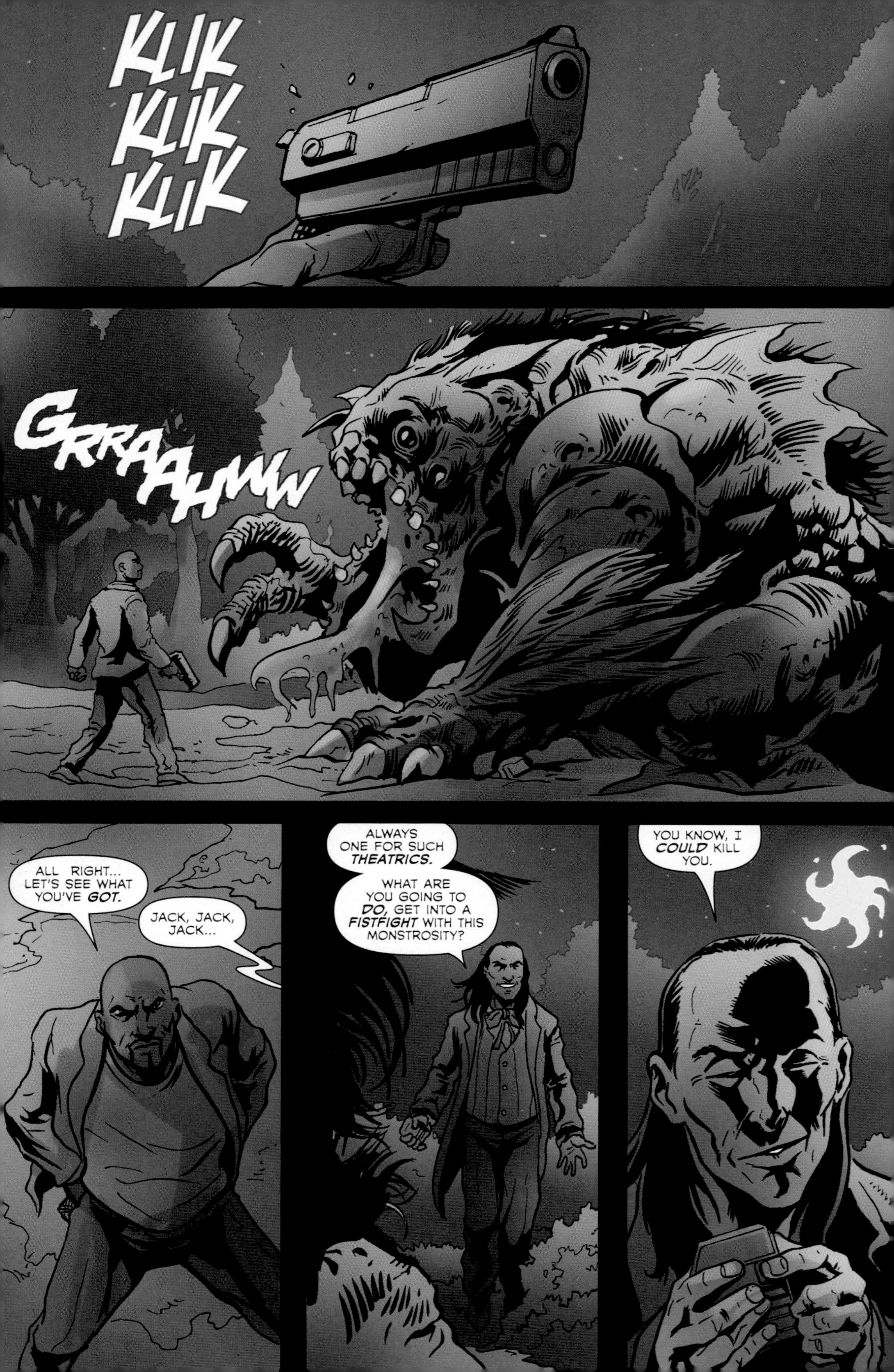
KLIK KLIK KLIK
GRRAAHMMW
ALL RIGHT... LET'S SEE WHAT YOU'VE GOT.
JACK, JACK, JACK...
ALWAYS ONE FOR SUCH THEATRICS.
WHAT ARE YOU GOING TO DO, GET INTO A FISTFIGHT WITH THIS MONSTROSITY?
YOU KNOW, I COULD KILL YOU.

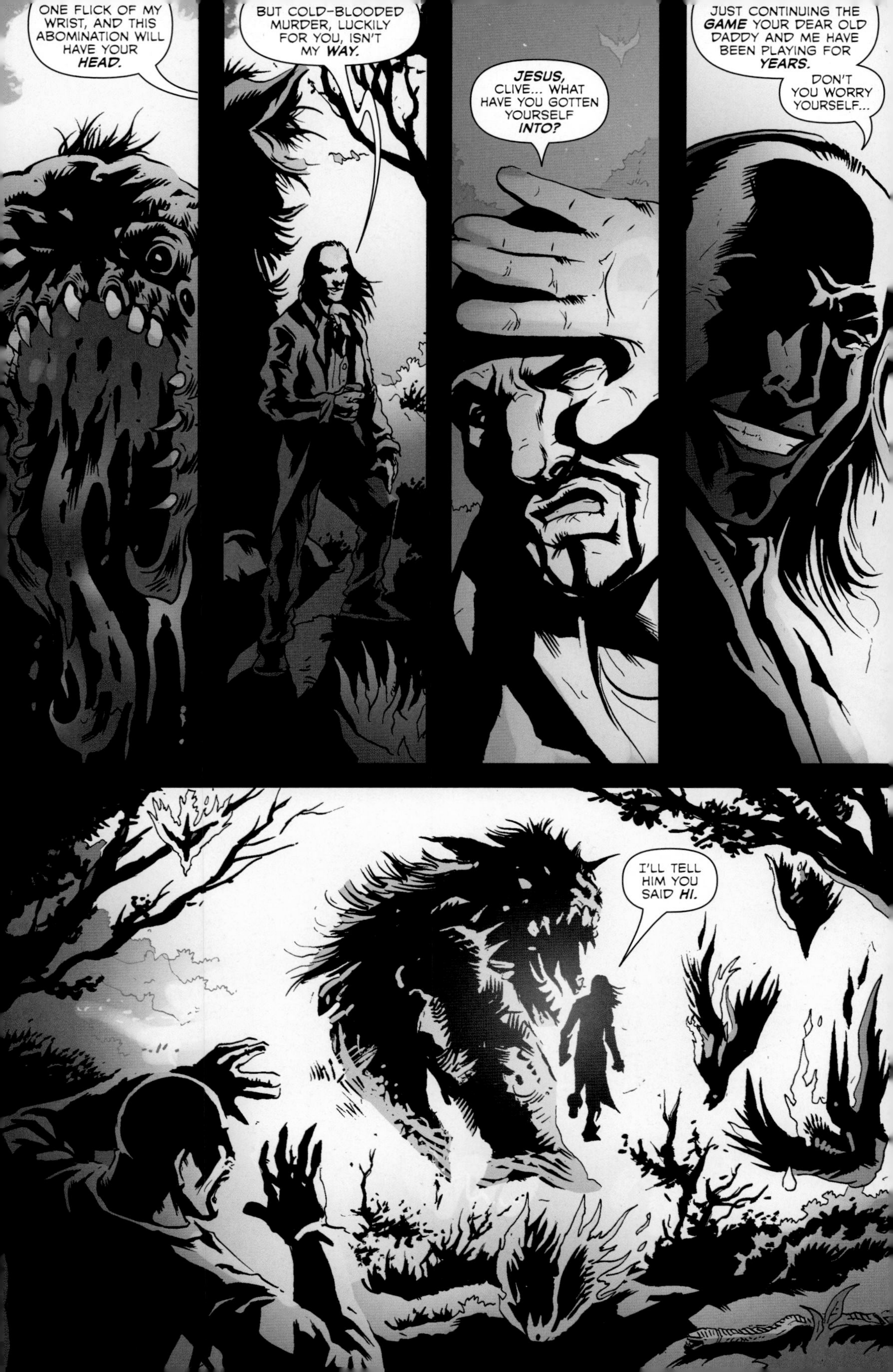

ONE FLICK OF MY WRIST, AND THIS ABOMINATION WILL HAVE YOUR **HEAD.**
BUT COLD-BLOODED MURDER, LUCKILY FOR YOU, ISN'T MY **WAY.**
JESUS, CLIVE... WHAT HAVE YOU GOTTEN YOURSELF **INTO?**
JUST CONTINUING THE **GAME** YOUR DEAR OLD DADDY AND ME HAVE BEEN PLAYING FOR **YEARS.**
DON'T YOU WORRY YOURSELF...
I'LL TELL HIM YOU SAID **HI.**

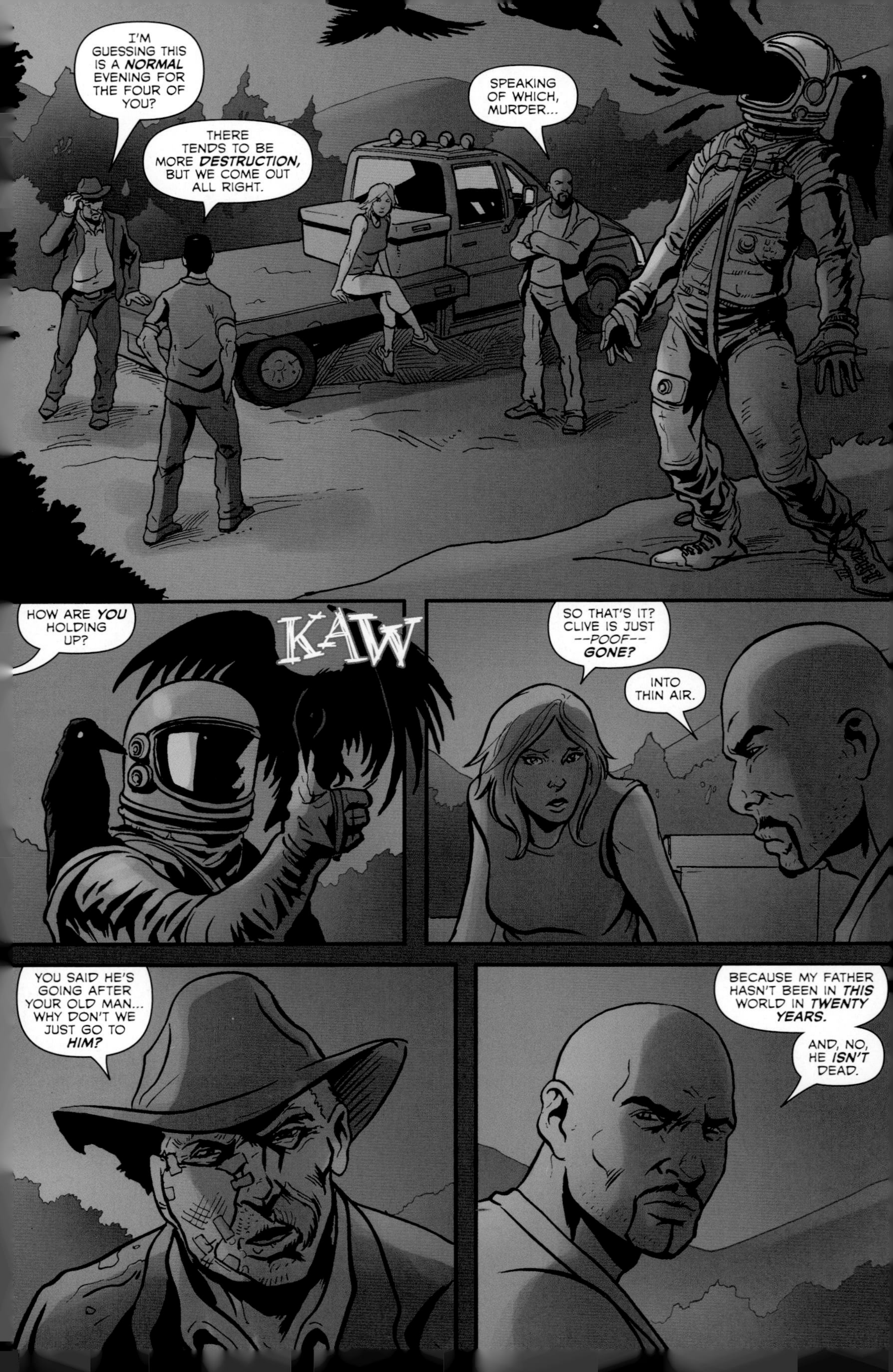
I'M GUESSING THIS IS A *NORMAL* EVENING FOR THE FOUR OF YOU?
THERE TENDS TO BE MORE *DESTRUCTION,* BUT WE COME OUT ALL RIGHT.
SPEAKING OF WHICH, MURDER...
HOW ARE *YOU* HOLDING UP?
KAW
SO THAT'S IT? CLIVE IS JUST *--POOF--* ***GONE?***
INTO THIN AIR.
YOU SAID HE'S GOING AFTER YOUR OLD MAN... WHY DON'T WE JUST GO TO *HIM?*
BECAUSE MY FATHER HASN'T BEEN IN *THIS* WORLD IN *TWENTY YEARS.*
AND, NO, HE *ISN'T* DEAD.

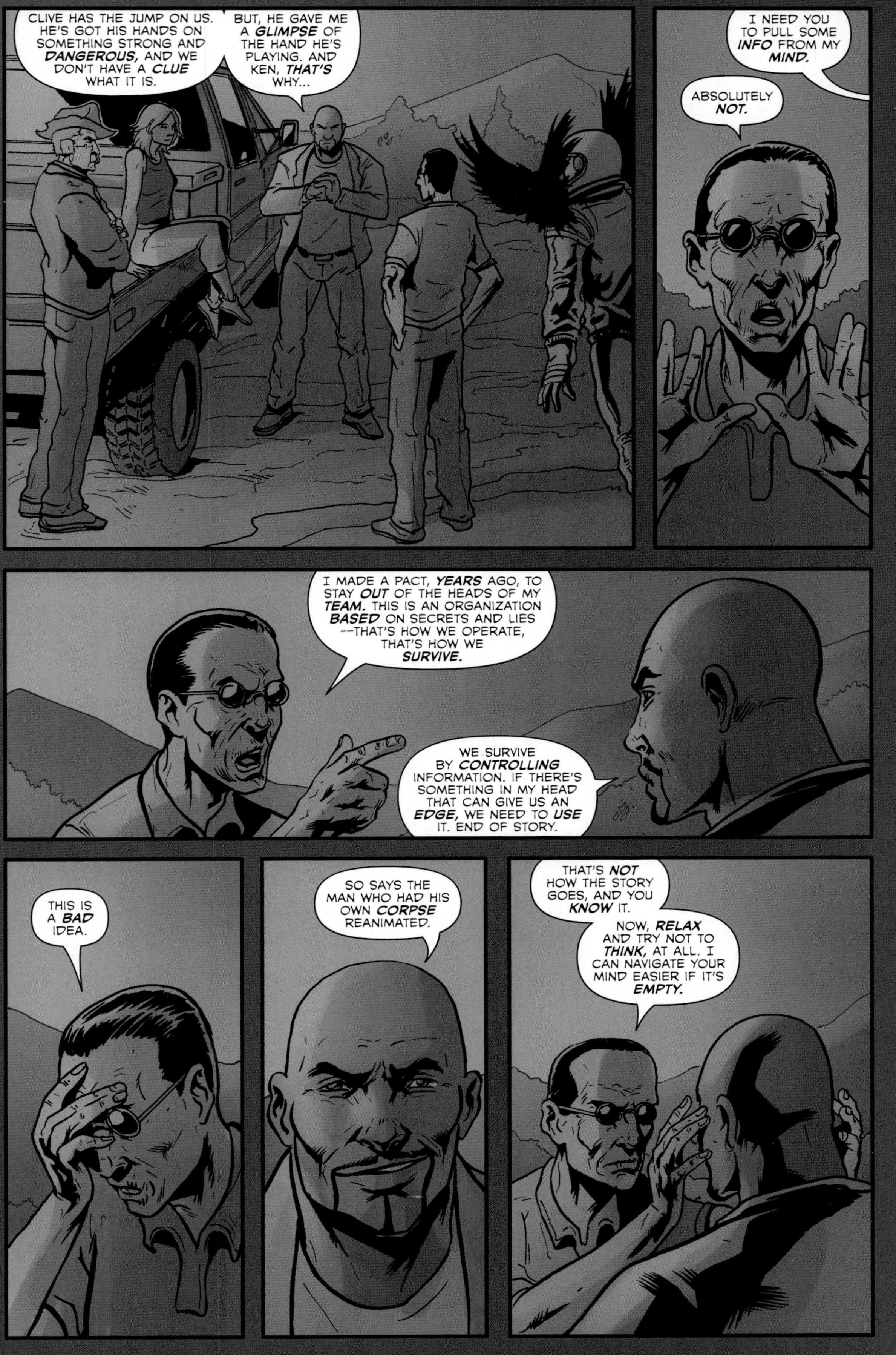
CLIVE HAS THE JUMP ON US. HE'S GOT HIS HANDS ON SOMETHING STRONG AND DANGEROUS, AND WE DON'T HAVE A CLUE WHAT IT IS.
BUT, HE GAVE ME A GLIMPSE OF THE HAND HE'S PLAYING. AND KEN, THAT'S WHY...
I NEED YOU TO PULL SOME INFO FROM MY MIND.
ABSOLUTELY NOT.
I MADE A PACT, YEARS AGO, TO STAY OUT OF THE HEADS OF MY TEAM. THIS IS AN ORGANIZATION BASED ON SECRETS AND LIES --THAT'S HOW WE OPERATE, THAT'S HOW WE SURVIVE.
WE SURVIVE BY CONTROLLING INFORMATION. IF THERE'S SOMETHING IN MY HEAD THAT CAN GIVE US AN EDGE, WE NEED TO USE IT. END OF STORY.
THIS IS A BAD IDEA.
SO SAYS THE MAN WHO HAD HIS OWN CORPSE REANIMATED.
THAT'S NOT HOW THE STORY GOES, AND YOU KNOW IT.
NOW, RELAX AND TRY NOT TO THINK, AT ALL. I CAN NAVIGATE YOUR MIND EASIER IF IT'S EMPTY.

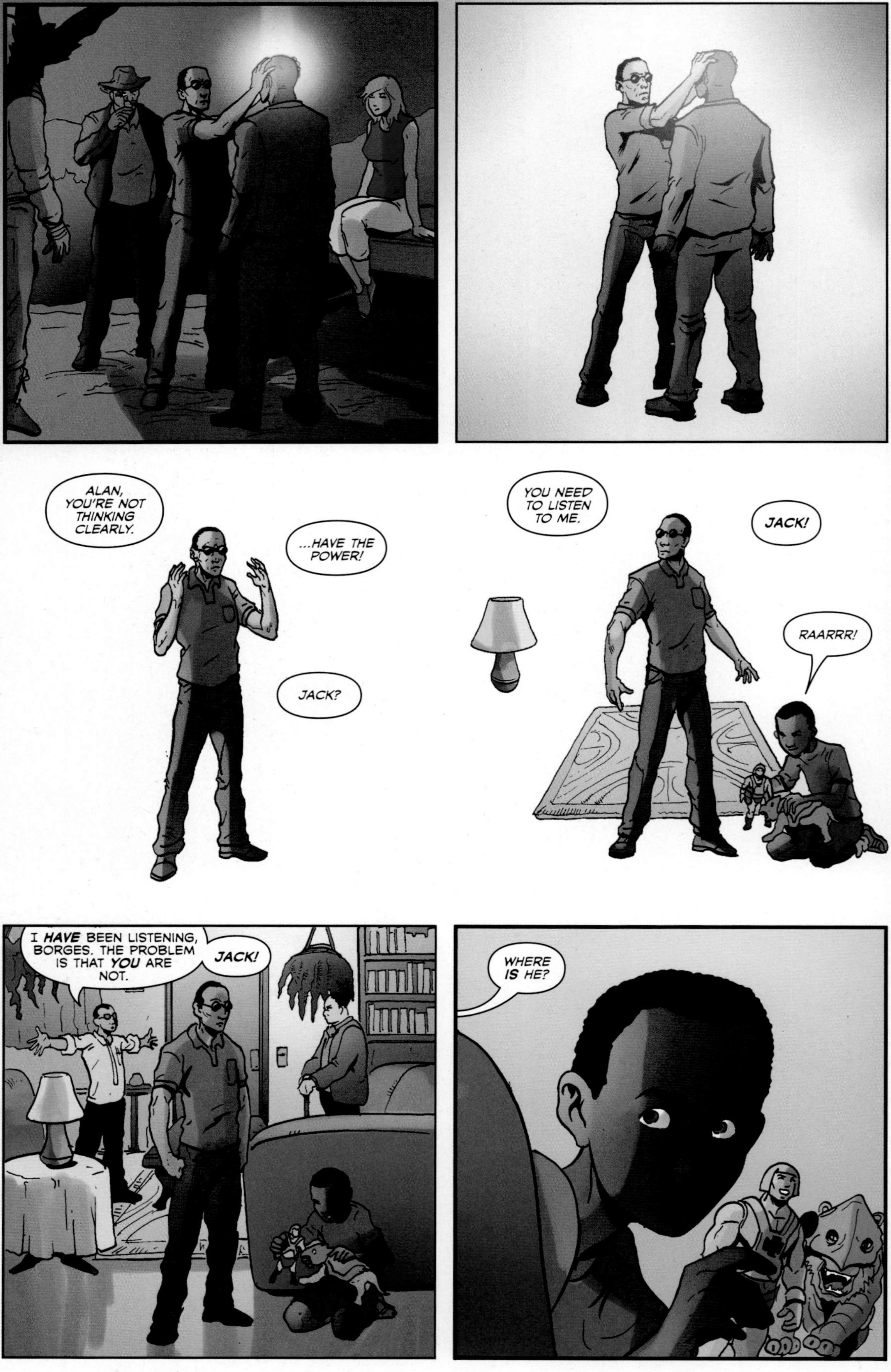
ALAN, YOU'RE NOT THINKING CLEARLY.
...HAVE THE POWER!
JACK?
YOU NEED TO LISTEN TO ME.
JACK!
RAARRR!
I HAVE BEEN LISTENING, BORGES. THE PROBLEM IS THAT YOU ARE NOT.
JACK!
WHERE IS HE?

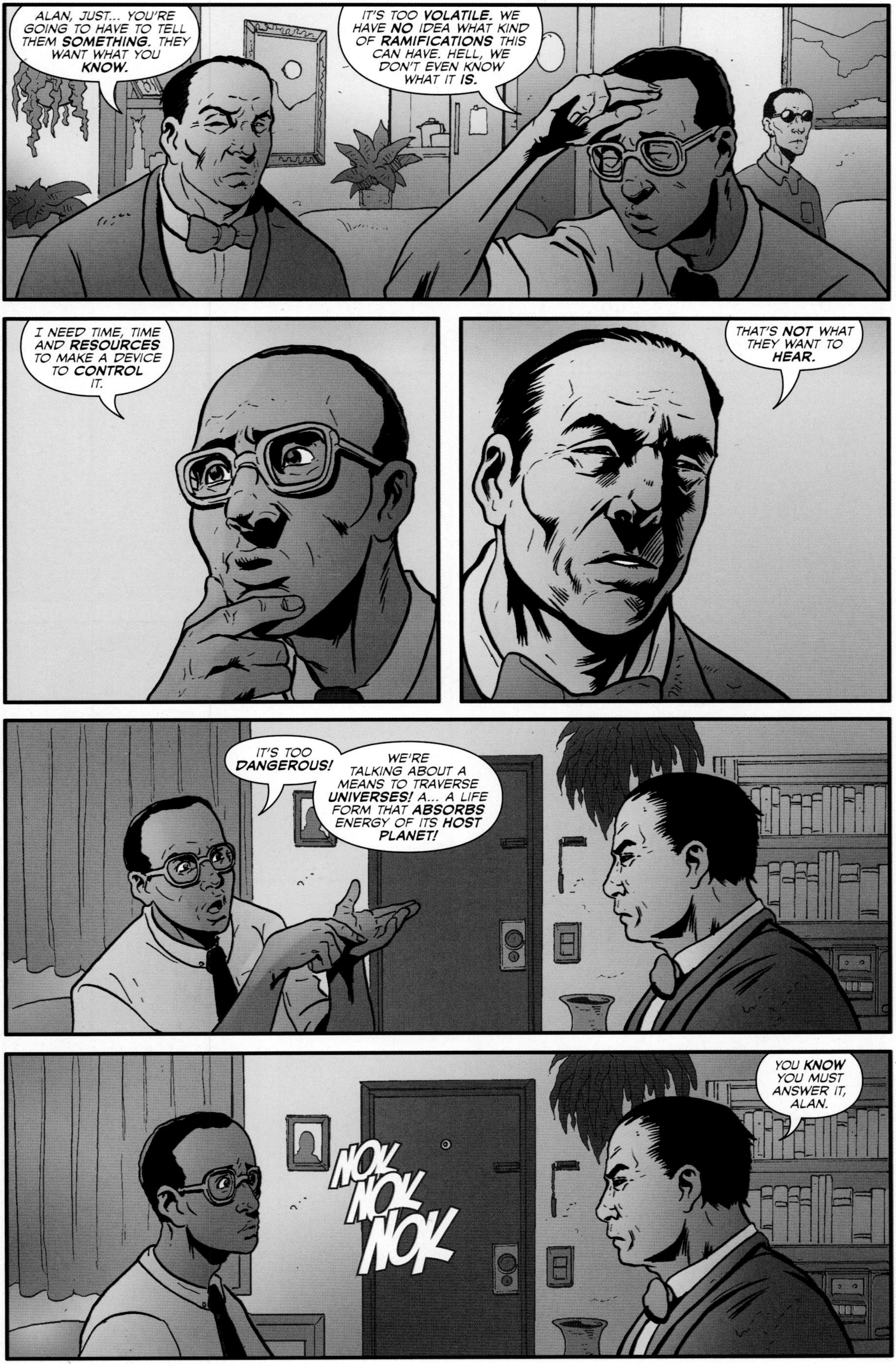
ALAN, JUST... YOU'RE GOING TO HAVE TO TELL THEM SOMETHING. THEY WANT WHAT YOU KNOW.
IT'S TOO VOLATILE. WE HAVE NO IDEA WHAT KIND OF RAMIFICATIONS THIS CAN HAVE. HELL, WE DON'T EVEN KNOW WHAT IT IS.
I NEED TIME, TIME AND RESOURCES TO MAKE A DEVICE TO CONTROL IT.
THAT'S NOT WHAT THEY WANT TO HEAR.
IT'S TOO DANGEROUS!
WE'RE TALKING ABOUT A MEANS TO TRAVERSE UNIVERSES! A... A LIFE FORM THAT ABSORBS ENERGY OF ITS HOST PLANET!
YOU KNOW YOU MUST ANSWER IT, ALAN.
NOK
NOK
NOK

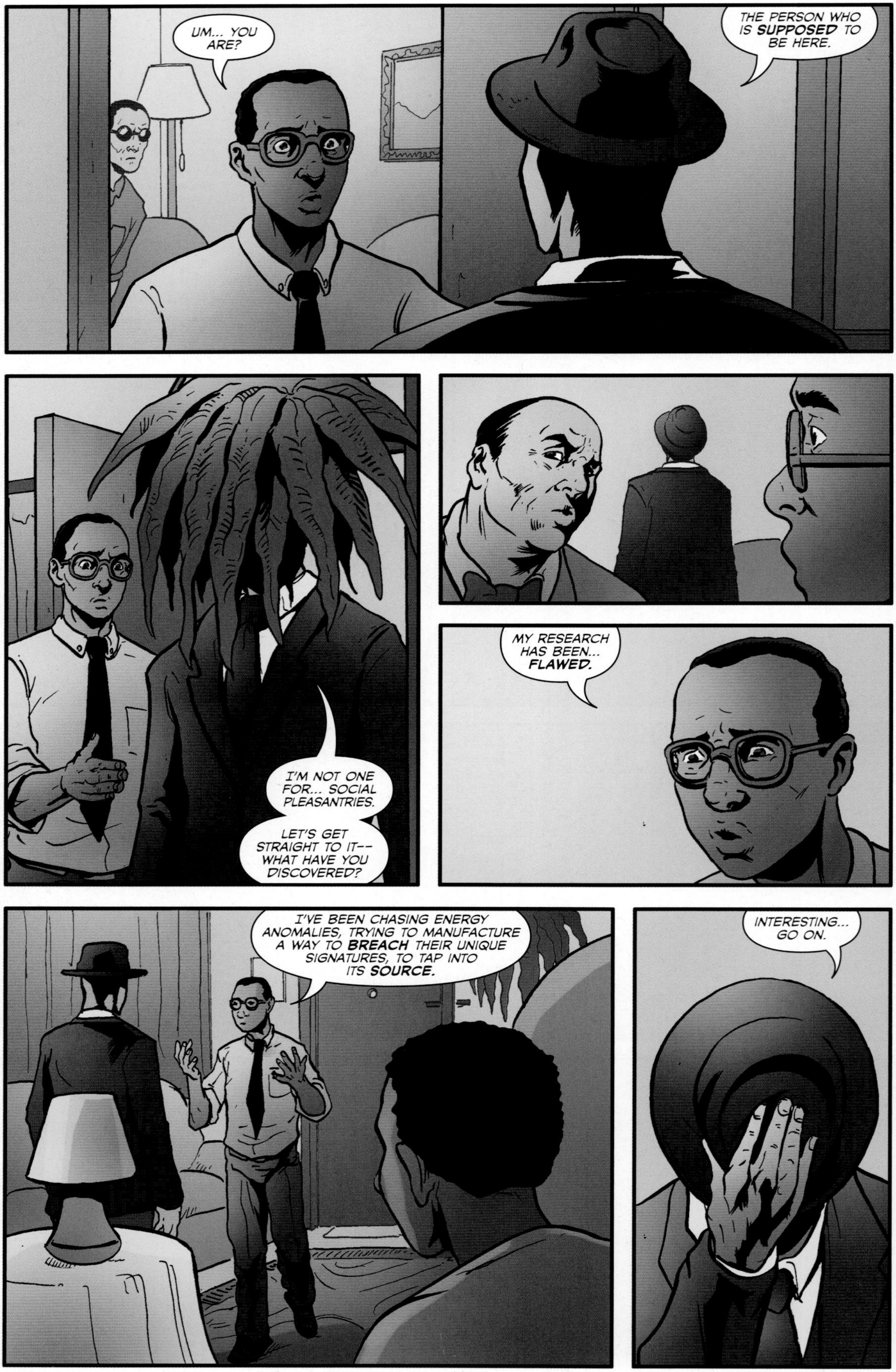
UM... YOU ARE?
THE PERSON WHO IS SUPPOSED TO BE HERE.
I'M NOT ONE FOR... SOCIAL PLEASANTRIES.
LET'S GET STRAIGHT TO IT-- WHAT HAVE YOU DISCOVERED?
MY RESEARCH HAS BEEN... FLAWED.
I'VE BEEN CHASING ENERGY ANOMALIES, TRYING TO MANUFACTURE A WAY TO BREACH THEIR UNIQUE SIGNATURES, TO TAP INTO ITS SOURCE.
INTERESTING... GO ON.

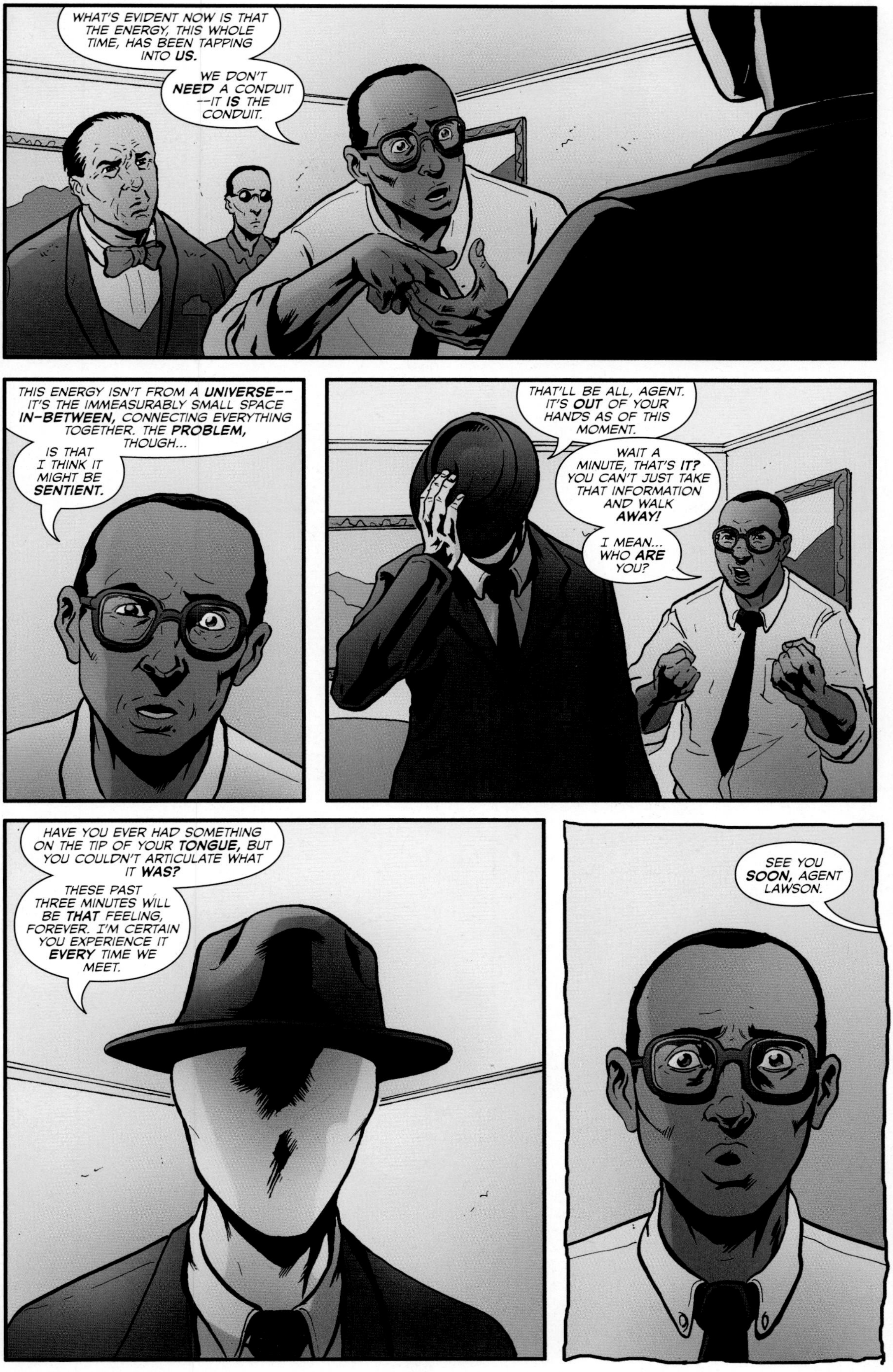
WHAT'S EVIDENT NOW IS THAT THE ENERGY, THIS WHOLE TIME, HAS BEEN TAPPING INTO US.
WE DON'T NEED A CONDUIT --IT IS THE CONDUIT.
THIS ENERGY ISN'T FROM A UNIVERSE-- IT'S THE IMMEASURABLY SMALL SPACE IN-BETWEEN, CONNECTING EVERYTHING TOGETHER. THE PROBLEM, THOUGH...
IS THAT I THINK IT MIGHT BE SENTIENT.
THAT'LL BE ALL, AGENT. IT'S OUT OF YOUR HANDS AS OF THIS MOMENT.
WAIT A MINUTE, THAT'S IT? YOU CAN'T JUST TAKE THAT INFORMATION AND WALK AWAY!
I MEAN... WHO ARE YOU?
HAVE YOU EVER HAD SOMETHING ON THE TIP OF YOUR TONGUE, BUT YOU COULDN'T ARTICULATE WHAT IT WAS?
THESE PAST THREE MINUTES WILL BE THAT FEELING, FOREVER. I'M CERTAIN YOU EXPERIENCE IT EVERY TIME WE MEET.
SEE YOU SOON, AGENT LAWSON.

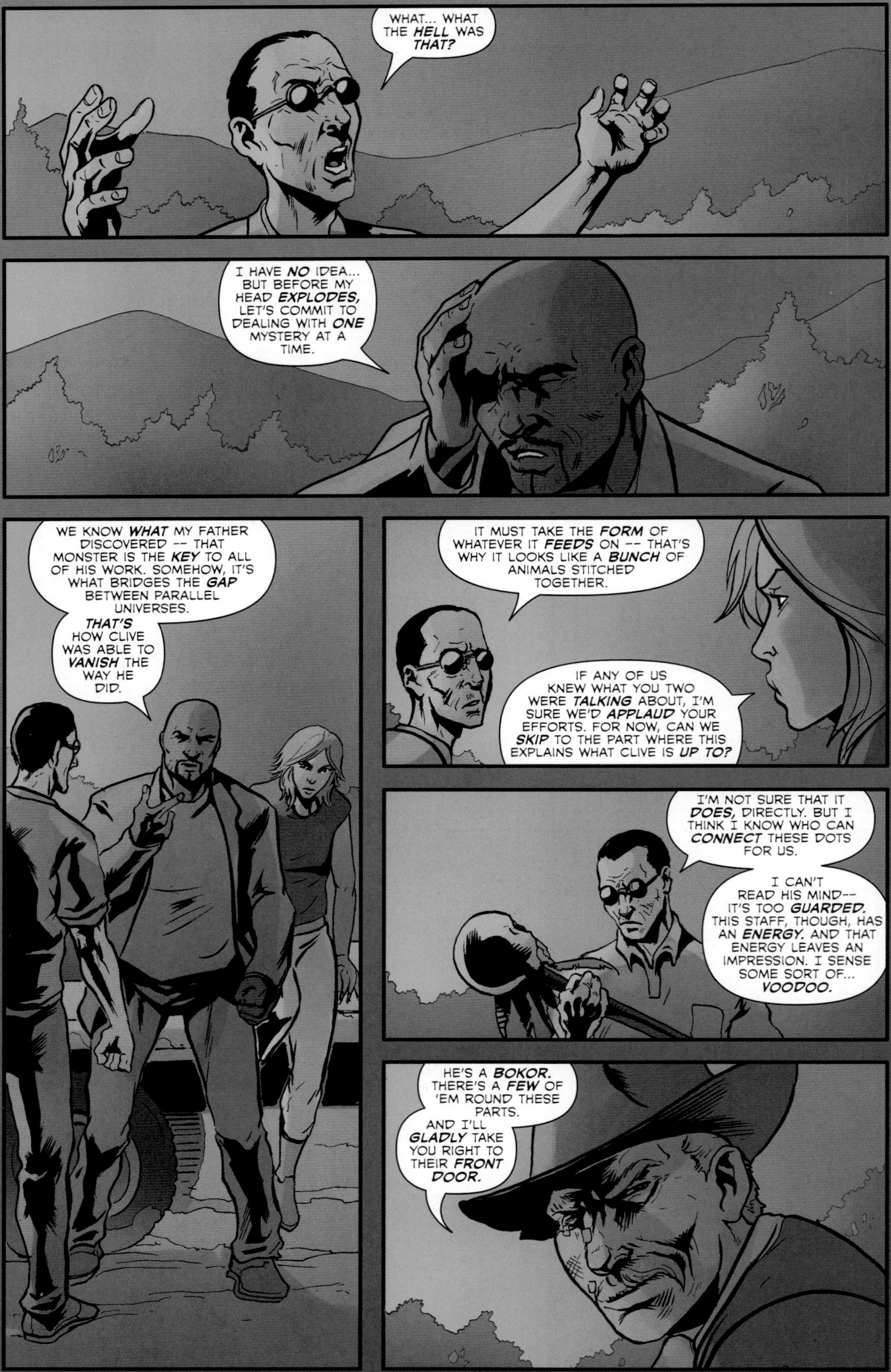
WHAT... WHAT THE HELL WAS THAT?
I HAVE NO IDEA... BUT BEFORE MY HEAD EXPLODES, LET'S COMMIT TO DEALING WITH ONE MYSTERY AT A TIME.
WE KNOW WHAT MY FATHER DISCOVERED -- THAT MONSTER IS THE KEY TO ALL OF HIS WORK. SOMEHOW, IT'S WHAT BRIDGES THE GAP BETWEEN PARALLEL UNIVERSES.
THAT'S HOW CLIVE WAS ABLE TO VANISH THE WAY HE DID.
IT MUST TAKE THE FORM OF WHATEVER IT FEEDS ON -- THAT'S WHY IT LOOKS LIKE A BUNCH OF ANIMALS STITCHED TOGETHER.
IF ANY OF US KNEW WHAT YOU TWO WERE TALKING ABOUT, I'M SURE WE'D APPLAUD YOUR EFFORTS. FOR NOW, CAN WE SKIP TO THE PART WHERE THIS EXPLAINS WHAT CLIVE IS UP TO?
I'M NOT SURE THAT IT DOES, DIRECTLY. BUT I THINK I KNOW WHO CAN CONNECT THESE DOTS FOR US.
I CAN'T READ HIS MIND-- IT'S TOO GUARDED. THIS STAFF, THOUGH, HAS AN ENERGY. AND THAT ENERGY LEAVES AN IMPRESSION. I SENSE SOME SORT OF... VOODOO.
HE'S A BOKOR. THERE'S A FEW OF 'EM ROUND THESE PARTS.
AND I'LL GLADLY TAKE YOU RIGHT TO THEIR FRONT DOOR.

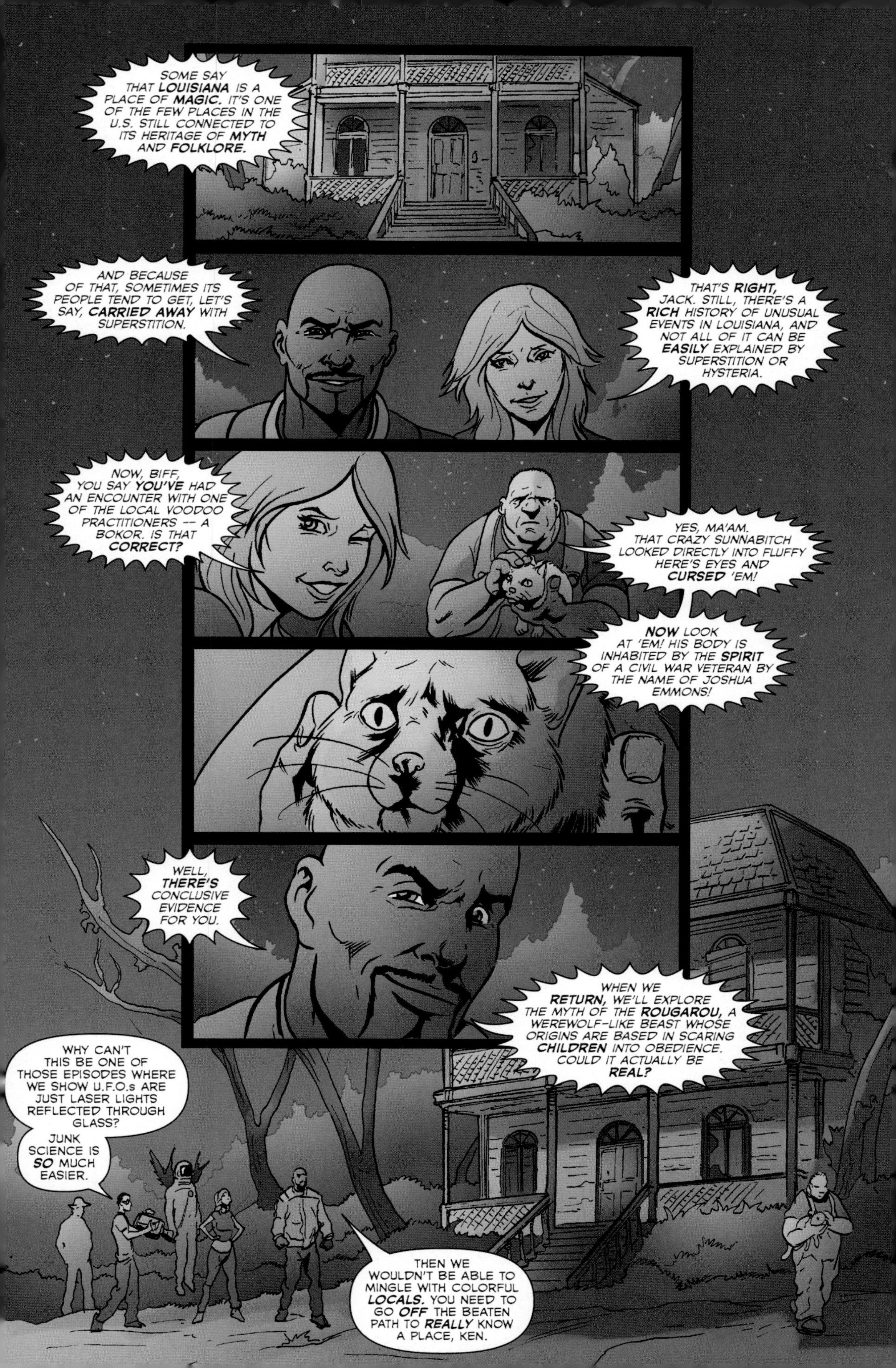
SOME SAY THAT LOUISIANA IS A PLACE OF MAGIC. IT'S ONE OF THE FEW PLACES IN THE U.S. STILL CONNECTED TO ITS HERITAGE OF MYTH AND FOLKLORE.
AND BECAUSE OF THAT, SOMETIMES ITS PEOPLE TEND TO GET, LET'S SAY, CARRIED AWAY WITH SUPERSTITION.
THAT'S RIGHT, JACK. STILL, THERE'S A RICH HISTORY OF UNUSUAL EVENTS IN LOUISIANA, AND NOT ALL OF IT CAN BE EASILY EXPLAINED BY SUPERSTITION OR HYSTERIA.
NOW, BIFF, YOU SAY YOU'VE HAD AN ENCOUNTER WITH ONE OF THE LOCAL VOODOO PRACTITIONERS -- A BOKOR. IS THAT CORRECT?
YES, MA'AM. THAT CRAZY SUNNABITCH LOOKED DIRECTLY INTO FLUFFY HERE'S EYES AND CURSED 'EM!
NOW LOOK AT 'EM! HIS BODY IS INHABITED BY THE SPIRIT OF A CIVIL WAR VETERAN BY THE NAME OF JOSHUA EMMONS!
WELL, THERE'S CONCLUSIVE EVIDENCE FOR YOU.
WHEN WE RETURN, WE'LL EXPLORE THE MYTH OF THE ROUGAROU, A WEREWOLF-LIKE BEAST WHOSE ORIGINS ARE BASED IN SCARING CHILDREN INTO OBEDIENCE. COULD IT ACTUALLY BE REAL?
WHY CAN'T THIS BE ONE OF THOSE EPISODES WHERE WE SHOW U.F.O.s ARE JUST LASER LIGHTS REFLECTED THROUGH GLASS?
JUNK SCIENCE IS SO MUCH EASIER.
THEN WE WOULDN'T BE ABLE TO MINGLE WITH COLORFUL LOCALS. YOU NEED TO GO OFF THE BEATEN PATH TO REALLY KNOW A PLACE, KEN.

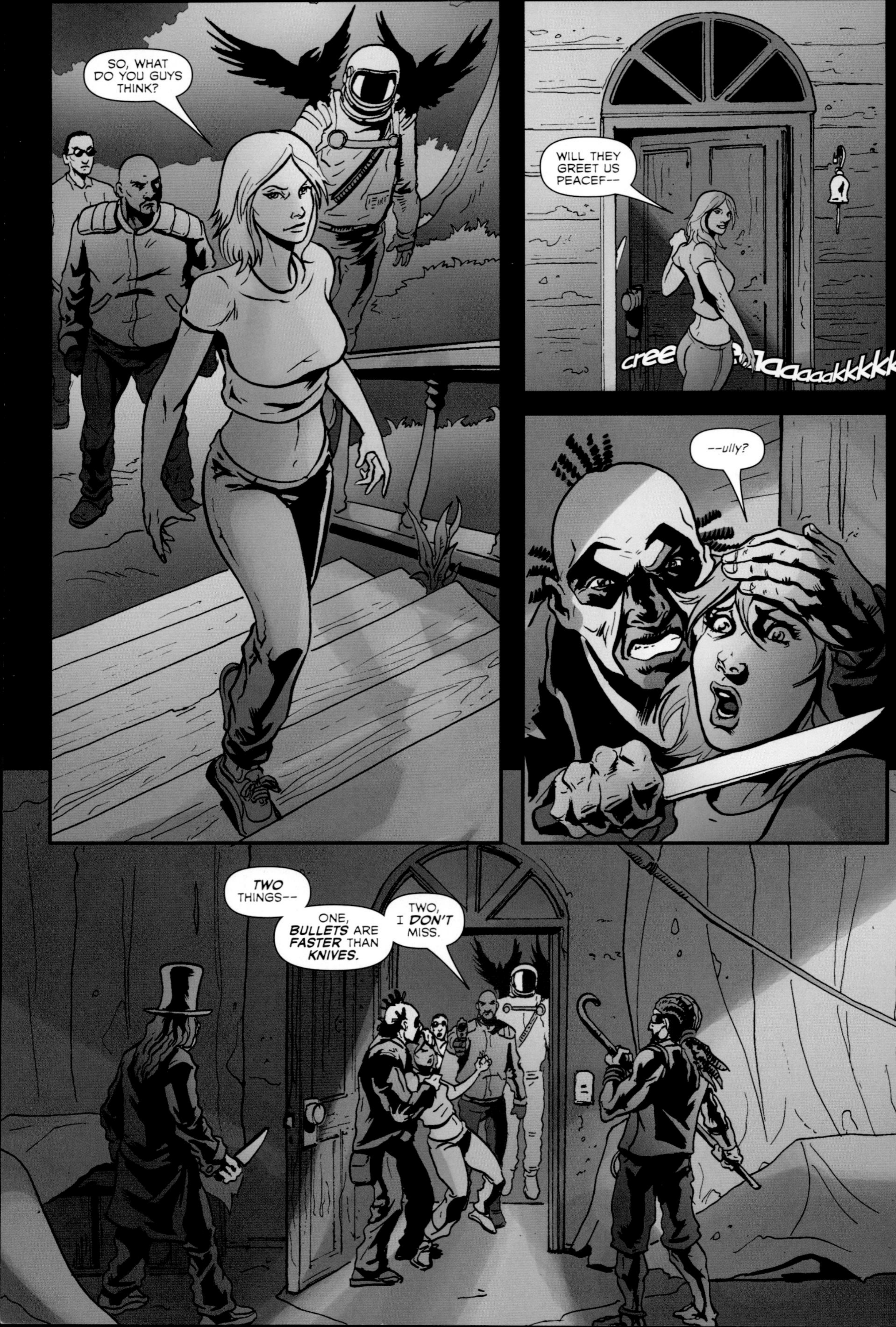
SO, WHAT DO YOU GUYS THINK?
WILL THEY GREET US PEACEF--
cree...aaaakkkkk
--ully?
TWO THINGS--
ONE, ***BULLETS*** ARE ***FASTER*** THAN ***KNIVES.***
TWO, I ***DON'T*** MISS.

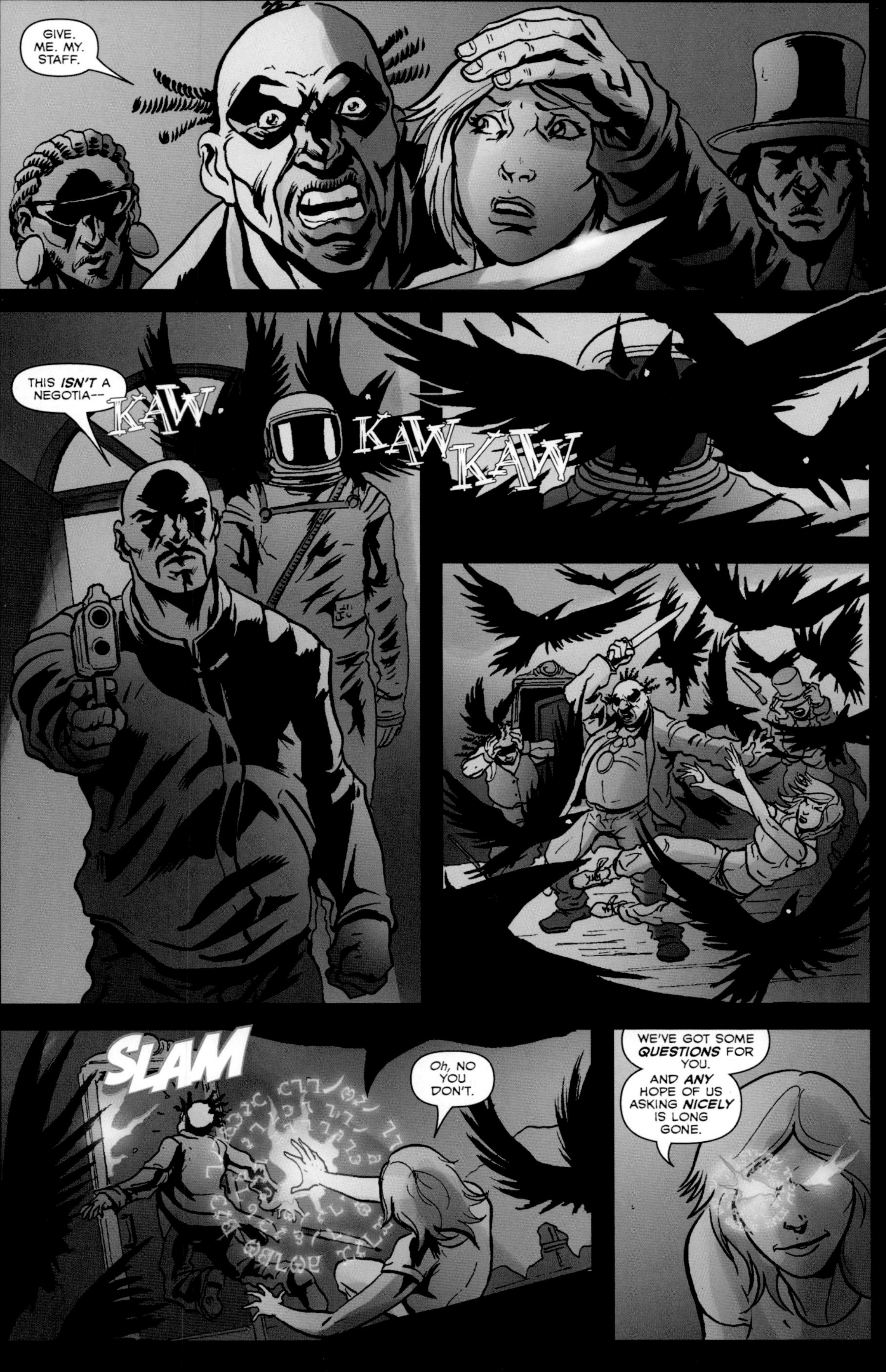
GIVE. ME. MY. STAFF.
THIS *ISN'T* A NEGOTIA--
KAW
KAW
KAW
SLAM
Oh, NO YOU DON'T.
WE'VE GOT SOME **QUESTIONS** FOR YOU.
AND **ANY** HOPE OF US ASKING **NICELY** IS LONG GONE.

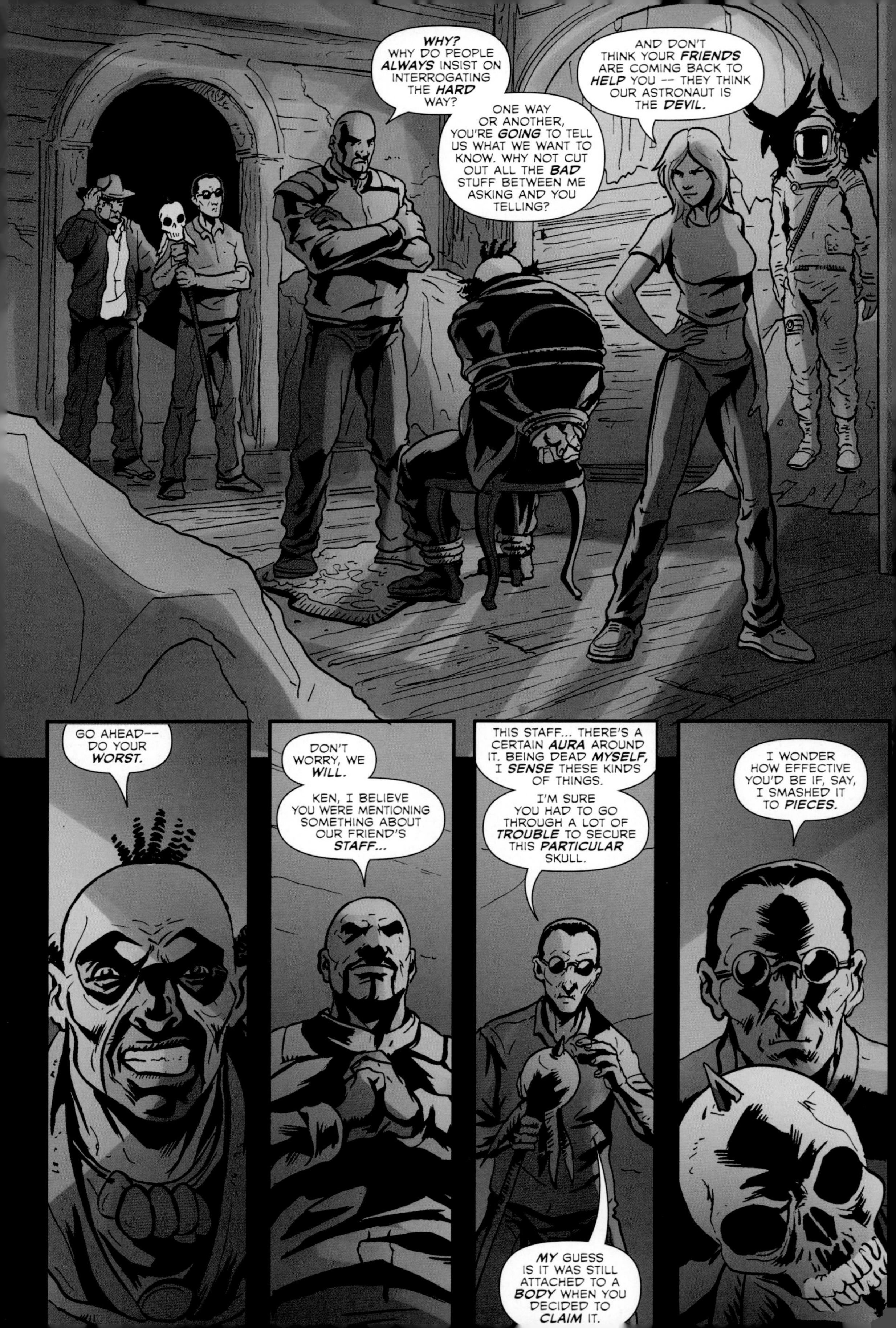
WHY? WHY DO PEOPLE ALWAYS INSIST ON INTERROGATING THE HARD WAY?
ONE WAY OR ANOTHER, YOU'RE GOING TO TELL US WHAT WE WANT TO KNOW. WHY NOT CUT OUT ALL THE BAD STUFF BETWEEN ME ASKING AND YOU TELLING?
AND DON'T THINK YOUR FRIENDS ARE COMING BACK TO HELP YOU -- THEY THINK OUR ASTRONAUT IS THE DEVIL.
GO AHEAD-- DO YOUR WORST.
DON'T WORRY, WE WILL.
KEN, I BELIEVE YOU WERE MENTIONING SOMETHING ABOUT OUR FRIEND'S STAFF...
THIS STAFF... THERE'S A CERTAIN AURA AROUND IT. BEING DEAD MYSELF, I SENSE THESE KINDS OF THINGS.
I'M SURE YOU HAD TO GO THROUGH A LOT OF TROUBLE TO SECURE THIS PARTICULAR SKULL.
MY GUESS IS IT WAS STILL ATTACHED TO A BODY WHEN YOU DECIDED TO CLAIM IT.
I WONDER HOW EFFECTIVE YOU'D BE IF, SAY, I SMASHED IT TO PIECES.

THEN TALK AND TALK *FAST!* HOW DOES CLIVE TRAVEL BETWEEN UNIVERSES? THAT DEVICE HE HOLDS-- HOW DOES IT *WORK?*

NO! YOU CAN'T DO *THAT!*

I DON'T *KNOW!* HE SAID SOMETHING ABOUT HOW UNIVERSES ARE SEPARATED FROM EACH OTHER LIKE *RADIO FREQUENCIES.*

THE DEVICE IS A *DIAL* -- YOU NEED TO GET IT JUST RIGHT IN ORDER TO GET A CLEAR *STATION.*

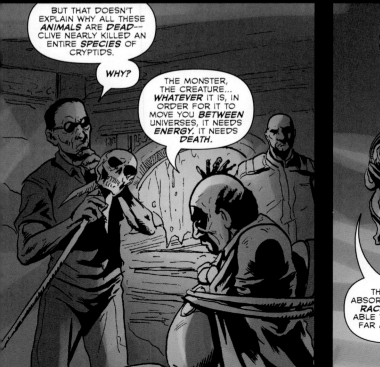

BUT THAT DOESN'T EXPLAIN WHY ALL THESE *ANIMALS* ARE *DEAD--* CLIVE NEARLY KILLED AN ENTIRE *SPECIES* OF CRYPTIDS.

WHY?

THE MONSTER, THE CREATURE... *WHATEVER* IT IS, IN ORDER FOR IT TO MOVE YOU *BETWEEN* UNIVERSES, IT NEEDS *ENERGY.* IT NEEDS *DEATH.*

WHAT *KIND* OF DEATH, AND HOW *MUCH?*

CLIVE THINKS IF IT ABSORBS AN ENTIRE *RACE,* WE'LL BE ABLE TO TRAVEL AS FAR AS WE NEED TO *GO.*

THAT'S WHY HE'S AFTER CRYPTIDS -- THEY'RE ISOLATED TOGETHER. DOESN'T TAKE MUCH TO CLEAN THEM ALL OUT.

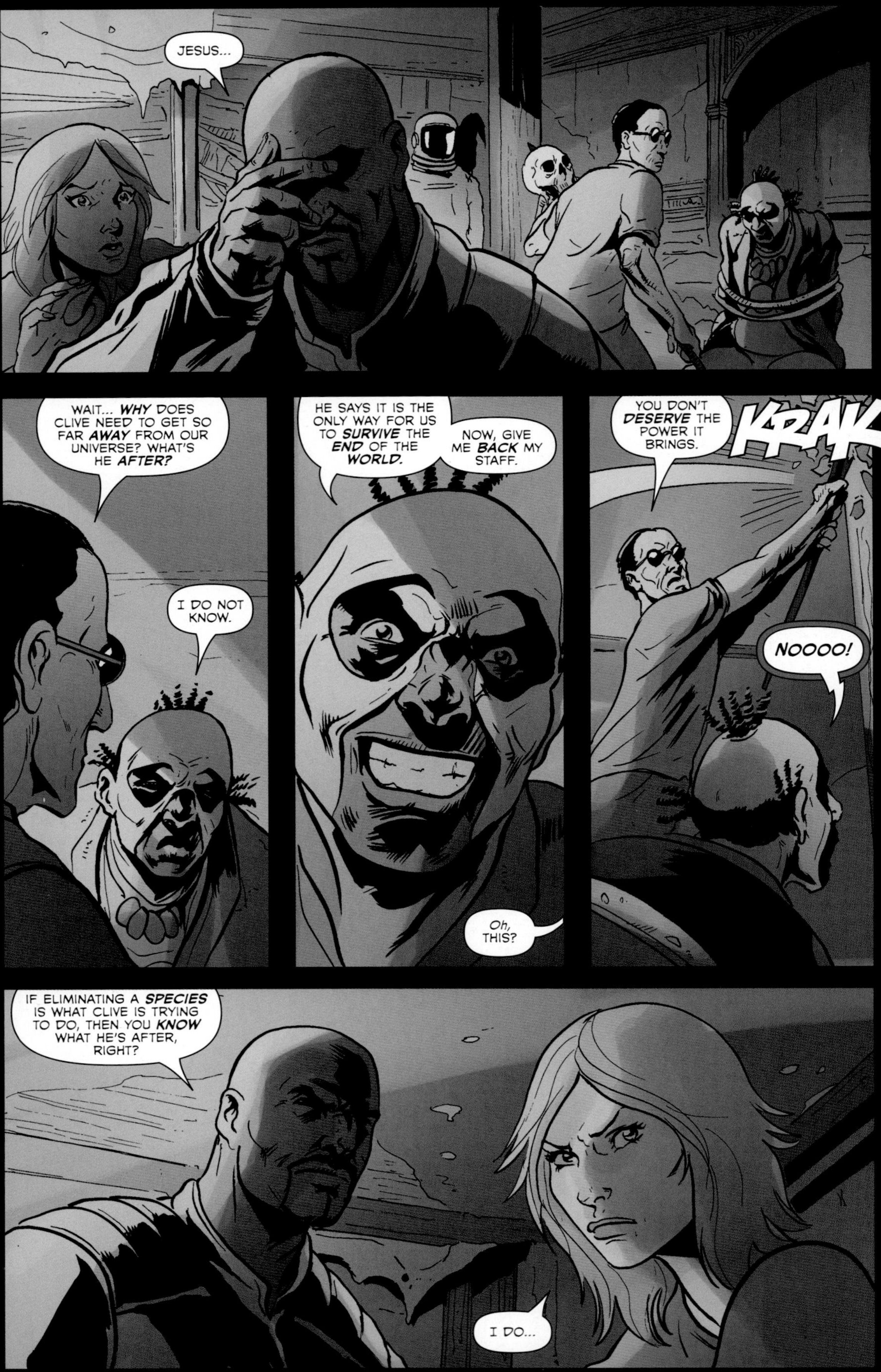
JESUS...
WAIT... WHY DOES CLIVE NEED TO GET SO FAR AWAY FROM OUR UNIVERSE? WHAT'S HE AFTER?
I DO NOT KNOW.
HE SAYS IT IS THE ONLY WAY FOR US TO SURVIVE THE END OF THE WORLD.
NOW, GIVE ME BACK MY STAFF.
Oh, THIS?
YOU DON'T DESERVE THE POWER IT BRINGS.
KRAK
NOOOO!
IF ELIMINATING A SPECIES IS WHAT CLIVE IS TRYING TO DO, THEN YOU KNOW WHAT HE'S AFTER, RIGHT?
I DO...

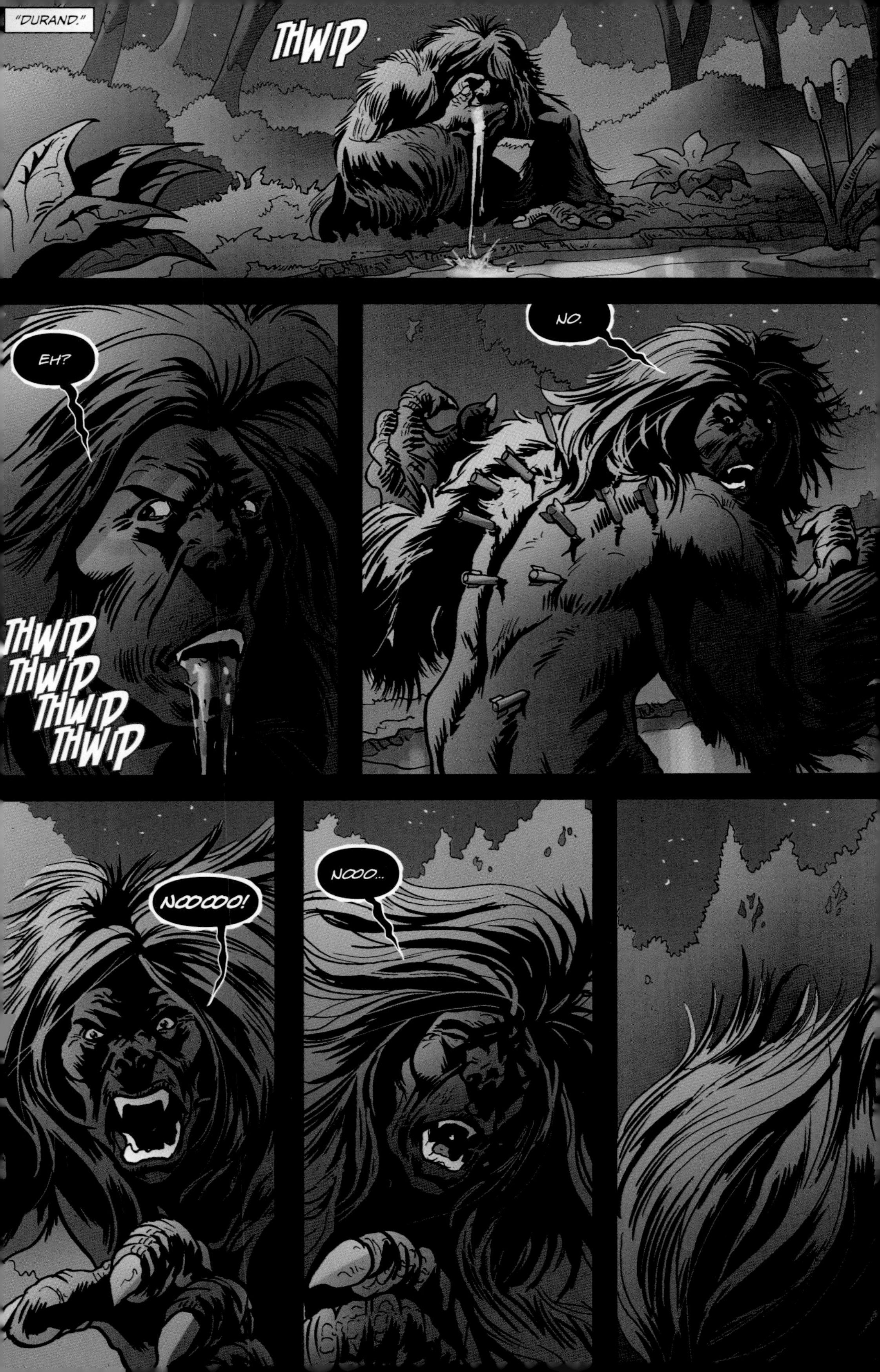
"DURAND."
THWIP
EH?
THWIP
THWIP
THWIP
THWIP
NO.
NOOOOO!
NOOO...

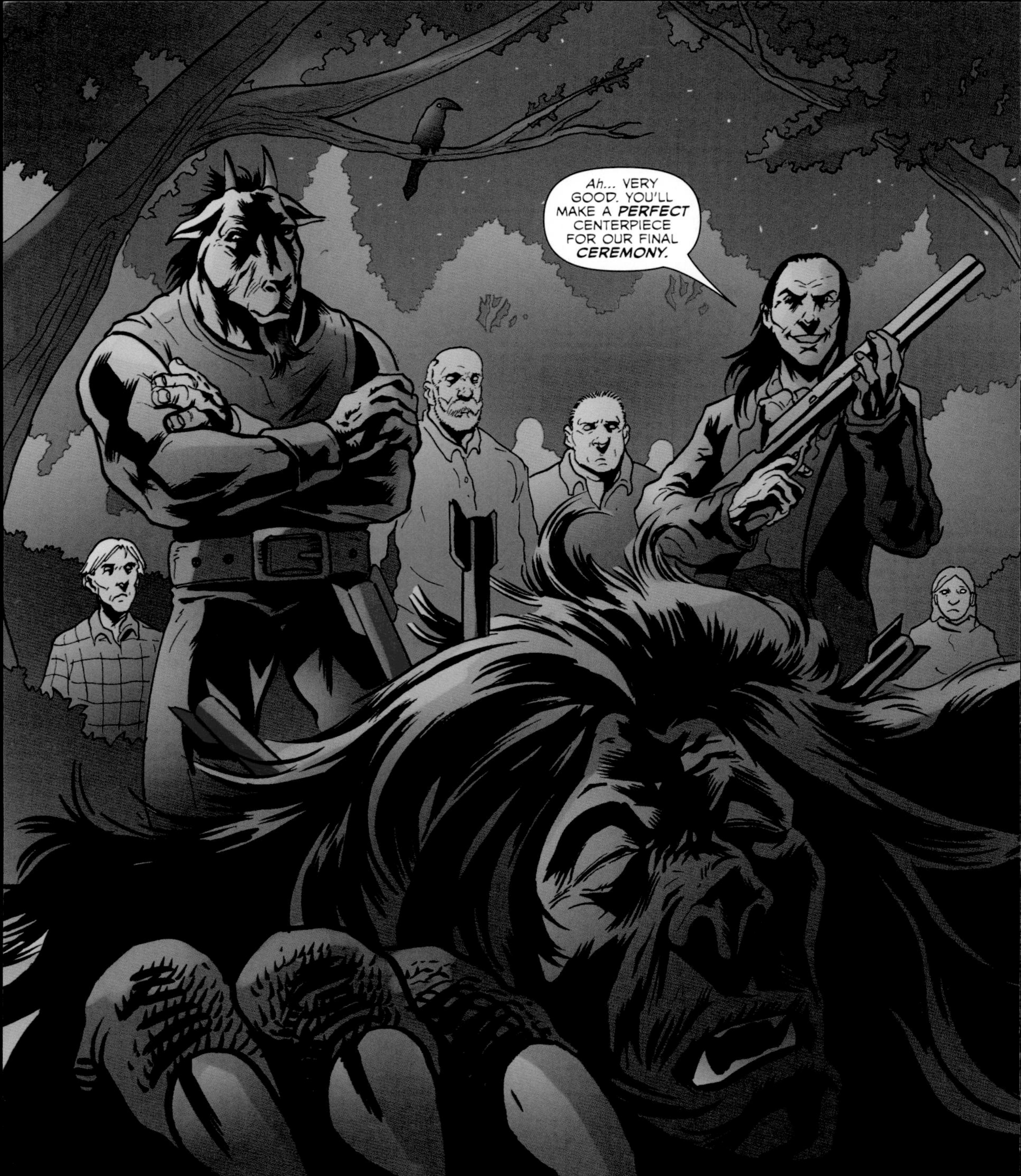
Ah... VERY GOOD. YOU'LL MAKE A PERFECT CENTERPIECE FOR OUR FINAL CEREMONY.

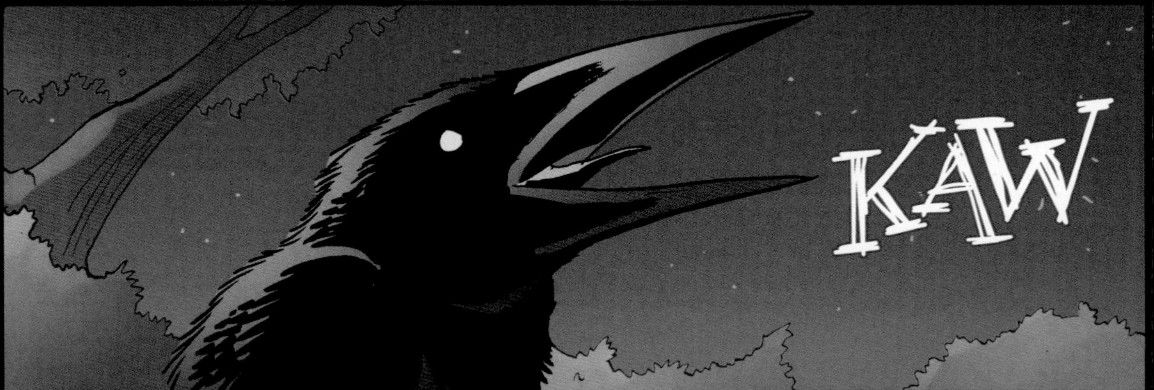
KAW

HOAX HUNTERS

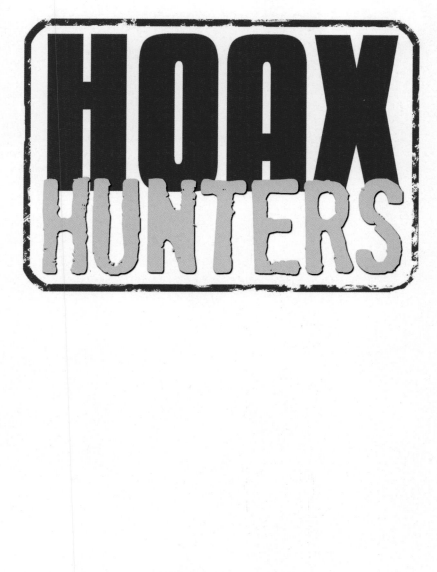

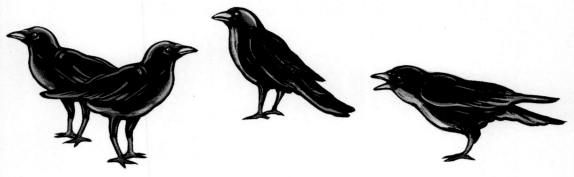

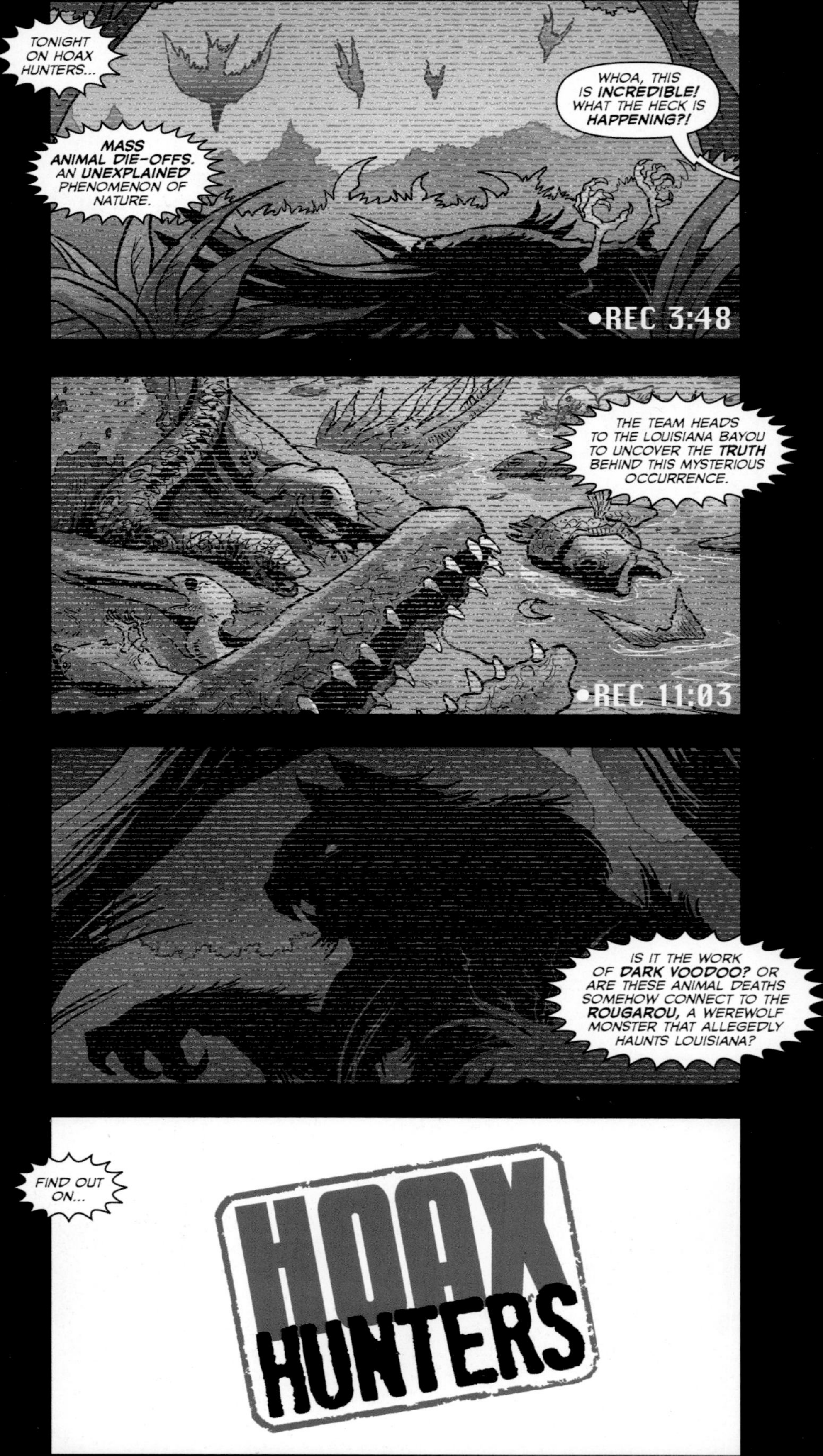
TONIGHT ON HOAX HUNTERS...
MASS ANIMAL DIE-OFFS. AN UNEXPLAINED PHENOMENON OF NATURE.
WHOA, THIS IS INCREDIBLE! WHAT THE HECK IS HAPPENING?!
•REC 3:48
THE TEAM HEADS TO THE LOUISIANA BAYOU TO UNCOVER THE TRUTH BEHIND THIS MYSTERIOUS OCCURRENCE.
•REC 11:03
IS IT THE WORK OF DARK VOODOO? OR ARE THESE ANIMAL DEATHS SOMEHOW CONNECT TO THE ROUGAROU, A WEREWOLF MONSTER THAT ALLEGEDLY HAUNTS LOUISIANA?
FIND OUT ON...
HOAX HUNTERS

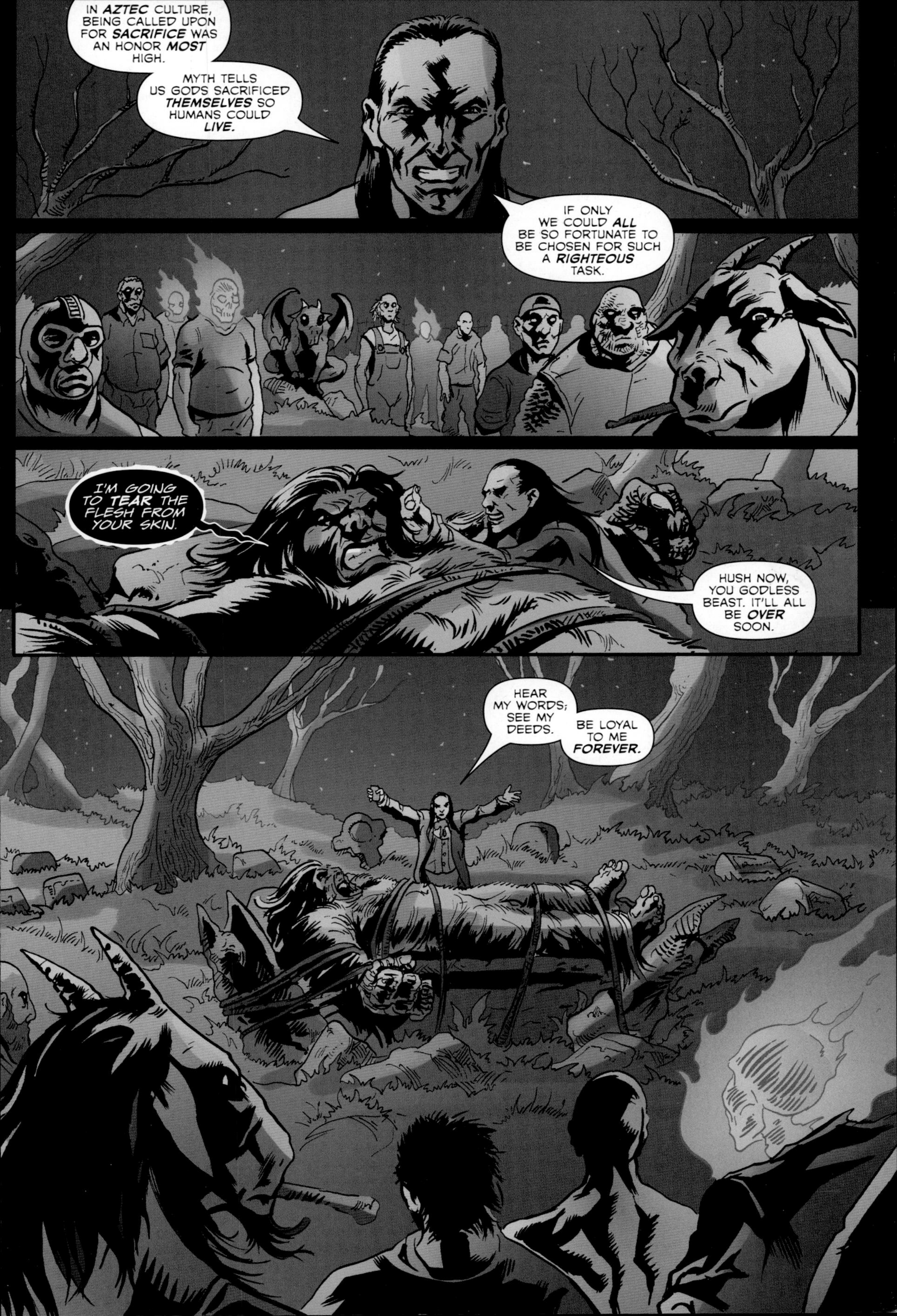
IN AZTEC CULTURE, BEING CALLED UPON FOR SACRIFICE WAS AN HONOR MOST HIGH.
MYTH TELLS US GODS SACRIFICED THEMSELVES SO HUMANS COULD LIVE.
IF ONLY WE COULD ALL BE SO FORTUNATE TO BE CHOSEN FOR SUCH A RIGHTEOUS TASK.
I'M GOING TO TEAR THE FLESH FROM YOUR SKIN.
HUSH NOW, YOU GODLESS BEAST. IT'LL ALL BE OVER SOON.
HEAR MY WORDS; SEE MY DEEDS.
BE LOYAL TO ME FOREVER.

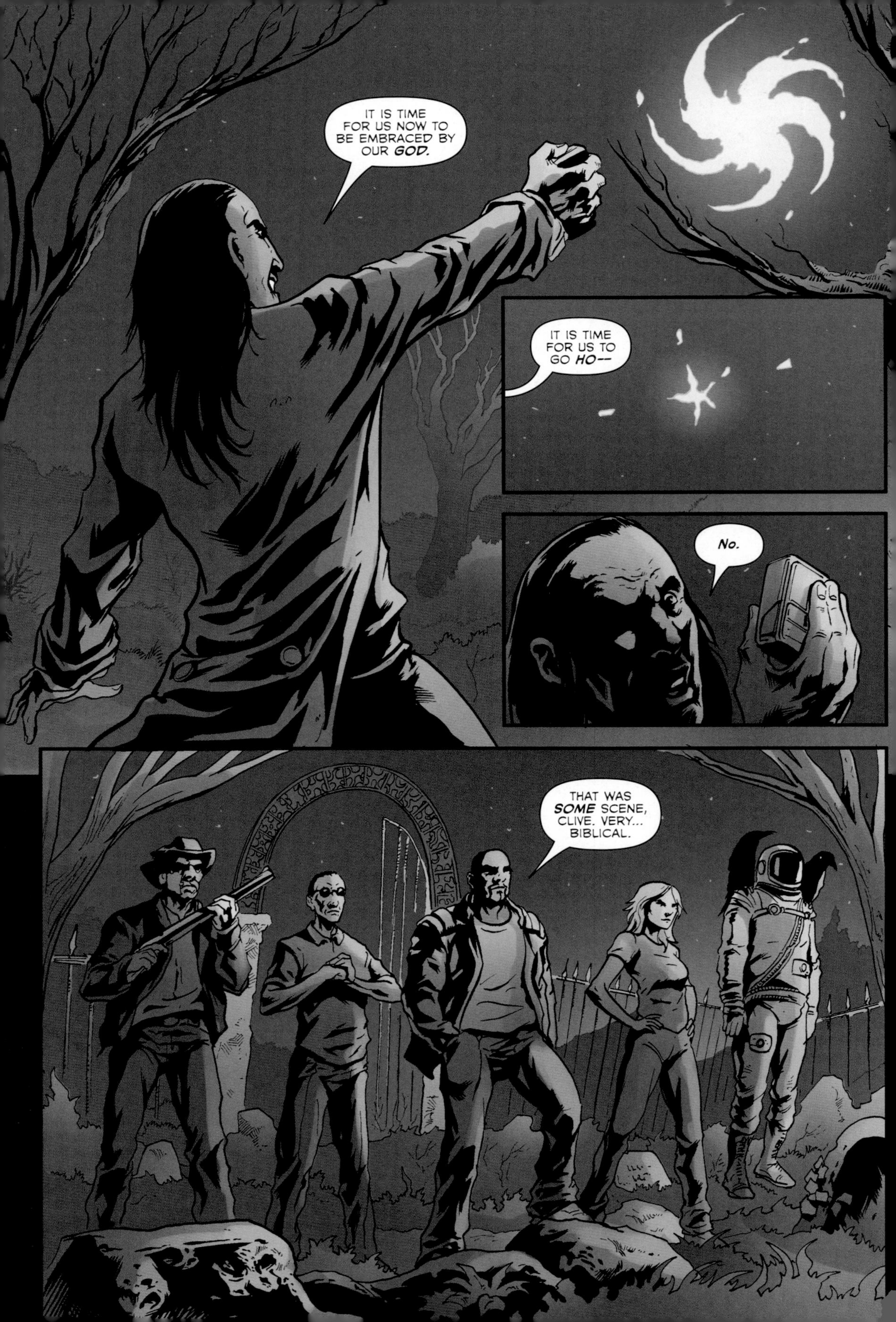
IT IS TIME FOR US NOW TO BE EMBRACED BY OUR GOD.
IT IS TIME FOR US TO GO HO--
No.
THAT WAS SOME SCENE, CLIVE. VERY... BIBLICAL.

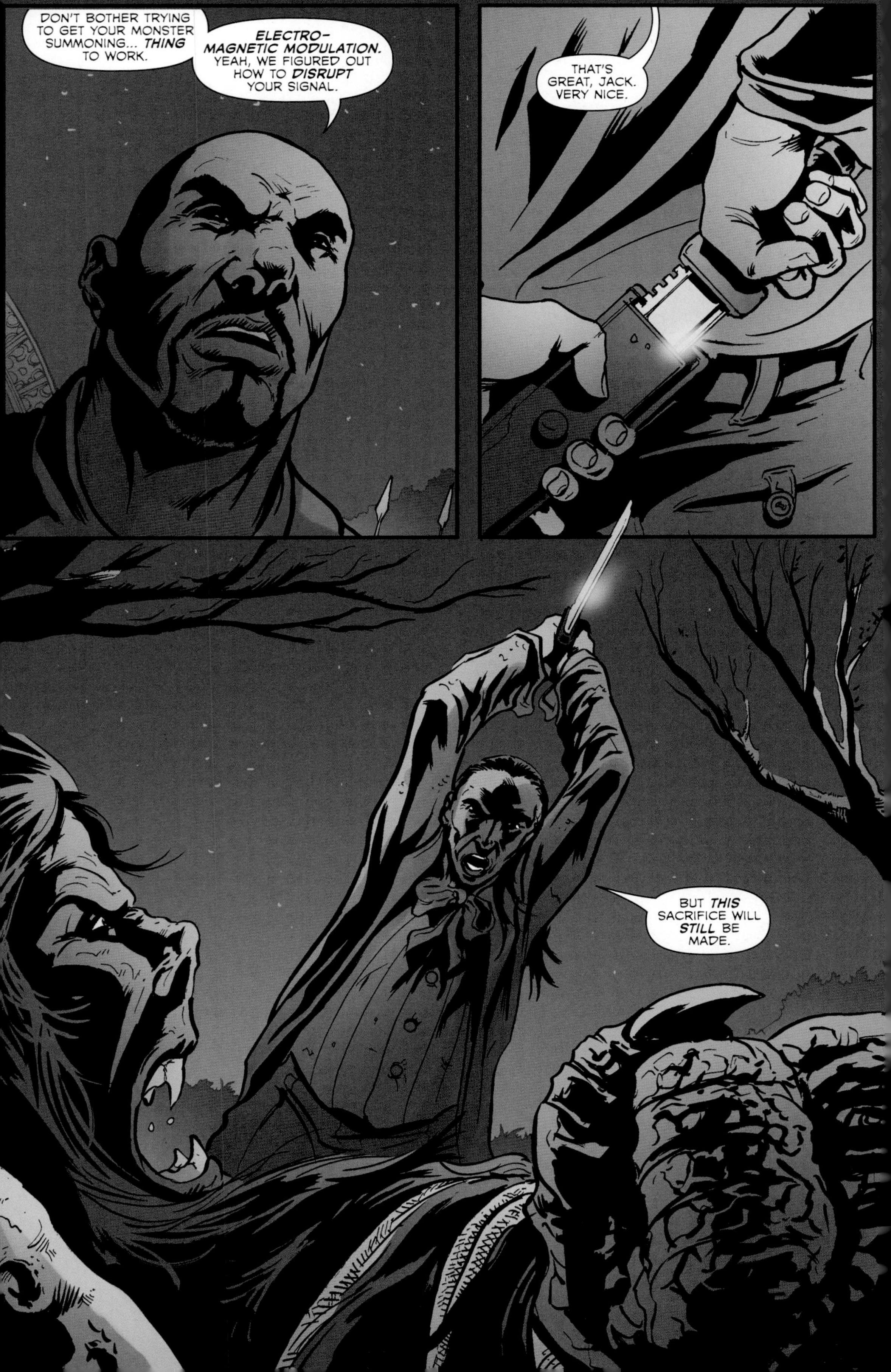
DON'T BOTHER TRYING TO GET YOUR MONSTER SUMMONING... THING TO WORK.
ELECTRO-MAGNETIC MODULATION. YEAH, WE FIGURED OUT HOW TO DISRUPT YOUR SIGNAL.
THAT'S GREAT, JACK. VERY NICE.
BUT THIS SACRIFICE WILL STILL BE MADE.

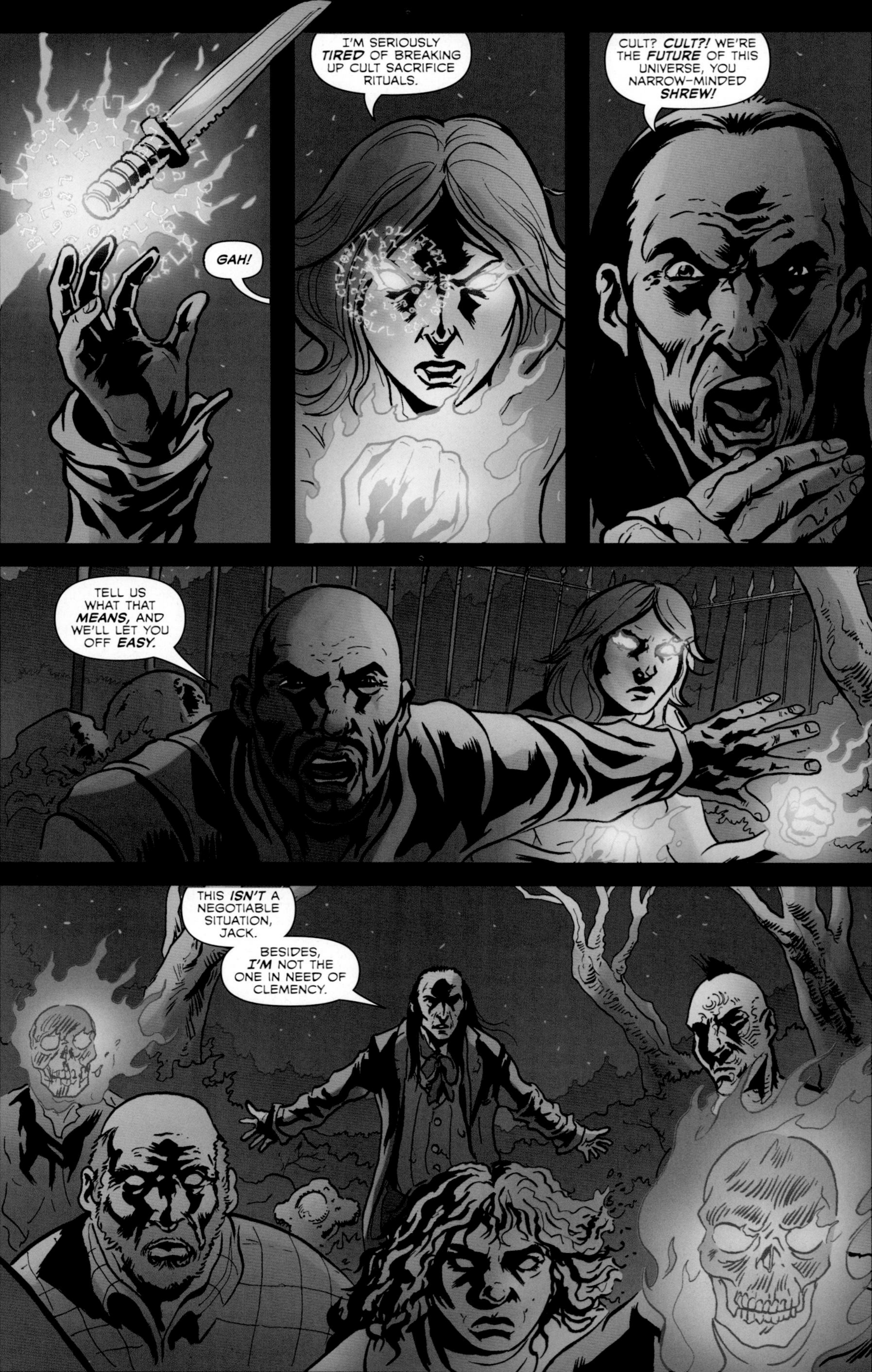
GAH!
I'M SERIOUSLY TIRED OF BREAKING UP CULT SACRIFICE RITUALS.
CULT? CULT?! WE'RE THE FUTURE OF THIS UNIVERSE, YOU NARROW-MINDED SHREW!
TELL US WHAT THAT MEANS, AND WE'LL LET YOU OFF EASY.
THIS ISN'T A NEGOTIABLE SITUATION, JACK.
BESIDES, I'M NOT THE ONE IN NEED OF CLEMENCY.

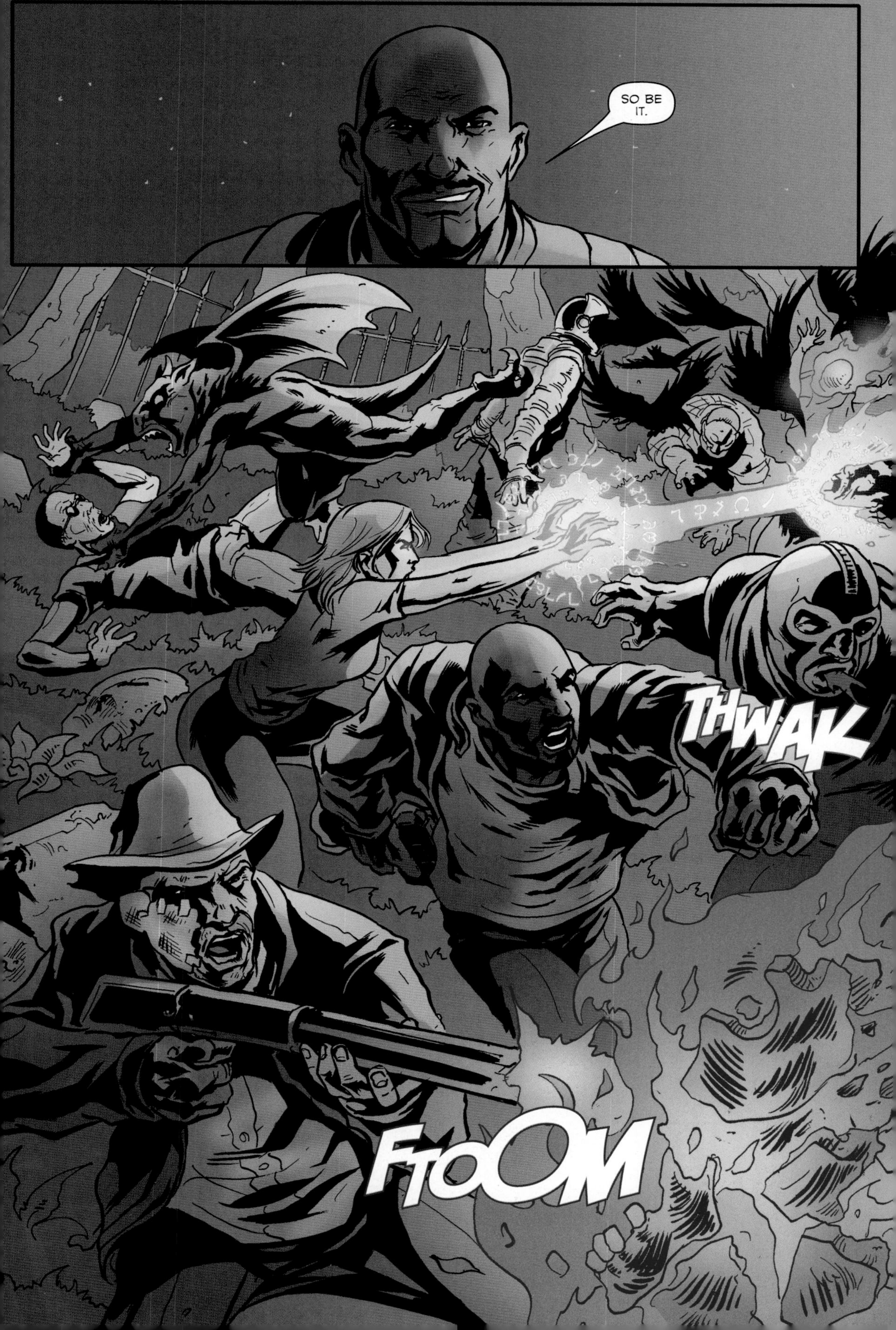
SO BE IT.
THWAK
FTOOM

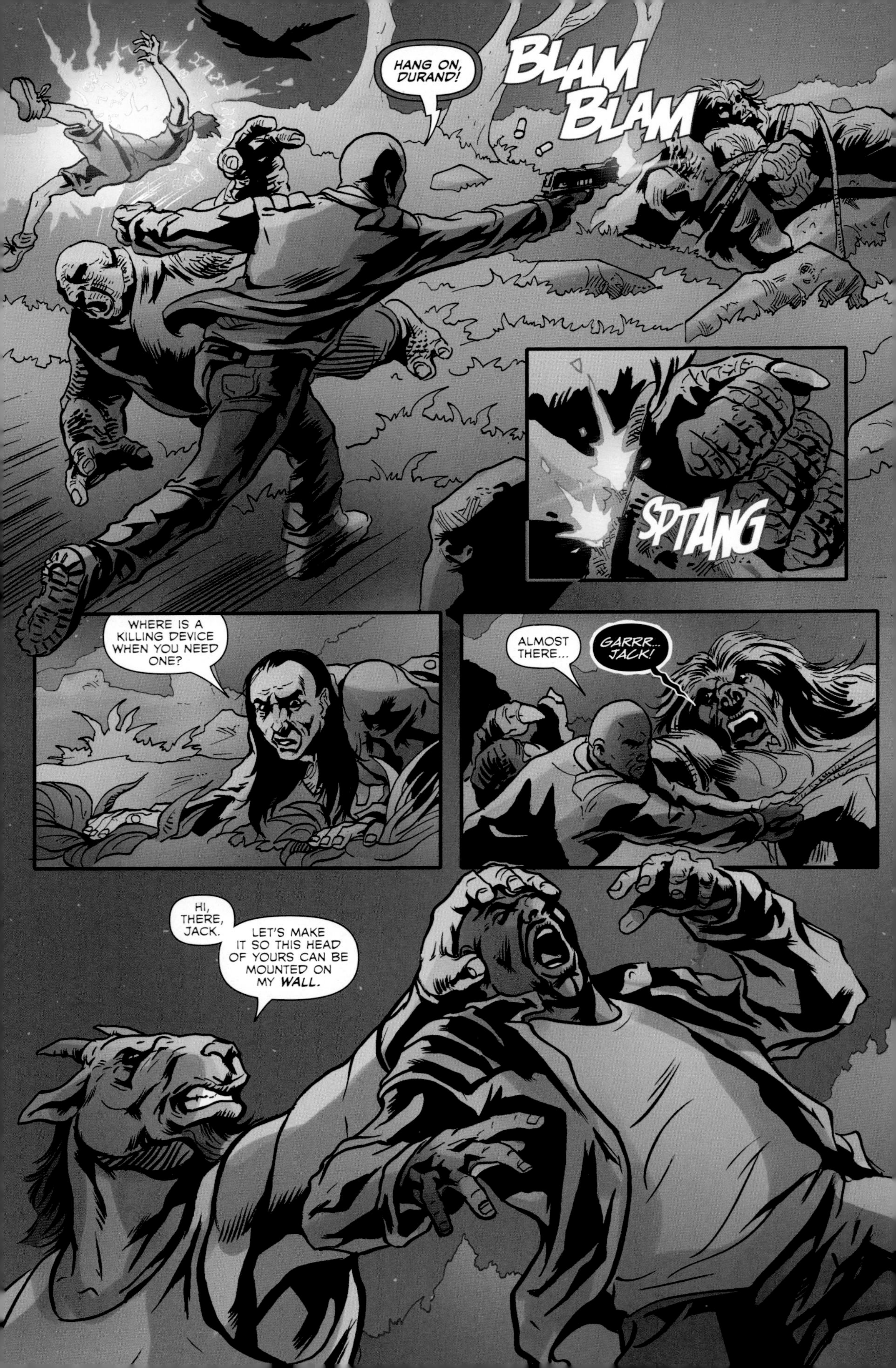
HANG ON, DURAND!
BLAM BLAM
SPTANG
WHERE IS A KILLING DEVICE WHEN YOU NEED ONE?
ALMOST THERE...
GARRR... JACK!
HI, THERE, JACK.
LET'S MAKE IT SO THIS HEAD OF YOURS CAN BE MOUNTED ON MY WALL.

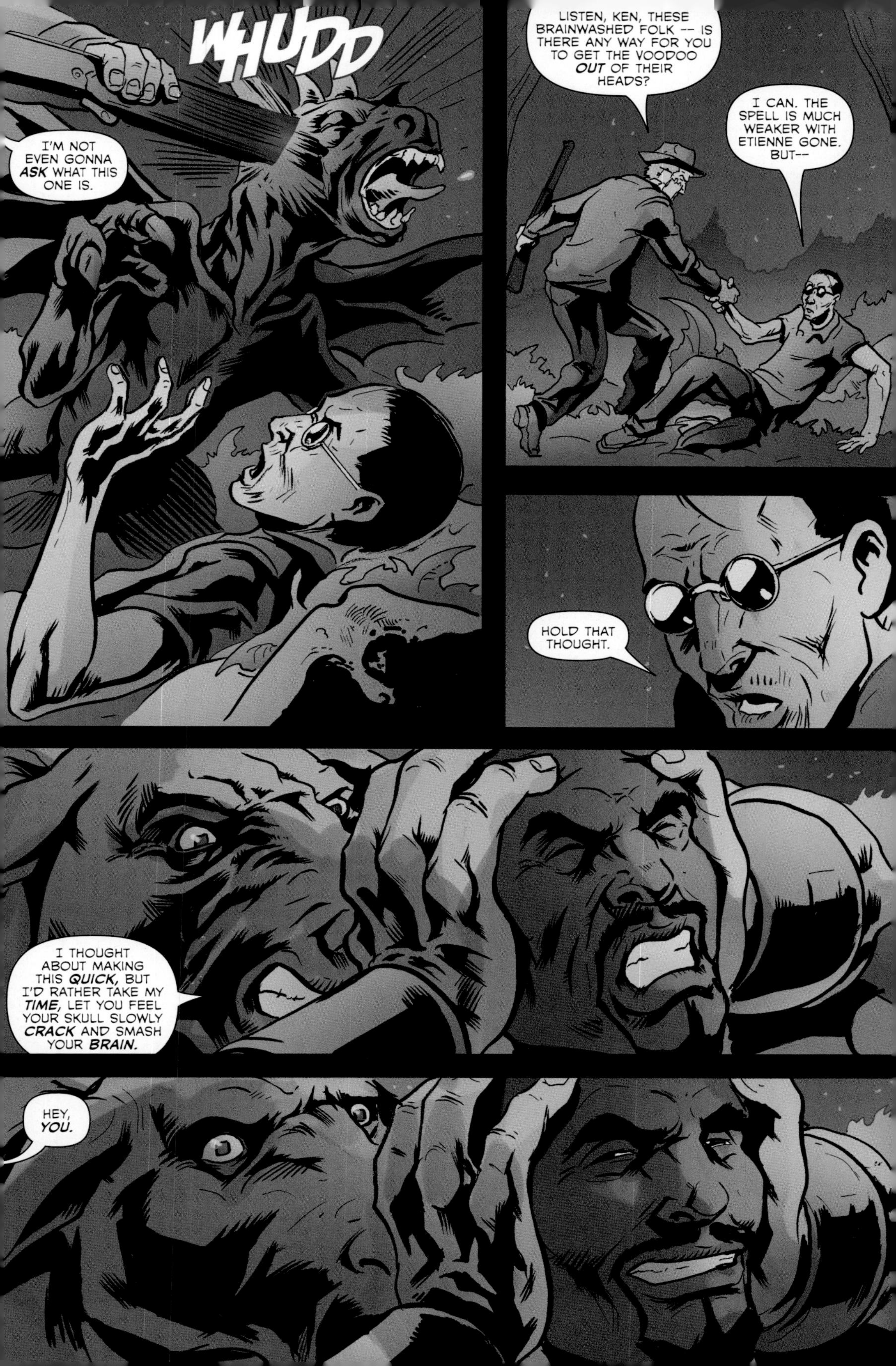
WHUDD
I'M NOT EVEN GONNA ASK WHAT THIS ONE IS.
LISTEN, KEN, THESE BRAINWASHED FOLK -- IS THERE ANY WAY FOR YOU TO GET THE VOODOO OUT OF THEIR HEADS?
I CAN. THE SPELL IS MUCH WEAKER WITH ETIENNE GONE. BUT--
HOLD THAT THOUGHT.
I THOUGHT ABOUT MAKING THIS QUICK, BUT I'D RATHER TAKE MY TIME, LET YOU FEEL YOUR SKULL SLOWLY CRACK AND SMASH YOUR BRAIN.
HEY, YOU.

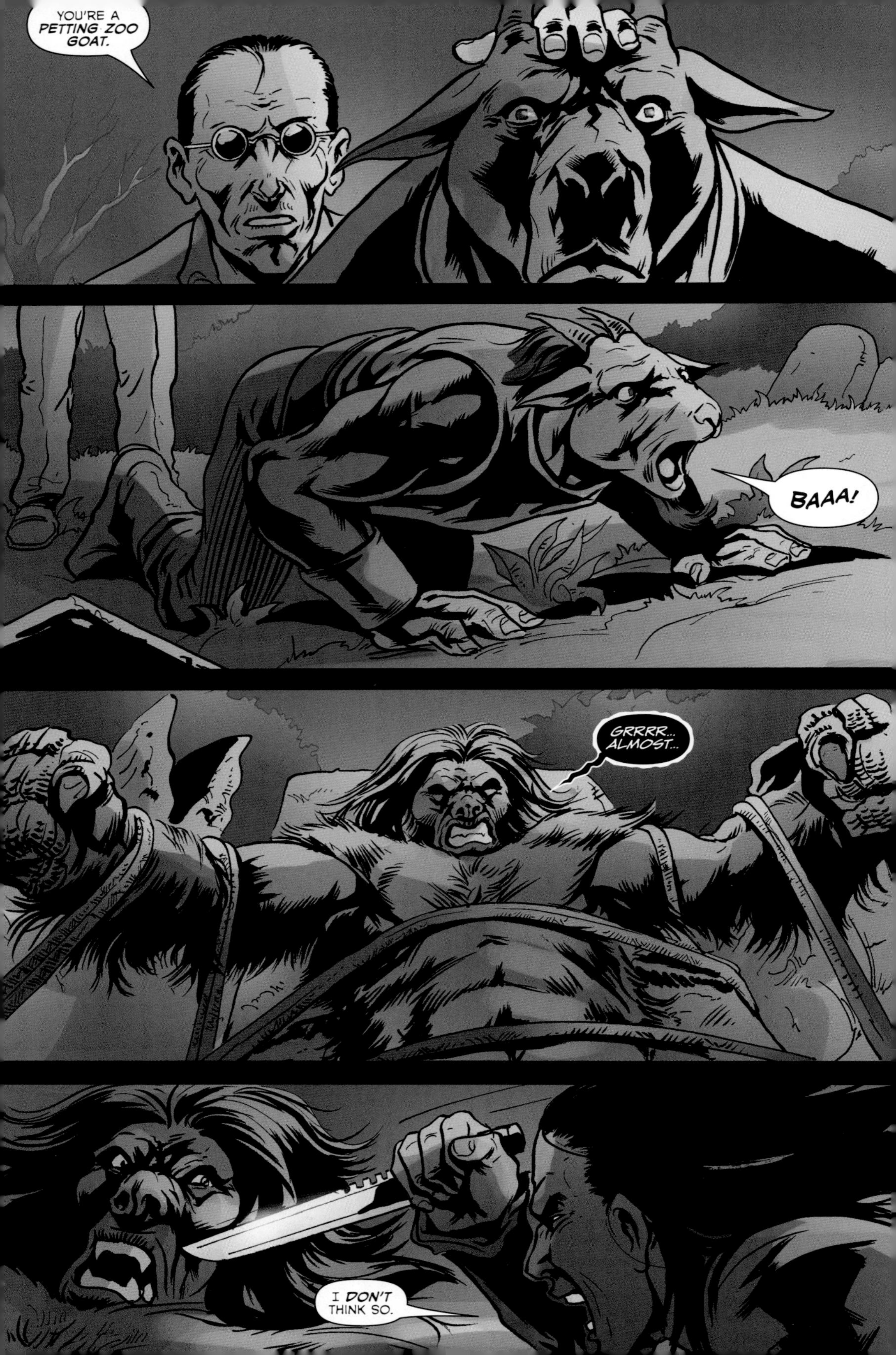
YOU'RE A PETTING ZOO GOAT.
BAAA!
GRRRR... ALMOST...
I DON'T THINK SO.

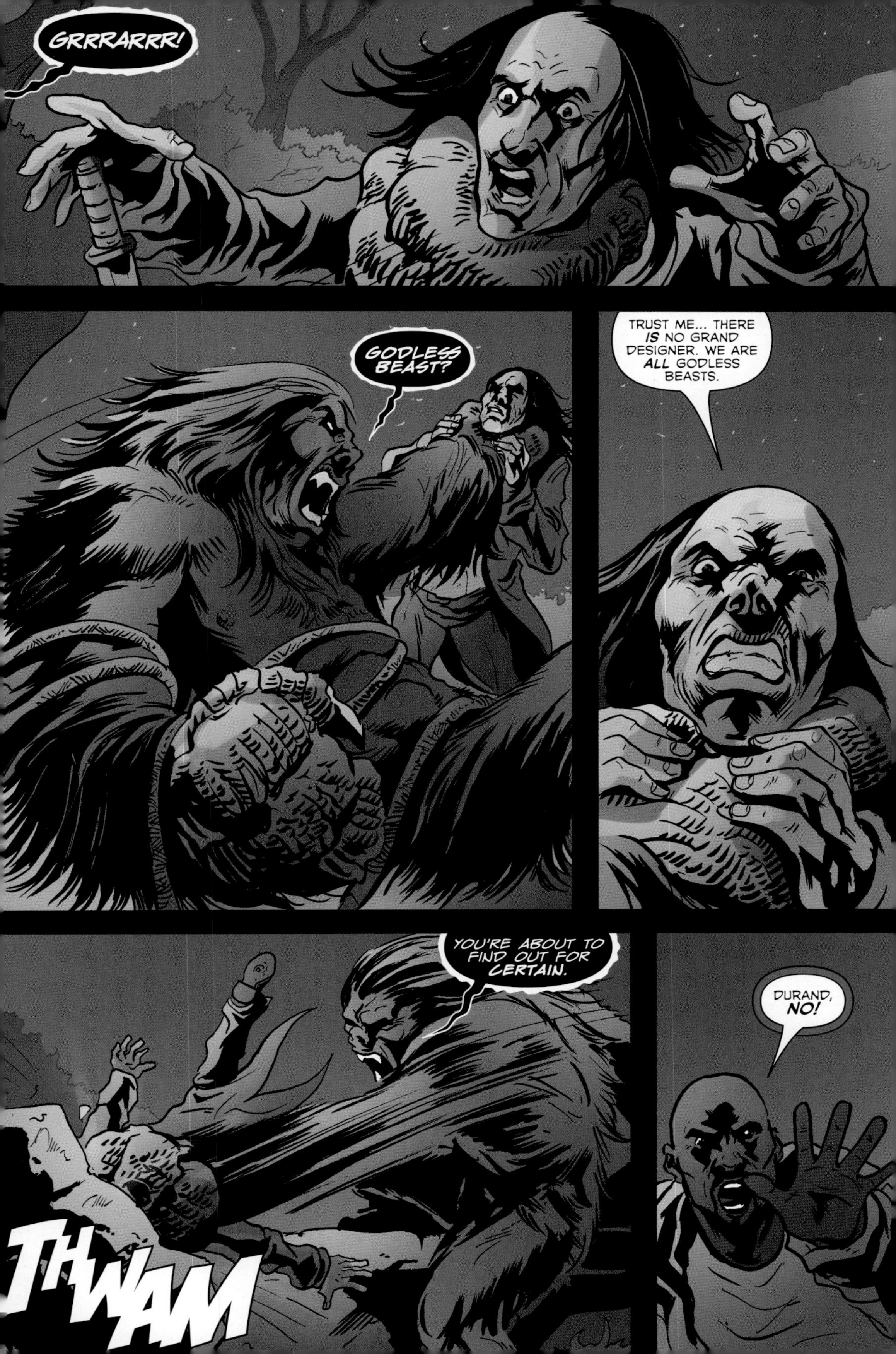
GRRRARRR!
GODLESS BEAST?
TRUST ME... THERE IS NO GRAND DESIGNER. WE ARE ALL GODLESS BEASTS.
YOU'RE ABOUT TO FIND OUT FOR CERTAIN.
THWAM
DURAND, NO!

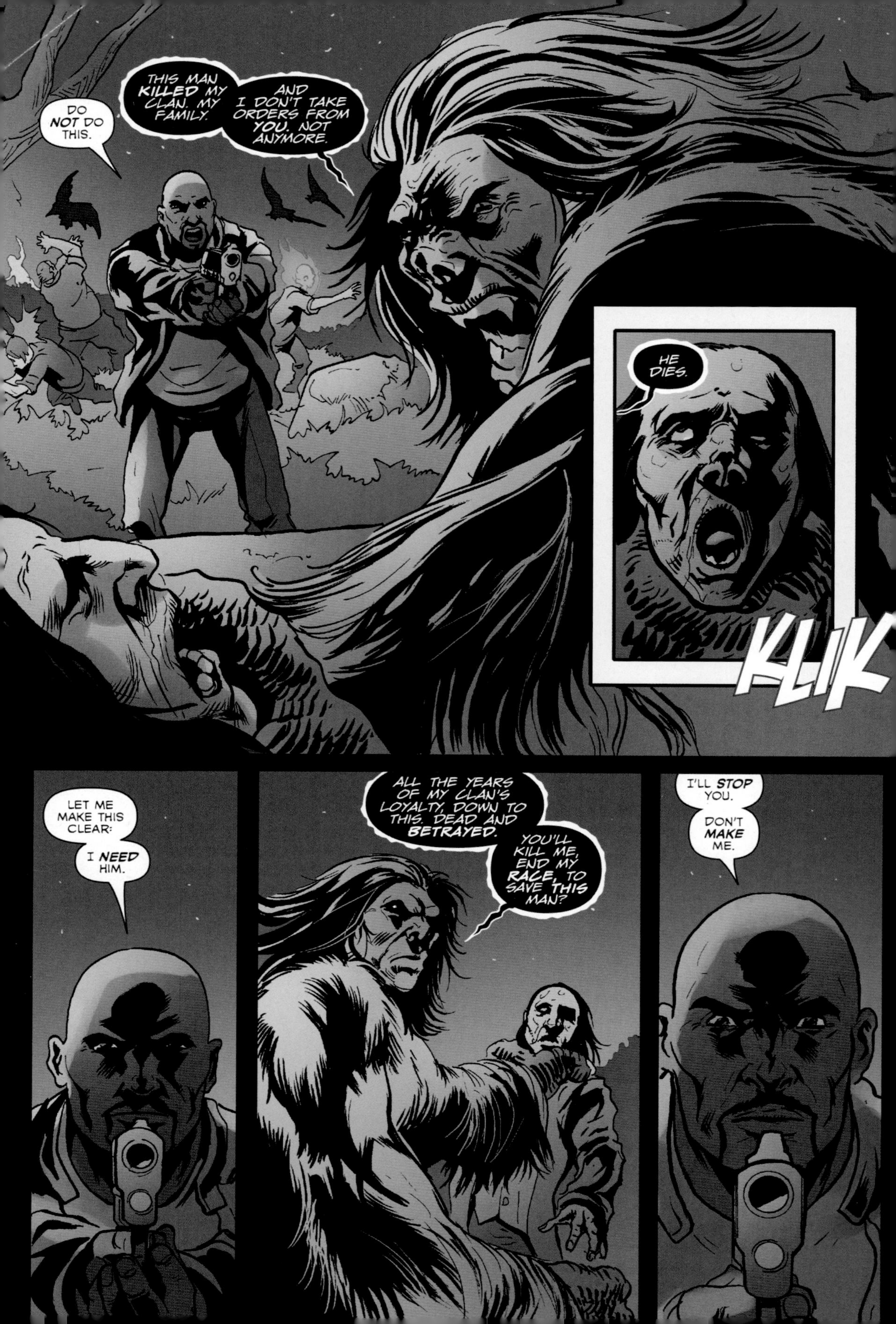
DO NOT DO THIS.
THIS MAN KILLED MY CLAN. MY FAMILY.
AND I DON'T TAKE ORDERS FROM YOU. NOT ANYMORE.
HE DIES.
KLIK
LET ME MAKE THIS CLEAR:
I NEED HIM.
ALL THE YEARS OF MY CLAN'S LOYALTY, DOWN TO THIS. DEAD AND BETRAYED.
YOU'LL KILL ME, END MY RACE, TO SAVE THIS MAN?
I'LL STOP YOU.
DON'T MAKE ME.

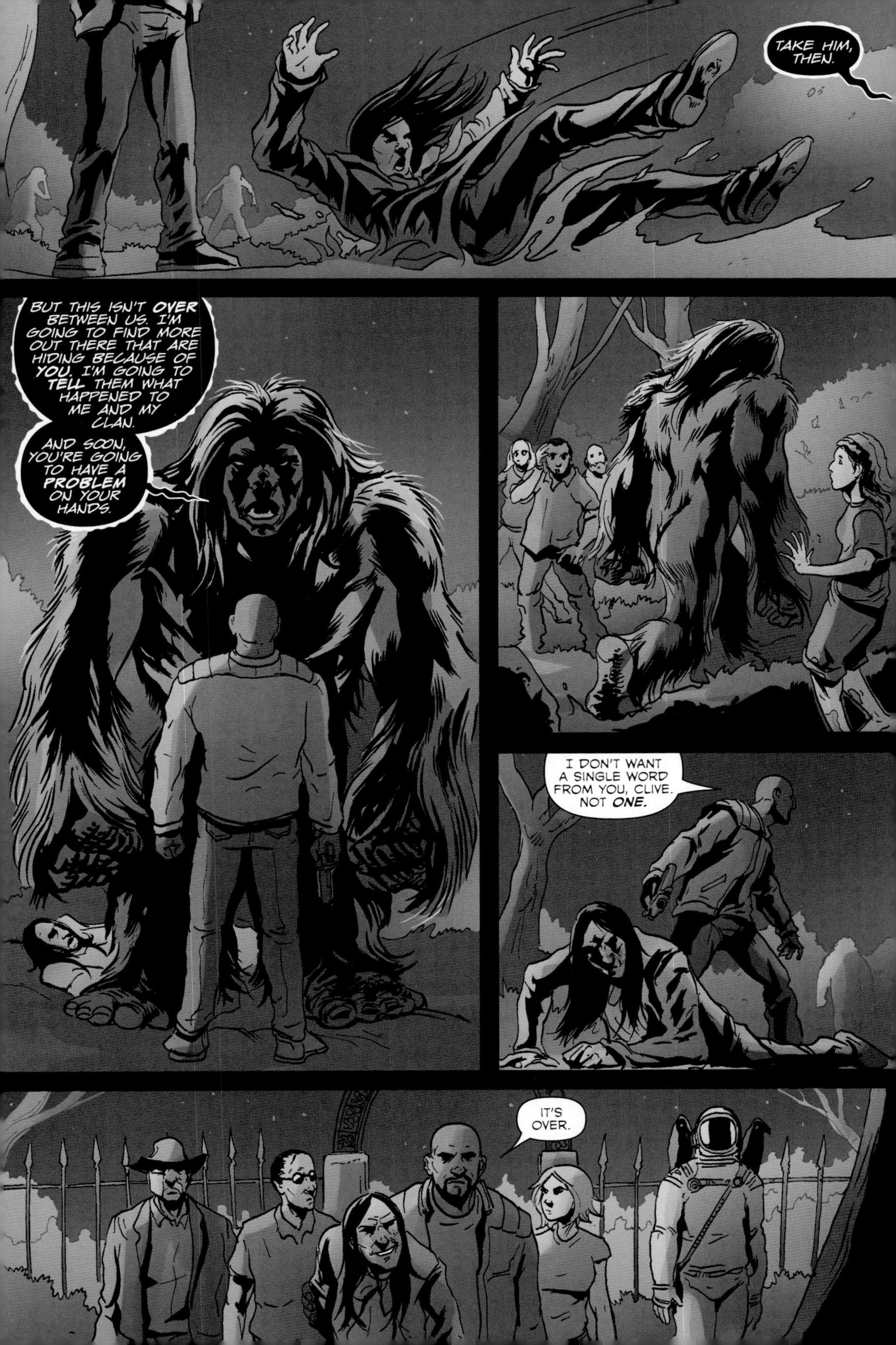
TAKE HIM, THEN.
BUT THIS ISN'T OVER BETWEEN US. I'M GOING TO FIND MORE OUT THERE THAT ARE HIDING BECAUSE OF YOU. I'M GOING TO TELL THEM WHAT HAPPENED TO ME AND MY CLAN.
AND SOON, YOU'RE GOING TO HAVE A PROBLEM ON YOUR HANDS.
I DON'T WANT A SINGLE WORD FROM YOU, CLIVE. NOT ONE.
IT'S OVER.

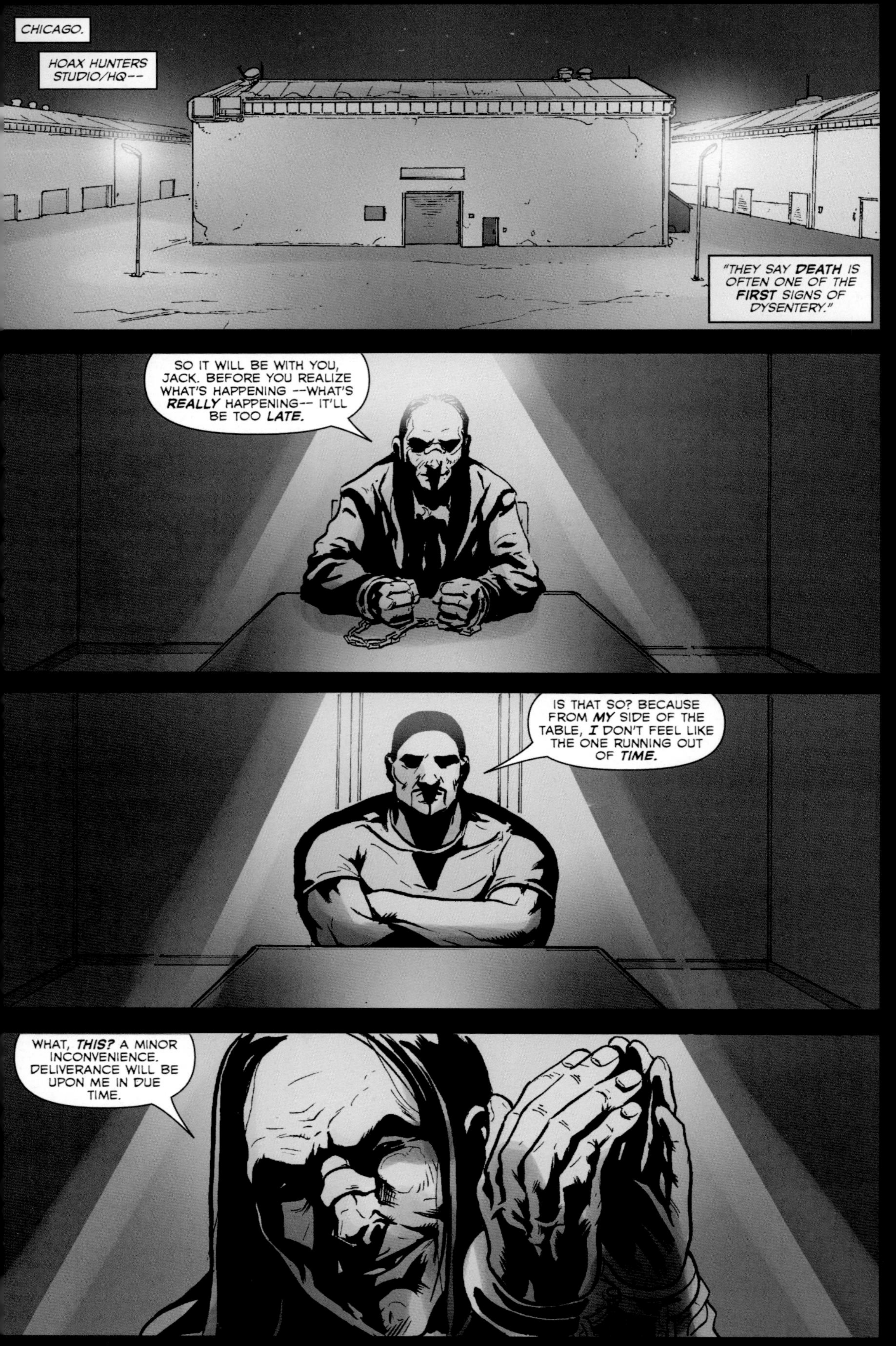
CHICAGO.
HOAX HUNTERS STUDIO/HQ--
"THEY SAY DEATH IS OFTEN ONE OF THE FIRST SIGNS OF DYSENTERY."
SO IT WILL BE WITH YOU, JACK. BEFORE YOU REALIZE WHAT'S HAPPENING --WHAT'S REALLY HAPPENING-- IT'LL BE TOO LATE.
IS THAT SO? BECAUSE FROM MY SIDE OF THE TABLE, I DON'T FEEL LIKE THE ONE RUNNING OUT OF TIME.
WHAT, THIS? A MINOR INCONVENIENCE. DELIVERANCE WILL BE UPON ME IN DUE TIME.

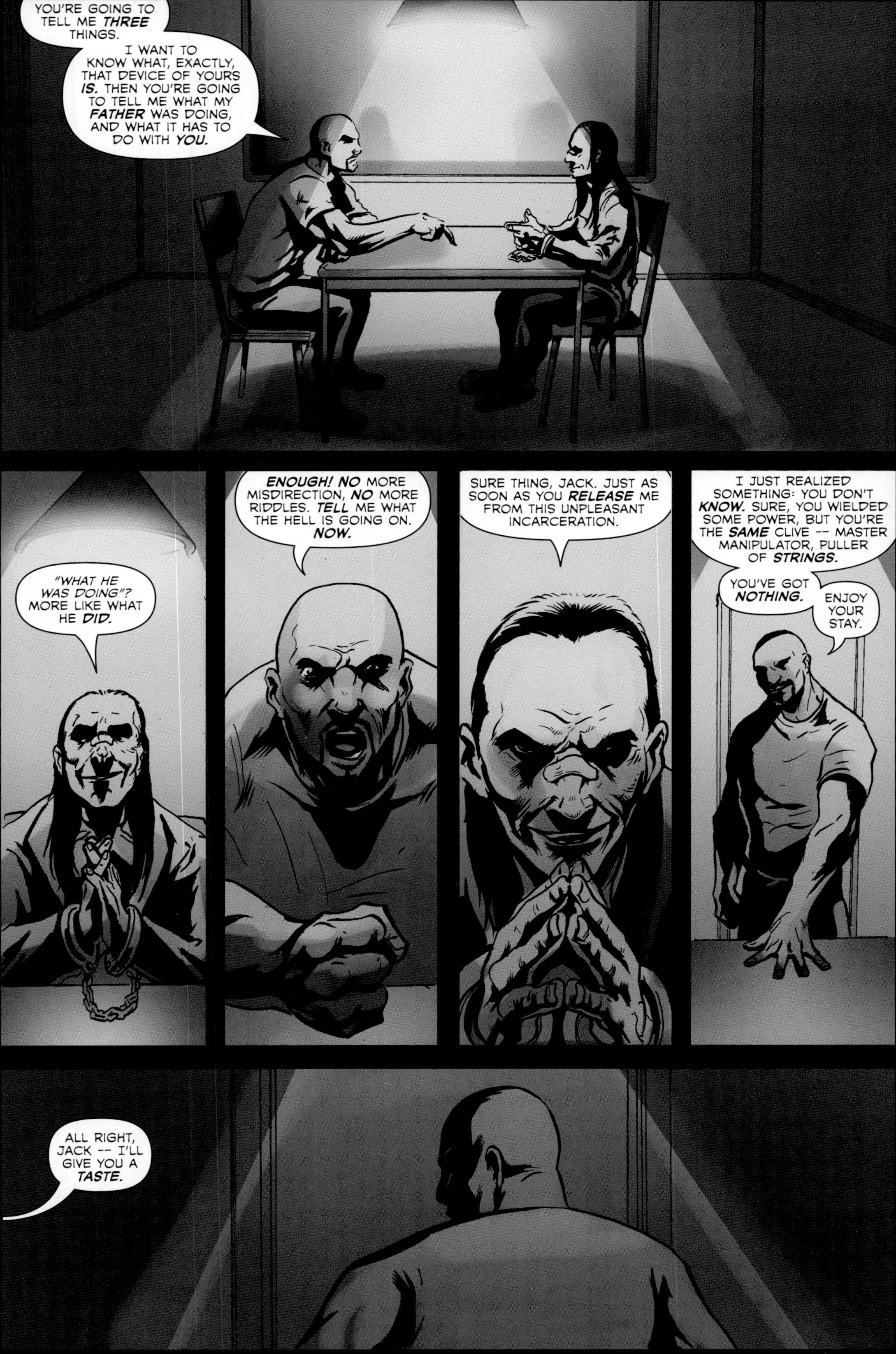
YOU'RE GOING TO TELL ME THREE THINGS.
I WANT TO KNOW WHAT, EXACTLY, THAT DEVICE OF YOURS IS. THEN YOU'RE GOING TO TELL ME WHAT MY FATHER WAS DOING, AND WHAT IT HAS TO DO WITH YOU.
"WHAT HE WAS DOING"? MORE LIKE WHAT HE DID.
ENOUGH! NO MORE MISDIRECTION, NO MORE RIDDLES. TELL ME WHAT THE HELL IS GOING ON. NOW.
SURE THING, JACK. JUST AS SOON AS YOU RELEASE ME FROM THIS UNPLEASANT INCARCERATION.
I JUST REALIZED SOMETHING: YOU DON'T KNOW. SURE, YOU WIELDED SOME POWER, BUT YOU'RE THE SAME CLIVE -- MASTER MANIPULATOR, PULLER OF STRINGS.
YOU'VE GOT NOTHING.
ENJOY YOUR STAY.
ALL RIGHT, JACK -- I'LL GIVE YOU A TASTE.

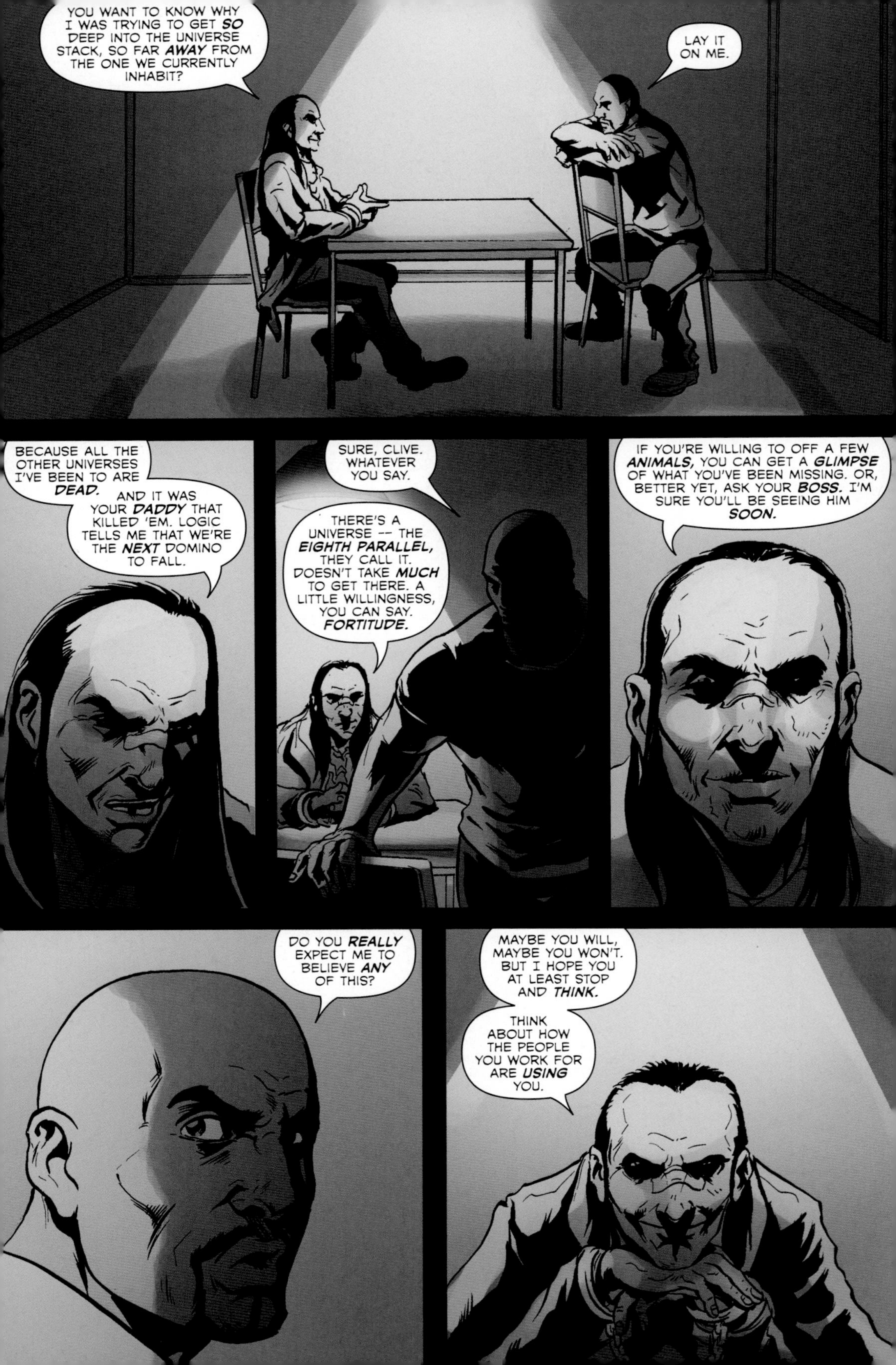
YOU WANT TO KNOW WHY I WAS TRYING TO GET SO DEEP INTO THE UNIVERSE STACK, SO FAR AWAY FROM THE ONE WE CURRENTLY INHABIT?
LAY IT ON ME.
BECAUSE ALL THE OTHER UNIVERSES I'VE BEEN TO ARE DEAD.
AND IT WAS YOUR DADDY THAT KILLED 'EM. LOGIC TELLS ME THAT WE'RE THE NEXT DOMINO TO FALL.
SURE, CLIVE. WHATEVER YOU SAY.
THERE'S A UNIVERSE -- THE EIGHTH PARALLEL, THEY CALL IT. DOESN'T TAKE MUCH TO GET THERE. A LITTLE WILLINGNESS, YOU CAN SAY. FORTITUDE.
IF YOU'RE WILLING TO OFF A FEW ANIMALS, YOU CAN GET A GLIMPSE OF WHAT YOU'VE BEEN MISSING. OR, BETTER YET, ASK YOUR BOSS. I'M SURE YOU'LL BE SEEING HIM SOON.
DO YOU REALLY EXPECT ME TO BELIEVE ANY OF THIS?
MAYBE YOU WILL, MAYBE YOU WON'T. BUT I HOPE YOU AT LEAST STOP AND THINK.
THINK ABOUT HOW THE PEOPLE YOU WORK FOR ARE USING YOU.

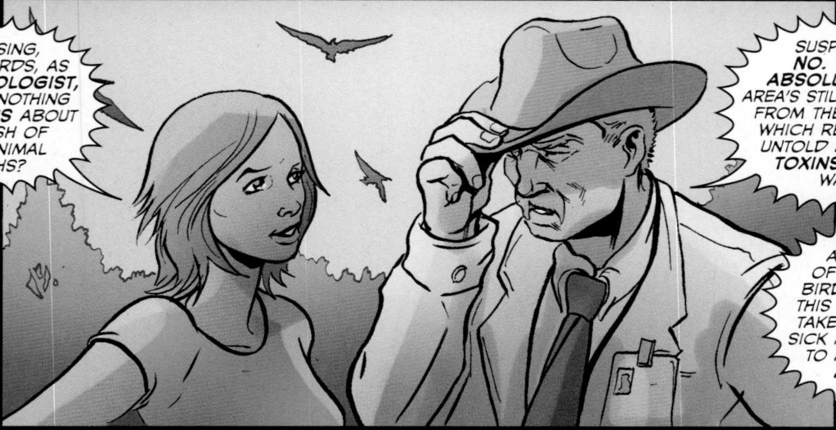
IN CLOSING, MR. EDWARDS, AS AN EPA BIOLOGIST, YOU FIND NOTHING SUSPICIOUS ABOUT THIS RASH OF MASS ANIMAL DEATHS?
SUSPICIOUS? NO. TRAGIC? ABSOLUTELY. THIS AREA'S STILL RECOVERING FROM THE OIL SPILL, WHICH RELEASED AN UNTOLD AMOUNT OF TOXINS INTO THE WATER.
ALL MANNER OF ANIMAL AND BIRD DRINK FROM THIS WATER. IT JUST TAKES ONE TO GET SICK AND PASS IT ON TO ANOTHER AND ANOTHER.

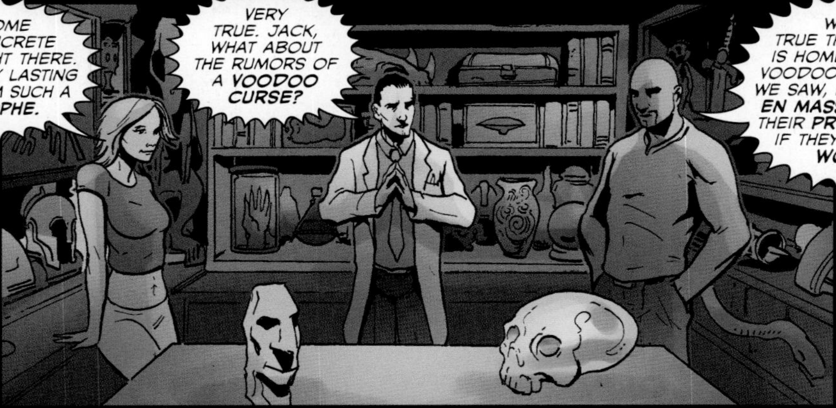
THAT'S SOME PRETTY CONCRETE SCIENCE RIGHT THERE. HARD TO DENY LASTING EFFECTS FROM SUCH A CATASTROPHE.
VERY TRUE. JACK, WHAT ABOUT THE RUMORS OF A VOODOO CURSE?
WHILE IT'S TRUE THAT LOUISIANA IS HOME TO VARIOUS VOODOO PRACTICES, AS WE SAW, KILLING ANIMALS EN MASSE DOESN'T FIT THEIR PRINCIPLES. EVEN IF THEY COULD, THEY WOULDN'T.

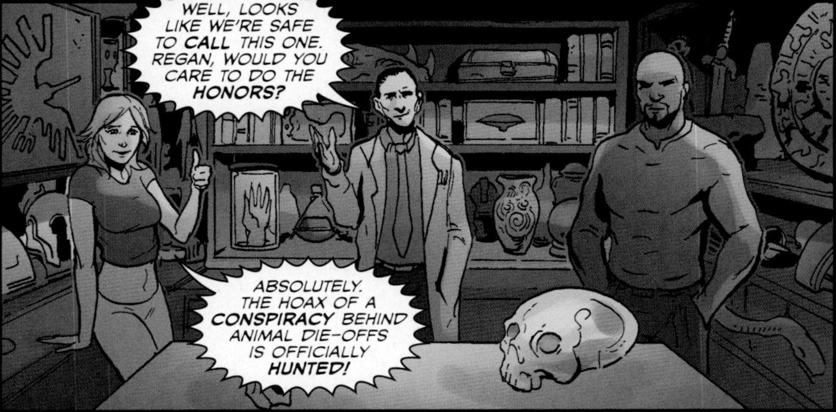
WELL, LOOKS LIKE WE'RE SAFE TO CALL THIS ONE. REGAN, WOULD YOU CARE TO DO THE HONORS?
ABSOLUTELY. THE HOAX OF A CONSPIRACY BEHIND ANIMAL DIE-OFFS IS OFFICIALLY HUNTED!

HOAX HUNTERS

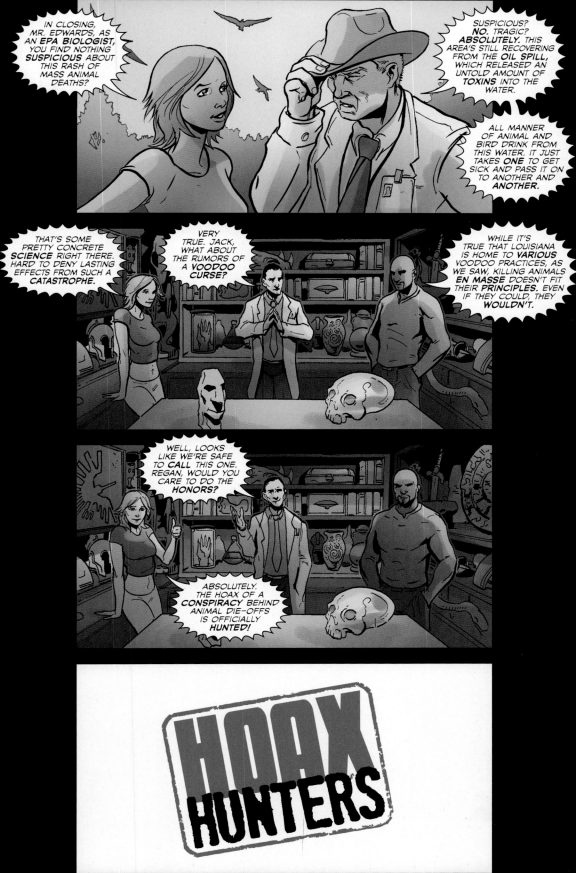

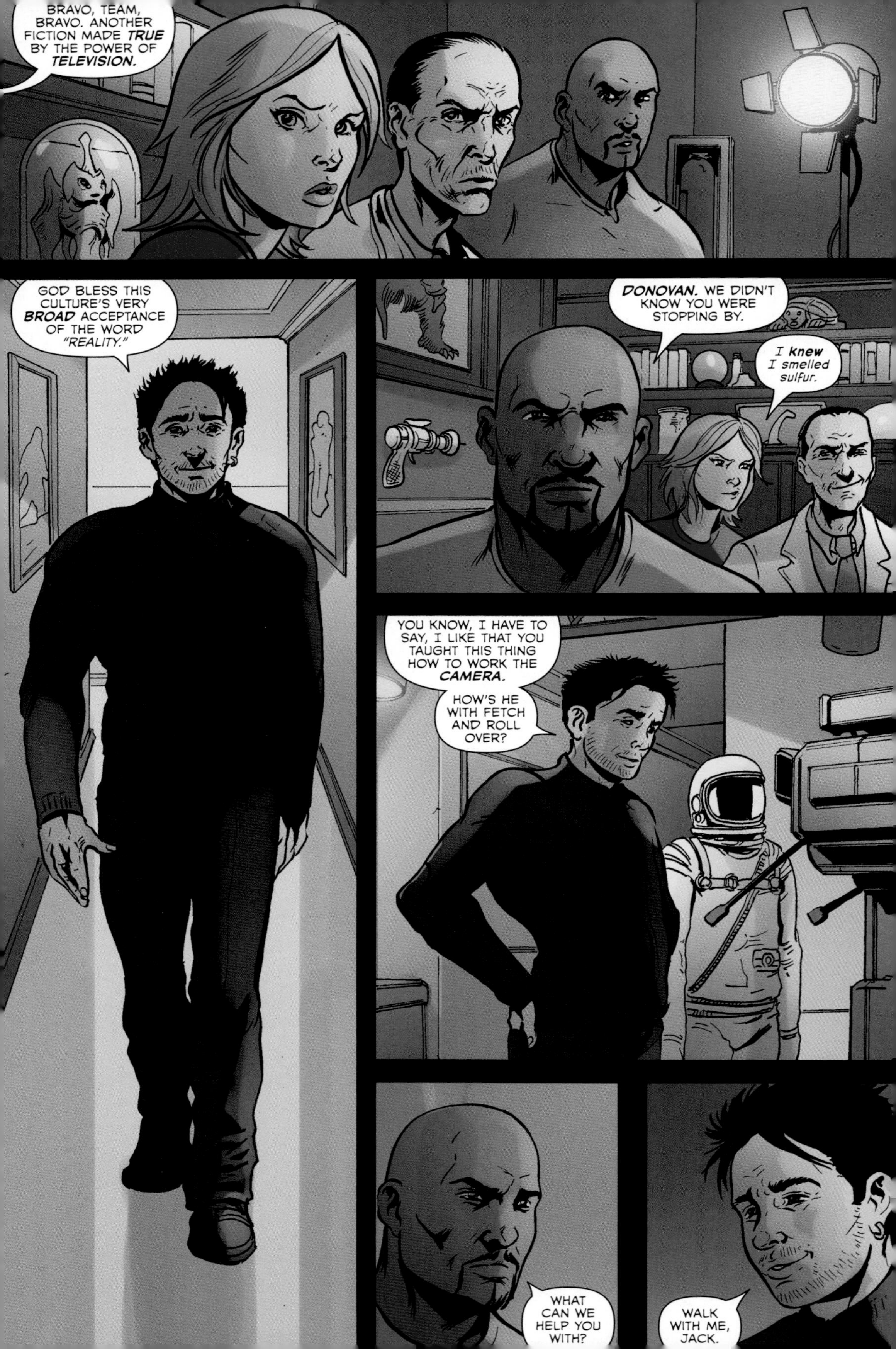
BRAVO, TEAM, BRAVO. ANOTHER FICTION MADE TRUE BY THE POWER OF TELEVISION.
GOD BLESS THIS CULTURE'S VERY BROAD ACCEPTANCE OF THE WORD "REALITY."
DONOVAN. WE DIDN'T KNOW YOU WERE STOPPING BY.
I knew I smelled sulfur.
YOU KNOW, I HAVE TO SAY, I LIKE THAT YOU TAUGHT THIS THING HOW TO WORK THE CAMERA.
HOW'S HE WITH FETCH AND ROLL OVER?
WHAT CAN WE HELP YOU WITH?
WALK WITH ME, JACK.

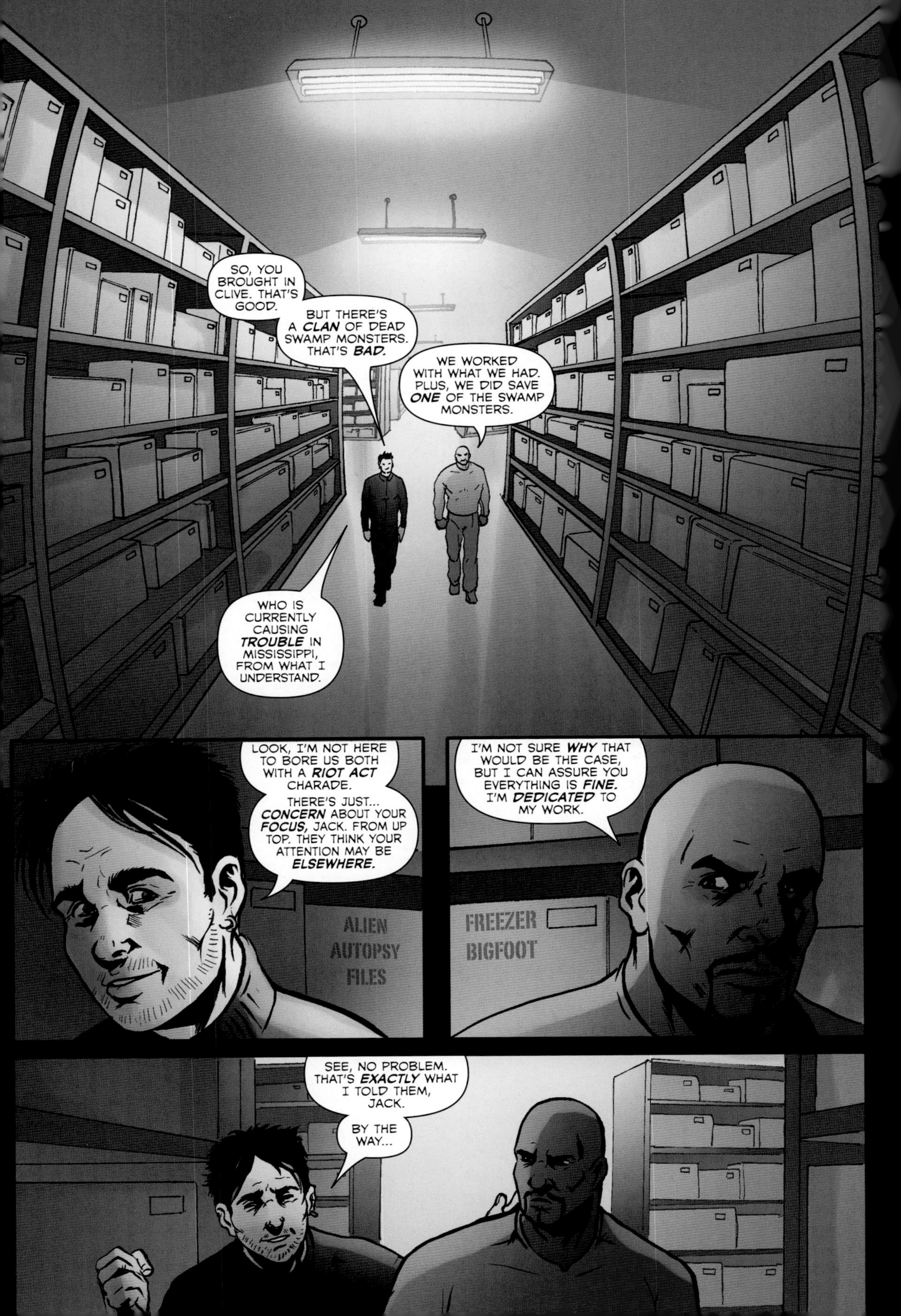
SO, YOU BROUGHT IN CLIVE. THAT'S GOOD.
BUT THERE'S A CLAN OF DEAD SWAMP MONSTERS. THAT'S BAD.
WE WORKED WITH WHAT WE HAD. PLUS, WE DID SAVE ONE OF THE SWAMP MONSTERS.
WHO IS CURRENTLY CAUSING TROUBLE IN MISSISSIPPI, FROM WHAT I UNDERSTAND.
LOOK, I'M NOT HERE TO BORE US BOTH WITH A RIOT ACT CHARADE.
THERE'S JUST... CONCERN ABOUT YOUR FOCUS, JACK. FROM UP TOP. THEY THINK YOUR ATTENTION MAY BE ELSEWHERE.
ALIEN AUTOPSY FILES
I'M NOT SURE WHY THAT WOULD BE THE CASE, BUT I CAN ASSURE YOU EVERYTHING IS FINE. I'M DEDICATED TO MY WORK.
FREEZER BIGFOOT
SEE, NO PROBLEM. THAT'S EXACTLY WHAT I TOLD THEM, JACK.
BY THE WAY...

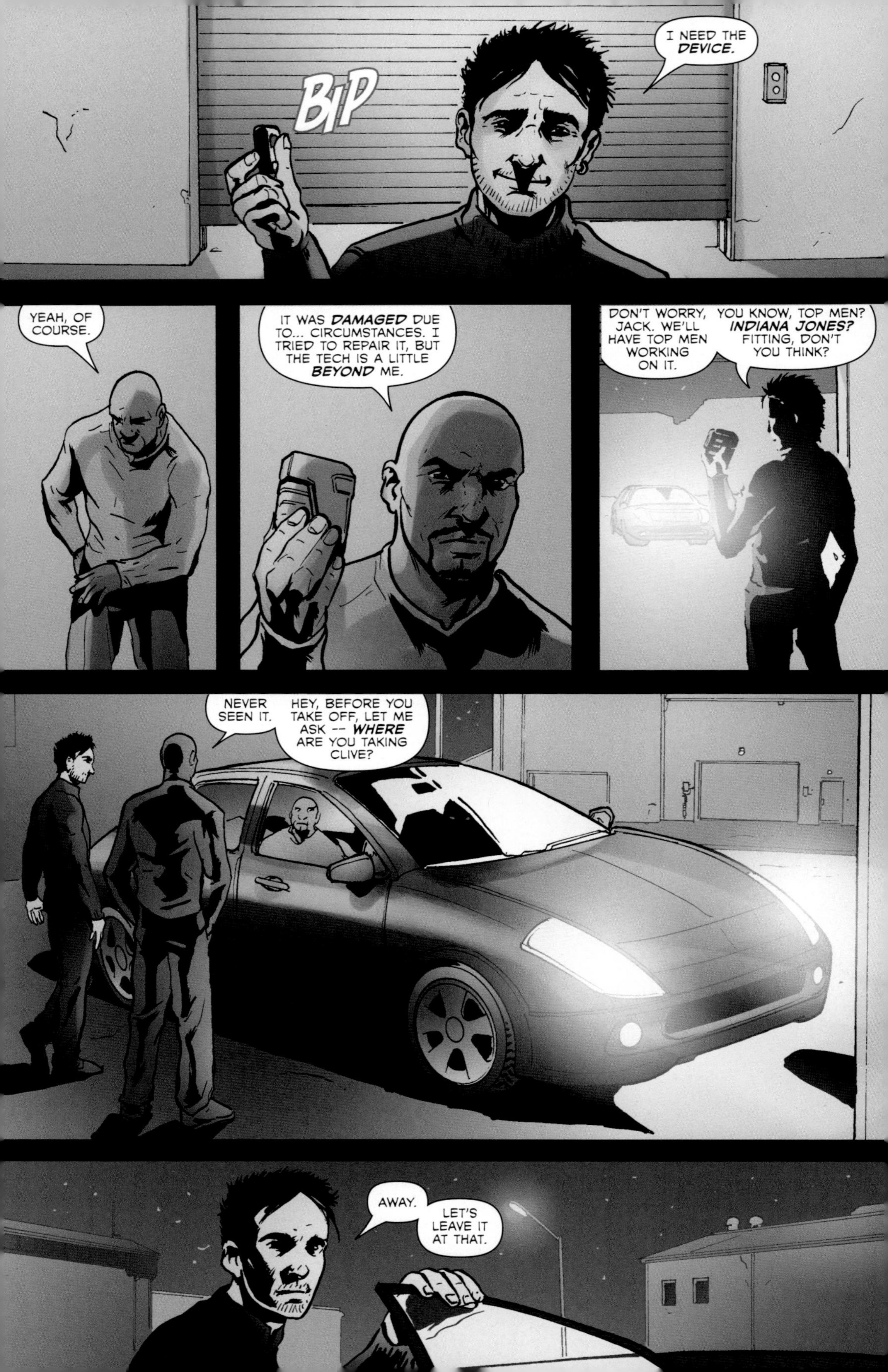
BIP
I NEED THE DEVICE.
YEAH, OF COURSE.
IT WAS DAMAGED DUE TO... CIRCUMSTANCES. I TRIED TO REPAIR IT, BUT THE TECH IS A LITTLE BEYOND ME.
DON'T WORRY, JACK. WE'LL HAVE TOP MEN WORKING ON IT.
YOU KNOW, TOP MEN? INDIANA JONES? FITTING, DON'T YOU THINK?
NEVER SEEN IT.
HEY, BEFORE YOU TAKE OFF, LET ME ASK -- WHERE ARE YOU TAKING CLIVE?
AWAY.
LET'S LEAVE IT AT THAT.

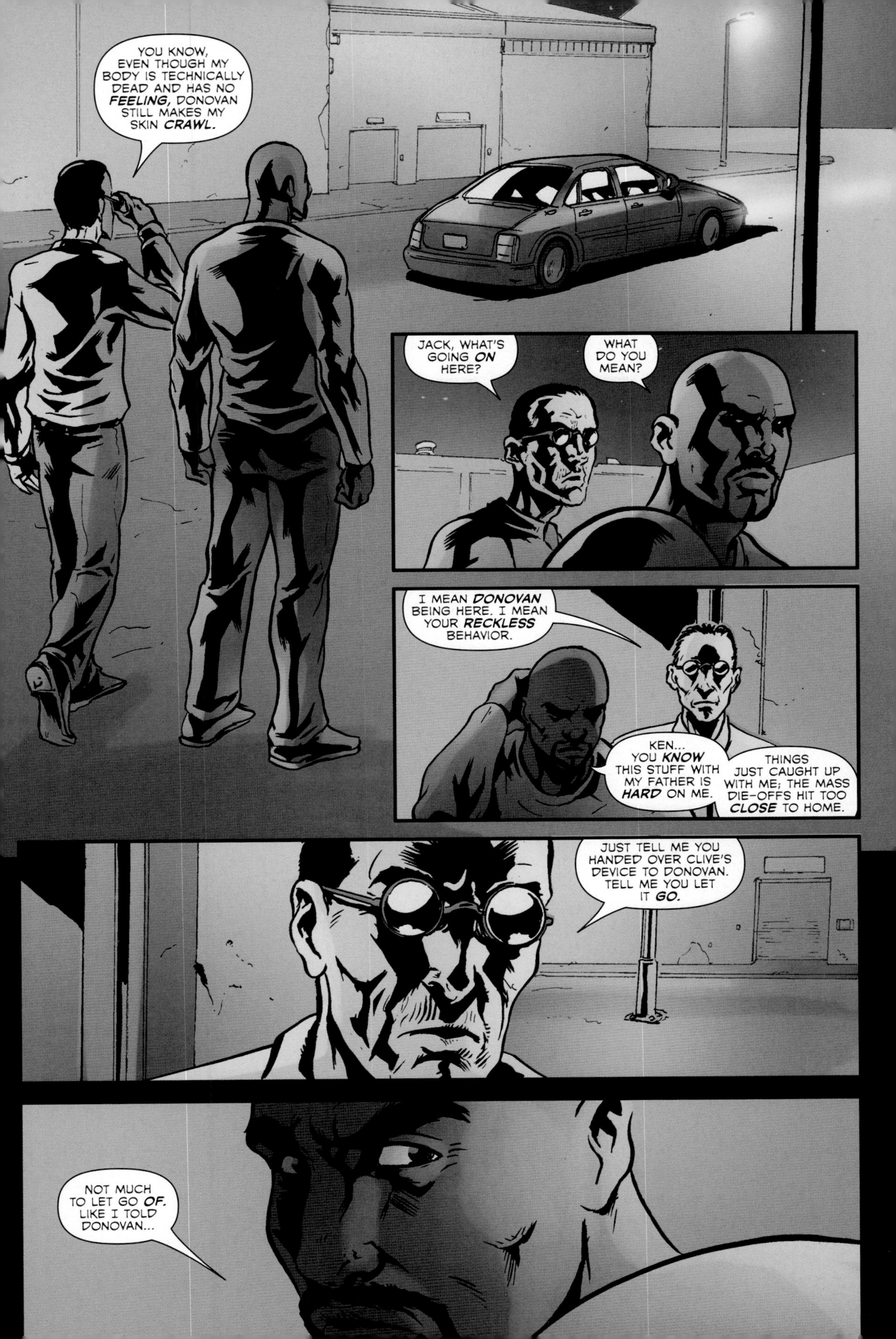
YOU KNOW, EVEN THOUGH MY BODY IS TECHNICALLY DEAD AND HAS NO FEELING, DONOVAN STILL MAKES MY SKIN CRAWL.
JACK, WHAT'S GOING ON HERE?
WHAT DO YOU MEAN?
I MEAN DONOVAN BEING HERE. I MEAN YOUR RECKLESS BEHAVIOR.
KEN... YOU KNOW THIS STUFF WITH MY FATHER IS HARD ON ME.
THINGS JUST CAUGHT UP WITH ME; THE MASS DIE-OFFS HIT TOO CLOSE TO HOME.
JUST TELL ME YOU HANDED OVER CLIVE'S DEVICE TO DONOVAN. TELL ME YOU LET IT GO.
NOT MUCH TO LET GO OF. LIKE I TOLD DONOVAN...

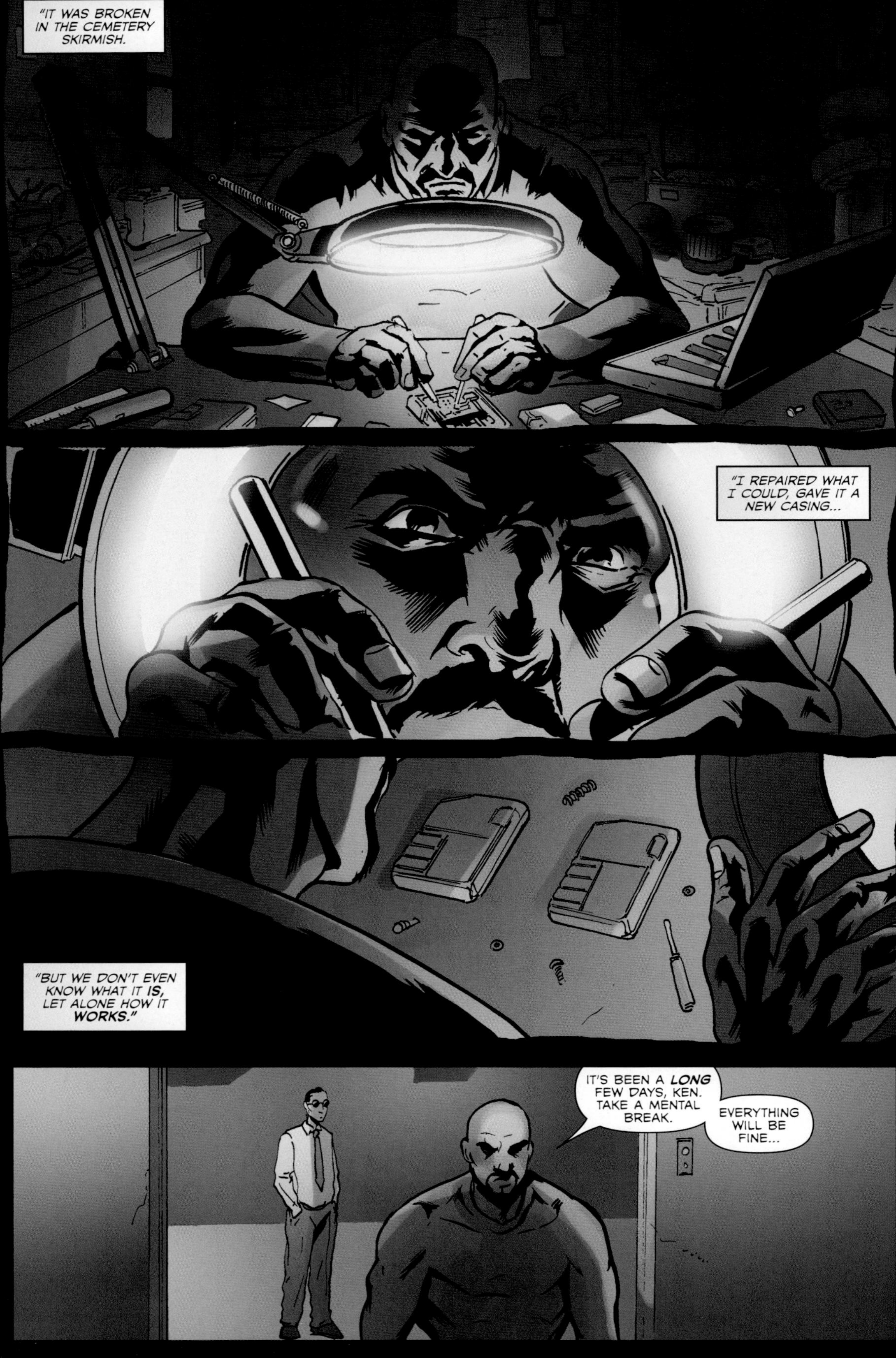
"IT WAS BROKEN IN THE CEMETERY SKIRMISH.
"I REPAIRED WHAT I COULD, GAVE IT A NEW CASING...
"BUT WE DON'T EVEN KNOW WHAT IT IS, LET ALONE HOW IT WORKS."
IT'S BEEN A LONG FEW DAYS, KEN. TAKE A MENTAL BREAK.
EVERYTHING WILL BE FINE...

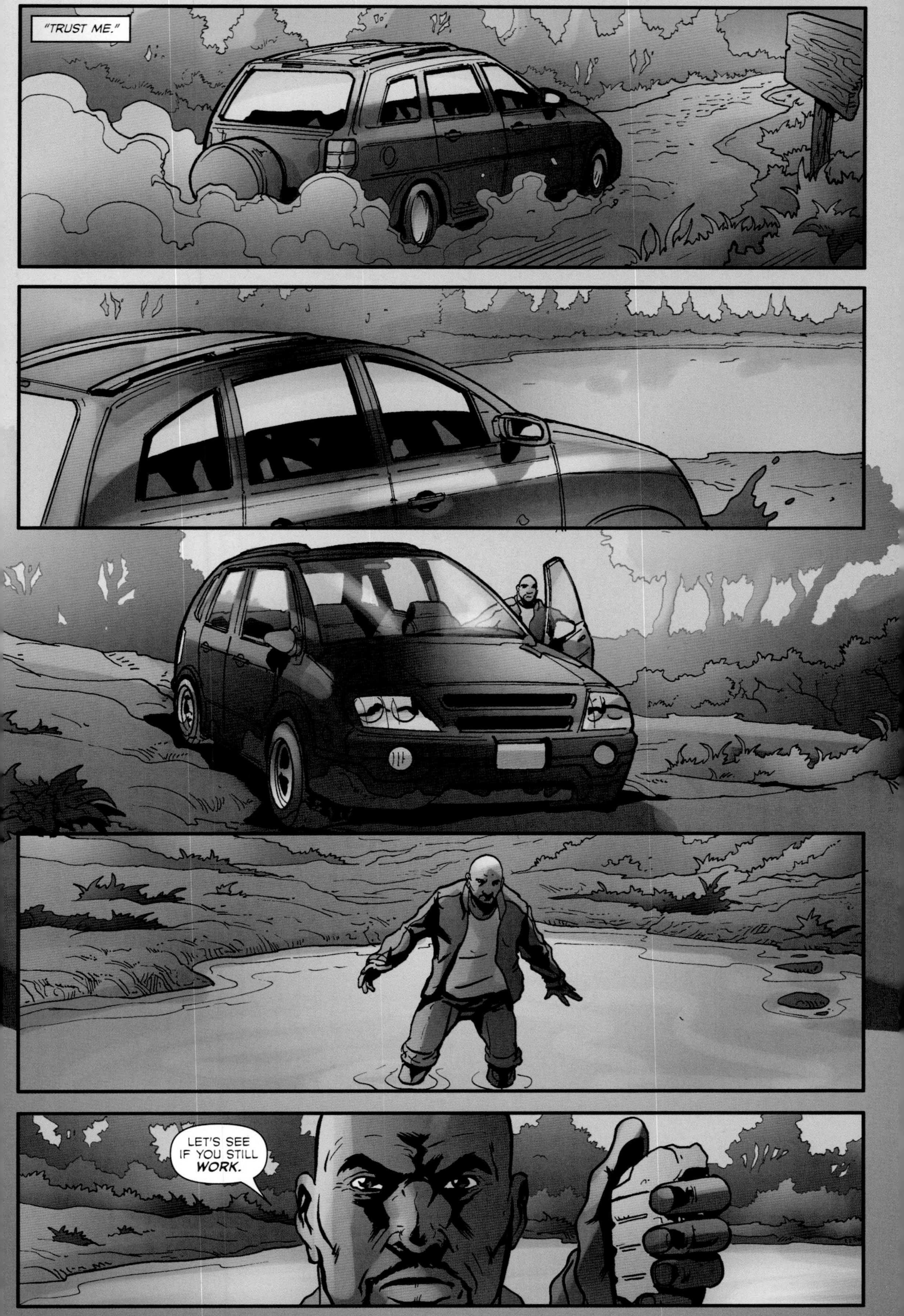
"TRUST ME."
LET'S SEE IF YOU STILL WORK.

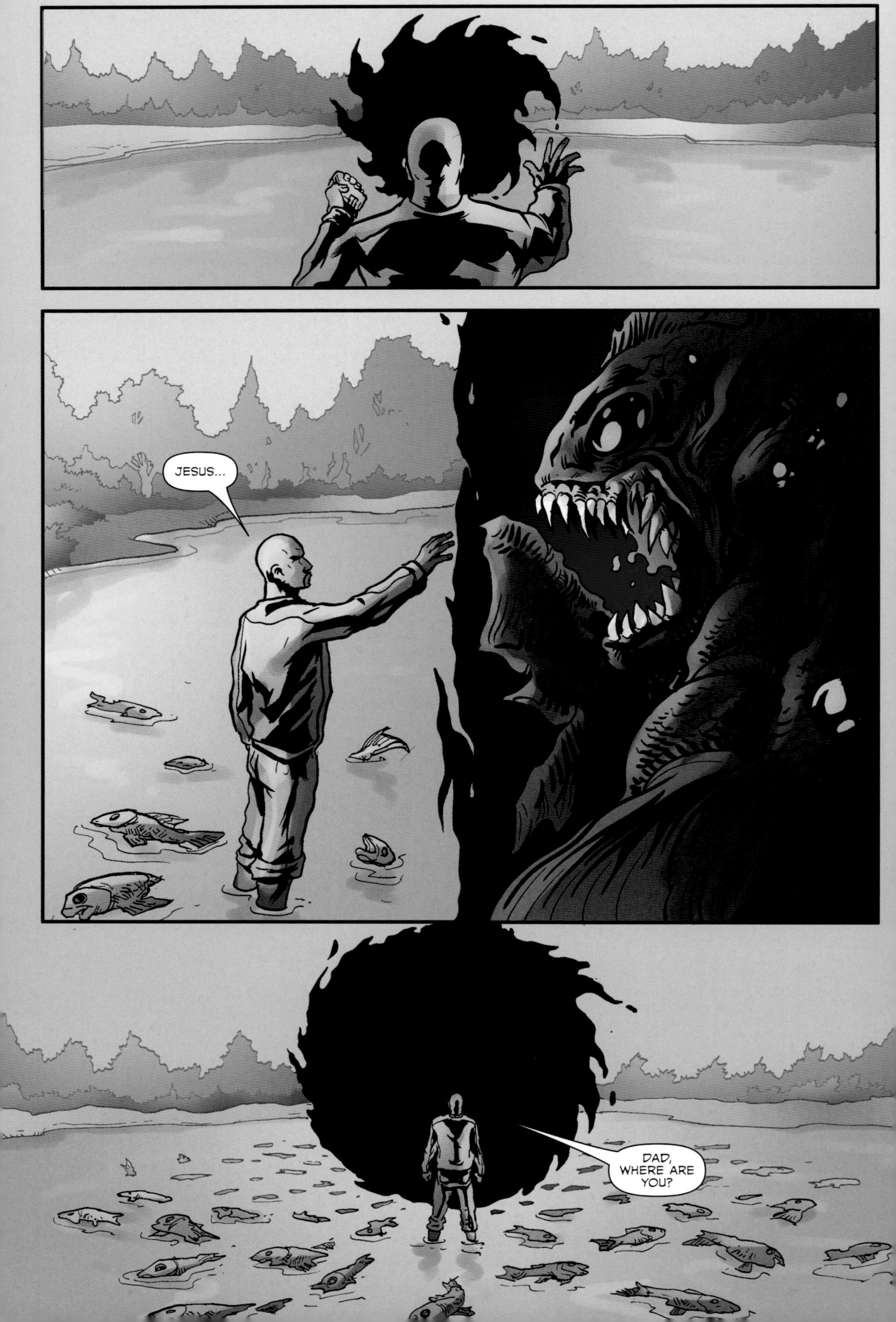
JESUS...
DAD, WHERE ARE YOU?

HOAX HUNTERS

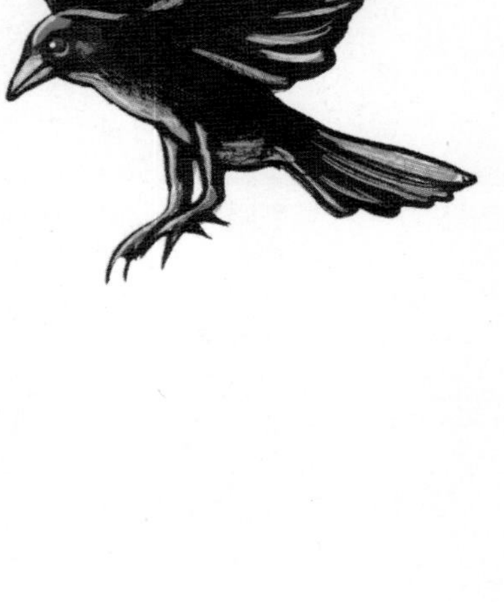

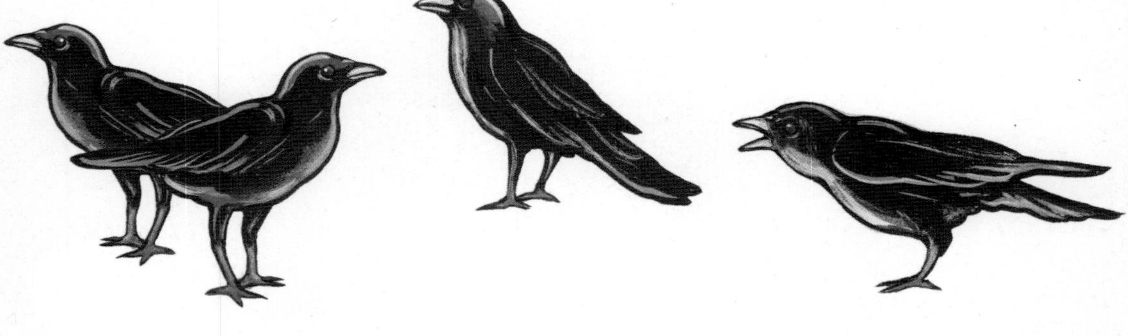

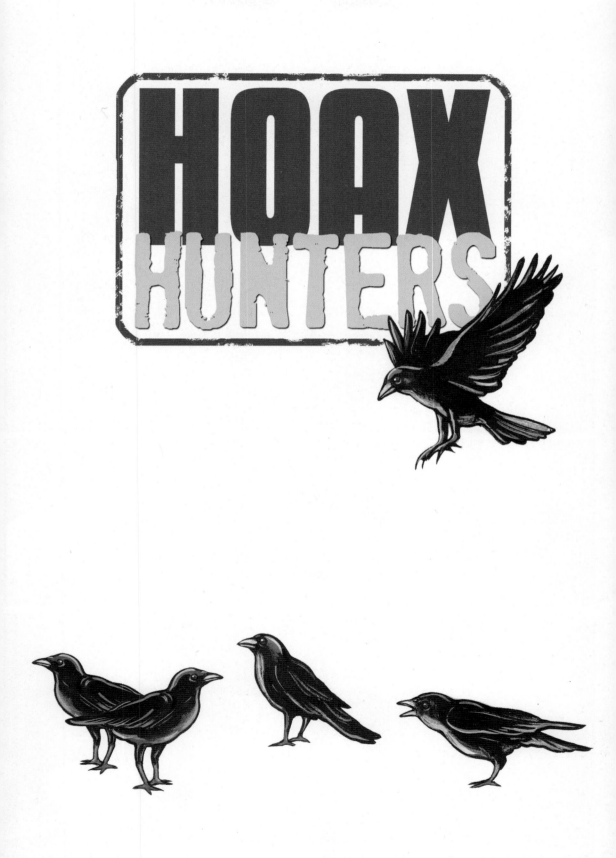

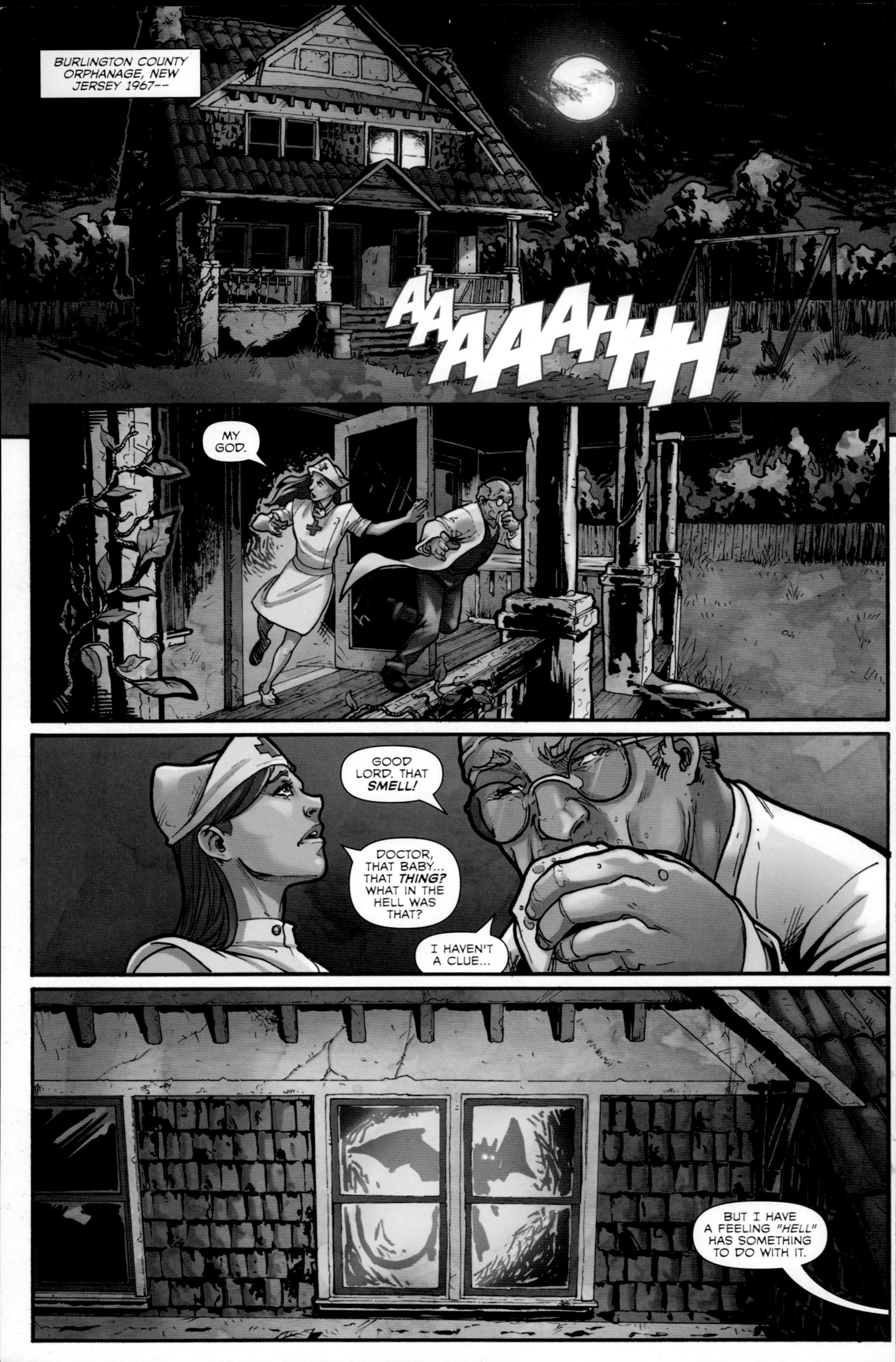
BURLINGTON COUNTY ORPHANAGE, NEW JERSEY 1967--
AAAAAAHHHH
MY GOD.
GOOD LORD. THAT *SMELL!*
DOCTOR, THAT BABY... THAT *THING?* WHAT IN THE HELL WAS THAT?
I HAVEN'T A CLUE...
BUT I HAVE A FEELING *"HELL"* HAS SOMETHING TO DO WITH IT.

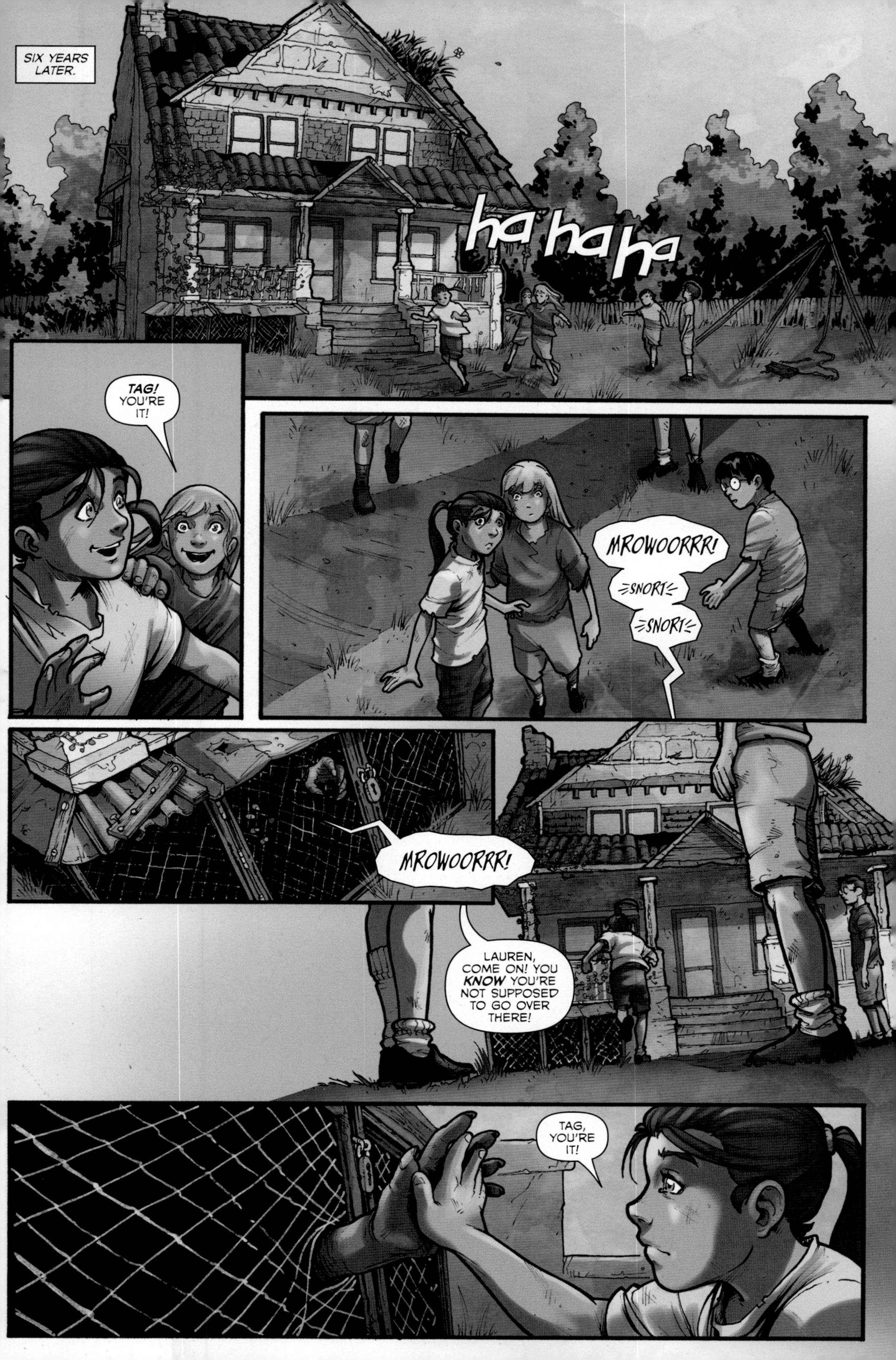
SIX YEARS LATER.
ha ha ha
TAG! YOU'RE IT!
MROWOORRR!
SNORT
SNORT
MROWOORRR!
LAUREN, COME ON! YOU KNOW YOU'RE NOT SUPPOSED TO GO OVER THERE!
TAG, YOU'RE IT!

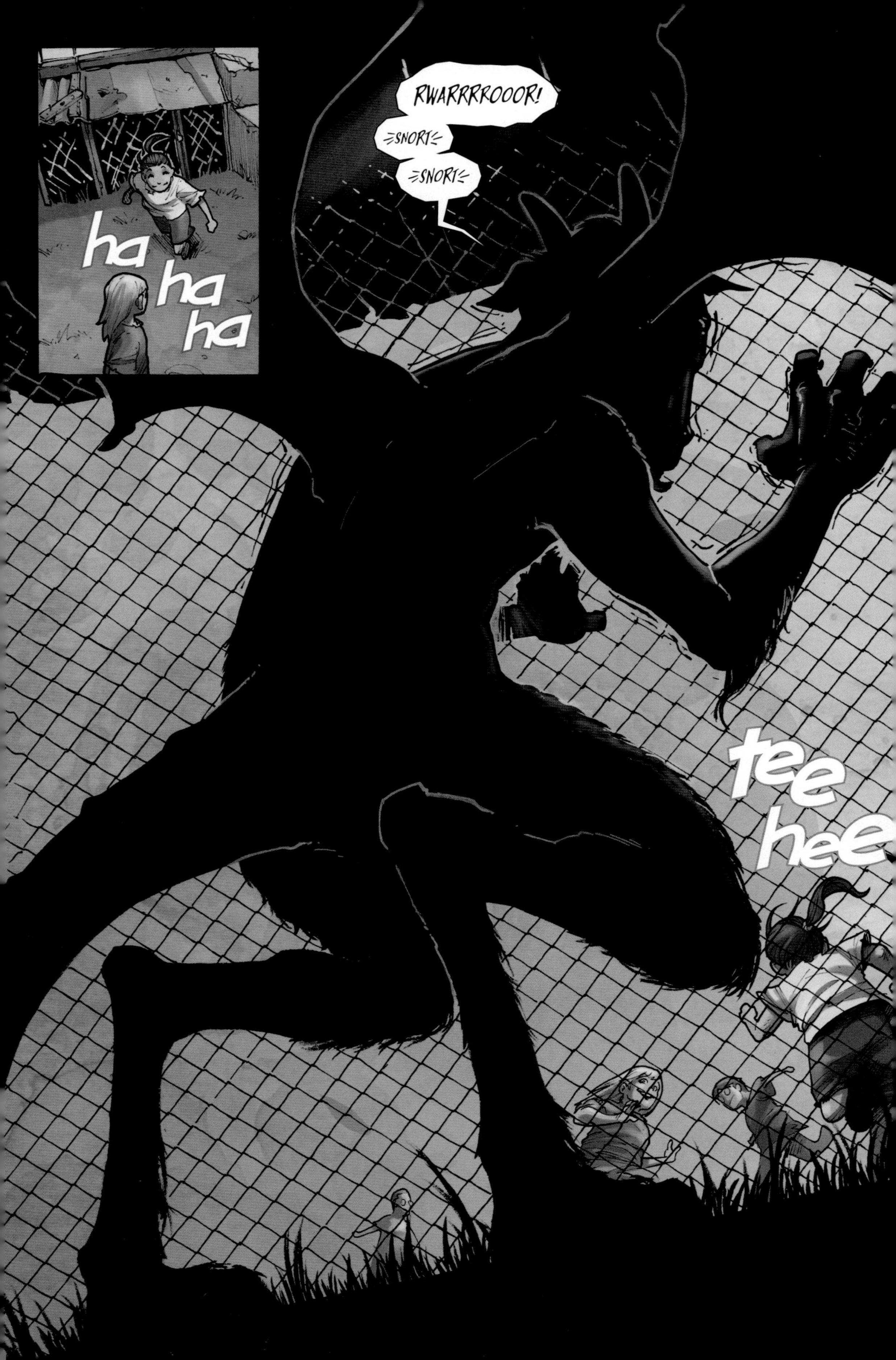
ha
ha
ha
RWARRRROOOR!
SNORT
SNORT
tee
hee

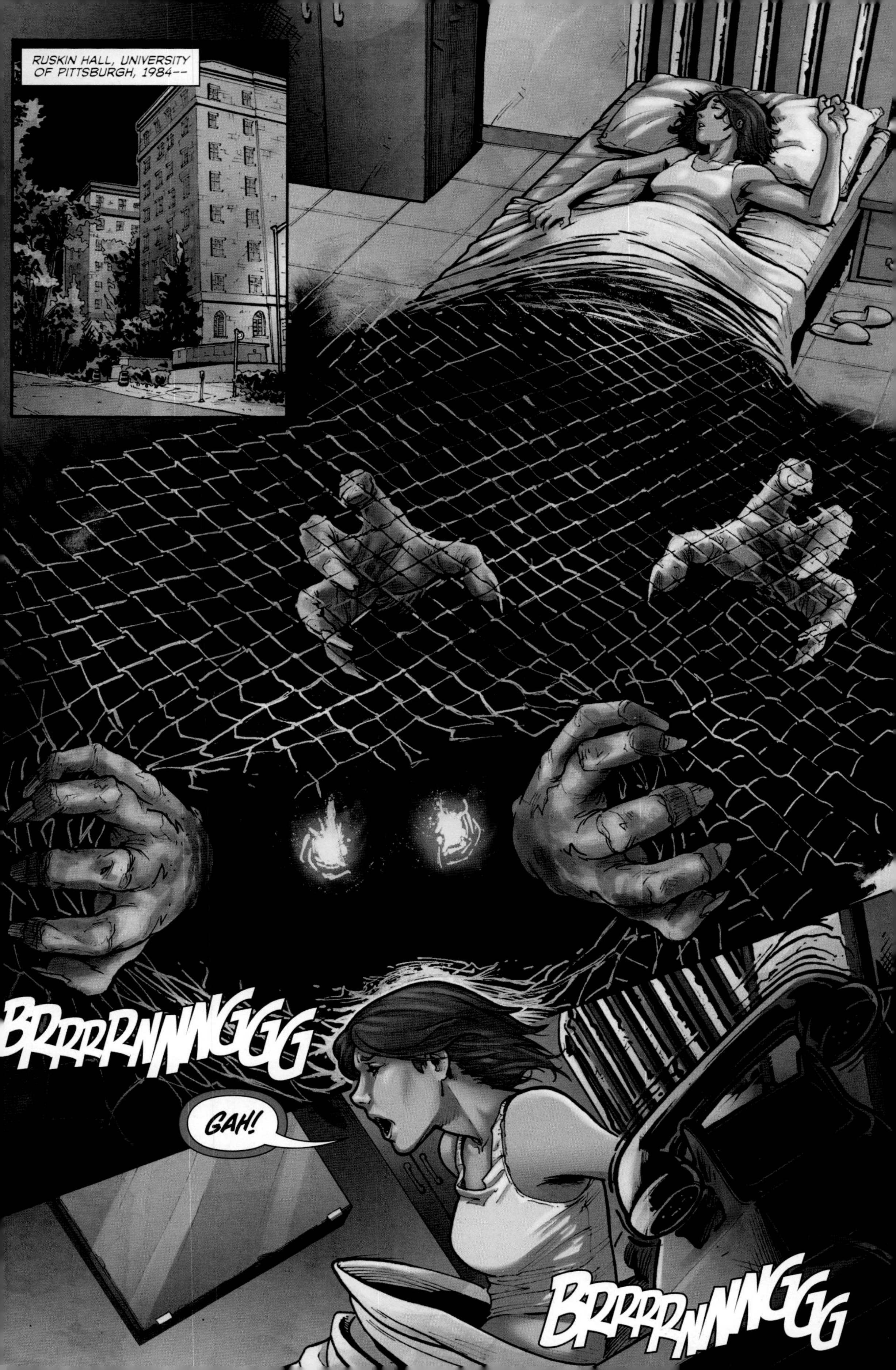
RUSKIN HALL, UNIVERSITY OF PITTSBURGH, 1984--
BRRRRRNNNGGG
GAH!
BRRRRRNNNGGG

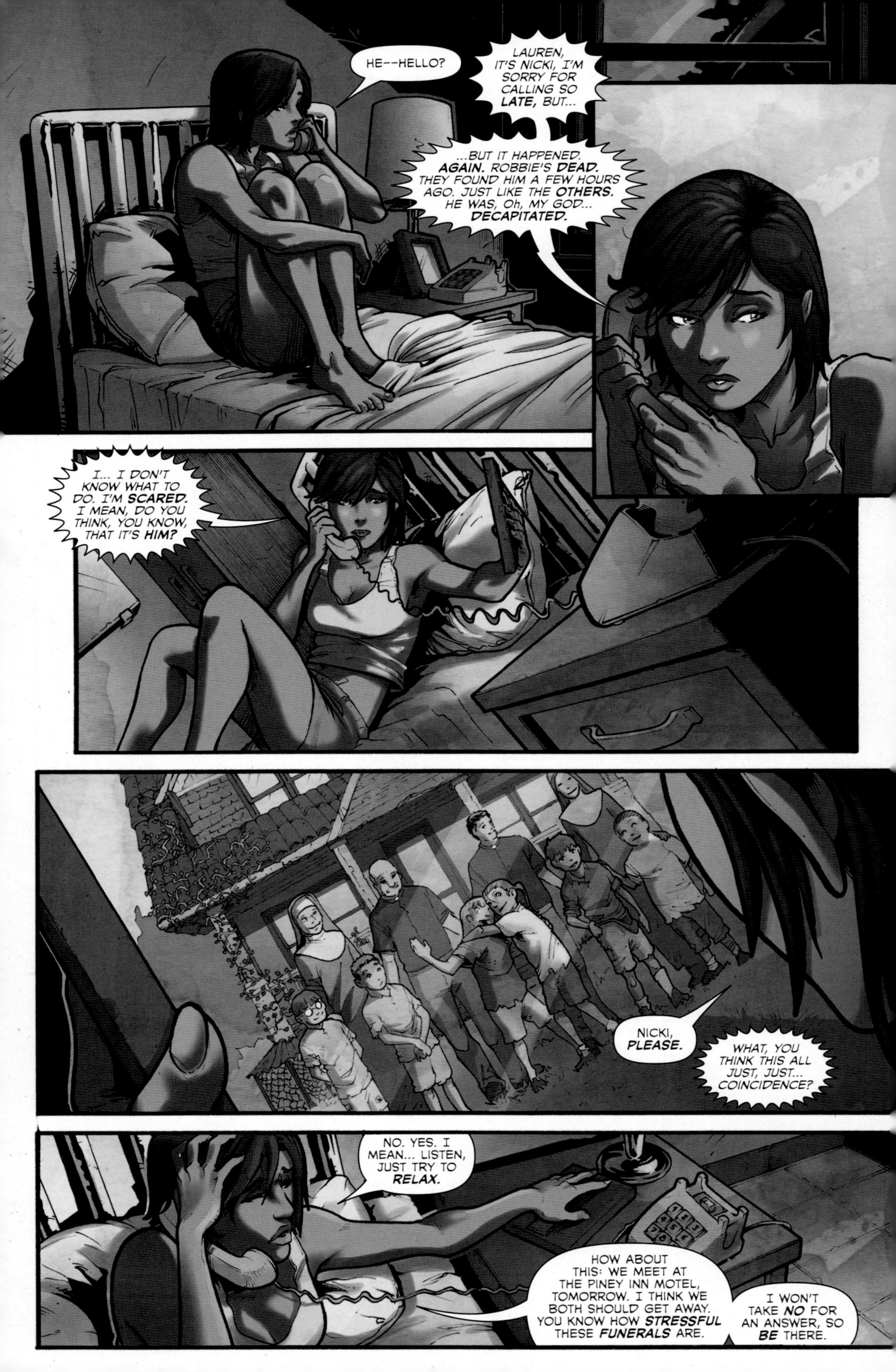
HE--HELLO?
LAUREN, IT'S NICKI, I'M SORRY FOR CALLING SO **LATE,** BUT...
...BUT IT HAPPENED. **AGAIN.** ROBBIE'S **DEAD.** THEY FOUND HIM A FEW HOURS AGO. JUST LIKE THE **OTHERS.** HE WAS, OH, MY GOD... **DECAPITATED.**
I... I DON'T KNOW WHAT TO DO. I'M **SCARED.** I MEAN, DO YOU THINK, YOU KNOW, THAT IT'S **HIM?**
NICKI, **PLEASE.**
WHAT, YOU THINK THIS ALL JUST, JUST... COINCIDENCE?
NO. YES. I MEAN... LISTEN, JUST TRY TO **RELAX.**
HOW ABOUT THIS: WE MEET AT THE PINEY INN MOTEL, TOMORROW. I THINK WE BOTH SHOULD GET AWAY. YOU KNOW HOW **STRESSFUL** THESE **FUNERALS** ARE.
I WON'T TAKE **NO** FOR AN ANSWER, SO **BE** THERE.

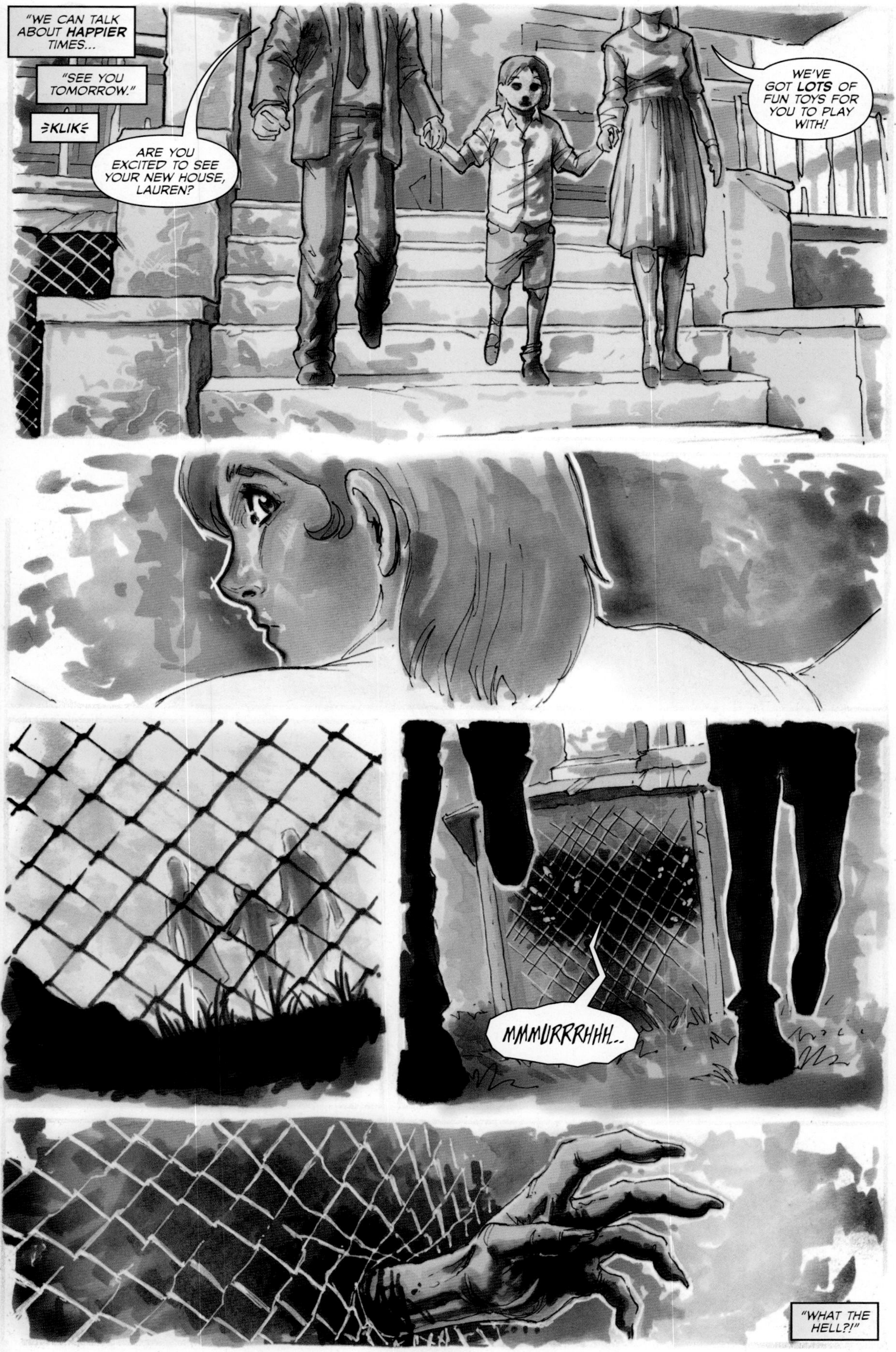
"WE CAN TALK ABOUT HAPPIER TIMES...
"SEE YOU TOMORROW."
KLIK
ARE YOU EXCITED TO SEE YOUR NEW HOUSE, LAUREN?
WE'VE GOT LOTS OF FUN TOYS FOR YOU TO PLAY WITH!
MMMURRRHHH...
"WHAT THE HELL?!"

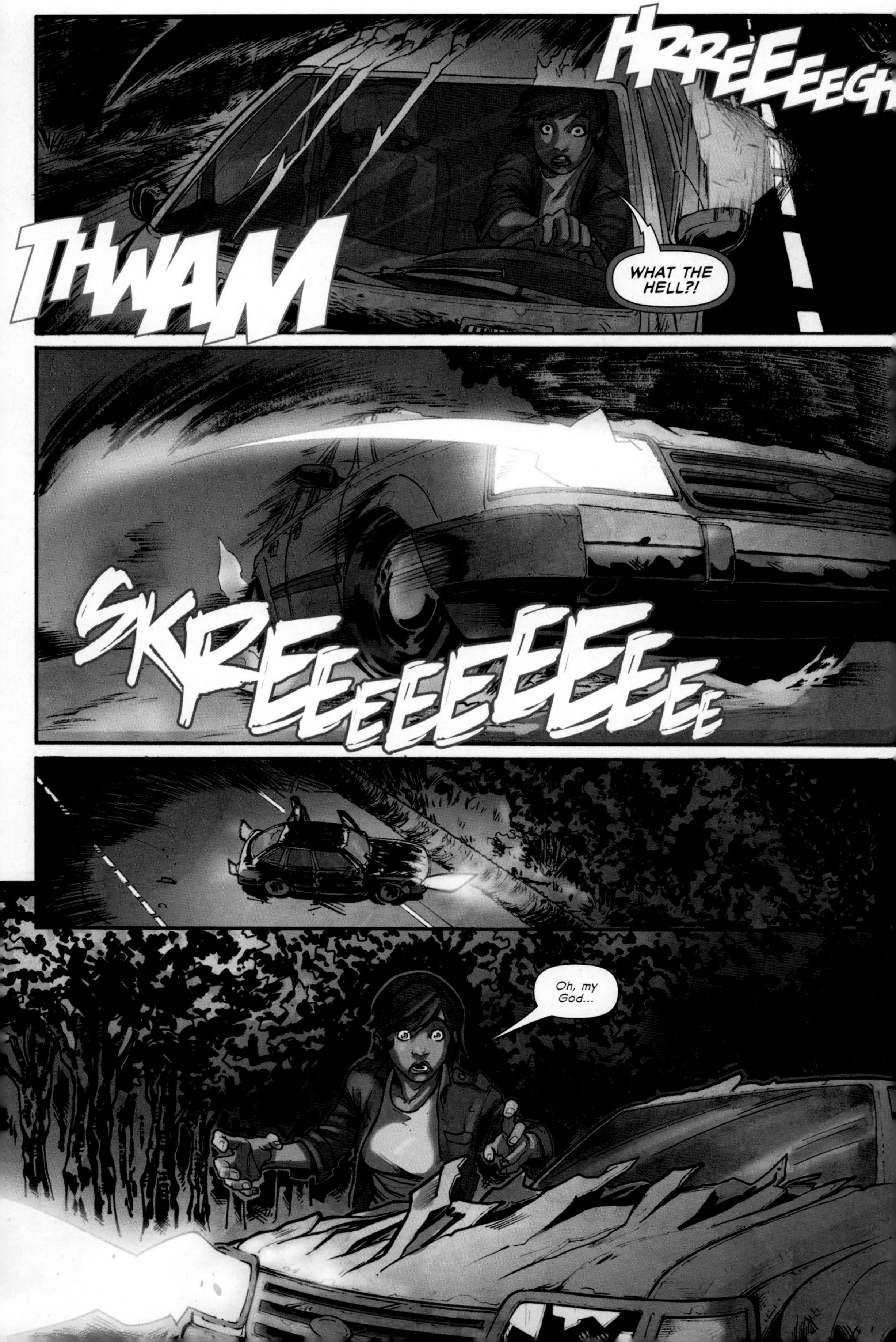
HRREEEEGH
THWAM
WHAT THE HELL?!
SKREEEEEEEEEEE
Oh, my God...

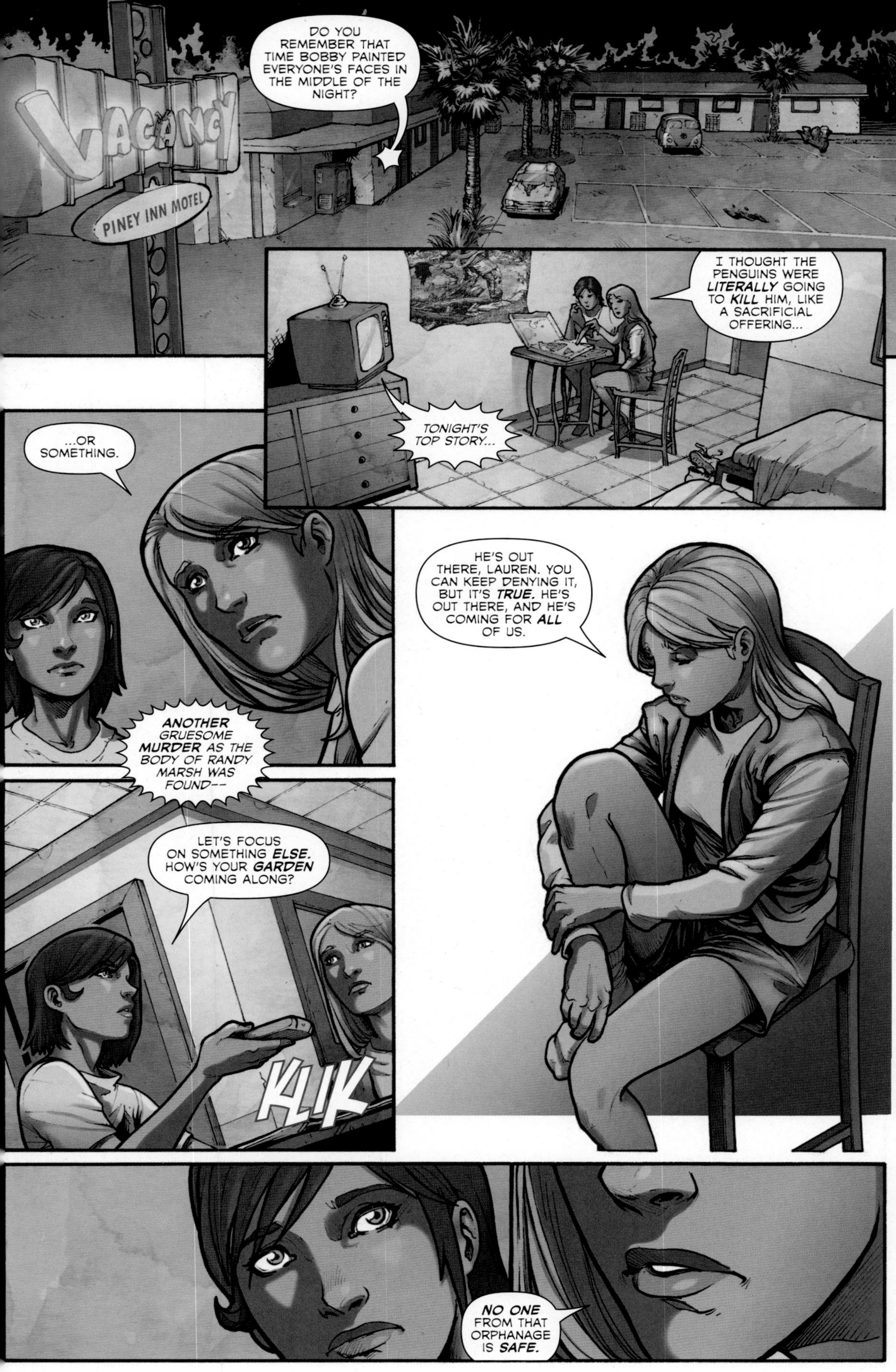
VACANCY
PINEY INN MOTEL
DO YOU REMEMBER THAT TIME BOBBY PAINTED EVERYONE'S FACES IN THE MIDDLE OF THE NIGHT?
I THOUGHT THE PENGUINS WERE LITERALLY GOING TO KILL HIM, LIKE A SACRIFICIAL OFFERING...
TONIGHT'S TOP STORY...
...OR SOMETHING.
ANOTHER GRUESOME MURDER AS THE BODY OF RANDY MARSH WAS FOUND--
HE'S OUT THERE, LAUREN. YOU CAN KEEP DENYING IT, BUT IT'S TRUE. HE'S OUT THERE, AND HE'S COMING FOR ALL OF US.
LET'S FOCUS ON SOMETHING ELSE. HOW'S YOUR GARDEN COMING ALONG?
KLIK
NO ONE FROM THAT ORPHANAGE IS SAFE.

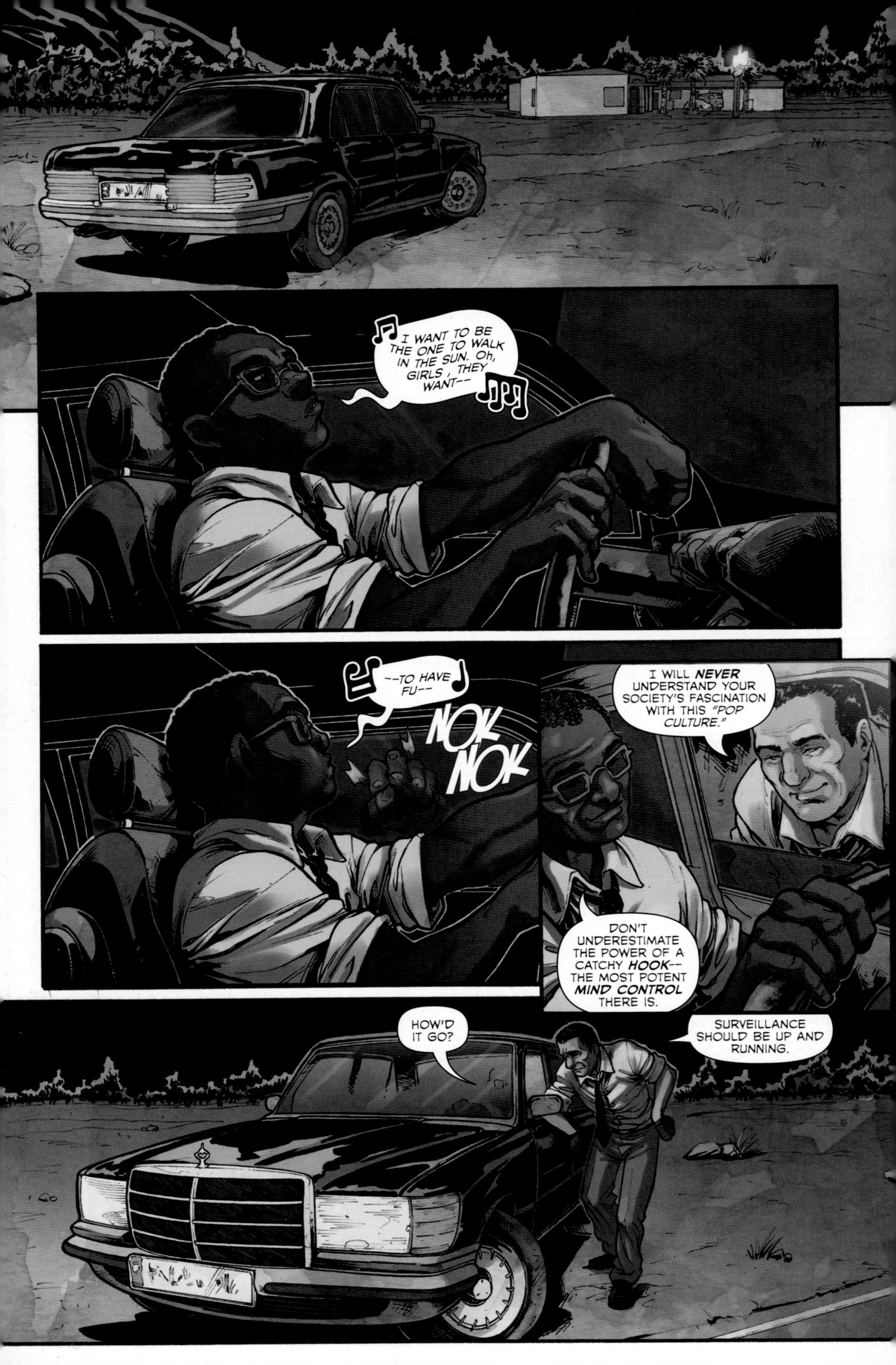
I WANT TO BE THE ONE TO WALK IN THE SUN. Oh, GIRLS, THEY WANT--
--TO HAVE FU--
NOK NOK
I WILL NEVER UNDERSTAND YOUR SOCIETY'S FASCINATION WITH THIS "POP CULTURE."
DON'T UNDERESTIMATE THE POWER OF A CATCHY HOOK-- THE MOST POTENT MIND CONTROL THERE IS.
HOW'D IT GO?
SURVEILLANCE SHOULD BE UP AND RUNNING.

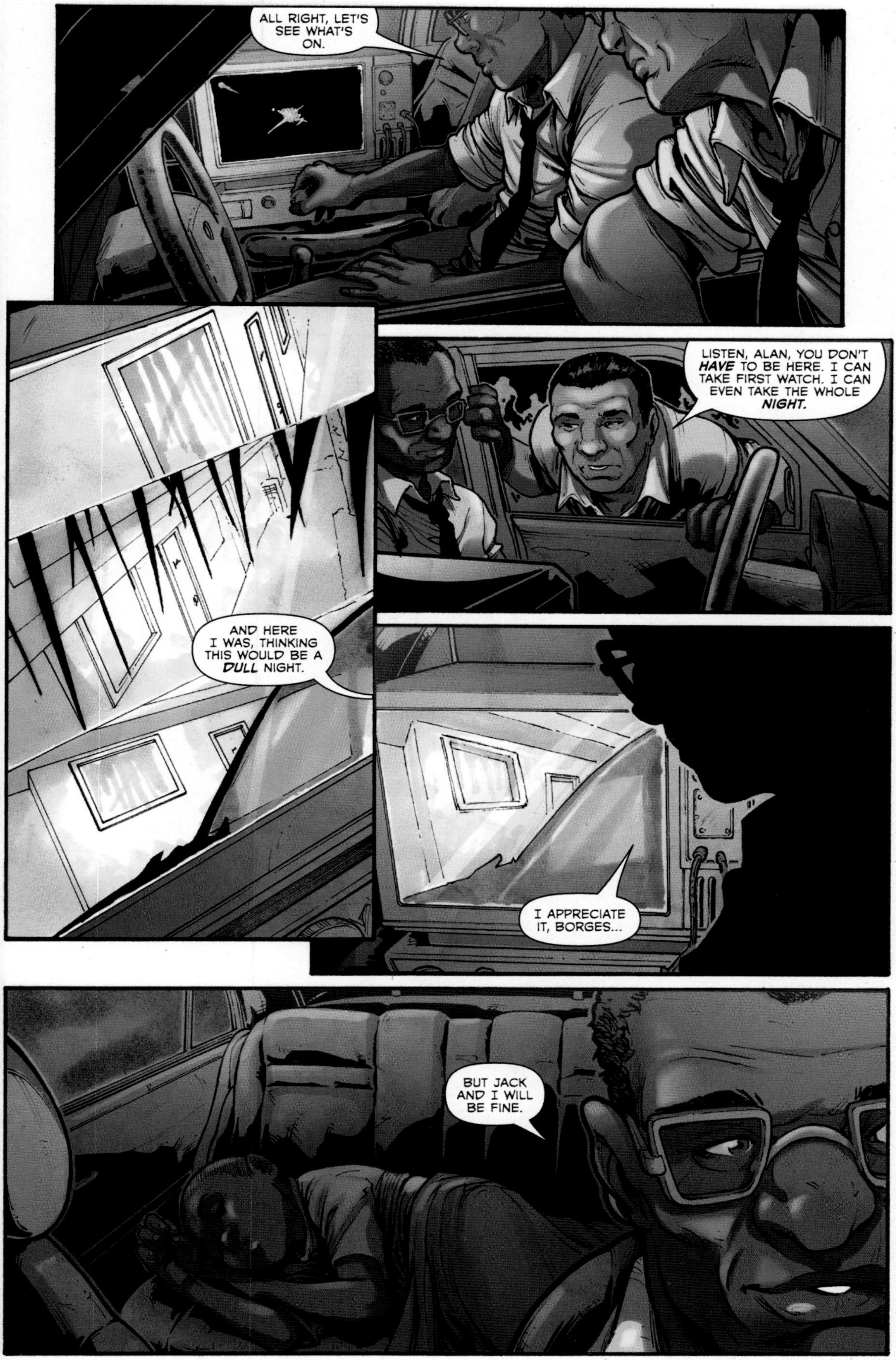
ALL RIGHT, LET'S SEE WHAT'S ON.
AND HERE I WAS, THINKING THIS WOULD BE A DULL NIGHT.
LISTEN, ALAN, YOU DON'T HAVE TO BE HERE. I CAN TAKE FIRST WATCH. I CAN EVEN TAKE THE WHOLE NIGHT.
I APPRECIATE IT, BORGES...
BUT JACK AND I WILL BE FINE.

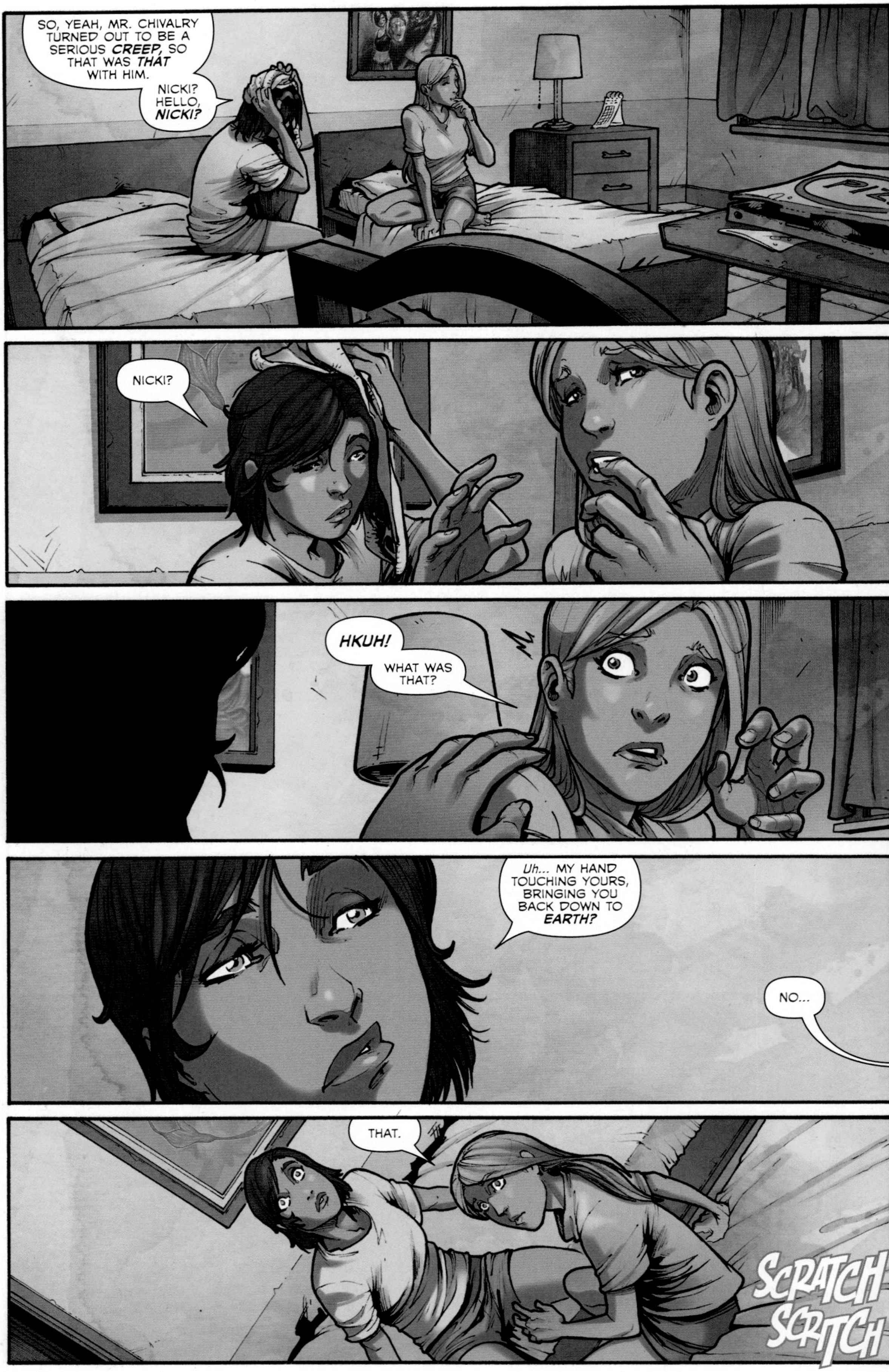

SO, YEAH, MR. CHIVALRY TURNED OUT TO BE A SERIOUS *CREEP,* SO THAT WAS *THAT* WITH HIM.
NICKI? HELLO, *NICKI?*
NICKI?
HKUH!
WHAT WAS THAT?
Uh... MY HAND TOUCHING YOURS, BRINGING YOU BACK DOWN TO *EARTH?*
NO...
THAT.
SCRATCH SCRITCH

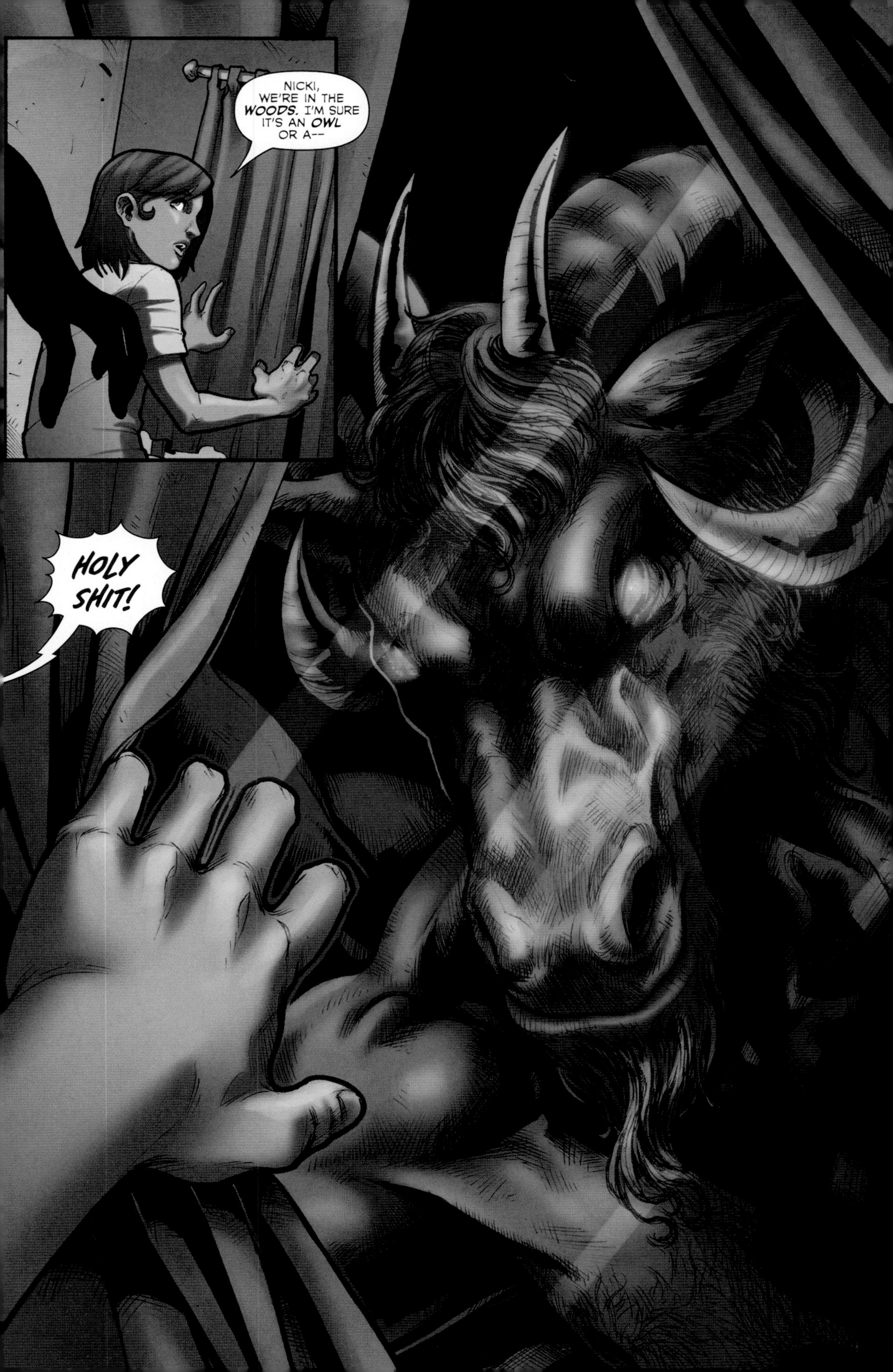
NICKI, WE'RE IN THE WOODS. I'M SURE IT'S AN OWL OR A--
HOLY SHIT!

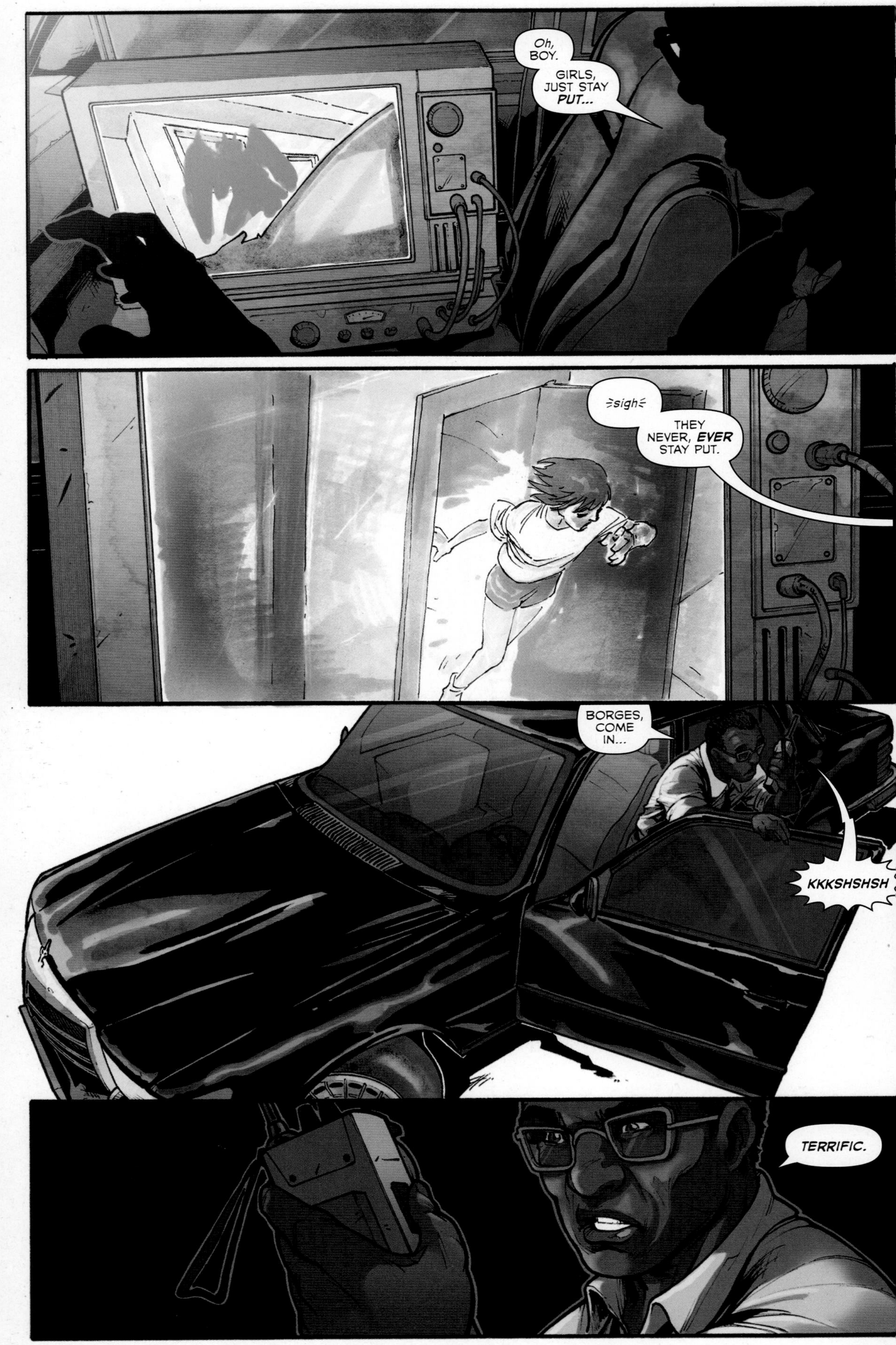
Oh, BOY.
GIRLS, JUST STAY PUT...
≈sigh≈
THEY NEVER, EVER STAY PUT.
BORGES, COME IN...
KKKSHSHSH
TERRIFIC.

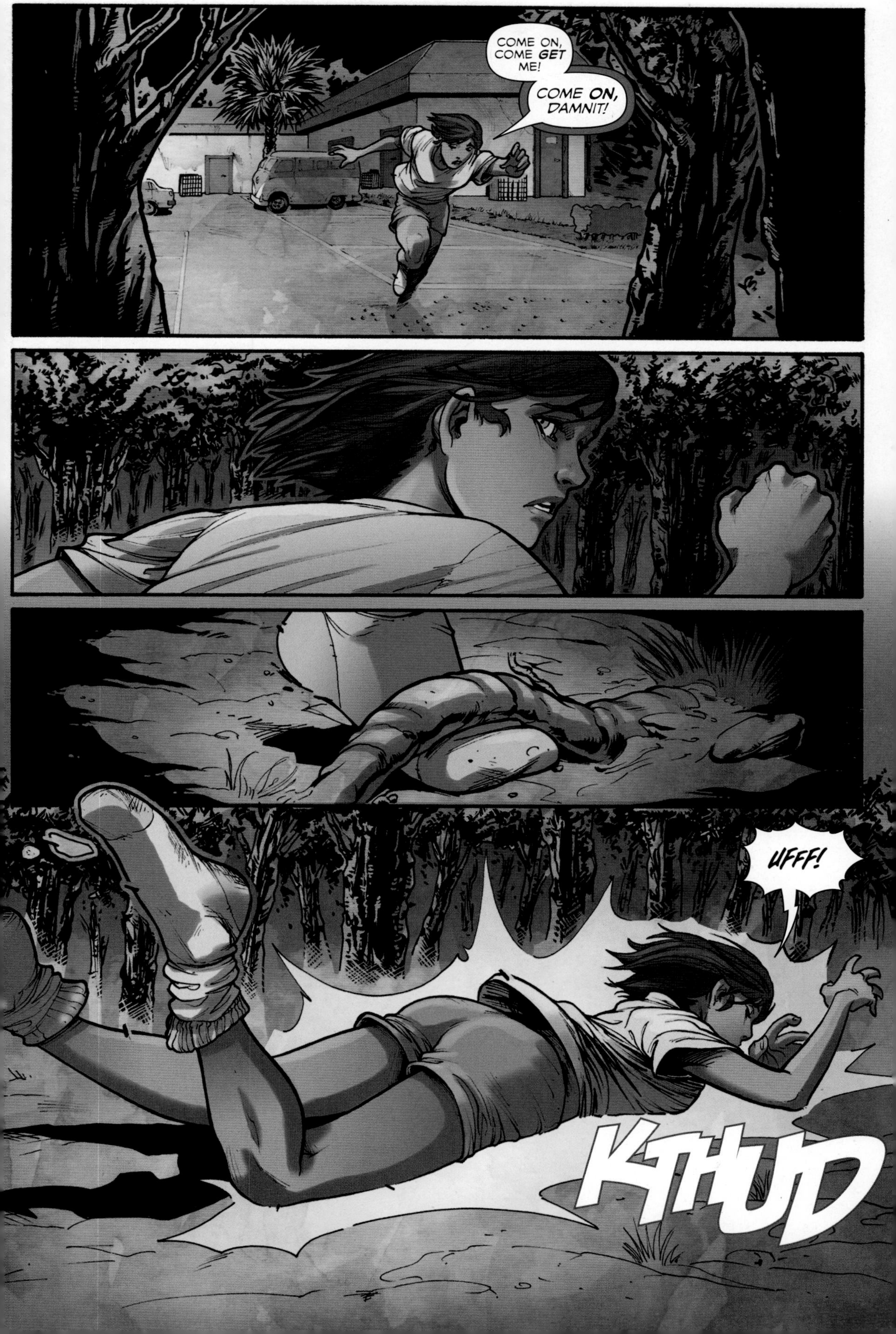
COME ON, COME GET ME!
COME ON, DAMNIT!
UFFF!
KTHUD

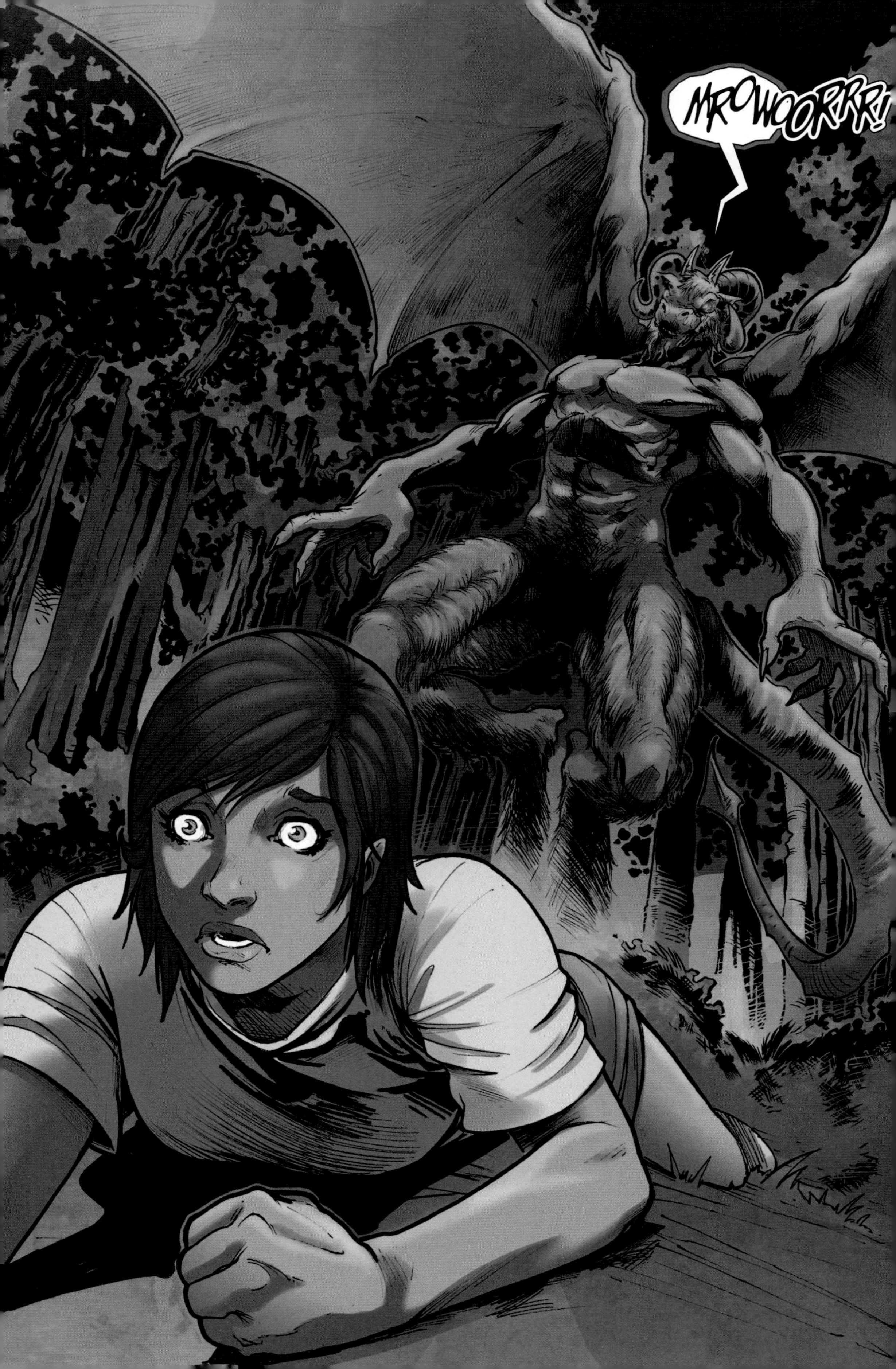
MROWOORRR!

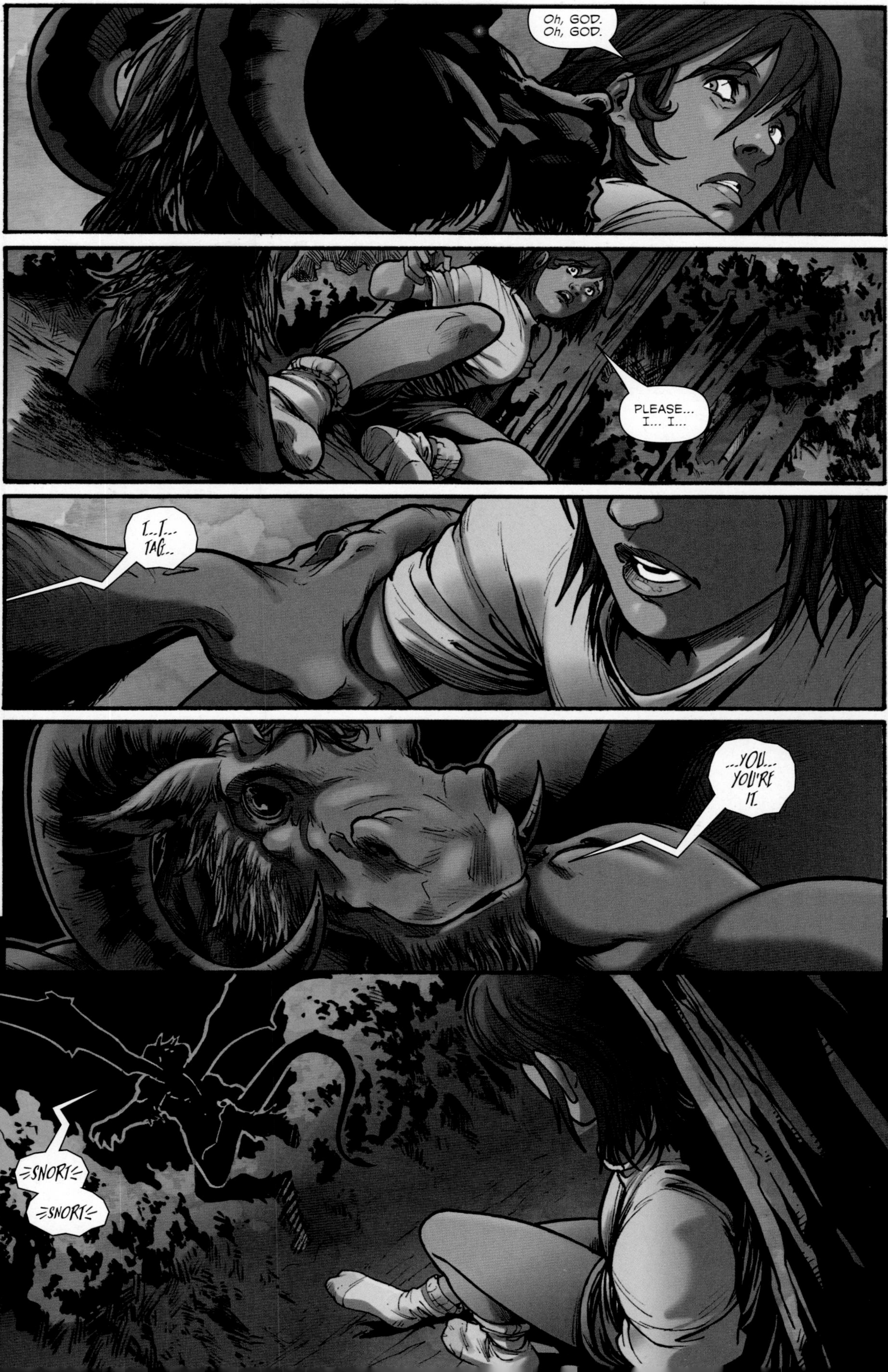
Oh, GOD.
Oh, GOD.
PLEASE...
I... I...
I...I...
TAG...
...YOU...
YOU'RE
IT.
SNORT
SNORT

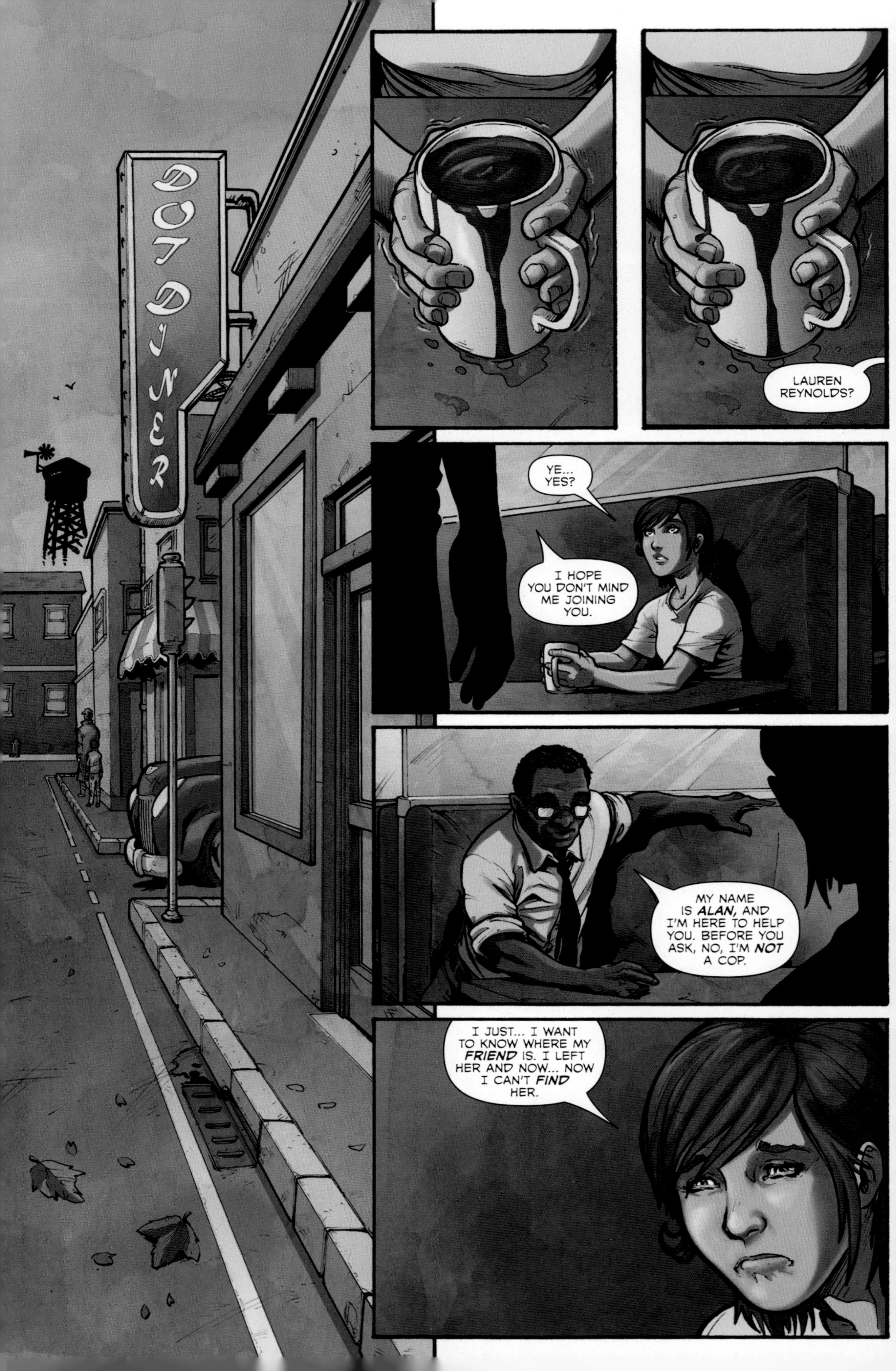
DOT DINER
LAUREN REYNOLDS?
YE... YES?
I HOPE YOU DON'T MIND ME JOINING YOU.
MY NAME IS ALAN, AND I'M HERE TO HELP YOU. BEFORE YOU ASK, NO, I'M NOT A COP.
I JUST... I WANT TO KNOW WHERE MY FRIEND IS. I LEFT HER AND NOW... NOW I CAN'T FIND HER.

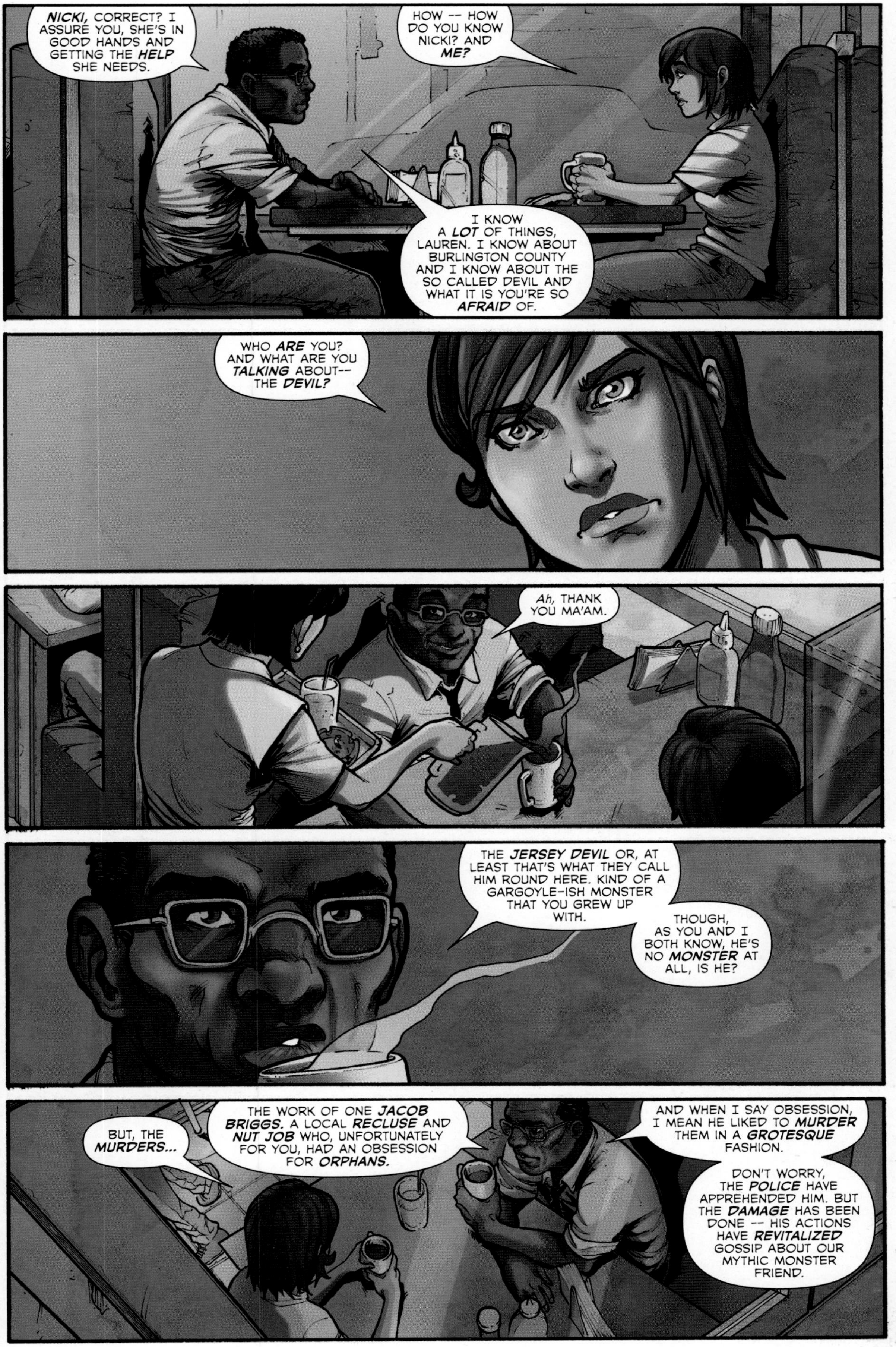
NICKI, CORRECT? I ASSURE YOU, SHE'S IN GOOD HANDS AND GETTING THE HELP SHE NEEDS.
HOW -- HOW DO YOU KNOW NICKI? AND ME?
I KNOW A LOT OF THINGS, LAUREN. I KNOW ABOUT BURLINGTON COUNTY AND I KNOW ABOUT THE SO CALLED DEVIL AND WHAT IT IS YOU'RE SO AFRAID OF.
WHO ARE YOU? AND WHAT ARE YOU TALKING ABOUT-- THE DEVIL?
Ah, THANK YOU MA'AM.
THE JERSEY DEVIL OR, AT LEAST THAT'S WHAT THEY CALL HIM ROUND HERE. KIND OF A GARGOYLE-ISH MONSTER THAT YOU GREW UP WITH.
THOUGH, AS YOU AND I BOTH KNOW, HE'S NO MONSTER AT ALL, IS HE?
BUT, THE MURDERS...
THE WORK OF ONE JACOB BRIGGS. A LOCAL RECLUSE AND NUT JOB WHO, UNFORTUNATELY FOR YOU, HAD AN OBSESSION FOR ORPHANS.
AND WHEN I SAY OBSESSION, I MEAN HE LIKED TO MURDER THEM IN A GROTESQUE FASHION.
DON'T WORRY, THE POLICE HAVE APPREHENDED HIM. BUT THE DAMAGE HAS BEEN DONE -- HIS ACTIONS HAVE REVITALIZED GOSSIP ABOUT OUR MYTHIC MONSTER FRIEND.

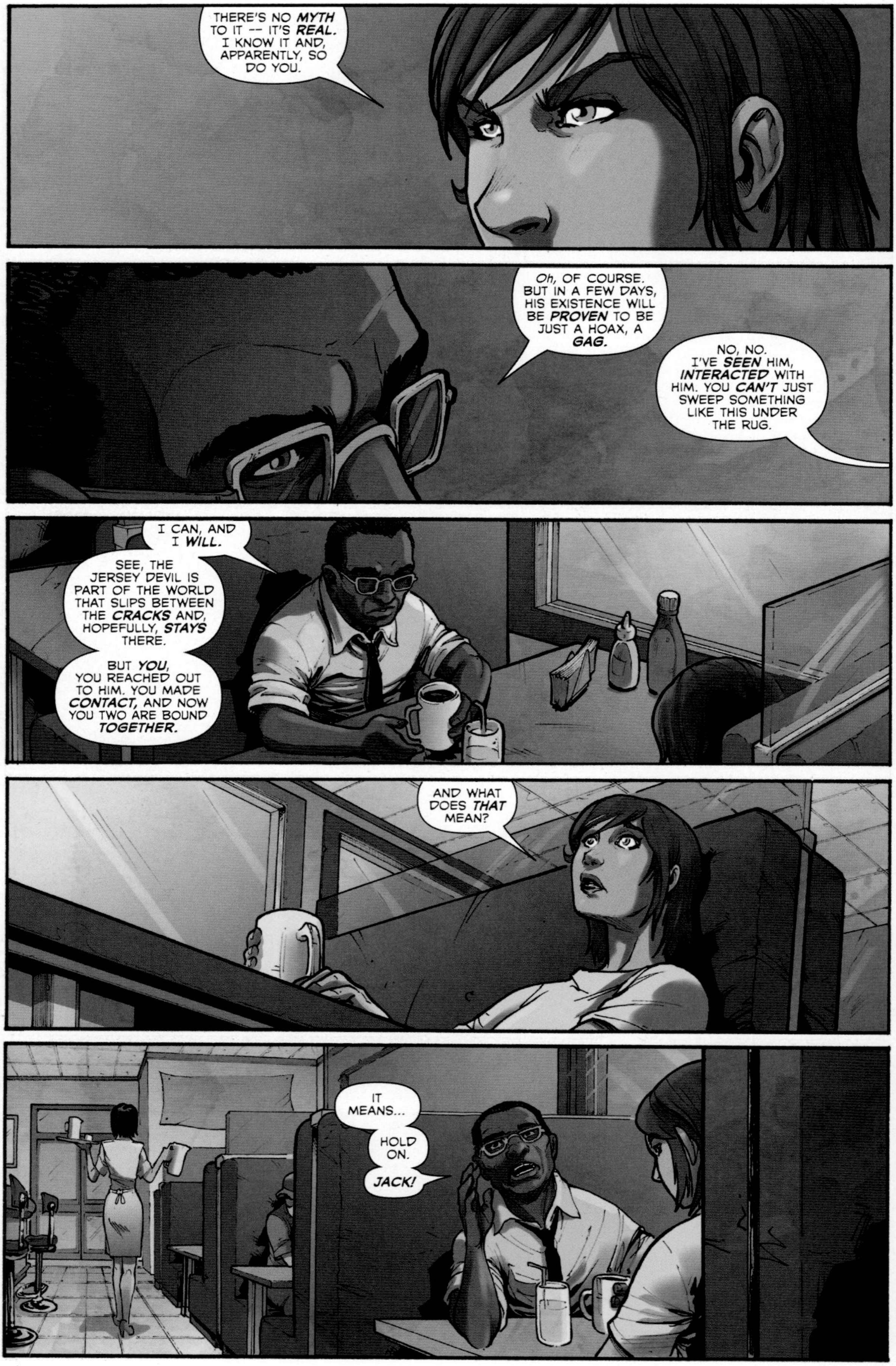
THERE'S NO MYTH TO IT -- IT'S REAL. I KNOW IT AND, APPARENTLY, SO DO YOU.
Oh, OF COURSE. BUT IN A FEW DAYS, HIS EXISTENCE WILL BE PROVEN TO BE JUST A HOAX, A GAG.
NO, NO. I'VE SEEN HIM, INTERACTED WITH HIM. YOU CAN'T JUST SWEEP SOMETHING LIKE THIS UNDER THE RUG.
I CAN, AND I WILL.
SEE, THE JERSEY DEVIL IS PART OF THE WORLD THAT SLIPS BETWEEN THE CRACKS AND, HOPEFULLY, STAYS THERE.
BUT YOU, YOU REACHED OUT TO HIM. YOU MADE CONTACT, AND NOW YOU TWO ARE BOUND TOGETHER.
AND WHAT DOES THAT MEAN?
IT MEANS...
HOLD ON.
JACK!

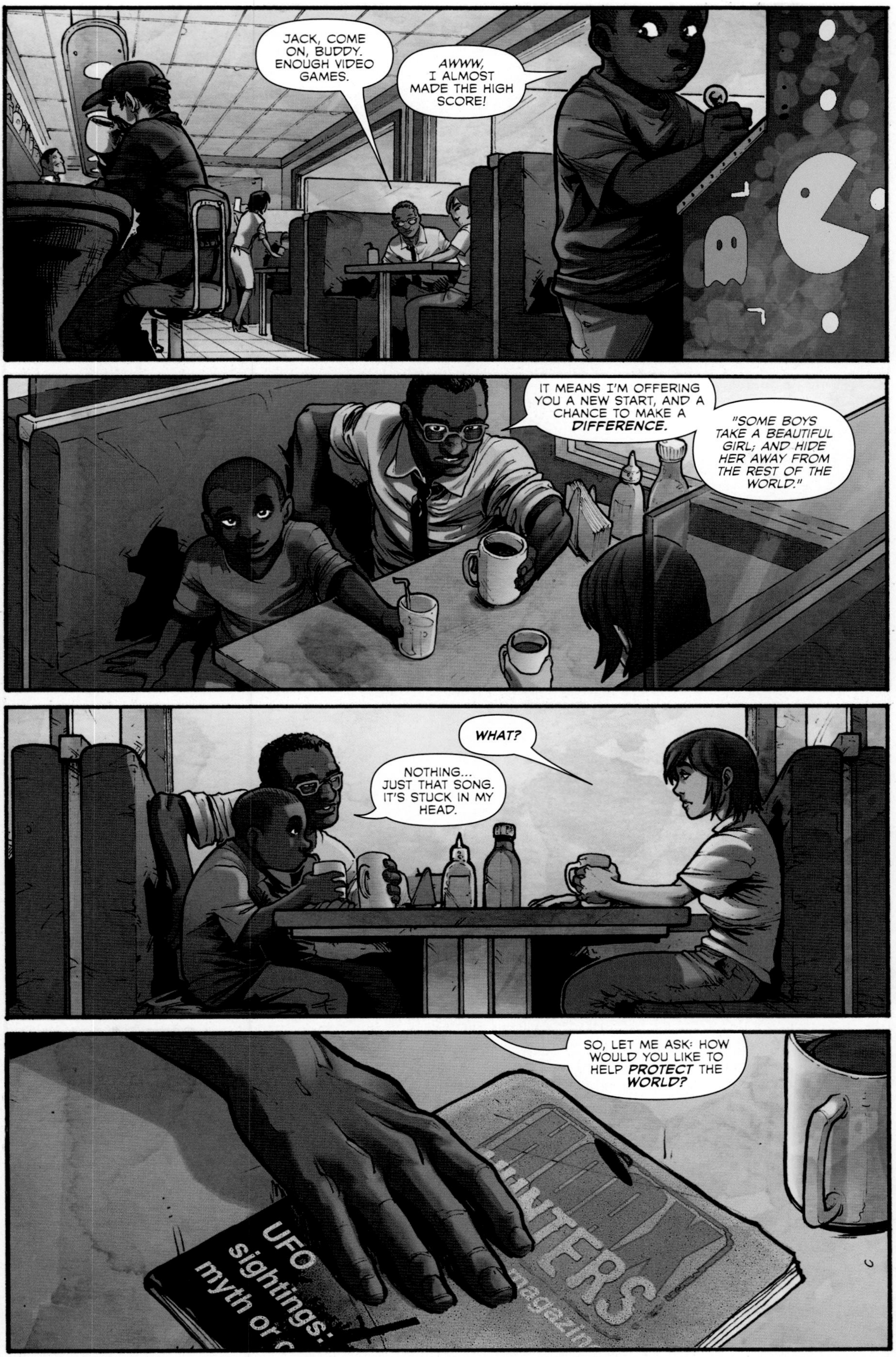
JACK, COME ON, BUDDY. ENOUGH VIDEO GAMES.
AWWW, I ALMOST MADE THE HIGH SCORE!
IT MEANS I'M OFFERING YOU A NEW START, AND A CHANCE TO MAKE A DIFFERENCE.
"SOME BOYS TAKE A BEAUTIFUL GIRL; AND HIDE HER AWAY FROM THE REST OF THE WORLD."
WHAT?
NOTHING... JUST THAT SONG. IT'S STUCK IN MY HEAD.
SO, LET ME ASK: HOW WOULD YOU LIKE TO HELP PROTECT THE WORLD?
UFO sightings: myth or
NTERS
magazin

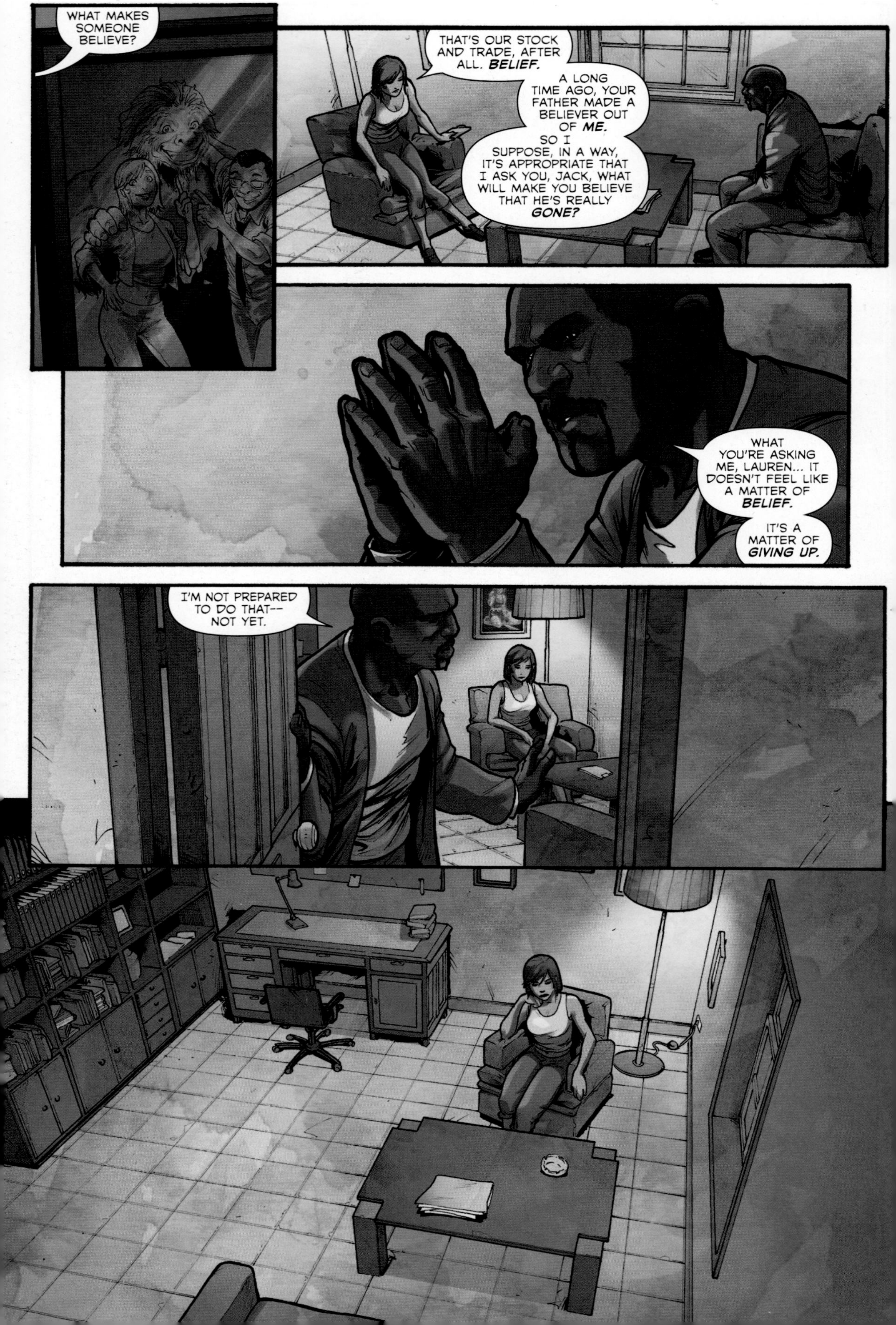
WHAT MAKES SOMEONE BELIEVE?
THAT'S OUR STOCK AND TRADE, AFTER ALL. BELIEF.
A LONG TIME AGO, YOUR FATHER MADE A BELIEVER OUT OF ME.
SO I SUPPOSE, IN A WAY, IT'S APPROPRIATE THAT I ASK YOU, JACK, WHAT WILL MAKE YOU BELIEVE THAT HE'S REALLY GONE?
WHAT YOU'RE ASKING ME, LAUREN... IT DOESN'T FEEL LIKE A MATTER OF BELIEF.
IT'S A MATTER OF GIVING UP.
I'M NOT PREPARED TO DO THAT-- NOT YET.

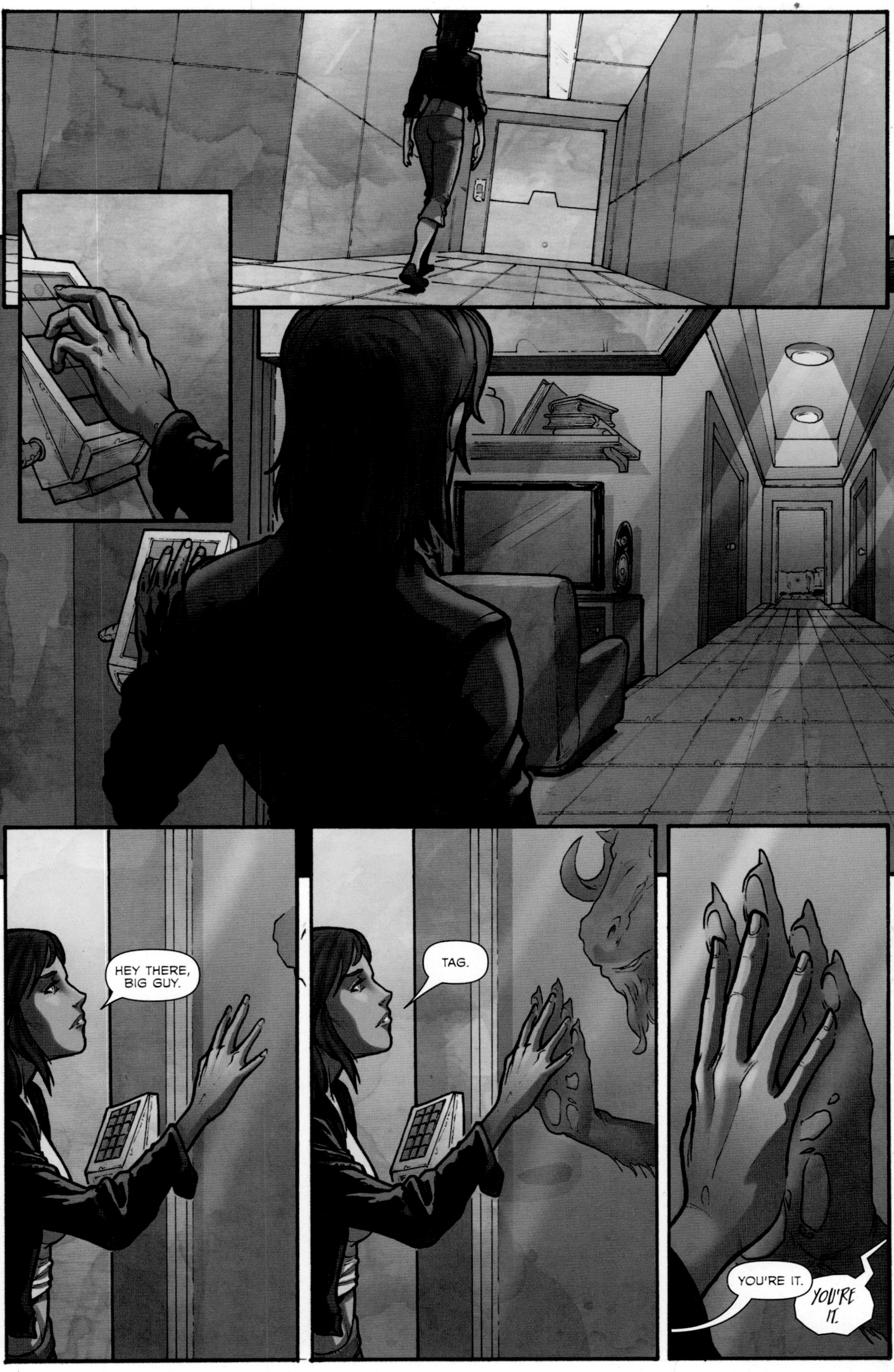
HEY THERE, BIG GUY.
TAG.
YOU'RE IT.
YOU'RE IT.

HOAX HUNTERS

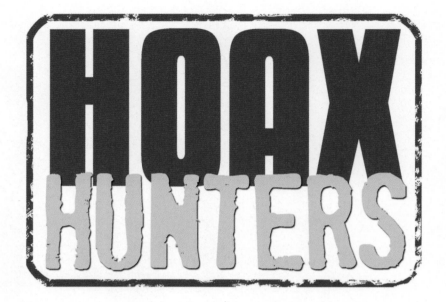

COVER GALLERY

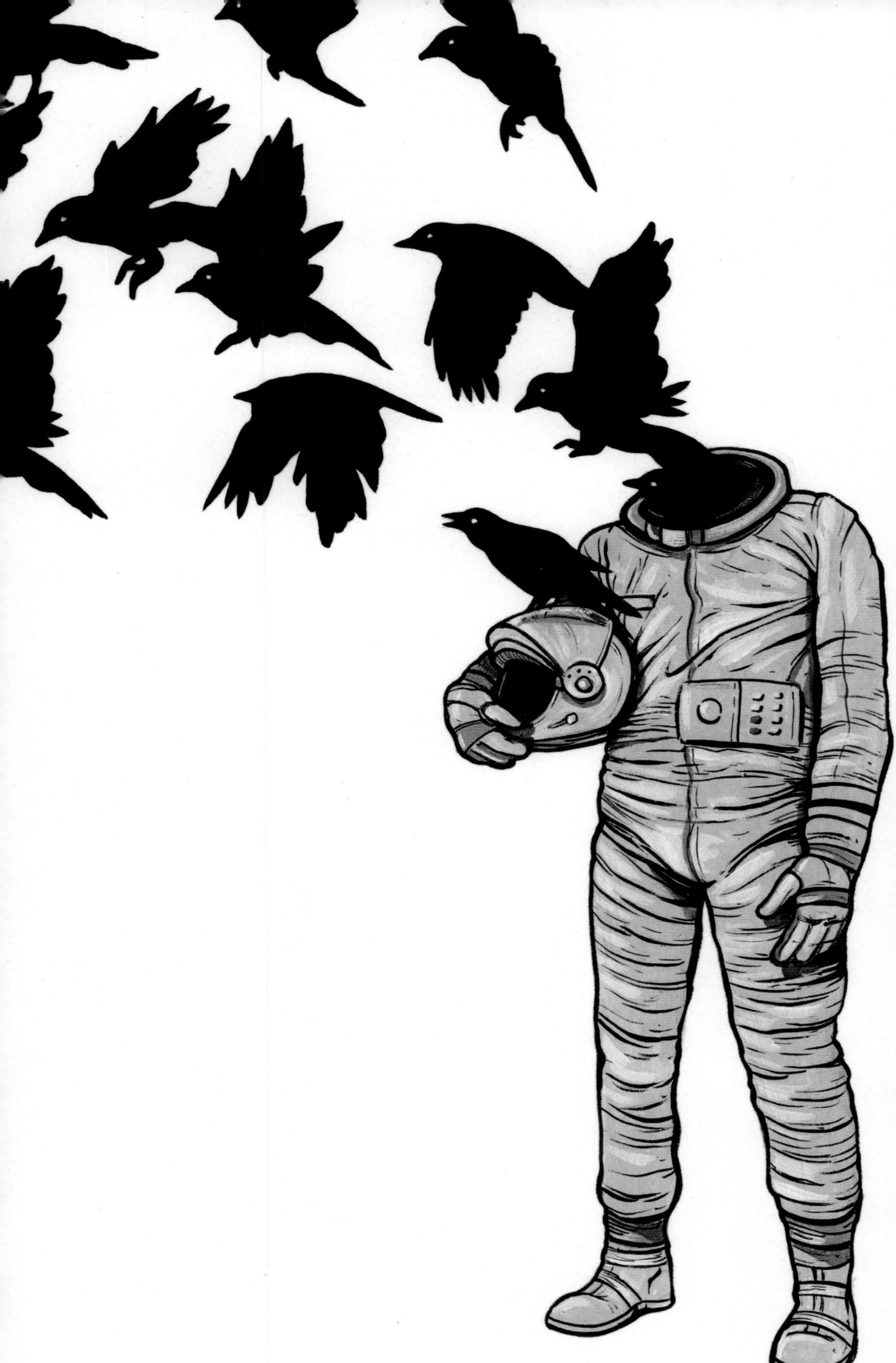

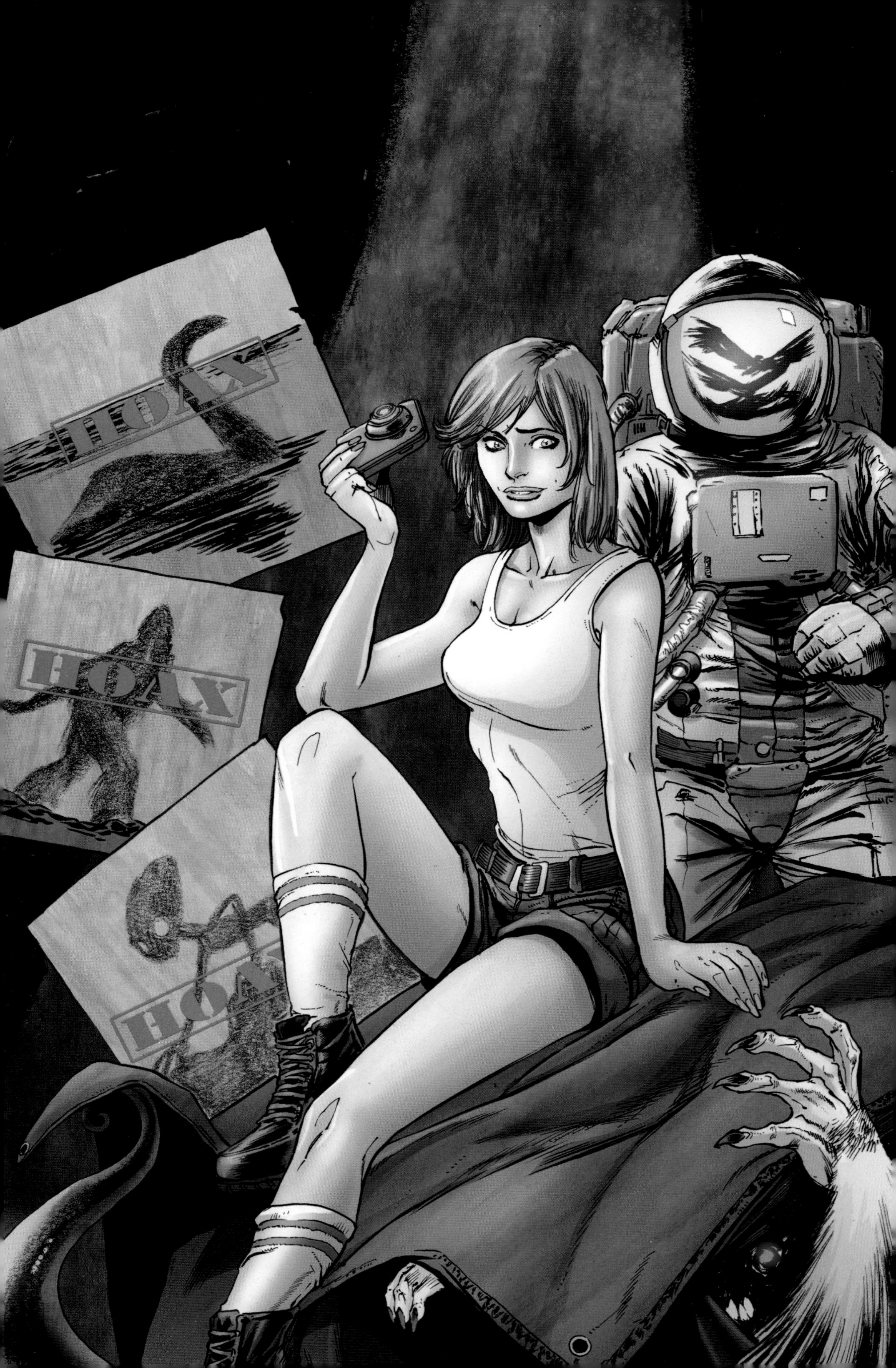
HOAX
HOAX

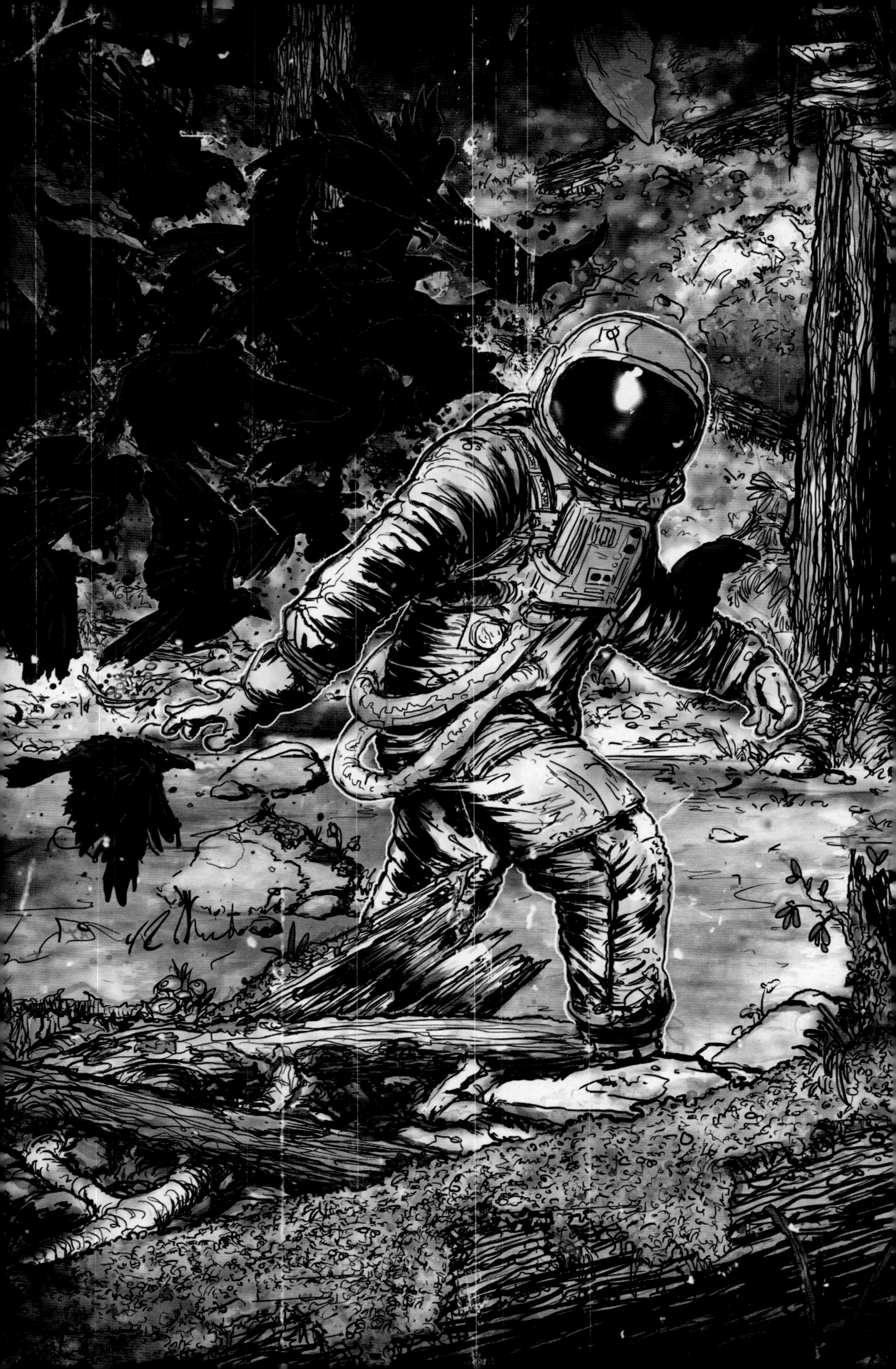

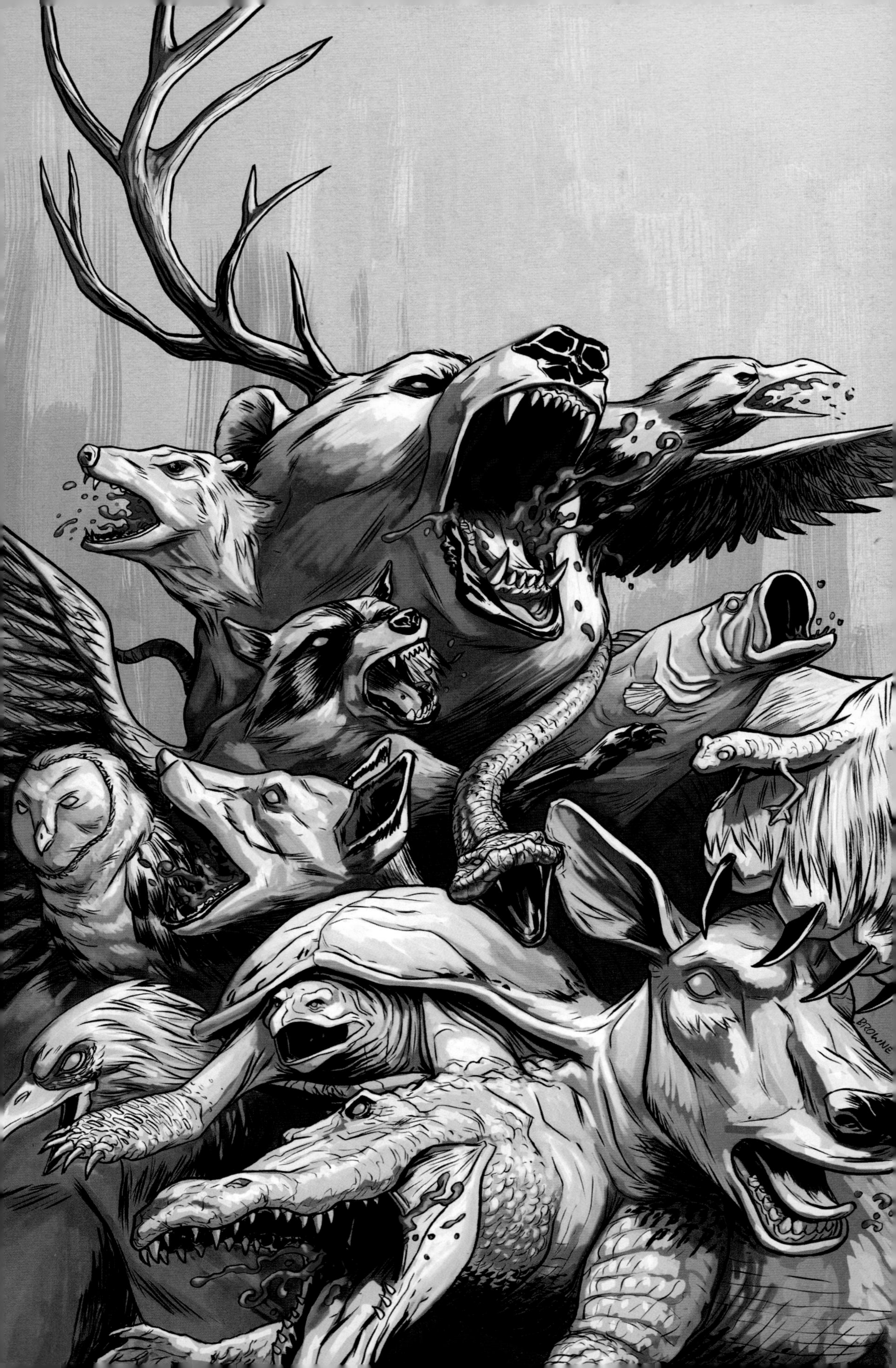
BROWNE

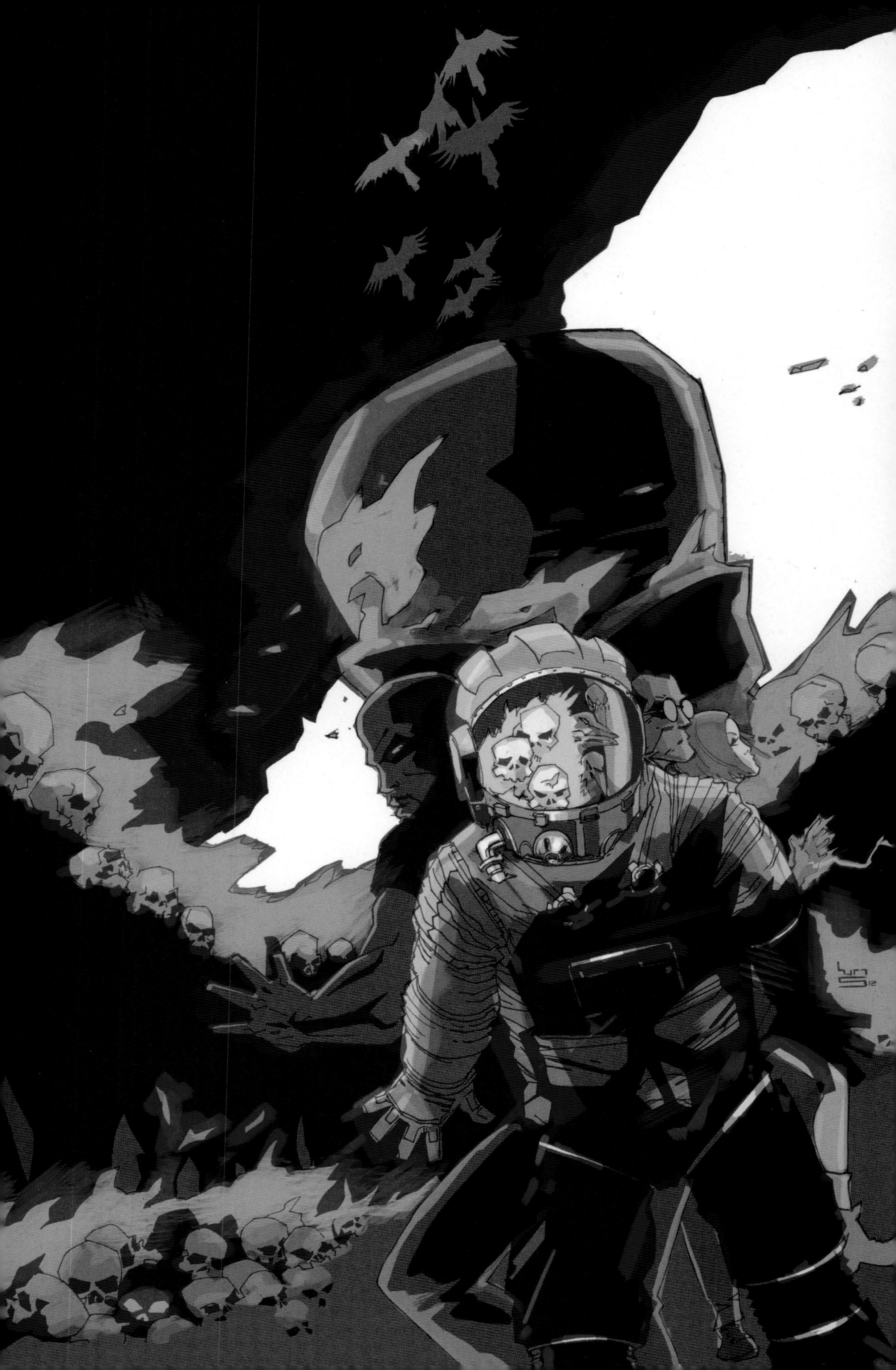

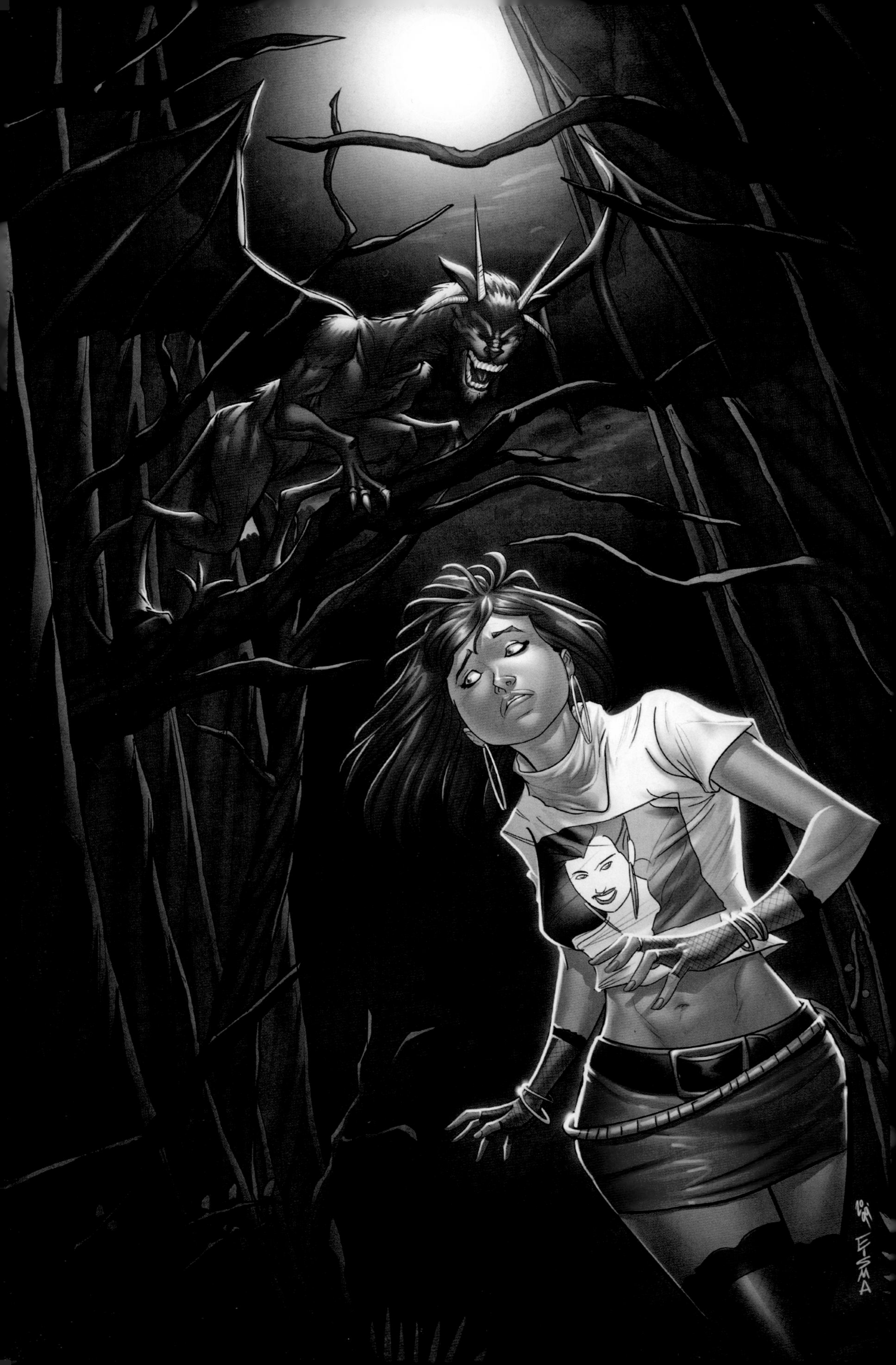

Here's the very first Murder design (circa 2004).
He was originally a giant robotic Kaiju filled with and
controlled by crows. (Those circles were glass
bubbles so the crows could see what they were doing.)
It was for an abandoned comic project about a
Japanese type superhero who worked at a fast food
restaurant and battled ridiculous Kaiju.

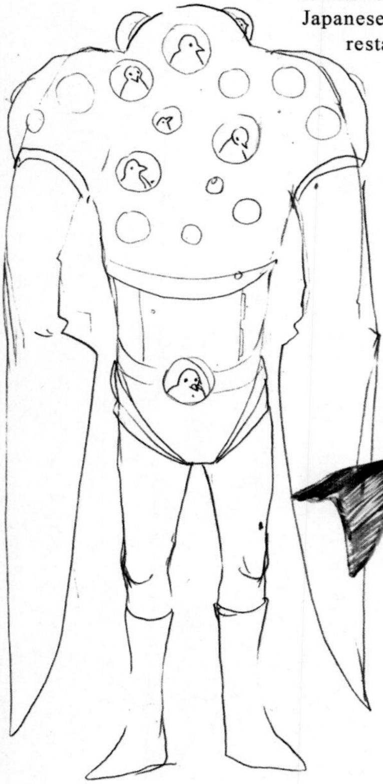

Note the poor crow
who had to control the groin.

In 2009 or so, Murder took the astronaut form
you see in Hoax Hunters. These early designs were
from (yet another) abandoned comic. This one was
to be a noir type crime/mystery that took place
in the 50s, simply called "Murder".

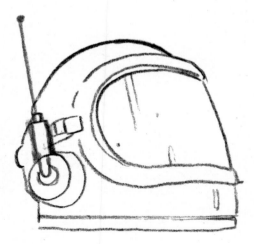

The original Murder (in astronaut suit) had
a skull floating in the head, but the skull idea was
dropped because it gave too much humanity
to the character.

Earlier designs had a more sci-fi feel as well, like
the helmet to the left.

- Steve.

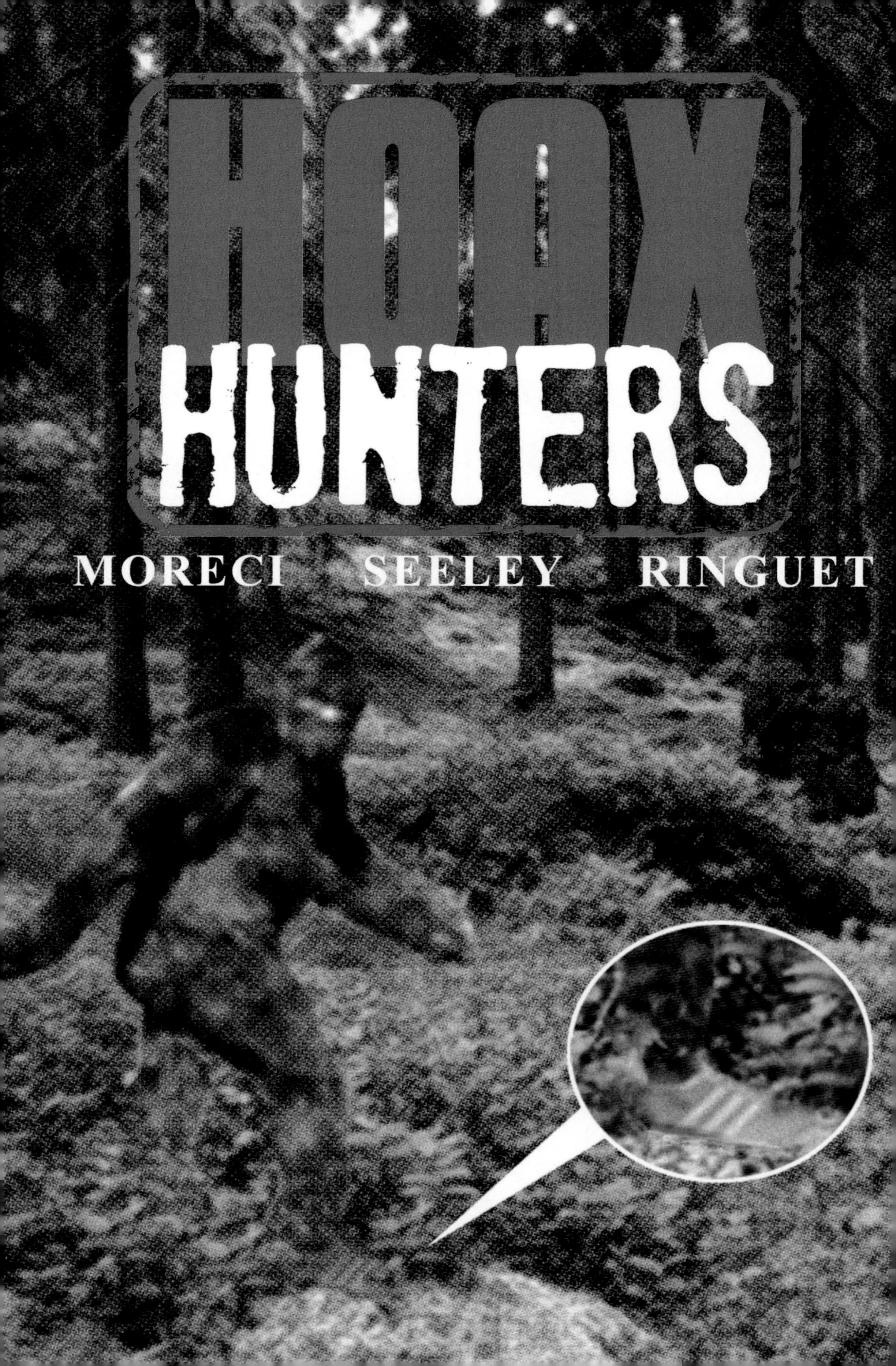
HOAX
HUNTERS
MORECI SEELEY RINGUET

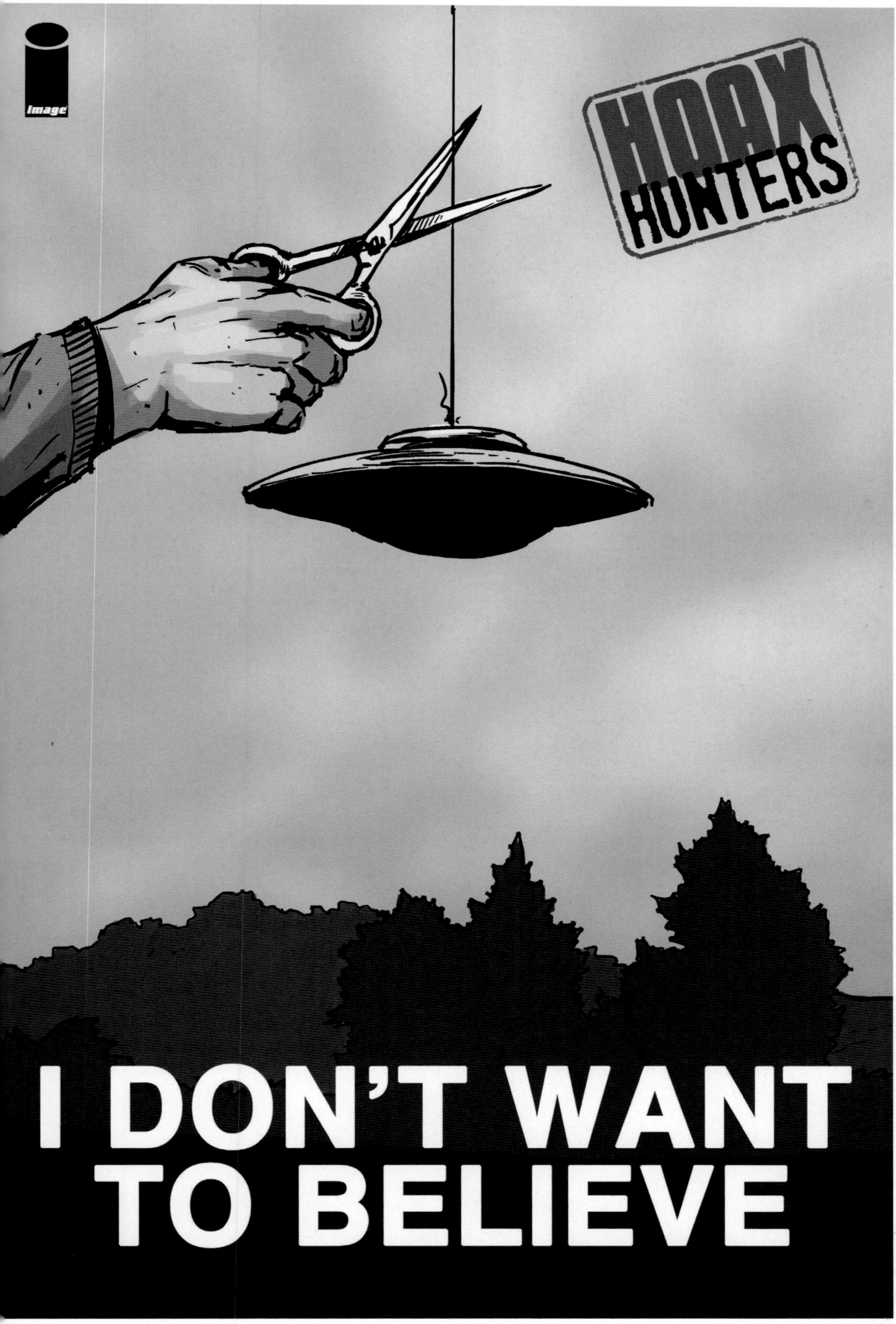
Image
HOAX HUNTERS
I DON'T WANT
TO BELIEVE

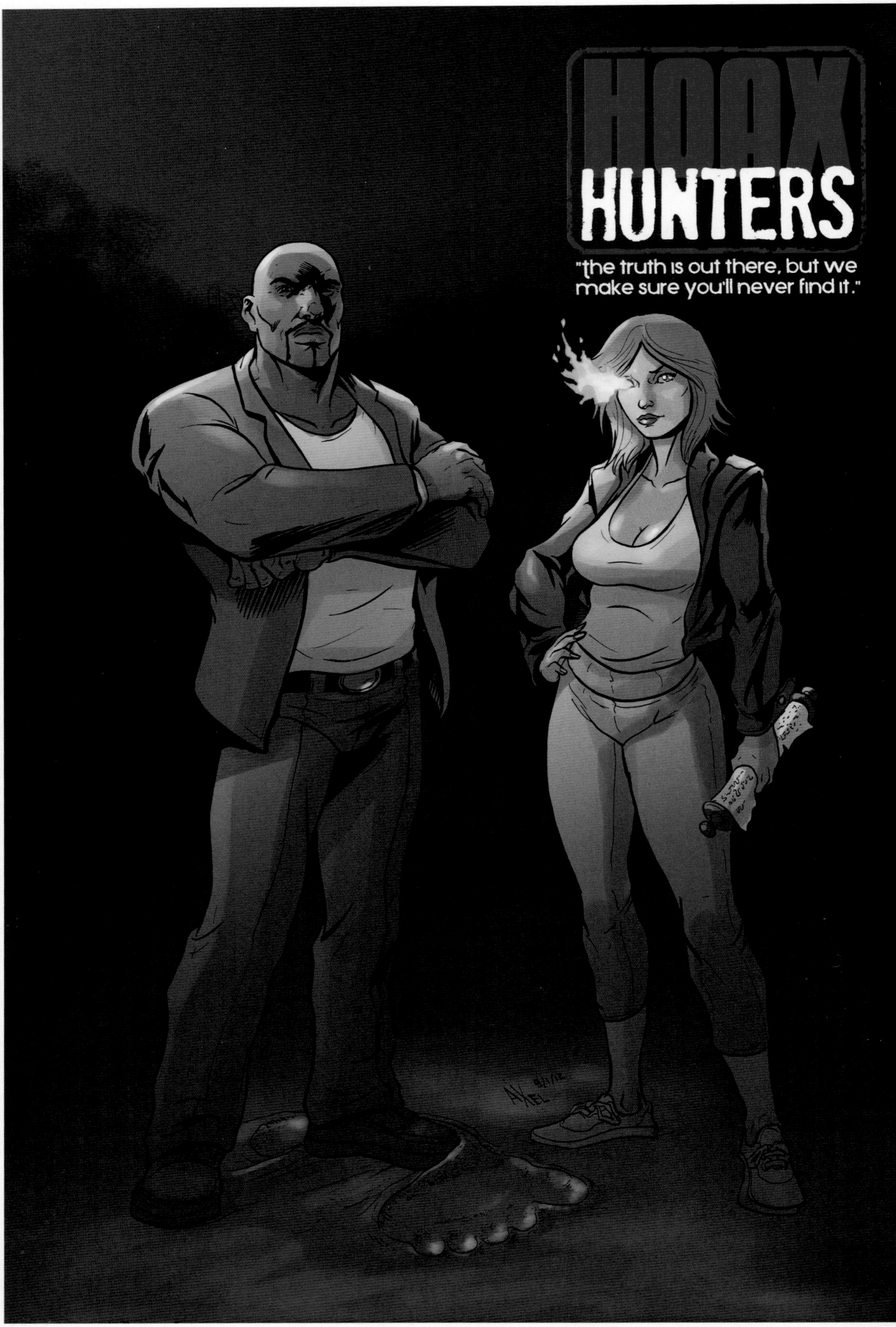
HOAX
HUNTERS
"the truth is out there, but we
make sure you'll never find it."

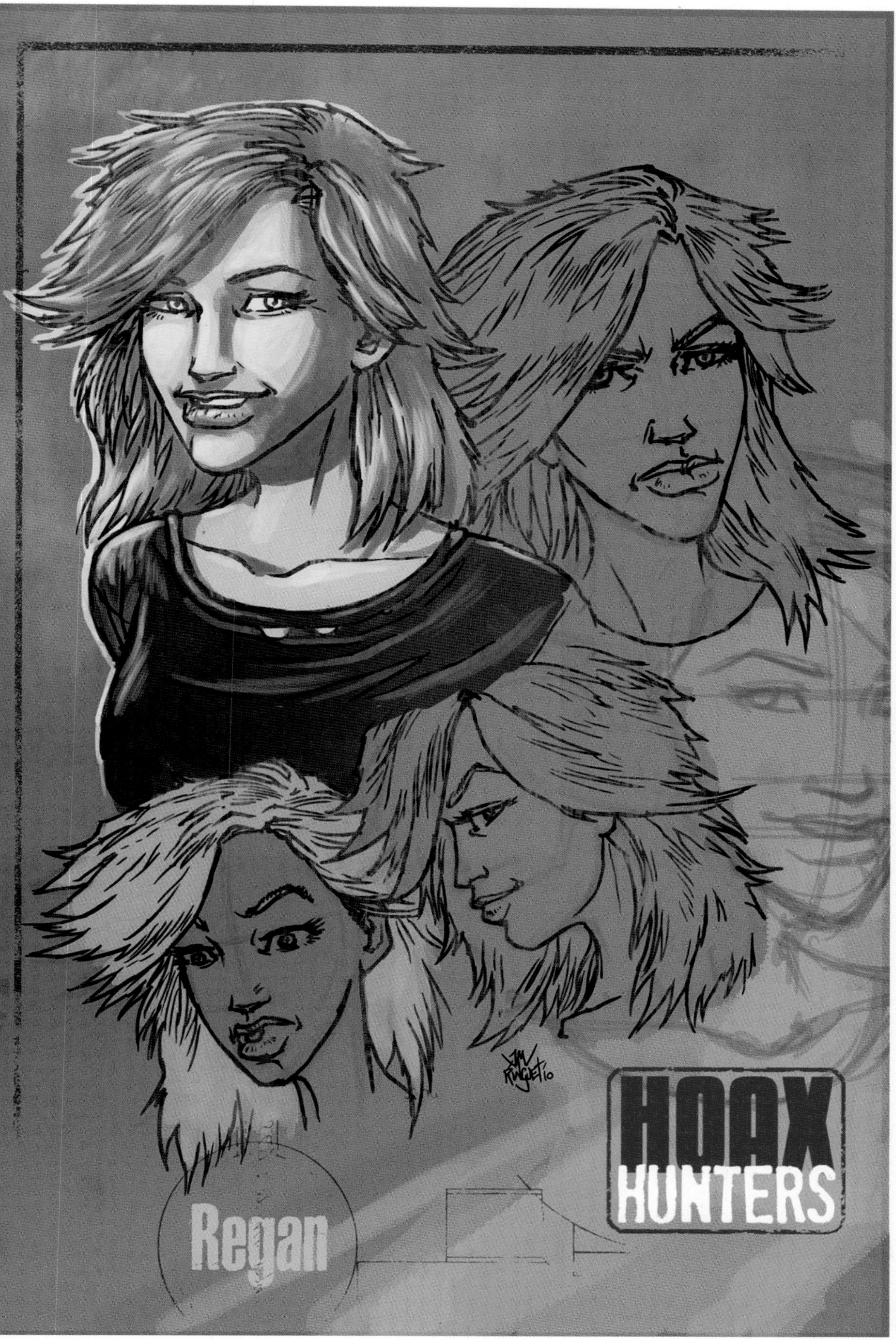

HOAX
HUNTERS
Regan

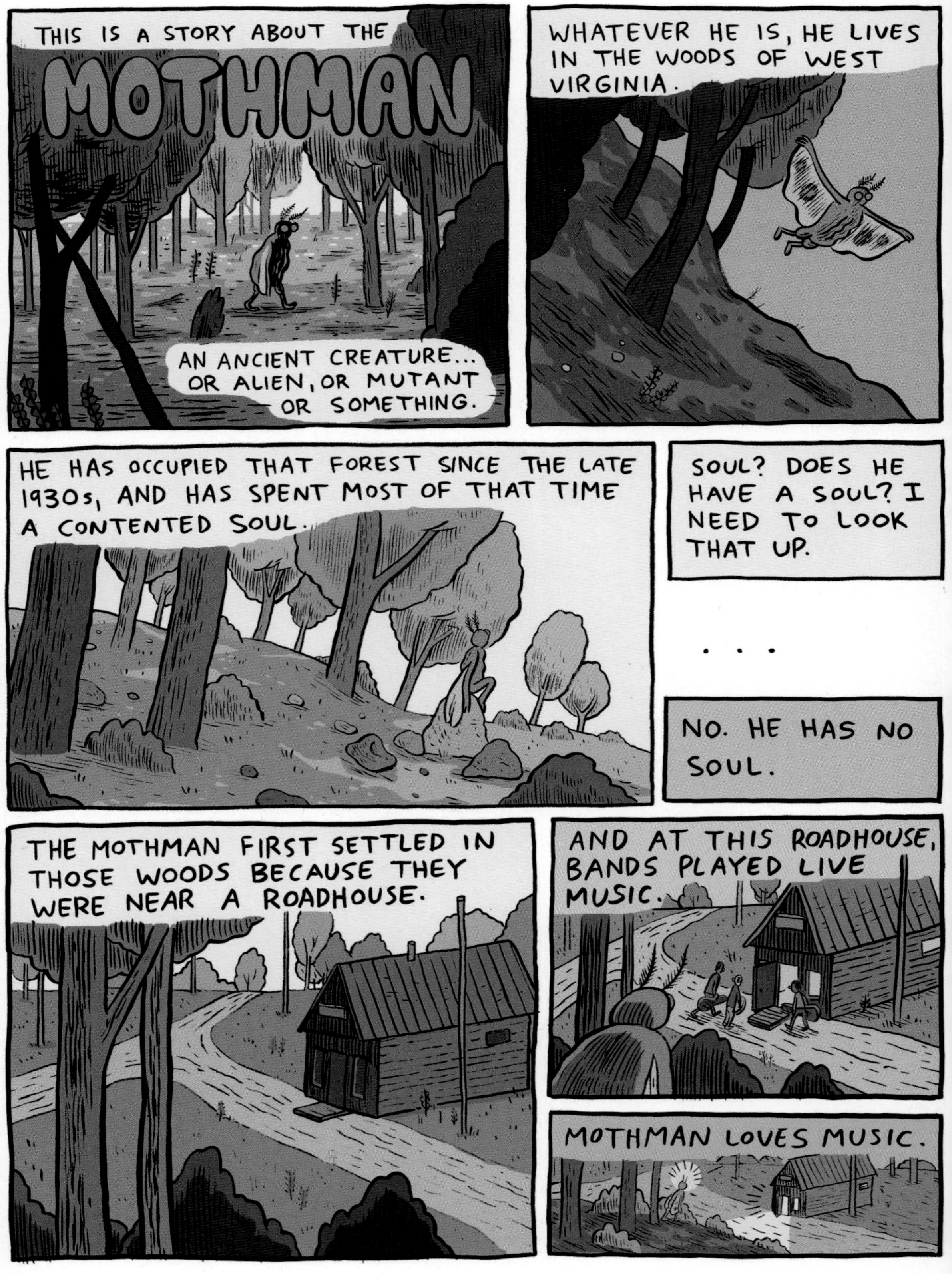
THIS IS A STORY ABOUT THE
MOTHMAN
AN ANCIENT CREATURE... OR ALIEN, OR MUTANT OR SOMETHING.
WHATEVER HE IS, HE LIVES IN THE WOODS OF WEST VIRGINIA.
HE HAS OCCUPIED THAT FOREST SINCE THE LATE 1930s, AND HAS SPENT MOST OF THAT TIME A CONTENTED SOUL.
SOUL? DOES HE HAVE A SOUL? I NEED TO LOOK THAT UP.
. . .
NO. HE HAS NO SOUL.
THE MOTHMAN FIRST SETTLED IN THOSE WOODS BECAUSE THEY WERE NEAR A ROADHOUSE.
AND AT THIS ROADHOUSE, BANDS PLAYED LIVE MUSIC.
MOTHMAN LOVES MUSIC.

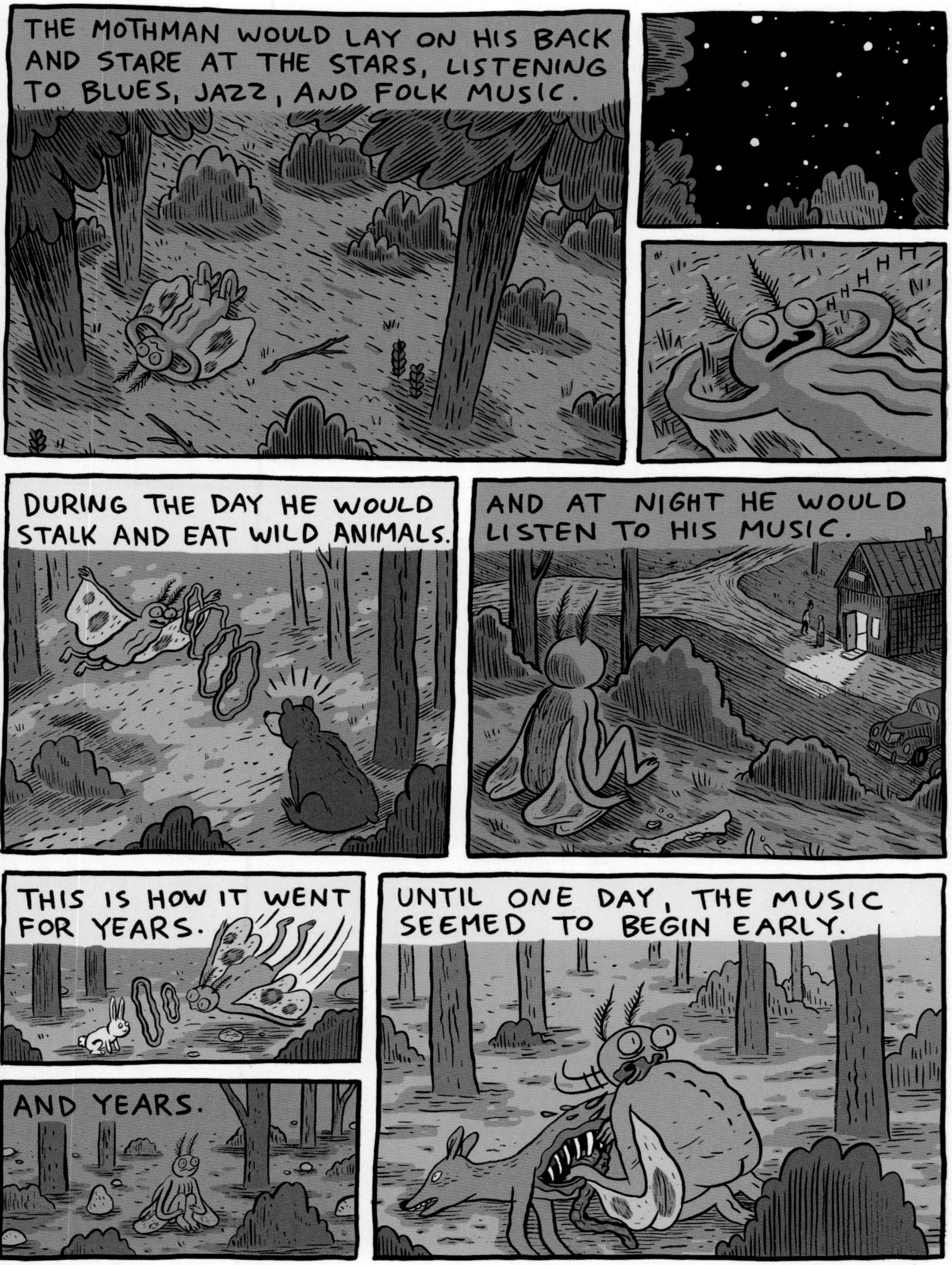
THE MOTHMAN WOULD LAY ON HIS BACK AND STARE AT THE STARS, LISTENING TO BLUES, JAZZ, AND FOLK MUSIC.
HHHHHH
DURING THE DAY HE WOULD STALK AND EAT WILD ANIMALS.
AND AT NIGHT HE WOULD LISTEN TO HIS MUSIC.
THIS IS HOW IT WENT FOR YEARS.
AND YEARS.
UNTIL ONE DAY, THE MUSIC SEEMED TO BEGIN EARLY.

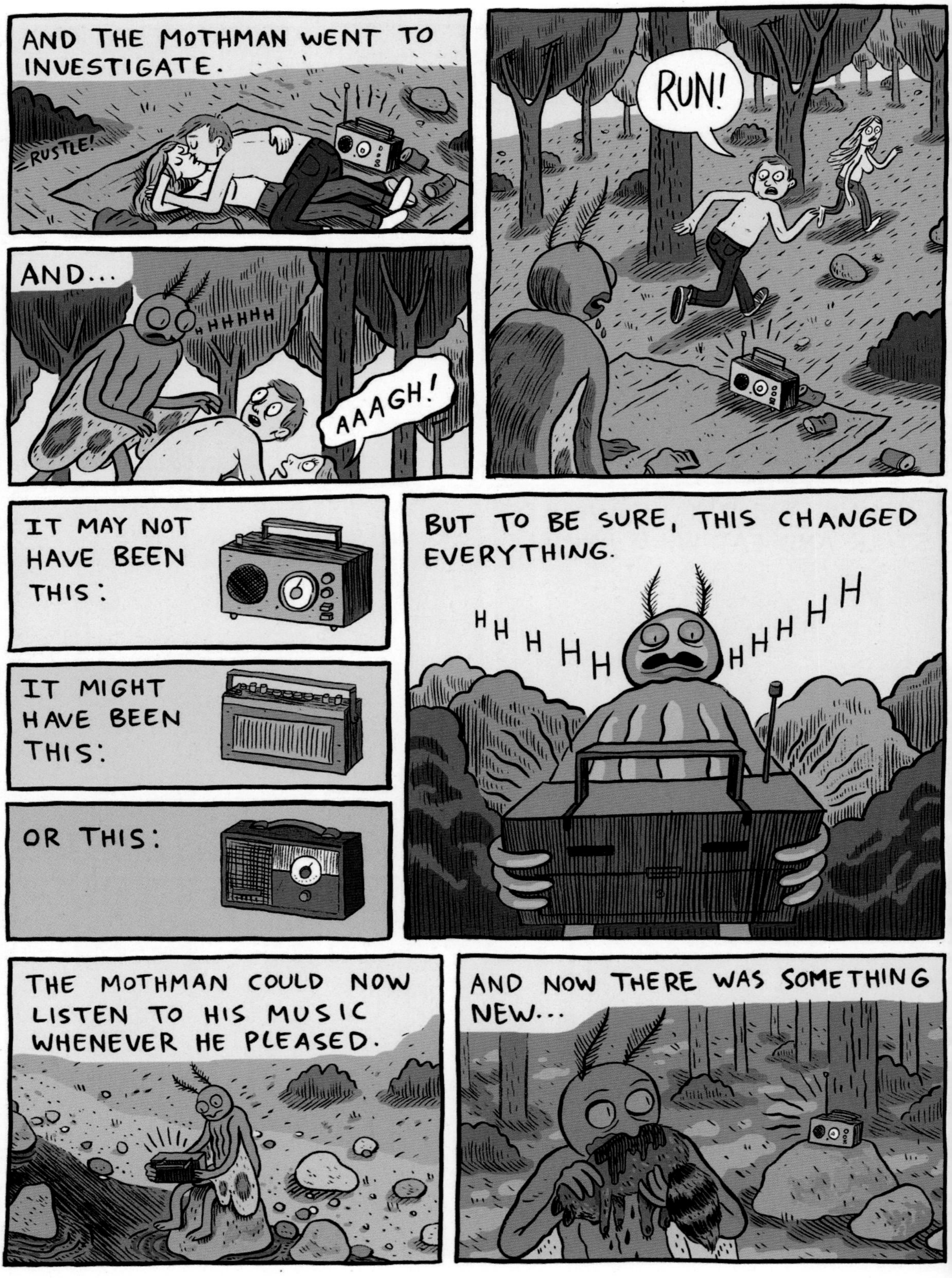
AND THE MOTHMAN WENT TO INVESTIGATE.
RUSTLE!
AND...
HHHHHH
AAAGH!
RUN!
IT MAY NOT HAVE BEEN THIS:
IT MIGHT HAVE BEEN THIS:
OR THIS:
BUT TO BE SURE, THIS CHANGED EVERYTHING.
HHHHHHHHHHHH
THE MOTHMAN COULD NOW LISTEN TO HIS MUSIC WHENEVER HE PLEASED.
AND NOW THERE WAS SOMETHING NEW...

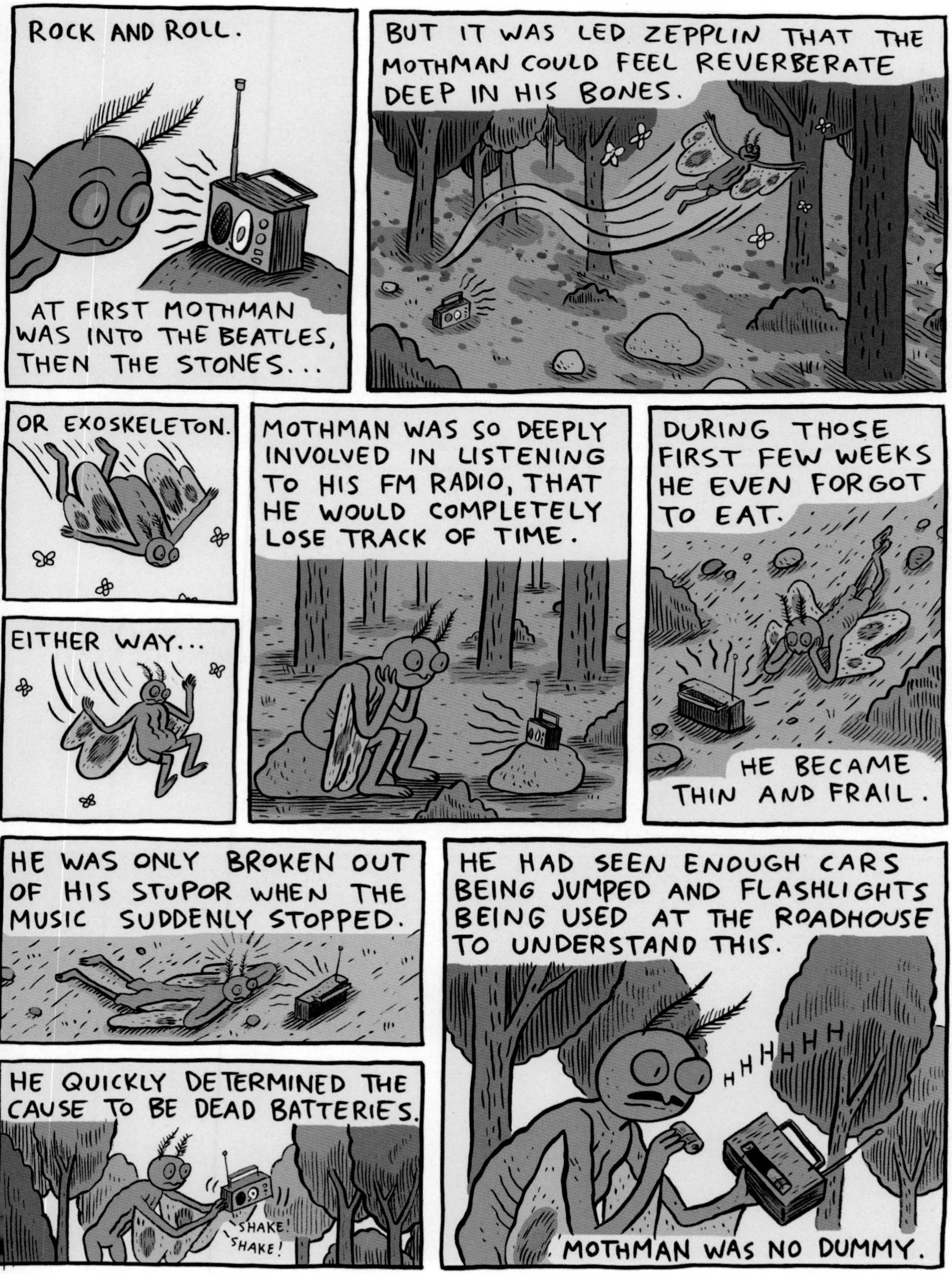
ROCK AND ROLL.
AT FIRST MOTHMAN WAS INTO THE BEATLES, THEN THE STONES...
BUT IT WAS LED ZEPPLIN THAT THE MOTHMAN COULD FEEL REVERBERATE DEEP IN HIS BONES.
OR EXOSKELETON.
EITHER WAY...
MOTHMAN WAS SO DEEPLY INVOLVED IN LISTENING TO HIS FM RADIO, THAT HE WOULD COMPLETELY LOSE TRACK OF TIME.
DURING THOSE FIRST FEW WEEKS HE EVEN FORGOT TO EAT.
HE BECAME THIN AND FRAIL.
HE WAS ONLY BROKEN OUT OF HIS STUPOR WHEN THE MUSIC SUDDENLY STOPPED.
HE QUICKLY DETERMINED THE CAUSE TO BE DEAD BATTERIES.
SHAKE!
SHAKE!
HE HAD SEEN ENOUGH CARS BEING JUMPED AND FLASHLIGHTS BEING USED AT THE ROADHOUSE TO UNDERSTAND THIS.
HHHHHHH
MOTHMAN WAS NO DUMMY.

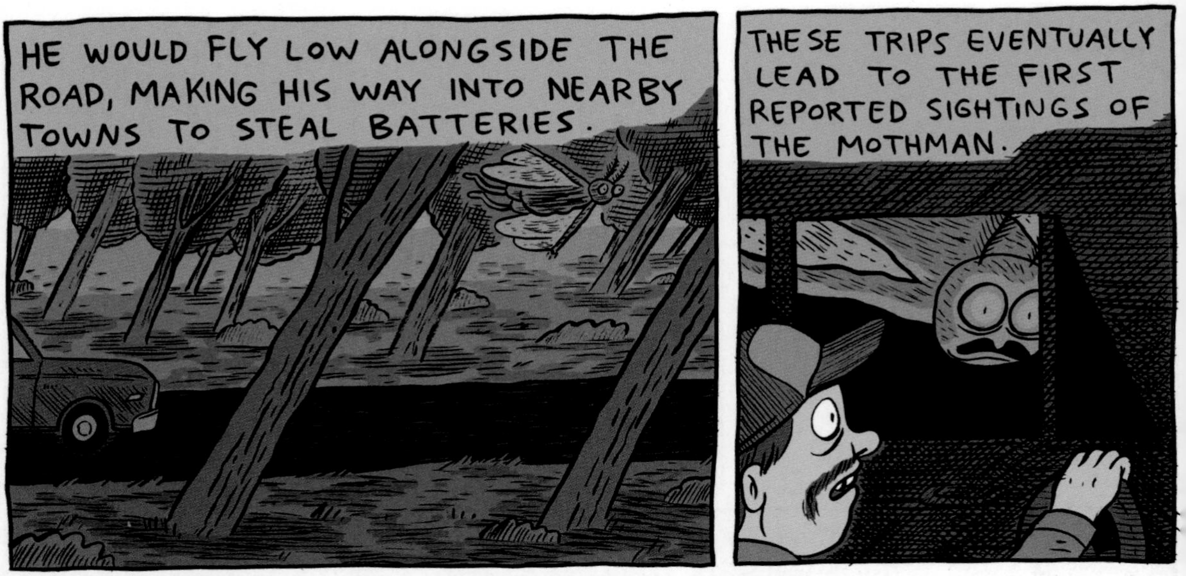
HE WOULD FLY LOW ALONGSIDE THE ROAD, MAKING HIS WAY INTO NEARBY TOWNS TO STEAL BATTERIES.
THESE TRIPS EVENTUALLY LEAD TO THE FIRST REPORTED SIGHTINGS OF THE MOTHMAN.

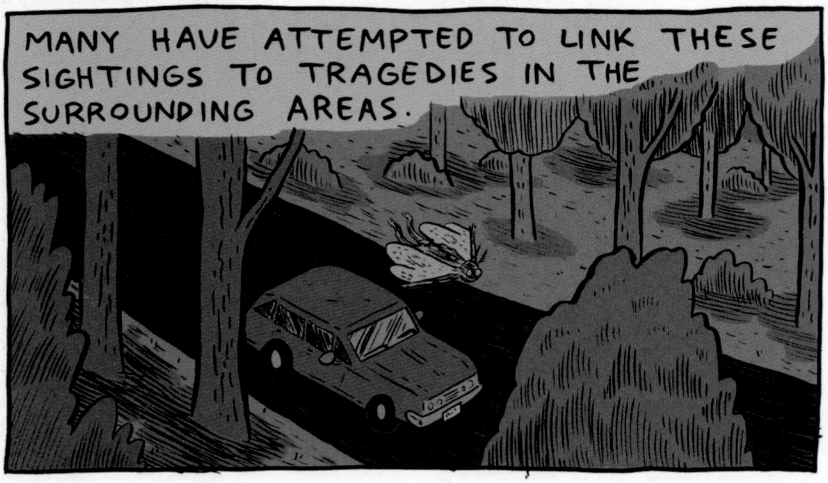
MANY HAVE ATTEMPTED TO LINK THESE SIGHTINGS TO TRAGEDIES IN THE SURROUNDING AREAS.

THESE ARE COINCIDENCES.

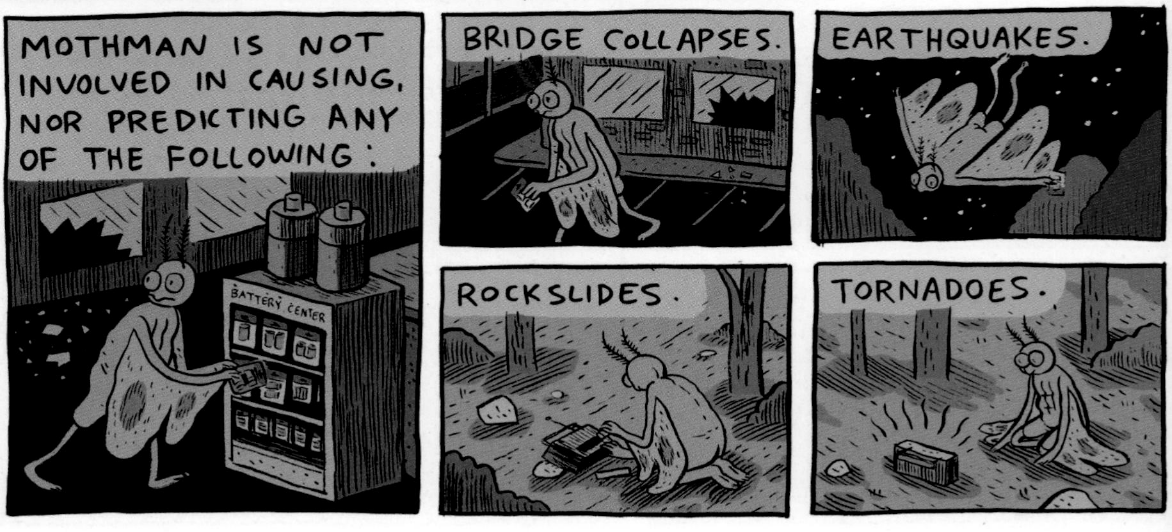
MOTHMAN IS NOT INVOLVED IN CAUSING, NOR PREDICTING ANY OF THE FOLLOWING:
BATTERY CENTER
BRIDGE COLLAPSES.
EARTHQUAKES.
ROCKSLIDES.
TORNADOES.

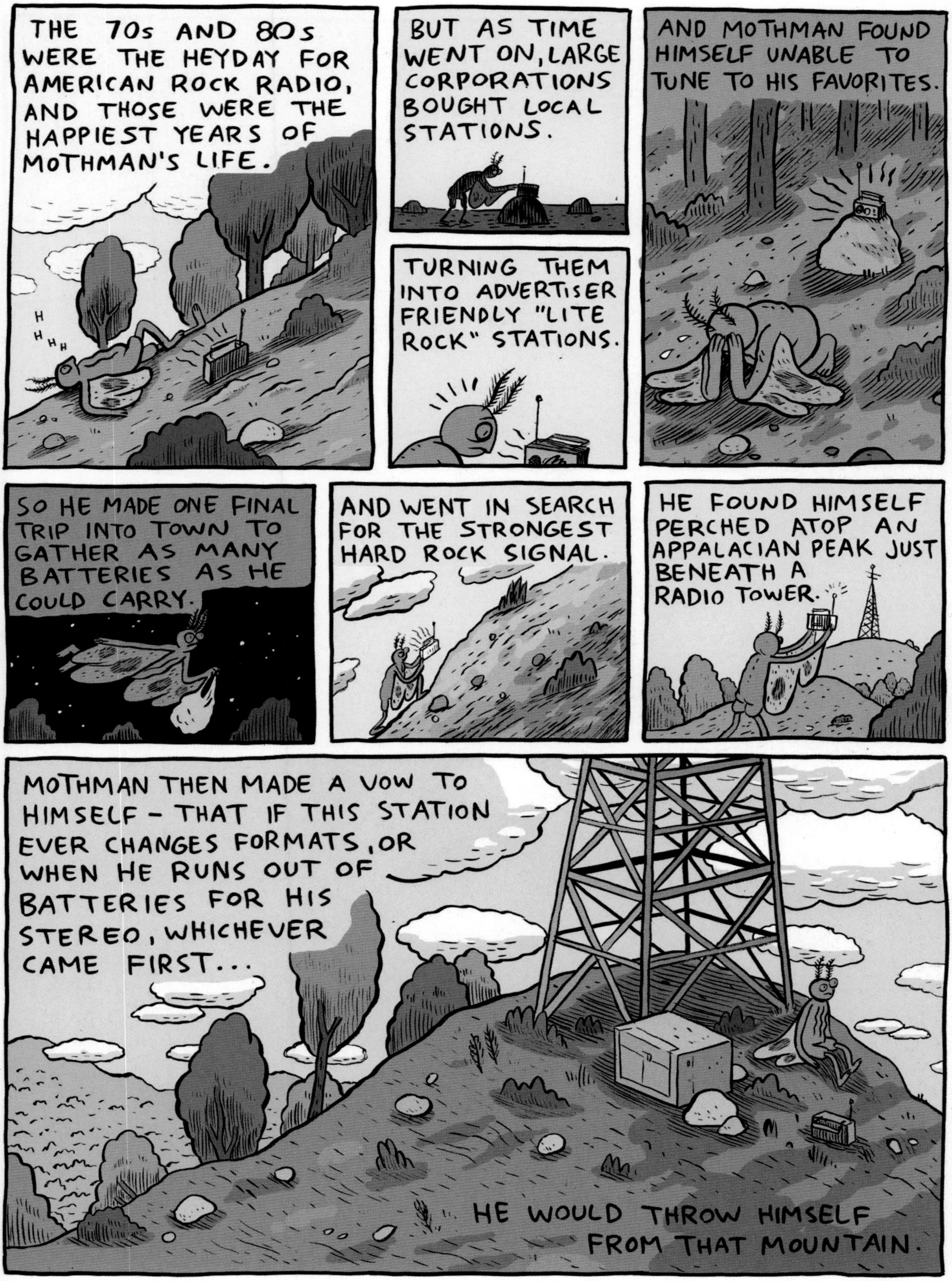
THE 70s AND 80s WERE THE HEYDAY FOR AMERICAN ROCK RADIO, AND THOSE WERE THE HAPPIEST YEARS OF MOTHMAN'S LIFE.
H H H H
BUT AS TIME WENT ON, LARGE CORPORATIONS BOUGHT LOCAL STATIONS.
TURNING THEM INTO ADVERTISER FRIENDLY "LITE ROCK" STATIONS.
AND MOTHMAN FOUND HIMSELF UNABLE TO TUNE TO HIS FAVORITES.
SO HE MADE ONE FINAL TRIP INTO TOWN TO GATHER AS MANY BATTERIES AS HE COULD CARRY.
AND WENT IN SEARCH FOR THE STRONGEST HARD ROCK SIGNAL.
HE FOUND HIMSELF PERCHED ATOP AN APPALACIAN PEAK JUST BENEATH A RADIO TOWER.
MOTHMAN THEN MADE A VOW TO HIMSELF - THAT IF THIS STATION EVER CHANGES FORMATS, OR WHEN HE RUNS OUT OF BATTERIES FOR HIS STEREO, WHICHEVER CAME FIRST...
HE WOULD THROW HIMSELF FROM THAT MOUNTAIN.

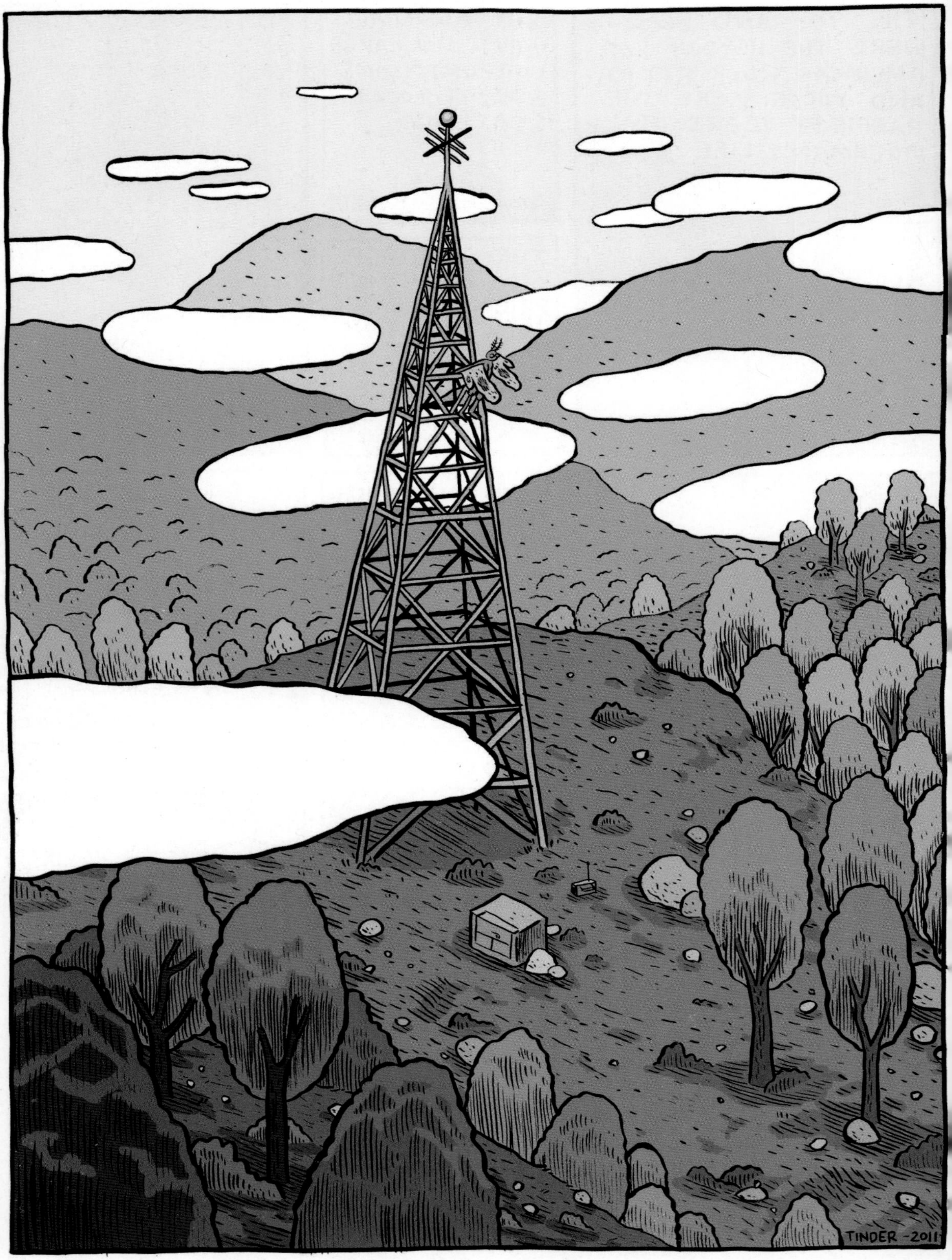
TINDER -2011